THE W.D. GANN
MASTER COMMODITIES COURSE

W. D. Gann

TABLE OF CONTENTS

LESSON 1

SPECULATION A PROFITABLE PROFESSION: A COURSE OF INSTRUCTIONS ON GRAINS

SPECULATION A PROFITABLE PROFESSION

A Course of Instructions With Time Tested Practical Rules of Trading in Grains.

In 1911 after I had made a great success trading in stocks and commodities, there was a public demand for a book with my rules for trading successfully. This demand was answered by my first small book, "Speculation A Profitable Profession". As the years went by I learned more about the market and realized that others needed the help that I could give them and I wrote more books to help others who were trying to help themselves.

In May 1954 I am nearing my 76th Birthday and am writing this new course of instructions not to make money for I have more income than I can spend but realizing the demand and the need for more knowledge about future trading by so many people I now give the benefit of my 52 years experience to help those who need it. The price of this course is made reasonable in order that men and women with a small account of money can get a market education and start with a small capital and make a success provided they follow the rules after they learn them.

My experience has proved that it is more profitable to trade in commodities than stocks and you can make larger profits on the same amount of capital with smaller risk. When you trade in commodities you are trading in the necessities of life. Commodity prices obey the law of supply and demand and follow a seasonal trend most of the time.

When you learn the rules and follow them you eliminate trading on Hope, Fear, and Guesswork which is nothing but gamble and you cannot afford to risk your money gambling. You must follow mathematical rules which I have proved to be realistic guide in trading. You must prove to yourself that the rules have always worked in the past and they will work in the future. When you have the proof follow the rules and you will make speculation a profitable profession.

HOW TO MAKE SPECULATION A PROFITABLE PROFESSION

Speculation or investment is the best business in the world if you make a business of it. But in order to make a success of it you must study and be prepared and not guess, follow inside information, or depend on hope or fear. If you do you will fail. Your success depends on knowing the right kind of rules and following them.

FUNDAMENTAL RULES

Keep this well in mind. For commodities to show up trend and continue to advance they must make higher bottoms and higher tops. When the trend is down they must make lower tops and lower bottoms and continue on down to lower levels. But remember prices can move in a narrower trading range for weeks or months or even years and not make a new high or a new low. But after a long period of time when commodities break into new lows they indicate lower prices and after a long period of time when they advance above old highs or old tops they are in a stronger position and indicate higher prices. This is the reason why you must have a chart long ways back in order to see just what position a commodity is in and at what stage it is between extreme high and extreme low.

THE KIND OF CHARTS TO KEEP UP

Remember the old Chinese proverb "One good picture is worth 10,000 words". You should make up charts and study the picture of a commodity before you make a trade. You should have a weekly high and low chart, a monthly high and low chart and a yearly high and low chart. A yearly high and low chart should run back 5, 10 or 20 years if you can get records that far. Monthly high and low chart should go back for at least 10 years and the weekly high and low should go back for 2 or 3 years. When commodities are very active you should have a daily high and low chart. This need not go back more than a few months. Start the daily chart after the commodity breaks into great activity.

FOLLOW THE MAIN TREND

You will always make money by following the main trend of commodities up or down. Remember that commodities are never too high to buy as long as the trend is up and they are never too low to sell as long as the trend is down. Never sell short just because the commodity is high or because you think it is too high. Never sell out and take profits just because the price is high. Buy and sell according to definite rules and not on hope, fear or guesswork. Never buy a commodity just because the commodity is low. There is usually a good reason why it is low and it can go lower.

RULES FOR BUYING AND SELLING

The first thing to remember before you start to apply any rules is that you must always use a STOP-LOSS order to protect your capital. When making a trade remember that you can be wrong or that the market may change its trend and the STOP-LOSS order will protect you and limit your loss. A small loss or several small losses can easily be made back with one large profit, but when you let large losses run against you it is hard to make them back.

PROVE ALL THINGS AND HOLD FAST TO THAT WHICH IS GOOD

The Bible tells us this and it is well worth remembering. Many people believe that it is wrong to buy at new high levels or to sell at new low levels but it is most profitable and you must prove this to yourself because when you do buy at new high levels or sell at new low levels you are going with the trend of the market and your chances for making profits are much better than guesswork or buying or selling on hope or fear.

PROLONGED ADVANCES

After commodities have had a prolonged advance and wind up with a fast, active, runaway market in most cases they come down very quickly and much faster or in a shorter period of time than when they go up. That is why you must keep up some daily charts at the end of a fast move and keep up the weekly charts to determine the first change in trend and be able to go with it.

SHARP DECLINE IN A SHORT PERIOD OF TIME

This usually follows a rapid advance and the first sharp declines which may last from one month to as much as seven weeks usually corrects an overbought position and leaves the market in position for a secondary advance.

When you are able to catch the extremes at the end of any great time cycle you can make a large amount of money in one year's time trading in fast active markets, and some very large profits in one month's time. It makes no difference whether you catch the extreme low or the extreme high – the opportunities are great for making money providing you select the commodity that will lead.

LARGE PROFITS ON SMALL RISKS

You can make large profits on small risks provided you use a STOP LOSS order, and apply all the rules and wait for a definite indication of a change in trend up or down before you make a trade.

FIXED IDEAS AND FIXED PRICES

Never get a fixed idea of just how high any price is going to go or just how low they are going. Never buy or sell on a price that you fix because you may be trading on hope or fear and not following the trend of the market and applying rules which will determine when the trend is changing.

HOW TO PROTECT PROFITS

After you have accumulated profits it is just as important to protect them with STOP-LOSS orders as it is to protect your original capital because once you have made profits it is your capital and STOP LOSS orders must be used to protect it. The most dangerous thing that you can do is to let a trade start going against you and lose back your profits. A STOP-LOSS order will protect the profits and you can always get in again when you are out, with capital. Remember when you are out of the market the only thing you can lose or miss is an opportunity.

My 52 years of experience has taught me that thousands of people have gone broke trying to hold on until the trend turned. Avoid getting out of the market too soon after move starts when you have a small profit. This can be a great mistake. Get out of the market quickly as soon as you see that you have made a mistake. If you place a STOP LOSS order this will put you out of the market automatically.

TOO LATE OR TOO SOON

You can lose money or miss opportunity by getting into the market too soon or getting out too late. That is not waiting until a definite change in trend is indicated, or failing to act in time when you see a definite change in trend. Wait until you have a well defined indication that the trend is changed, then buy or sell. Follow all the rules in my book "How to Make Profits on Commodities". There are many rules in my book "How to Make Profits Trading in Commodities" which are not in this course of instruction and by using all the rules you will make a greater success.

HOPE AND FEAR

I repeat this because I have seen so many people go broke trading on hope or fear. You will never succeed buying or selling when you hope the market is going up or down. You will never succeed by making a trade because you fear the market is going up or down. Hope will ruin you, because it is nothing more than wishful thinking and provides no basis for action. Fear will often save you if you act quickly when you see that you are wrong. "The fear of the market is the beginning of wisdom". Knowledge which you can only obtain by deep study will help you make a success. The more you study past records the surer you are to be able to detect the trend of the future.

MAKE THE MARKET MOVE YOUR WAY

You must learn to realize that you cannot make the market go your way, you must go the market's way and must follow the trend. Many successful business men who are accustomed to giving orders to others and have them carried out will often when they get into the market, especially for the first time, expect the market to follow their orders or move their way. They must learn that they <u>cannot</u> <u>make</u> the <u>market</u> <u>trend</u> go <u>their</u> <u>way</u>. They must follow the market trend as is indicated by fixed rules and protect their capital and profits by the use of STOP LOSS orders. There is no harm in making a few mistakes and a few small losses because small losses are the expense of a successful speculator. If you intend to make <u>speculation</u> a <u>profitable</u> <u>profession</u> you must <u>learn</u> all the <u>rules</u> and <u>apply</u> <u>all of them</u> to <u>determine</u> the <u>trend</u>. Professional men, such as lawyers, doctors, accountants and engineers spend years in training and a large amount of money to learn how to succeed in their chosen profession. You must spend time and money to learn the profession and become a successful speculator or investor.

HOW TO MAKE THE MOST MONEY IN THE SHORTEST PERIOD OF TIME

Most people want to get rich too quick, that is why they lose their money. They start speculating or investing without first preparing themselves or getting a Commodity education. They do not have the knowledge to start with and the result is they make serious mistakes which cost them money. When you do have knowledge and are prepared you can make the most money in the shortest period of time. You must learn to follow the rules which I have laid down and proved to you by examples that you can make a large amount of money in a short period of time when the market is at the right stage for fast advances and fast declines occur.

Do not try to lead the market or make the market. Follow the trend which is made by big men who make big money and you will make money. Buy when the big market makers are ready for prices to move up fast, sell when they are ready for prices to move down fast and you will make large profits in a short period of time. Trade only when the market shows a definite trend and trade according to definite rules.

Study the chart on Soy Beans for 1953 and 1954 and the examples which I have given and you cannot fail to make profits provided you use STOP LOSS orders as advised.

From March 8, 1954 to April 27, 1954 May Soy Beans advanced from 343½ to 422, a gain of 78½¢ per bushel in 50 calendar days and 35 actual market days. This would give a profit of $7,800 on 10,000 bushels and you were buying after the price was up $1.05 per bushel from the low in August 1953 which proves that you can buy at new highs in the last stage of a bull market and make large profits in a short period of time. This is without guessing but following rules and buying when the big people buy and of course you are with the trend made by the big traders.

Refer to the trading examples on May Rye and you will see how large profits could be made in a short period of time by selling short after prices were down to comparatively low levels against the extreme high levels.

WHY PEOPLE DO NOT MAKE MONEY BUYING AND SELLING COMMODITIES

I have stated in my books many times the market does not beat you, it is your own human weakness that causes you to defeat yourself. The average man or woman nearly always wants to buy low and sell high. The farmer wants to sell at high prices whatever he produces but he wants to buy what he needs at low prices.
The labouring man wants high wages all the time but wants low prices for what he buys to eat or wear. This is a violation of a fundamental economic law and it just will not work. To make a success in speculation you cannot expect to buy low and sell high. You will make money when you do exactly the opposite of what the average man or woman wants to do or tries to do and makes a failure and loses as a result of what they are trying to do.

You will make profits when you learn to BUY HIGH AND SELL LOW. You must learn to follow the trend of prices and realize that they are NEVER too HIGH TO BUY as LONG as the TREND is UP and NEVER TOO LOW TO SELL AS LONG AS THE TREND IS DOWN.

ONE GRAIN GOES UP WHILE ANOTHER GOES DOWN AT THE SAME TIME

May Beans and May Rye 1953-54

Example: May 7, 1946 May Rye sold at 286½, the highest price in history. Many people remember this high price and buy all the way down instead of selling. Why do they buy? Because after May Rye sold at 286½ it looked cheap at $2.00 and they buy it; at 150 it looks still cheaper and they buy it but the trend is down and it goes lower. At 125 it looks still cheaper but it goes lower because the MAIN TREND IS DOWN and the supply exceeds the demand or the selling is better than the buying.

May Soy Beans 1948 high 436-3/4. The price had moved up from 334 in October 1947, and after the trend turned down in less than one month's time, May Beans sold at 320½ and three months later advanced to 425. These wide fluctuations were the result of buying and selling. Too many people got bullish too late and bought too late and later became pessimistic when prices were down $1 per bushel.

They then sold and prices went up again.

1953 August 20th May Beans low 239½. They had sold at 309 in April 1953.

After May Beans started up traders decided prices were TOO HIGH and
at 270 they SOLD SHORT. The WISE MAN who KNEW the TREND was up,

BOUGHT. When May Beans reached the previous old high of 311¼ in December 1953, which was the high of April 1953, the public decided that prices were too high because in four months' time, or since August, prices went up over 70¢ per bushel so they sold out anything that they had bought and sold short, hoping to buy lower.

Dec. 17, 1953 May Beans declined to 295-3/4 and made bottom, then advanced to 310 around the high of December 1953. The public decided prices were TOO HIGH and SOLD SHORT while the WISE TRADERS BOUGHT AT NEW HIGHS following MY RULES and continued to BUY AT NEW HIGHS because the TREND WAS UP.

1954 April 27th May Beans sold at 422, an advance of $1.82 per bushel in eight months and seven days. The greatest advance in history and the greatest range in any option.

Not only the small traders but men who had millions of dollars bucked the trend and sold Soy Beans all the way up until May Beans crossed $4 per bushel, then they all got panicky and bought to cover shorts and take losses and many became so bullish that they bought hoping prices would advance to $5 per bushel. There was talk of a corner and a squeeze and a shortage of supply. The talk scared people into buying.

April 26th May and July closed at the limit, up 10¢ per bushel in one day.

This news was in the newspapers, that the market has closed at the limit with nothing offered. People who were Bears and selling short when prices were 50¢ to 75¢ per bushel lower, bought on fear hoping for higher prices.

This meant that the shorts had lost hope and that hope had turned into despair and that they were covering shorts or buying. May Beans sold at 422 on April 27th but closed at 411, lower than they closed on April 26th when there were no beans offered. July Beans sold at 415 on April 27th and closed at 405, lower by 4¢ per bushel than the night before when none was offered for sale. THE PICTURE HAD CHANGED OVERNIGHT. THE WISE BUYERS who had BOUGHT all the way up from 240 became sellers; they had been BUYING AT NEW HIGH LEVELS, now they SOLD AT NEW LOW LEVELS, reversing their position and selling at new low levels.

Prices rallied to April 30 but failed to reach highs of April 27th. On May 3rd the real selling started and prices declined the limit of 10¢ per bushel. May closing at 400-5/8 July closing at 398-1/8, down the limit of 10¢ for one day. Why did prices go down like this? Because the wise traders, when prices broke the low of April 20, SOLD AT NEW LOWS AND they will continue to sell as prices continue to go lower, while the man who WANTS TO BUY LOW and SELL HIGH will BUY all the way down and LOSE. When Beans sell at 350, 250 and eventually below $2 they will look like great bargains and the bargain hunters will remember 422 and 415 highs on April 27, 1954 and will BUY because they HOPE that PRICES will go up to HIGH LEVELS again. And the result can be but one thing, they will lose their money, while the man who follows the TREND will SELL SHORT all the way down and SELL AT NEW LOW LEVELS and make a fortune.

The way to make profits is to go the market's way. Do not try to make the market go your way. Apply all the rules in my book, HOW TO MAKE PROFITS TRADING IN COMMODITIES, follow the MAIN TREND and SELL REGARDLESS of HOW LOW prices go as long as the trend is down and continue to BUY AT NEW HIGHS AS LONG as the prices go up. In this way you will make SPECULATION A PROFITABLE PROFESSION and will have profits instead of losses.

RULES FOR TRADING IN COMMODITIES

RULE 1. Buy at new high prices or old top levels.

RULE 2. Buy when prices advance above old low price levels.

RULE 3. Sell when prices decline below old top levels or high prices.

RULE 4. Sell at new low price levels. As a general rule it is safer to wait until prices advance at least 2¢ above high levels and still more important to wait until they close above these levels before buying and at the same time it is safer to wait until prices decline 1/2¢ below old levels and still safer to wait until they close below these old levels before making a trade.

RULE 5. <u>Closing Prices</u>. Wait to buy or sell until prices close above old highs or below old lows on the daily or weekly charts when markets are very active and moving fast; it is important to use the daily high and low chart and the closing price above highs or below lows. Prices may advance rapidly during the day but when it comes to closing time they may run off several cents and close lower than the previous day, and at the same time when there is a sharp decline, prices may go below the low of the previous day but when they close they close near the high levels; therefore, it is the closing price that is always important to keep up on the daily, weekly or monthly high or low charts. The longer the time period in days, weeks, months or years when prices exceed old highs or break old lows, the greater the importance of the change in trend and the move up or down. Remember the general rule, when prices advance to new high levels they generally react back to the old tops, which is a safe place to buy and when they decline below old lows, as a rule they rally back to the old lows, which is a safe place to sell. Always, of course, protect with STOP LOSS orders.

RULE 6. STOP LOSS ORDERS. Your capital and your profits must be protected at all times with STOP LOSS orders which must be placed when you make the trade and not later.

RULE 7. AMOUNT OF CAPITAL REQUIRED. It is very important to know exactly how much of your capital that you can risk on any one trade and never lose all your capital. When you make a trade you should never risk more than 10% of the capital you have to trade with, and if you have one or two losses, reduce your units of trading.

For trading in Rye and Soy Beans, you should have at least $1500.00 for trading in 5000 bushels. Suppose you risk 3¢ a bushel on a trade; you would have to lose 10 consecutive times to wipe out your capital. You could hardly lose it this way just guessing and by following the rules it is impossible to lose all of your capital. For trading in Soy Beans, especially at high levels, you should have at least $3000.00 capital for each 5000 bushels that you trade in because it is often necessary to risk as much as 5¢ a bushel on Soy Beans. But the profits are much greater than anything you can trade in.

Should you wish to trade in job lots of 1000 bushels, or 2000 bushels, you, of course, can start on a capital of $500.00 and limit losses not more than 3¢ on any trade and by following the rules, in many cases your risks will not be more than 1¢ a bushel. The same rules apply to Wheat, Corn, and Lard.

Oats move in a narrower range and require about half as much capital as Rye or Wheat to trade with.

RULE 8. THIS RULE IS FOR BOTH BUYING AND SELLING: When prices decline 50% of the highest selling level, you can buy with a STOP LOSS order of 3¢ below the low prices. Next strongest buying point is 50% between the extreme low and the extreme high. For example, May Rye, the highest price it ever sold was 286½ ; 50% of this is 143½ and when this level is broken by 3¢ it is in a very weak position. The lowest level May Rye ever sold was 30¢ per bushel; 50% of this 286½ and 30¢ is 158¼. The highest price that cash Rye ever sold was $3.35; one half of this is 167½ and we have given an example of what happens when May Rye and other options decline below 167½, 158¼ and 143½.

SELLING LEVEL. When prices advance after being far below the 50% point and reach it for the first time, it is a selling level or place to sell short, protected with a STOP LOSS order of not more than 3¢ above the 50% price level. Example: Suppose that May Rye advances to 143½. The first time it reaches this price, if the indications on the daily chart show it is making top, it is a short sale with a stop at 146½. The next point is 158¼ which is 50% of the range between 30¢ and 286½; this is 158¼. When May Rye advances to this point you would watch for resistance and sell short with a STOP LOSS order at 161½.

After this point the next selling level is 167½ or 50% of 335. Next the range between 30¢ and 335½; 50% of this is 182½ which would be the strongest resistance and the most important selling level protected with STOP LOSS order at 185½.

When you start trading be sure that you know all of the rules and that you follow them, and be sure that you place a STOP LOSS ORDER.

WHERE TO PLACE STOP LOSS ORDERS:

You must place STOP LOSS orders below the lows of swings and not just below the lows on the daily chart. STOPS must be above old tops or below old bottoms on a weekly or monthly chart. STOP LOSS orders placed below closing prices on the daily or weekly chart are much safer and less likely to be caught because you are moving your STOPS according to the trend. STOPS placed above closing prices on the daily or weekly chart are caught a smaller number of times than if you place them below a daily bottom or a daily top. The swings or reversals in a market are the prices to place STOP LOSS orders one way or the other. It is of great importance to know where to place a STOP LOSS order properly. Grains selling below $1 a bushel, a STOP LOSS order is as a rule safe and caught less of the time when you place it 1¢ below the bottom and especially 1¢ under closing prices, or 1¢ above closing prices. When prices are moving from $1 to $2 per bushel the STOPS should be at least 2¢ above highs or 2¢ below lows or 2¢ above closing prices or 2¢ below closing prices.

Prices at $2 to $3 per bushel. At this range of prices STOPS should be at least 3¢ under the lows or above the highs.

Prices $3 to $4 per bushel. At this range of high levels fluctuations are fast and wide and STOPS, to be safe, must be placed farther away, at least 4¢ to 5¢ per bushel above highs or under the lows. It makes no difference where your STOPS are placed so long as it is safe and not caught until the time is right when there is a definite change of trend. At the end of high prices, from $3.50 to $4. per bushel which seldom occurs, STOPS can be placed 1¢ to 2¢ below the daily closing price or at 1¢ to 2¢ above the daily closing prices. At extreme high prices you must depend on the daily high and low chart to give you the first indication of a change in trend which later will be confirmed by the weekly high and low chart of price moves.

When prices are selling at extreme high levels, follow all the rules in my book, HOW TO MAKE PROFITS TRADING IN COMMODITIES, and if you have taken my Master Forecasting Course, apply the rules on Great Time Cycles as well as the minor time periods.

Remember you can never have too much knowledge. Continue to study and learn more for knowledge can always be turned into profits later.

WHAT TO DO BEFORE YOU MAKE A TRADE: Check all records of prices, daily, weekly, monthly and yearly and note all time periods. Note when the prices are near some old high levels or near some old low levels of recent weeks or years. Then calculate just what your risk will be before you make the trade and after you make it, place the STOP LOSS order for your protection in case you are wrong.

WEEKLY HIGH AND LOW CHART: The weekly high and low chart is a very important trend indicator. When prices get above a series of weekly highs or lows, or decline below a series of weekly lows, it is of greater importance and indicates a greater change in trend which may last for many weeks.

MONTHLY HIGHS AND LOWS: When prices advance above or decline below prices which have occurred for many months past it means a greater change in trend which can last for several months.

YEARLY HIGHS AND LOWS: When prices advance above or decline below the prices made several years in the past, it is nearly always a sure sign of big moves which will last for a long period of time, or at least have a greater advance or decline in a short period of time, and when old highs are crossed, or lows broken, always watch for a reaction to come back to around the old highs or slightly lower, and after they are broken, expect the rally to advance back around the old highs or slightly below.

Study the yearly highs and lows and you will see the proof. Remember the greater the time period, when it is exceeded, the greater the move up or down.

We will prove the rules by starting with a capital of $3000, and trading in Rye, based on the rules given above. First, we are going to trade in May Rye and we must know something about the history of May Rye.

1951, July 23 low 169 holding 1½¢ above the 50% price indicated strength and good buying because August 20 was low at 169, making two supports at this time level. We are now buying 10,000 bushels at 169 and place STOP at 165½ or 2¢ below the 50% point.

The market advances. September 20 we buy 10,000 more at 181 because it is above two tops or high levels. November 1951 we buy 10,000 more at 210 because the price is above an old top of 208 of April 3, 1951. 1951, December 10 and 12th high 221½ and 221, a top against the high at 218. We had bought 10 at

169, 10 at 181 and 10 at 210. We sell all these out at 219 which gives a total profit of 94¢ per bushel or $9,400. We now withdraw the capital of $3,000 and start trading on the profits alone.

1951, December 12; we sell 20,000 bushels at 218 and place a STOP at 223½. 1952, January, we sell 20,000 at 204 and move the STOPS down to 208. February 5, 11, and 27th and March 4 the lows are 194, 192½, 193½ and 193. We cover the shorts at 195 and buy 40,000 at 195, making a STOP at 190. The profits on these deals are $8,200. added to the other profit gives a $17,600 to trade with.

1952, March high 211, a lower top. We sell short 40,000 bushels.

May 1 low 193, same low as March 4; we cover shorts at 194 making a profit of 13¢ per bushel or $5,200 added to $17,600 gives $22,800 capital. We stop trading in this May option because it will expire on May 20. We could trade in July, September or December but we wait for the May Rye for the 1953 delivery to start trading and show a trend and then we start trading again.

1952, July 23 high 218½ under the old top of 221½. It declined to 207 on July 19, August 14 high 219, a second high and slightly below the 1951 high. We sell short 50,000 at 218 and place the STOP at 222½. The trend moves down. August 18, 19th and 29th and September 20 prices are 196½, 195½, the same as May 1952. Because we know that the seasonal trend is usually low in the latter part of August or early September, we cover all the shorts, 50,000 at 197 and buy 50,000 at 197 for long accounts and place STOP at 194. November 13 high 213-3/4 a lower top than August 14, but we wait to sell until we get a definite indication. November 24 and 28th lows 204, we raise STOP to 203. This STOP was caught and we sold 50,000 longs at 203 and sold short 50,000 bushels. This gave us a total profit or working capital of $26,3000.00. We sold 50,000 short at 203 and raised the STOP to 209.

December the market broke the price of 195, the old low. We sold 25,000 more at 193 and made STOP on 75,000 at 196. 1953 January prices broke the lows of July 1952 at 190. We sell 25,000 at 188 making STOP on 100,000 at 193.

January 1953 – 12th – low 180. January 15 high 187, reduce STOP on 100,000 to 189½.

February 13 low 171.

March 3 high 182½, reduce STOP to 186.

Later in March the price broke 171 low. We sell 25,000 more at 166 when the price breaks the low of 169 of July 21, 1927 and it had broke 50% of 335½ which is 167-3/4, putting it in a very weak position with the main trend down.

May 11 low 154

March 3 high 182½, reduce STOP to 186.

Later in March the price broke 171 low. We sell 25,000 more at 166 when the price breaks the low of 169 of July 21, 1951 and it has broke 50% of 335½ which is 167-3/4 putting it in a very weak position with the main trend down.

May 11 low 154. We buy 125,000 at 156 to cover because the May option will expire about May 20 [1953]. We now have a total profit of $69,550 to work with. We can now trade safely on 100,000 bushels which gives 70¢ per bushel margin and a loss of 3¢ on 100,000 bushels would be $3,000 and if we lost for ten consecutive times we would still have more than half or 50% of our capital to trade with, which is perfectly safe.

We wait for May Rye for 1954 delivery to give an indication of what it is going to do.

1953, July 6. The option opened at 153, a new low. July 7 high 156 when it breaks 153 we sell 100,000 bushels at 152 and make the STOP 157. It declines very fast and we sell 25,000 more at 140 because it is 3½¢ below the 50% of 286½ which is 143½ , the high of May 7, 1946 and we wait until the price is 3¢ below this level which puts it in a very weak position before going short.

1953, July 28 low 133½, August 6 high 140-3/4 and 140; we make the STOP on 125,000 at 145, the decline continues and breaks the low of 133½. We sell 25,000 more at 131½ and make STOP at 142½.

August 13 low 121, August 17 high 135½, reduce STOP to 137. August 28 and September 15 and September 23 low 116½, 114-3/4, 115. We know that the seasonal lows are often made in August and September and the trend turns up so we reduce the STOP to 121 on the shorts. The STOP was caught and we buy 150,000 at 121. We now have a capital of $127.500 to work with. We buy 100,000 at 121 and make STOP 114.

November 2, high 134, November 17 and 30th low 133½; we make STOP 120½. December 14 high 133½, a slightly lower top, we raise STOP to 129. STOP was caught. We sold 100,000 at 129 with 8½ profit which gives us a working capital of $135,500. We sold short 100,000 bushels at 129 and placed the STOP at 136.

December 23 low 120.

1954, January 3 and 14th low 120½ and 121-3/4, higher bottom. We buy 100,000 at 124, profit 5¢ which now gives a capital of $140,500. We buy 100,000 at 124.

1954, January 22 - 27th high 128, a lower top. We raise the STOPS to 124. STOPS were caught and we are out even losing only commission.

We sold short 100,000 at 124 with STOP 125. March 29 low 101½, April 2 high 110½, we reduce the STOP to 112½. April 19 high 108-3/4, we reduce the STOP to 110-3/4. April 30 low 93½ with the main trend still down and we would remain short with a stop at 104½ or 3¢ above the low of March 29, 1954. We will assume that we covered shorts at 96, this would give us a profit of $173,700 in 33 months starting with a capital of $3,000. Suppose we cut this 50%, the profit would still be $86,850. This is proof from the records based on rules that if you do not guess you can make large profits on small risks.

This also proves that no matter how low the price is you can make big profits by selling short and no matter how high the price is you can make money buying so long as you are going with the trend up or down. The question naturally arises, "Why do not more people make fortunes trading in Commodities"? The answer is weakness of the human element. They trade on hope, fear, and think prices are too low to sell or too high to buy and if they do act they do different from what the rules indicate, but remember that there are always some big traders who do buy and sell no matter how low the price is or how high it is, and these are the people who make big money. The late Jesse Livermore traded this way and accumulated as much as $15,000,000 at one time. Men like Dr. Crawford have the nerve to buy and sell at extreme low levels or extreme high levels where the trend is down and to make millions, while the man who fears or trades on hope does not have the nerve and he not only misses big profits but he makes losses. If you expect to succeed you must learn to follow rules and after you have proved to yourself the rules will work, have the nerve to follow them and profits are assured.

SOY BEANS – RECORD OF HIGHS AND LOWS.
MAY SOY BEANS. Trading in Futures started October 5, 1936 and May Soy Beans opened at that time at 120 and advanced to 164 in January 1937.

1938, October low 69; 1937, July 27 low 67. This was the lowest price that May Soy Beans ever sold.

1940, August low 69. From this level prices advanced to September 14, 1941, high 202.

October 19 low 154½.

1942, January high 203, just 1¢ above the high of September 1941.

December low 166.

1943, January high 186. At this time the Government stopped trading in Soy Beans and there was no trading until October 1947 when trading was resumed. In October 1947 May Beans started up from 334 which was above all tops since February 1920 when the high was 405, so you would buy at 334 or 336, because they were at new high levels and hold for a definite indication to sell.

1948, January 15 high 436-3/4, the highest price in history. At this time you would have to keep up a daily high and low chart and a weekly high and low chart to tell when the trend changed and know where to place STOPS and where to sell out longs and go short. This indication was given on January 19, 1948 and you would be short. A big decline followed to February 9, 1948, low for May Beans 320½, where the daily chart again gave indications to cover shorts and buy. After that time the price advanced to 425 in May 1948. In October 1948 the 1949 option opened and declined to 239, which was 50% from the low of 44¢ in December 1932 to the extreme high of 436-3/4, making this a buying level protected with STOP LOSS order at 236.

1948, November high 276-3/4. The daily and weekly high and low chart indicated that this was a selling level and a time to sell out longs and sell short. A rapid decline followed on heavy liquidation.

1949, February 14 low 201½, down to the old low levels of 1941 and a buying level because it was just above $2.00 per bushel.

1950, May high 323½. The Korean War started on June 25, 1950 and war is always bullish on commodities, and therefore we would look for buying opportunities. A big advance followed and most options went to above 280 in July 1950.

1950, October 16 low for May Beans 232½. A rapid advance followed from this level.

1951, February 8 high 344½. At this time the Government placed a ceiling on May Beans at 333, and in fact on all other Beans. November Beans started down at this time from a high of 334 and declined to 262 in July.

1951, May Beans for 1952 delivered, opened in June at 287.

1951, July 9 low 268-3/4. In October prices crossed the highs of 3-months at 281 to 283. You would buy at this time because prices were again at new highs and you should buy based on the rules.

1952, March, April and early May prices reached the low of 282. Buy because it was 3-months at the same low level.

1952, May high 314. Same high as December 1951, a selling level.

1952, August – the new option low 291 and the end of August high 314-3/4, 3 tops at the same level. Sell with STOP at 317.

1952, October low 298.

1952, December high 311, a lower top and selling level.

1953, February low 282, not 3¢ below the lows at 284 in March, April and May, 1952, a buying level with a STOP at 279.

1953, April high 309, a lower top than December 1952, a selling level.

1953, the May option declined to 292.

THE GREATEST ADVANCE IN MAY BEANS IN HISTORY

When I state the greatest advance I mean the greatest advance from low to high levels of any option.

BUYING CAMPAIGN IN MAY BEANS. We will start with a capital of $3,000 and buy according to the rules outlined. August 20, 1953 May Beans low 239½.

We would buy 10,000 bushels at 240, place a STOP-LOSS order at 3¢ below, making a risk of 10% of the capital or $300.00.

Why do we buy here? Because it was the same low as October 1948 and for the same mathematical rule. 1932 low 44¢, 1948 high 436-3/4, 50% of this is 240-3/8, a sure buying level protected with a STOP LOSS order.

The May 1954 option opened at 256 and advanced to 259-3/4 and then declined to 239½.

1953, September 2, high 263, closed the same day at 259. While we now have an indication that prices are going higher we do not buy more but wait for the closing rule and for the price to close above 260, which was the high of the life of the option after it started.

September 16, low 248-3/4. We raise STOP to 246-3/4 on the 10 bought at 240.

During the week ending October 10 May Beans closed at 261. We now buy 10 more at 261 and raise the STOP on all of the beans to 255 or 1¢ below the low of the week.

The advance was rapid and for the week ending October 31, the price closed at 282, above the old low at 280 in February 1953. This was an indication of higher prices and as we have big profits we can buy 5,000 at 282 and raise STOPS to 275.

Look up the record to see where the new old highs are so we will know when resistance should be made. We find these highs at 314-3/4, 313½, 311, and 309.

These highs were made in 1952 and 1953; therefore, we would expect some reaction from around these levels.

1953, December 2, high 311¼, same high as December 1952. We sell out 25,000 at 310 giving a profit of $12,300.00 and with the capital investment of $3,000.00, makes a $15,3000.00 capital to operate on. We sell 25,000 short at 311 and place the STOP at 316. While we know the trend is up we expect a reaction from these old high levels. A fast decline followed December 17, low 295-3/4 at old low levels of March, April and May 1953. We cover 25,000 bushels at 297 with a profit of 13¢ which gives a working capital of $18,800.00. At this price we can figure safely 30% margin per bushel is enough or $3,000.00 on 10,000 bushels or $7,500.00 on 25,000. This is conservative trading.

We buy 25,000 for long account at 297 and place STOP at 293. The price starts up from December 17 low and makes higher bottoms and higher tops indicating up trend.

We follow the closing rule which is that when prices close above old highs that have been made months or years past it is an indication that prices must go very much higher.

1954, January 19, high 315½, closed 314½, not yet enough above the old highs. We wait for close at 316½ to buy.

January 22, closed at 317. We buy 25,000 more at 317.

February 22, low 309¼, down for the last old top in 1953. We make STOPS at 307.

From previous records we know that the next old top is 344¼ on February, 1951 so expect that this is the next price to watch.

February 24 and 25th, high 340½ and 342. Low for three days at 335½ we raise STOPS to 333½ until price goes above 344½, the old top and an indication of higher prices.

March 4, high 359-3/4, closed at 359. March 5, low 349, March 8, low 343½, at the old top level and a buying level. We buy 15,000 more at 345 and raise STOPS on all to 341.

March 19, prices crossed the previous high of 359½, which was the high of March 4, indicating higher. March 19 we buy 15,000 more at 361. March 25, high 371. April 1, low 354½, a higher bottom than March 11 and 16th. We raise STOPS to 352 on all our line of May Beans that was bought. April 9, prices make a new high closing at 375, indicating much higher prices.

April 13, high 382½, April 14, low 376½. Raise STOP to 373. April 15, high 388, closed at 387¼. We buy 10,000 more at 387.

April 20, high 402, closed at 396. We know that when it does close above $4.00 it will indicate higher prices. We know the last high in May 1948 was 425 so the indications are that May Beans will reach somewhere near these old highs but now is the time to protect profits and not buy more.

April 27, high 407½, closed at 402, under the high but above $4.00, which indicated higher prices.

April 23, low 398¼, closed at 403½. We now raise STOPS on all longs to 395.

April 27, high 422, within 3¢ of 425, the high of May 1948, and up from 239½ to 422. The price has advanced 182½ cents, the greatest in history.

April 27, after high of 422 the market declined fast and closed at 411, which was the lowest price of the day. We now place a STOP 5¢ below this low or at 406.

April 28, low 406½, missed the STOP by 1/2¢. April 28, 29th and 30th, high 317½, 315½ and 316-3/4. When prices made 316-3/4 on April 30 we raise STOP to 411-3/4 or 5¢ per bushel down from this top because the prices have started to make lower tops and we must pull up STOPS and protect profits that have accumulated.

April 30, late in the day May Beans declined to 410¼ and the STOP was caught. We sold out all longs at 411. Total profits $92,6000.00 in 8 months and 10 days time on a capital of $3,000.00 and the trading was very conservative, the risks were conservative at all times.

This is proof beyond any doubt that prices are never too high to buy if you follow the rules and protect with STOP LOSS orders. When these great extremes occur, fortunes are made by men who have the nerve and the knowledge to follow the rules. In this campaign we have not done any guessing as to where to buy or sell. We have let the market prove itself. We have bought on definite rules and placed the STOP LOSS orders based on definite rules and sold out at an extreme high level on a definite rule because the option was nearing the end or reaching the 1st of May when we do not trade in an option. This great advance in Soy Beans is no exception. It has happened in other commodities – Coffee, Cocoa, Cotton, Cottonseed Oil, Lard, Rye, Wheat, and Corn. If you will only learn the rules and when the market runs into these extreme levels, not try to guess where the highs are going to be but simply follow the trend and follow up with STOP LOSS orders and buy regardless of price when new highs are made, you cannot fail to make enormous amounts of money.

MAY CORN

You will find the chart on May Corn covering all the main swings from January, 1925 up to date. Study this chart and apply all the rules just the same as we have applied them in the examples on Soy Beans and Wheat.

You will note this chart from January 1925 where the price started down from 137. It made lower tops and lower bottoms until 1926 when there were two bottoms around the same level at 67 and 69. This was a buying level. From there the price moved up and when it crossed the other top at 97 you would buy more. The high in August 1927 was 122, a selling level. After that the price declined and made a slightly higher bottom in 1928 and rallied until May 1928. Following this there were three bottoms just below 80. These occurred in 1928 and 1929 and the tops were up to around 110 and 112.

July 1930 was the last high where you would sell short against the old tops and when prices broke the lows of 77 and 78 you would sell more. When prices broke below the lows of 1926, which was 67, you would sell more. The decline continued making lower bottoms and lower tops until May 1932 when the low was 28¢ per bushel. There was a rally to 41 and final low was in February 1933 when the low was 24¢ per bushel. After President Roosevelt took office in March 1933 and the Exchanges [re]opened, the trend on all commodities as well as all stocks turned up and when prices crossed the tops, as you can see on the chart, you would buy. There was a rapid advance. May Corn high in July 1933, 82½¢ per bushel. This was just under the old lows and it was a selling indication.

April 1934, low 40¢ per bushel, higher than previous bottoms and around the other bottoms. From this level the main trend turned up again and advanced until May 1935. Then the next option in September 1935 made low at 56¢ per bushel. When it started crossing tops and making higher levels, you would continue to buy at high levels. You can see that the main trend swings continued up without ever breaking a swing bottom, finally crossing the high of May 1937 and advancing to 187½ in April 1947, declined to 142 in June 1947 and then the advance was resumed. When prices crossed the high of 173 and the high of 187½ you would buy more. There was a rapid advance with small reactions until September 1947, high 288. This was above all previous highs for May Corn and you would wait until there was an indication on the weekly and daily charts to show that the trend had turned down. From this time on the main trend continued down making lower bottoms and lower tops until February 1949 when final low was reached at 110. Look back over your charts and you will find old tops at 112 and 108, therefore, when May Corn declined to 110 in February 1949, it was a buy because there had been a drastic decline and the long interest had been cleaned out. You would watch the daily and weekly chart here and you would see where they showed a change in trend. Note two higher bottoms following this time, the last bottoms occurring in February 1950, low 124. Here you would buy and when prices crossed 137, the high of May 1949, you would buy more at new high levels.

Again, when prices crossed the high of December 1948, 152½, you would buy more. The market continued to advance reaching final high in December 1951, 198½. You would always expect selling around the even figure of $2.00 per bushel and this would be the place to sell out longs and sell short as the price was just above the old bottom at 192 and lower than any other bottom. From this high the main trend turned down and you could remain short. May Corn continued down making low in September 1953, when the low was 138.

The market advanced to 162½ in December 1953; failing again to cross the high of March 1953 you would again sell short. The decline was resumed and the low of 148 was made in April 1954, and the rally after that was very small. Up to this writing the main trend on May Corn is down but the option will expire in the month of May so you will follow July and December as the trend indicates, December option being the best trend indicator because the new crop can be delivered in December. Therefore, you would get up a chart weekly, daily and monthly on December Corn and follow the indications on it for the balance of 1954. You would always keep up a May, July and December chart on Corn. The record that I have given covering the May option back to 1925 is all that you will need except daily, weekly and monthly charts on December and July options.

Again I repeat, you must always use a STOP LOSS order and must always continue to study and learn more and more about the records and you will make a success with Corn as well as anything else.

MAY CORN SWINGS 1925 TO 1954

The main trend turned down from a high of 136 in January 1925 and continued down until May 1926, low 67¢, then in April 1927 there was a bottom that was slightly higher. This was a buying level. Prices advanced to August 1927, high 122, a selling level against an old top, and after that the main trend was down making lower tops and lower bottoms.

1928 and 1929 the lows were around 76¢ per bushel. There were 3 lows at these prices. When the low was broken at these levels you would sell short and then sell more when it broke 65¢ per bushel. Final low was reached at 24¢ in February 1933. For many years back in 1860, 1893 and 1896 low on Corn had been 20¢ per bushel. Therefore, when it was around these low levels it was a buy for a long term investment. You can see that the main trend continued up after the February lows until July 1933 when the price advanced to 83¢ per bushel, just above a series of old bottoms. It was a rapid advance and indicated selling. Then there was a decline to April 1934 making two bottoms and making bottoms at the same level as the old tops which would be a buying level. The price then advanced until 1935 reaching 95¢ per bushel. August 1935, low 56¢ per bushel. This was a buying level and when it crossed 68¢ you would buy more and hold selling around 96¢, a series of old tops, and reacted. When it crossed 97¢ you would buy more.

1937 May high 139, a selling level as indicated by the daily and weekly high and low chart. After this the main trend was down making lower bottoms and lower tops until August 1939, low 42¢ per bushel, around the same low as April 1934, and a buying level. From this time on the bottoms were higher and the tops were higher. You would buy every time an old top was crossed and buy heavily when it crossed the old tops at 142. The advance continued until September 1947, high 288. The daily and weekly charts showed that this was top for a fast decline. The decline continued making lower tops and lower bottoms until February 1949 when there was panicky decline and May Corn sold at 110. Look back in the years 1928 and 1929; you will find a series of tops around 112 and 110 making this a buying level. After this the main trend turned up making higher bottoms. When prices crossed 135 you would buy more and when they crossed 150 you would buy more. The advance continued until December 1951, high 198. Corn is always a sale just under $2.00 as there is always a reaction even in a bull market. However, at this time the main trend turned down and prices continued to work lower until September 1953, low 137. December 1953 high 162, same high as March 1953 and a selling level.

In March 1954 the price declined to 148 per bushel and up to this time has been in a narrow trading range. However, the main trend is down but at this time you would make up charts on December Corn daily and weekly and study it and follow the short side as long as the trend is down.

Apply all of the same rules on Corn that we used on all of the commodities and you will make a success trading in it. Many times Corn has very wide swings and when it is active there are excellent opportunities for profits.

MAY RYE SWINGS 1932 TO 1954

Rye is very profitable to trade in and most of the time it shows profits in comparison with wheat and runs Soy Beans a close second at certain times. You can see by the chart how bottoms and tops are formed and you should buy when it declines to a new low level and sell when it breaks into new high levels. Note 1938 to 1945 when lows were around 42¢ and 40¢ a bushel – a series of bottoms making this a buying level as a real investment. February 1941 – when final low was reached at 41¢ the price started to move up and when it crossed 54¢ you would buy more. The advance continued until January 1942 high 93¢; the trend turned down temporarily from this level and declined until May and November 1952, low 68¢ and 66¢, higher bottoms than October 1941, a buying level. You would buy more when it crossed 81¢ and then later after it reacted to April 1943 and crossed 90¢, you would buy more and when it crossed 95¢ you would buy more and finally when the price crossed the highs of 1933, 1936, and 1937 you would buy more, as it indicated very much higher prices. The last low was September 1944 at 94¢; from this level there was a rapid advance crossing the highs of 1944 where you would buy more and then when it crossed 152 you would buy more. The advance was rapid until May 7, 1946, high 286½, the highest price in history. Here you would be keeping up the daily high and low chart and this indicated high, a selling level, and you would have sold short. A rapid decline followed.

1948, July. The next option started at 196 and being far below where other option expired, you would sell short. The main trend continued down making lower tops and lower bottoms until February 1949, low 115. A buying level against the high of July 1943. From this level the advance was rapid making higher bottoms and higher tops. You would buy more when it crossed 160, buy more when it crossed 165.

1951, May high 210½. The option was about to expire and of course you would stop trading.

1951, August low 168. The daily chart showed up trend and you would buy.

1951, December high 221½. The daily high and low charts showed selling level and you would go short.

1952, March low 190. The indications were that this was bottom and you would buy again.

1952, August high 219. A lower top and a selling level.

1952, October low 193. A higher bottom and a buying level.

1952, November – final high at 214, the third lower top and a selling level; you would sell short all the way down. When it broke 193 you would sell more; when it broke 190 you would sell more, after that time the rallies were very small and the option expired in May 1953 at 153. The new option started in July 1953 at 156; you would sell short and sell just as soon as it declined to 152 which was under the old bottoms.

1953, September 15 low 115; same low as February 1949 and a buying level. Prices advanced to 134 November 2, reacted to November 17, advanced to 134 again on December 14, making a double top and a selling level. After this it continued to work lower making lower bottoms and lower tops. When the price broke 118 you would sell more. When it broke 115, the lows of 1949 and 1953, you would sell more. The decline continued until May 1954 when the May option sold at 88-3/4 and the July option declined to 91½ and the December option to $1. This was a drastic decline and a final liquidation when the open interest dropped to the lowest level for many years.

At this writing the indications are that Rye is low enough for at least a rally. You will note that the low in May came down to the old top level of March 1943, and there was a series of tops around 87¢ to 90¢. However, for trading in the future in 1954 and 1955, you should keep up the July and December options and then when the May option starts for 1955, keep up the daily and weekly high and low chart and you will be able to determine the trend on Rye and make large profits trading in it.

Follow all the rules in SPECULATION A PROFITABLE PROFESSION, as well as read carefully all the rules on Rye in my book, HOW TO MAKE PROFITS TRADING IN COMMODITIES. If you do this and study and place STOP LOSS orders for protection, and trade only definite indications, you can make substantial profits trading in Rye Futures.

MAY SOY BEAN SWINGS OF 10¢ PER BUSHEL OR MORE FROM OCTOBER 16, 1950 TO MAY 1954.

The reason that we have shown the swings on this chart, starting October 16, 1950, is because that was the low after a sharp decline from the big advance in August after the Korean war started. You can see that from October 16, 1950, low 232½ the advance was rapid until February 8, 1951, high 344¼ when the Government placed a ceiling on Beans at 333. I have marked "B" for buying levels on the chart and "S" for selling levels.

In 1951 when the Government placed a ceiling on Soy Beans at 333, if you had a chart on November Beans you could see that it indicated top and you would go short of the November option.

1951, July 9 – May Soy Beans declined to 268-3/4 and the main trend turned up again and advanced to December 10, 1951, high 314.

1952, February 27 and April 21, lows at 381 and 328; this was a buying level as indicated and the price advanced to 311 May 21, 1952. This was a selling level against the top of December 1951; however, the May option expired and you would, of course, wait for the new option which started July 24, 1952 at 291. The trend turned up and it advanced to 314. August 14 it declined to 306; August 26 made double top and September 3 at 314 which was a selling level with a STOP at 316. The main trend continued down until February 13, 1953, low 280, around the same lows as April 1952, a buying level. There was a rapid advance to April 16, high 309, which was the last high and the option declined to 296½ and expired.

1953, July 25; the new option opened at 256 and advanced to 259½. You would sell it short when it broke 256 because it was below all previous bottoms and indicated lower. The price declined to August 20 low of 239½. This was a buying level as indicated by the weekly and daily charts. The market advanced to 263 on September 3, reacted to 248-3/4 September 16. You will note that I have marked "B", the buying levels all the way up on this chart and that bottoms were higher and tops were higher showing the main trend up.

1954, January 22, high 317½. This was above all of the tops at 314, 311, and 309, a definite indication that prices were going very much higher. February 2, when a reaction came to 309¼, which was down to the old top levels, you would buy. When it crossed 317 buy more, and continue to buy all the way up. When it crossed 345 you would buy more. March 4, high 359-3/4, March 8, low 343½, just back to the old top level of February 8, 1951 and a buying level. Protect with STOP LOSS order at 342. The advance continued making higher bottoms and higher tops and you would buy every time it advanced to new high levels until April 27, 1954, extreme high 422. April 28, low 406½; April 29, high 417½, a lower top and a selling level; however, there was definite indication for weakness and selling when it broke to 406.

1954, May 12; May Beans declined to 372, a decline of 50¢ per bushel since April 27. The July option made high on April 27 at 415 and sold at 368-1/8 on May 12, 1954, down 47¢ per bushel. The writer sold July Beans short at 412 on April 30, and sold more at 400½; sold again at 396 and at 390½ because prices were breaking the previous low levels and indicated a definite down trend. We covered shorts at 370 on May 12 because our daily high and low chart and hourly high and low chart indicated that the market was making bottom for a one to two day rally. You should keep up a daily high and low chart and a weekly chart on May, July and November Soy Beans and if you trade according to the rules you can make a vast amount of money. Soy Beans is really the "millionaire money maker" but remember that if you buck the trend on Soy Beans, it can break a millionaire; therefore, use STOP LOSS orders every time you make a trade and LIMIT YOUR RISK and do not OVERTRADE and you can make enormous profits trading in Soy Beans.

WHEAT

You always need to know the record of prices for a long period of time on Wheat as well as anything else. 1852 Wheat low 28¢ per bushel; 1867 high $3 per bushel; 1877 high 176; 1888 high 165; 1898 high 185, 1905 high 122, 1909 high 135; 1912 high 119, 1915 high 167.

1914, June low 84¢ per bushel. This was just before the war started; when it crossed 119 and 122 you would buy and expect the next important resistance level to be the old high of 165.

1915, September high 167. Did not go 3¢ above 165 making this a SELLING LEVEL with a STOP at 168.

1916, when May Wheat advanced above 167 you would FOLLOW the RULES and BUY AT NEW HIGH LEVELS and then watch the next old high at 185. When this was crossed you would BUY MORE AT NEW HIGHS because it had been so long since 185 was made back in 1898 and so much time had elapsed you would expect very much higher prices, especially in a war market.

The next old high was $3 a bushel, the extreme in 1867; when this was crossed the next high had to be shown by a change in trend because there was no other high to use as a guide.

1917, May 11 high 325. The Government stopped trading and Futures Trading was not resumed until 1920. This is the May option that we refer to and from this time on we will refer to the May option and give trading indications on the May option.

In 1920, from that time on you could see what old lows were broken and when prices declined below old top levels and old low levels showing the main trend as down and you would continue to sell. Refer to chart on Wheat 1914 to 1954. Note 1921 to 1924 lows of 105, 104, and 101; the last low, 101, was made in March 1924, a buying level with STOP at 99.

The next tops were 127, 150 and 181; when these highs were exceeded you would follow the rules and buy at new highs.

1925, January high 205-7/8; from this high the trend turned down and you can see by the chart that TOPS were LOWER and BOTTOMS were LOWER indicating DOWN TREND. Here you would follow all the rules and SELL SHORT.

1928, April last high 171; you would sell more when 116, 112, 93 and 84 were broken. 84 was the low of June 1914, and declining below this level indicated much lower prices.

1932, December; final low 43-3/8 for the May option. This was the lowest that May Futures ever sold and the lowest since January 1895 when the last low was 49¢ per bushel.

After the low in December 1932 you would look up the last old highs and watch them. These were 62, 73, 130, 135, 150, 164, 171, 181, 185 and 205-7/8.

In 1933, when the main trend had turned up, you would buy when the prices crossed 62, 73, and watch 130, the last old high in February 1929.

1933, July, May Wheat made a high of 128, just below 130, making this a SELLING LEVEL.

1939, September. Hitler started the war and war is always bullish on Wheat and you should always buy when war starts. May Wheat was selling around 62½ in August 1939, the old top level of May 1932, making this a BUYING LEVEL protected, of course, with STOP around 60. You would buy when prices advanced above the previous highs, 86, 117, 128, 164, 171, 185 and 205-7/8.

Note 1937 high 145 and September 1944 last low 144 – you would buy here because it was at the OLD TOP LEVEL and place a STOP 3¢ below.

1944 and 1945. The Government put ceilings on Wheat and these ceilings were not removed until 1946.

1946, September May Wheat last low 180. When it advanced above 185 you would buy more at new high levels and then when it crossed 205-7/8, the high of 1925, you would follow the rule and BUY AT NEW HIGH LEVELS and watch 300 to 325, the highest Futures had ever sold for resistance levels.

1947, November and January 1948, May Wheat high 306-7/8. Study the weekly and daily chart at the time these highs are made and you will see how the TREND TURNED DOWN and it was time to sell out all long Wheat and sell short.

The first decline after the high in January 1948 was very rapid and in less than one month's time it declined to 229 in February 1948, then rallied to 252 and in February 1949 declined to 196½. You can see by the chart July 1949 low was 191- 3/4 and after this the trend turned up and made higher bottoms and higher tops.

1951, February high 261 made the next low at 235.

December high 265½, this was final high of this upswing. You would sell short and sell more on the way down after prices declined below 235.

1953, August low 186-3/4; from this level the minor trend turned up and in March

1954 the high was 231, failing to advance to 235 the low of May 1951, indicating weakness and lower prices. The trend turned down and on May 12, 1954 May Wheat declined to 195¼ and July Wheat to 189½, and at this writing the main trend is still down.

Follow all the rules in this course of instruction, SPECULATION A PROFITABLE PROFESSION and the rules in my book HOW TO MAKE PROFITS TRADING IN COMMODITIES. Never decide that you know it all.

Continue to keep up charts and study and you will make speculation a profitable profession.

I have never thought that I had learned all there was to learn and have made some of my greatest discoveries after I was 75 years old, having perfected my Master Charts, my 3-Dimension Chart proving the relation between price, time and volume, which shows velocity or speed and trend. Also discovered new Master Time Charts.

I have spent over $20,000.00 since my 75th birthday making researches and preparing trends for the future.

Learn to work hard and study. The more you study the greater your success will be. KNOWLEDGE IS THE GREATEST THING YOU CAN HAVE. It is better than money in the bank. You can never lose KNOWLEDGE and no one can STEAL it from YOU; therefore, get all the KNOWLEDGE YOU possibly can.

CONCLUSION

I have written this course of instructions, SPECULATION A PROFITABLE PROFESSION to help others make a success trading in Commodities. There is no greater pleasure in life than rendering good service to others. The Bible tells us that a man should not hide his candle under a bushel; I believe in passing on my secret discoveries to help others and have always found greater happiness and made greater success by helping others.

> "He who has the truth and keeps it,
> Keeps what not to him belongs;
> Keeps a pearl from him who needs it,
> And a fellow mortal wrongs."
>
> (Anon.)

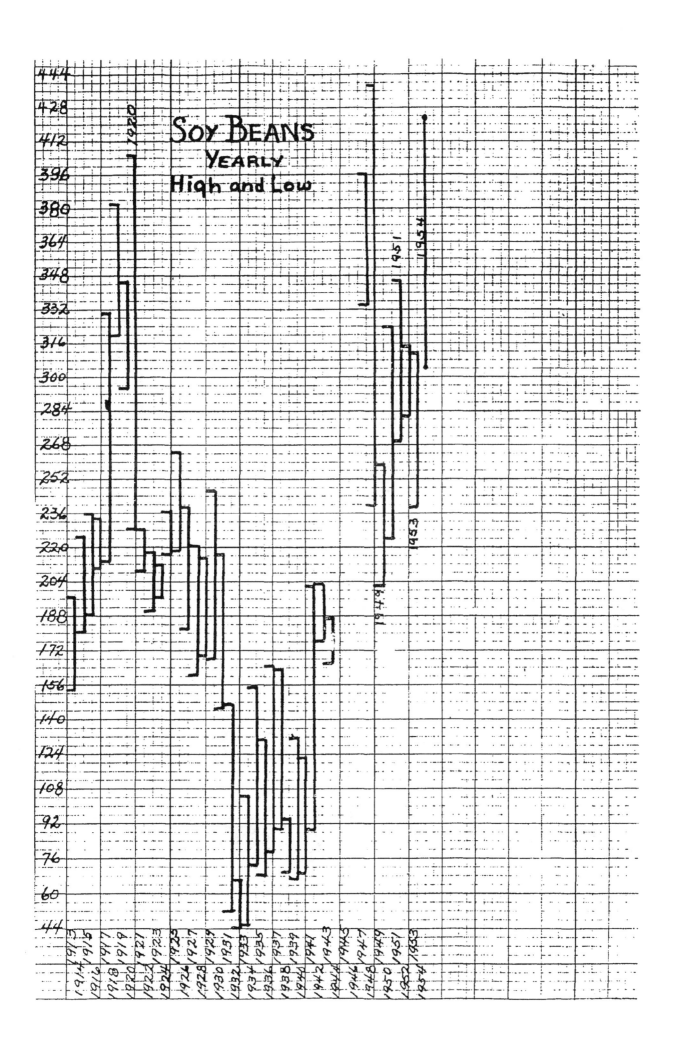

SOY BEANS
YEARLY
High and Low

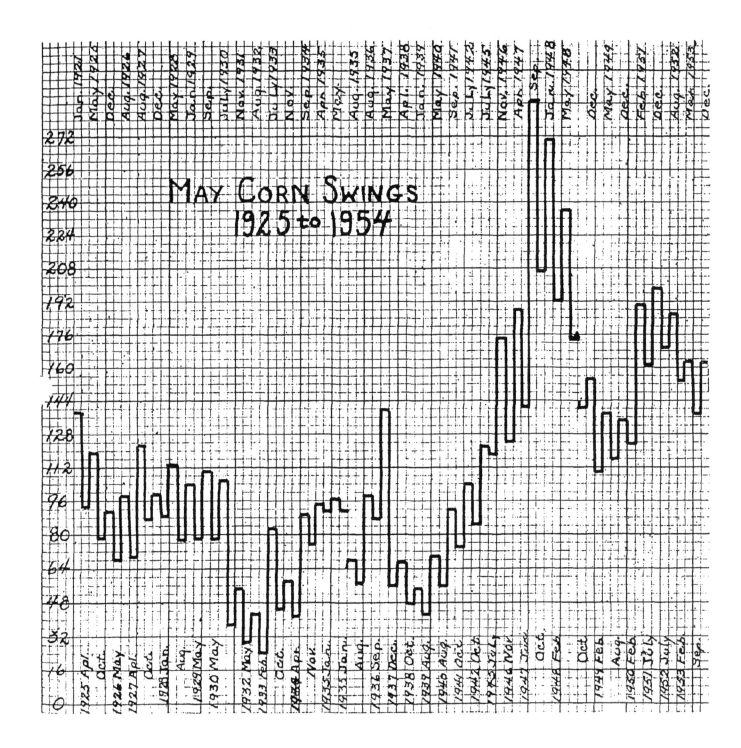

MAY CORN SWINGS
1925 to 1954

—40—

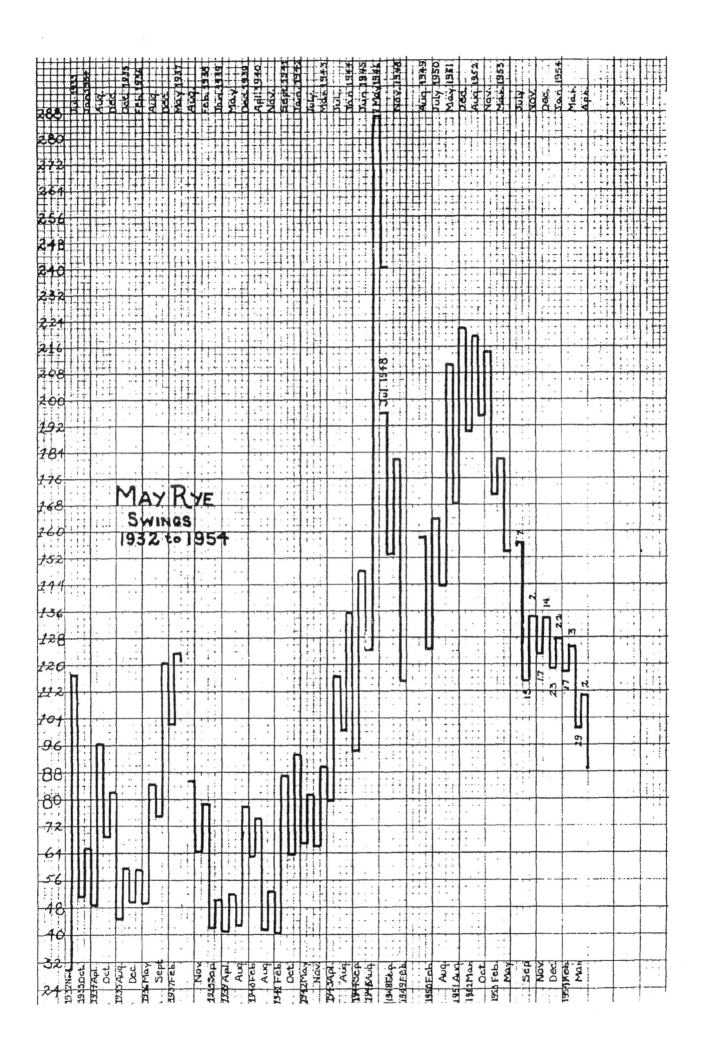

MAY RYE
SWINGS
1932 to 1954

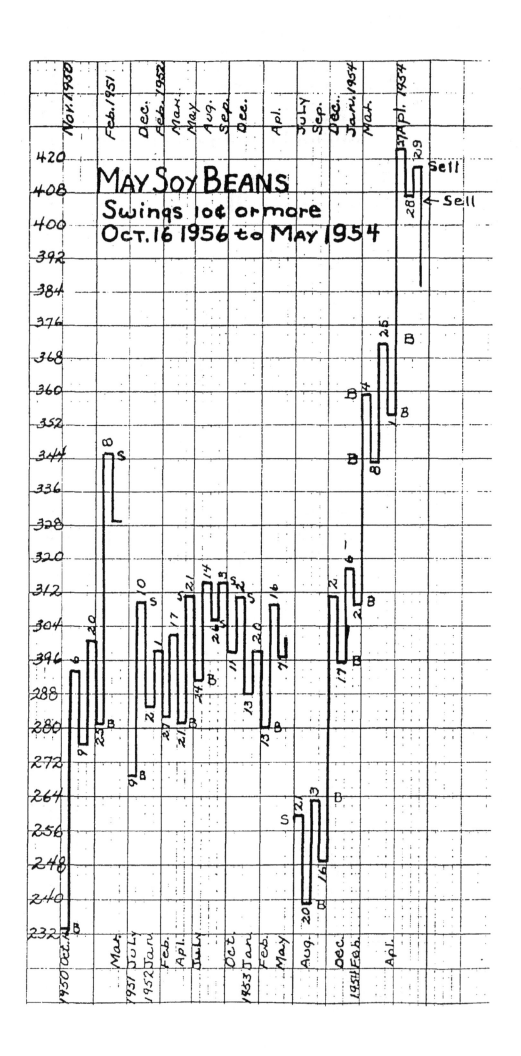

MAY SOY BEANS
Swings 10¢ or more
Oct. 16 1956 to May 1954

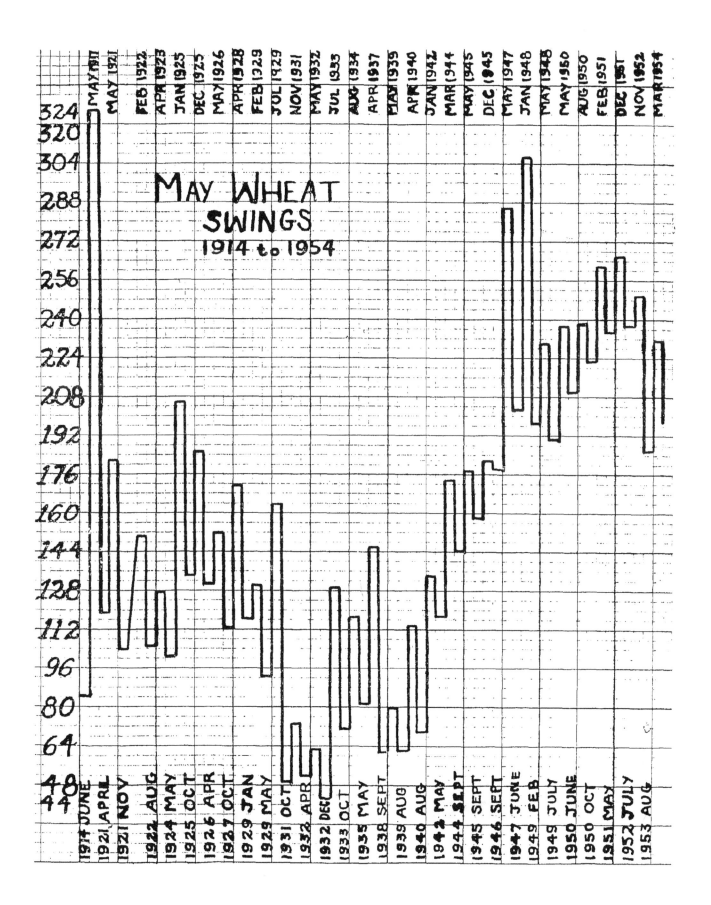

MAY WHEAT
SWINGS
1914 to 1954

LESSON 2

MECHANICAL METHOD AND TREND INDICATOR FOR TRADING IN GRAINS

CONTENTS

CONTENTS *(Contd.)*

AUTHOR OF
TRUTH OF THE STOCK TAPE
WALL STREET STOCK SELECTOR
NEW STOCK TREND DETECTOR
HOW TO MAKE PROFITS IN COMMODITIES

W. D. GANN

82 WALL STREET
NEW YORK 5. N.Y.

MEMBER
AMERICAN ECONOMIC ASS'N
ROYAL ECONOMIC SOCIETY

MECHANICAL METHOD AND TREND INDICATOR

FOR TRADING IN WHEAT, CORN, RYE OR OATS

****

CAPITAL REQUIRED

The first and most important thing to know when you start to trade is the amount of capital required that will enable you to continue to trade 1, 2, 3, 5 or 20 years and never lose your capital. If you always have capital to start trading again, you can recoup losses and make money, but if you risk all of your capital on one or two trades and lose it, then the chances are against you. "Safety first" is the rule to apply.

The unit of trading in Wheat on the Chicago Board of Trade is 5,000 bushels, although you can trade in job lots of 1,000 bushels. When Wheat is selling between 50 and 75¢ per bushel, you need a capital of $750 to trade in 5,000 bushels. Your stop loss orders should be 1 to 2¢ per bushel under a daily bottom or under the Trend Line bottom, according to the rules.

If your average risk is 1½¢ per bushel or $75 on each 5,000 bushels, you could lose 10 consecutive times before your capital of $750 would be wiped out. This has never happened and never will happen if you trade according to the rules and buy and sell on Trend Line bottoms and tops and on double or triple bottoms and tops. It is seldom that you will ever have three consecutive losses. However, should you have three consecutive losses, which would reduce your capital 200 to $250, then try to make your next trade of 5,000 bushels where your risk will only be 1¢ per bushel.

If you have three trades that show a total loss of 5¢ per bushel and then you get a market running and make 10¢ per bushel, you are 5¢ per bushel ahead. Of course, many times in very active markets, with wide range, you will start a pyramid which will result in profits of 50¢ per bushel or even $1 per bushel before your pyramid is closed out. The main thing to do is to always go with the trend and never buck the trend, regardless of how much capital you have.

When Wheat is selling between 75¢ and $1, then you should have a capital of $1,000 to trade in 5,000-bushel lots. When Wheat is selling between $1.00 and $1.50 per bushel, your capital should be $1,500. When Wheat is selling between $1.50 and $2.00, your capital should be $2,000.00 for each 5,000-bushel lot.

CORN AND RYE: Your capital for trading in these grains when they are selling between 25 and 40¢ per bushel should be $500. When they are selling between 40 and 75¢ per bushel, your capital should be $750. When they are selling between $1.00 and $1.75 per bushel, the capital required is $2,000. However, brokers may require more margin at the higher price levels.

KIND OF CHARTS YOU SHOULD KEEP

You should always keep up a daily high and low chart with opening and closing on it and keep your Trend Line on this Daily Chart.

You should also keep up a 3-day Chart separately, and a Weekly high and low chart.
Your should have a monthly chart going back 15 to 20 years so you will know where the important tops and bottoms are, where old Resistance Levels have been made. This is often very helpful.

CHART FOR THE TREND LINE INDICATOR

Keep up a daily high and low chart on two of the active options and mark the opening and closing prices on this chart.
The Trend Indicator or Trend Line is obtained by following the daily moves. As long as the option is advancing and making higher bottoms and higher tops, the Indicator or Trend Line moves up each day to the highest price and continues to move up as long as the market makes higher tops and higher bottoms.
The first day that the option reverses and makes a lower bottom by 1/4¢ or more, you move the Trend Line down to that bottom. Then, if on the following day the option moves down to a lower bottom, you move the Trend Line to the low of that day and continue to move it down as long as it makes lower bottoms.
Then, the first day that the option records a higher bottom and a higher top, you move the Trend Line up again to the top of that day.
This Trend Lime simply follows the swings of an option.

NEW HIGH AND NEW LOW THE SAME DAY
If an option makes a higher top in the early part of the day than the previous day, then before the market closes, goes down and makes a lower bottom than the previous day, you move the Trend Line up to the higher top reached in the early party of the day, then move it down to the bottom made later in the day.
The idea of the Trend Indicator is to show each higher top and lower bottom so that you will always know where an option starts down from the last top or starts up from the last bottom.

WITHIN DAY
By a "within day" I mean a day when an option makes a higher bottom but does not make a higher top than a previous day; in other words, it remains within the range of the previous day.

If an option is declining and only rallies one day, making a higher bottom but not making a higher top, then breaks to new lows, I do not consider it important or advisable to move the Trend Line up; neither would I move the stop loss order down above this "within day" top unless it was after a prolonged decline in a fast-moving market.

Apply this same rule when an option is advancing and makes a lower top but not a lower bottom the same day, remaining within the range of the previous day; then if it advances to higher levels the following day, the Trend Line should not be moved down and stop loss orders should not be moved up under this bottom unless there has been a prolonged advance in a fast-moving market.

Within moves last sometimes as much as 2 or 3 days, that is, remaining 2 or 3 days on a side move without breaking the bottom of a previous active day or crossing the top of that day. When a change occurs after a move of this kind, go with it. If it breaks the bottom after a series of within days, go short. If it crosses the top after a series of within days, consider the trend up and go long.

HOW TO USE STOP LOSS ORDERS

With this Method you must always use a stop loss order 1, 2, or 3¢ below the bottom or above the tops made by the Trend Indicator.

Remember that stops are placed above or below the top of bottom on the Trend Line Indicator, and NOT placed above or below the high and low for the day, except when you are applying the 7 to 10-day Rule and following a pyramiding move up or down, or where there is a Signal Top or Bottom day, when you place stop loss orders above the top of the signal day or below the bottom of the signal day.

When the market is moving slowly, you can use 1¢ stop loss orders with greater success and larger profits, but when an option fluctuates rapidly the move will often go 1½¢ over a top or under a bottom and not go 2¢, therefore a 2¢ stop loss order will not be caught as often. A stop loss order 3¢ under a Trend Line Bottom or over a Trend Line top will be caught less frequently than a 1 or 2¢ stop loss orders. However, as a general rule, I only advocate using 3¢ stop loss orders in very active markets.

When Wheat is selling at very high prices, then you have to put your stop loss orders further away, but in most cases I never advise using a stop loss order more than 3¢ per bushel away. However, after Wheat has had a big advance or a big decline and you have big profits, then you can either follow up with stop loss orders 1¢ under each day's bottom or
3¢ per bushel below each day's bottom , or follow down with a stop loss order
5¢ above the top level of each day or follow up with a stop loss 5¢ under the bottom of each day until your stop is caught. Never risk 5¢ per bushel on any one trade to start with, only when you have big profits can you afford to have your stop loss order 5¢ per bushel away.

1/2-POINT MOVES AND STOPS

After Wheat has made a series of bottoms or tops around the same level and becomes very active, then it is just as well to move your stop loss order up 1/2¢ under the series of bottoms or place your stop 1/2¢ above the series of tops. As a rule, when it breaks 1/2¢ under or crosses 1/2¢ over, it indicates a further move in that direction.

WHEN NOT TO TRADE

Never trade in any option after delivery day. In other words, on April 30 always get out of May Wheat and do not trade during May. Never trade in July during the month of July; nor in September option during the month of September; nor in December option during the month of December. It never pays to trade when you can be called on any minute for delivery. Keep your trades in the distant options.

TRADING INSTRUCTIONS

BUYING AND SELLING POINTS

Rule 1 – TRADING ON TREND LINE INDICATIONS ONLY

The simplest and easiest rule to use is to buy 10,000 bushels, 5,000 bushels, or any other unit that you start trading in, and place a stop loss order 1¢ under the last Trend Line bottom; then follow up with a stop loss order 1¢ under the last Trend Line bottom and never use any other indication to sell out until the Trend Line breaks 1¢ under the previous Trend Line bottom, where your stop is caught. Then reverse, selling 10,000 bushels or whatever your unit is and following that down with a stop loss order 1¢ above each Trend Line top until your stop loss order is caught. Then reverse and go long again.

Remember, always allow your Trend Indicator to be your guide and when it turns down, follow it and do not expect a change until the Trend Indicator shows it. That is what your Trend Indicator is for – to keep you with the trend of the market, and when it changes, you must change and reverse your position accordingly.

This rule will make the cautious investor or trader a very large percentage of profits each year if he trades when the market is active. The higher price at which an option is selling, the more money this rule will make.

Rule 2 – BUYING AT DOUBLE OR TRIPLE BOTTOMS

Buy against double or triple bottoms and protect with stop loss order 1, 2, or 3¢ away according to the price and activity. When an option makes the same price level a few days apart, it makes what we call a double bottom on the Trend Indicator. A triple bottom is when an option makes bottom around the same level of prices the third time. A second or third bottom can be slightly higher or lower than the previous bottom, but remember this rule:

When you buy at the time an option reaches the third bottom, you should never risk more than 1¢, for when the third bottom is broken, especially if this bottom is around the same level, and your stop is caught, it will indicate that the main trend has changes and you should double up and go short.

Always reverse position when the trend changes. If you are long of the market and your stop is caught, you must go short. If you are short of the market and the trend changes and your stop is caught, you must go long or buy an equal amount.

The safest buying point is when an option makes a triple bottom near the same level, protected with a stop loss order not more than 1¢ under the lowest level of the triple bottom.

Rule 3 – SELLING AT DOUBLE OR TRIPLE TOPS

This rule is just the reverse of Rule 2. Sell against double or triple tops with stop loss order 1, 2, or 3 points above the top, but on a third top never use more than a 1¢ stop loss order because, as a general rule, when an option reaches the same price level the fourth time, it goes through and goes higher. Therefore, it is always a sure indication when it goes above the third top, you can buy it for higher prices.

The safest selling point is when an option makes a triple top near the same level, protected with a stop loss order not more than 1¢ above the highest level of the triple top.

Rule 4 – FOURTH TIME AT THE SAME LEVEL

Triple bottoms are the strongest and triple tops the strongest, but it is very important to watch an option when it reaches the same level the fourth time as it nearly always goes through. Therefore it is safe to reverse position and pyramid when an option goes through a triple top or crosses the same price level the fourth time.

Reverse the rule on the down side. Where triple bottoms are made close together, when an option goes to this level the fourth time, it nearly always goes thru. Therefore, when triple bottoms are broken, reverse, sell out all longs and go short, always going with the trend and never against it.

Rule 5 – ASCENDING OR RISING BOTTOMS AFTER A TRIPLE BOTTOM

After an option makes a third or triple bottom, then has a rally and from this rally reacts again, making a fourth bottom higher than the previous bottoms, it is a sign of strong support and indication of higher prices. Then if the fifth bottom is higher, it is a still stronger indication that a greater advance will take place.

Rule 6 – DESCENDING OR LOWER TOPS AFTER A TRIPLE TOP

After a triple top, watch the fourth top or the first rally after an option breaks away from the triple top. If this fourth top is lower than the previous tops, it is a sign of weakness and lower prices. Then after a decline, if the next top of a rally, which would be the firth top counting from the first, is still lower, it is a sign of extreme weakness and indicates much lower prices.

Rule 7 – 7 TO 10-DAY RULE FOR AN ACTIVE, FAST-MOVING MARKET

When an option of grain is very active, declining fast and making lower tops and lower bottoms each day, after is has declined 7 days or more, you should make your stop loss order 1¢ above each day's top, and when your stops are caught, reverse position and buy, placing stop loss order 1¢ under the previous day's bottom.

When an option is very active and advancing fast, after it has advanced 7 to 10 days or more without breaking a previous day's bottom, you should follow your purchase up with a stop loss order 1¢ under each day's low until the stop is caught. Then reverse and go short, placing a stop loss order 1¢ above the previous day's top.

But do not consider that the main trend has changed up or down until an option crosses a Trend Line top or breaks under the last Trend Line bottom.

PYRAMIDING

Rule 8 – HOW TO PYRAMID

Much larger profits can be made pyramiding, and it is just as safe to pyramid if you adhere strictly to the rules.

If you are trading in 5,000 bushels and using a capital of $750 to $1,000 after you buy or sell the first 5,000 bushels, when the market moves 5¢ in your favor or when you have $250 profit, buy or sell 5,000 bushels more so long as the Trend Indicator shows that the main trend is still up or down. Continue to buy or sell 5,000 bushels more every time the market moves 5¢ in your favor, always placing a stop loss order not more than 1¢ below the Trend Line bottom or 1¢ below each day's lowest, if you are long, and not more than 1¢ above Trend line top or 1¢ above each day's highest if you are short. If you have pyramided until you have 25,000 bushels, then you should have an order in to sell 30,000 bushels on stop, which would put you short 5,000 bushels to start a new deal. Pyramid again in the same way or as long as the market moves in your favor.

But remember that when an option selling between 60¢ to $1.00 per bushel has moved 15 to 25¢ in your favor, you must watch for a change in trend and be careful about buying or selling another lot on which you would have to take a loss.

Rule 9 – THE RUN OR PYRAMIDING MOVE

The big money in pyramiding is made in the run between accumulation and distribution. Pyramids should be started after double or triple bottoms. Then, when you get into this run, buy every 5¢ up, protecting with a stop loss order 1¢ under each day's bottom or 1¢ under the last Trend Line bottom. By following up with a stop loss order 1¢ under the Trend Line bottom, you not get out until the main trend has changed. But in fast-moving markets, after you have bought the 5th or 6th lot, then it is safest to keep your stop loss orders 1¢ under each day's bottom, because in active fast-moving markets at high levels, an option often declines 10 to 12¢ in two days without breaking the Trend Line bottom or without declining and moving the 3-day Chart down. If you use your rule for determining the top day, then you can get out before the trend changes or even before the option breaks the bottom of a previous day.

Rule 10 – PYRAMIDING ON TREND LINE INDICATIONS ONLY

The pyramiding plan is simple and easy to use. You simply use Rule 1 to make your first trade, buying the first lot after the Trend Line Indicator shows up trend by crossing a Trend Line top by 1¢, then use Rule 9 for buying the second lot after the option breaks out of a trading range, but, remember, never buy the second lot until the option crosses the highest top of the trading range.

In a declining market, sell the first lot after the Trend Line shows down trend by breaking a Trend Line bottom by 1¢; then use Rule 9 for selling the second lot after the option breaks out of a trading range, only selling the second lot when the option breaks the lowest bottom of the trading range.

Rule 11 – *SAFEST PYRAMIDING RULE*

One of the safest rules to use for pyramiding when an option is at extremely high levels or extremely low levels is to start with 5,000 bushels and when the market moves 5¢ in your favor, buy another 5,000 bushels; then when it moves 5¢ more, buy or sell 5,000 bushels; then on the next 5¢ move in your favor, buy or sell 5,000 bushels. Continue to follow the market up or down with this amount until there is a change in the main trend.

Rule 12 – *FAST MARKET AND WIDE FLUCTUATIONS*

In fast-moving markets, like 1915 to 1917, and 1929, 1933, 1945 and 1946, when you pyramid and have very large profits, you should follow down with a stop loss order about 7 to 10¢ away from the market. Then, after a severe decline reduce stop loss orders, placing them about 3 to 5¢ above the low level, because when a market is moving as fast as this, you should not wait for the Trend Indicator to show a change in trend by crossing a Trend Line top or even a previous day's top before changing position; also apply the rules for determining bottom by Signal Day and Opening and Closing Prices. Reverse this rule in an advancing market.

Rule 13 – *WHEN NOT TO PYRAMID*

Never buy a second lot for a pyramid when an option is near a double top or sell a second lot when an option is near a double bottom.

Safety is the first consideration in starting or continuing a pyramiding campaign in an option of grain. Mistakes are made by buying or selling a second lot too near the accumulation or the distribution point. After a big run up or down, you must always wait for a definite change in trend before starting to pyramid.

An option often holds for several days or weeks in a range or 10 to 12¢, moving up and down, not crossing the highest top or breaking the last bottom made. When it does get out of this range, crossing the highest top or breaking the lowest bottom, it indicates a bigger move and you should start to pyramid, buying the second lot after it makes a new high or selling when it breaks to a new low.

The Wheat market has peculiar and unusual moves. It often has straight moves up or down with very small reactions, often only a 2-day rally or a 2-day reaction until the long trend has run out. After these long periods of advances or declines, then Wheat will go thru a narrow trading range for days, weeks or months. While it is in this trading range, whether it is accumulating or distributing, then you must trade against the bottoms and tops and wait until it breaks out of the trading range up or down before starting a new pyramid. You have to trade for small profits when Wheat is in these narrow ranges.

HOW TO DETERMINE CHANGE IN TREND

Rule 14 – MINOR TREND INDICATOR

In a declining market, never consider the minor trend has turned up until the trend changes on the Trend Line Chart. To change the trend on the Trend Indicator, an option must advance 1 or more cents above the last top on the Trend Indicator, according to the activity and price of the option, whether you are using 1, 2, or 3¢ stop loss orders above the previous top.

In an advancing market, never consider that the minor trend has turned down until an option breaks 1 or more cents under the last bottom on the Trend Indicator or Trend Line Chart.

Remember that breaking one cent under a daily bottom or going one cent over a daily top does not change the trend.

Rule 15 – MAIN TREND INDICATOR

After a prolonged advance, never consider that the main trend has changed until a bottom made by the 3-day chart has been broken.

After a prolonged decline, never consider that the main trend has changed until a top made by the 3-day Chart has been crossed.

Rule 16 – BREAKAWAY POINTS

Watch the point and price where the last move starts up from and when that price is broken, consider that the main trend is changing to the down side.

When an option is in strong position at high levels, watch the last bottom or starting point of the last move to new highs. When this level is broken it is an indication that the main trend is turning down.

Watch the point and price where the last move starts down from and when that price is crossed, consider that the main trend is changing to the up side.

When an option is in a weak position at low levels and slowly working lower, making lower tops and lower bottoms, it is important to watch the last top or the point where an option breaks away from and makes new lows and never decide that the main trend has turned until the option begins to cross some of these levels from which it broke away.

Rule 17 – SECOND AND THIRD HIGHER BOTTOMS AND LOWER TOPS

Watch the second and third higher bottoms. When an option breaks a second higher bottom, consider the main trend has changed to the down side.

Watch the second and third lower tops. When an option crosses the third lower top, consider the trend has turned up, at least temporarily, and go with it.

Rule 18 – SECTIONS OF A MOVE

It is important to study the different sections or moves that an option makes between the first low level and the first, second, third, fourth, or fifth tops of a move. After an option has had several moves up and reacted, when it is near the end of the move, the gains over the last previous top will be less and the run from the last bottom to the last top will be less than in the early stages of the movement, an indication that the move has run out and that a culmination is near. Then apply your other rules and watch the Trend Indicator and 3-day Chart for a reversal in trend.

In a declining market, apply the same rule. When the declines or sections of a move become shorter, it indicates that the selling pressure is waning.

Rule 19 – 3 FULL-CENT INDICATION AT BOTTOM OR TOP

In very weak markets watch for the first advance of 3 full-cents from any low level and in very strong markets for the first reaction of 3 full-cents which will indicate a change in the minor trend.

By 3 full-cents I mean, for example, from 60 low, a rally to 63 would be 3 full cents. If this low was 59½¢, we would not count 3 full cents until the option rallied to 63.

Reverse this rule when an option is advancing. Suppose it advances to 50-7/8 and has not had a 3 full-cent reaction for some time; then if it declines to 47, I would consider it a 3 full-cent reaction and an indication that the minor trend was reversing. In this case, if the option only declined to 47½ or even to 47¼, we would not count it a full 3-cent reaction, because full points are based on even figures.

Rule 20 – SHARP 2-DAY SIGNAL MOVE

After a prolonged decline an option often has a sharp 2-day rally, making a very wide range in price, then moves in this same range for several days or weeks without getting higher than the top of the 2-day rally or without breaking the previous bottom. This shows support or accumulation. Then when the top of the 2-day rally is crossed, it is an indication that you should buy a second lot to start a pyramid.

Apply the same rule after a sharp 2-day decline, which does not change the main trend because the option does not decline into the 3rd day, but later when the bottom of this sharp 2-day decline is broken, it is an indication that the main trend has turned down and you can start to pyramid again.

IMPORTANCE OF OPENING AND CLOSING PRICES

Rule 21 – SIGNAL TOP DAY

The opening and closing prices are very important when an option is very active and reaches extreme high and low.

On the day that extreme high price of a move is reached after a big advance, if option closes near the low of the day or closes below the halfway point of the day's range or closes below the opening, it indicates that the selling is better than the buying and that the option is getting ready to turn the trend down, at least temporarily. When there is a move of this kind, you should sell out and go short without waiting, placing a stop loss order on the shorts 1¢ above the final day's high.

Rule 22 – SIGNAL BOTTOM DAY

On the day that an option has a sharp break after a prolonged decline, if it closes higher than the opening or above the halfway point or better still if it closes at the extreme high, after making a wide range and going lower than the previous day, it is an indication that the buying is better than the selling and that the trend is getting ready to turn up or that a bigger rally may be expected. Therefore you should cover shorts and buy without waiting for the option to make a higher top than a previous day or without waiting until the trend turns up by crossing a Trend Line top.

Rule 23 – CLOSING NEARER THE TOP OR BOTTOM AND OPENING LOWER OR HIGHER

If an option has a big advance and closes near the top or at the exact top, then the next morning opens 1 to 2¢ lower, it is a sign of weakness and an indication that the option is going lower, especially if it fails to cross the high of the previous day.

When an option is declining and closes near the lowers levels of the day, then next morning opens 1 to 2¢ higher and never breaks the opening price and closes near the highest level of the day, it is a sure sign of good support and indicates that the option is going higher. If the option opens higher after closing weak and holds until 11 o'clock the same day without breaking the opening, it is a sign of higher prices and you should buy.

Rule 24 – A NARROW DAY AFTER A SHARPER DECLINE OR A SHARP ADVANCE

After an option has been declining for some time and has a sharp break, closing weak or near the low level, if on the following day the range is very narrow and the option goes only slightly lower and closes about the same level, it is an indication that the move has a run out and your stop loss order should be moved down 1¢ above the top of the narrow day.

After an option has been advancing for some time and had a sharp advance, closing strong or near the high level, if on the following day the range is very narrow, it is an indication that a culmination is near and your stop loss order should be moved up 1¢ under the bottom of the narrow day.

Rule 25 – CLOSING AT THE SAME LEVELS FOR A SERIES OF DAYS

Watch the closing price of an option after a prolonged decline or a prolonged advance.

If an option closes for a series of days around the same level, it is an indication that it is receiving support or meeting resistance around this level. Then the first day that it closes above or below this series of closings, it will be an indication of a change in trend and you should go with it.

Rule 26 – THREE TOPS OR BOTTOMS NEAR THE SAME LEVEL AND CLOSING PRICE

Watch how an option closes when it had a sharp run up and makes a top. If it closes below the halfway point or near the low of the day, it is an indication that it is making top. Then, when it advances to the same level the second or third time, if it reacts the same day and closes near the low, it is a sure indication of good selling and that the trend is getting ready to turn down.

Reverse this rule in a declining market. If three bottoms occur around the same level and each time the option closes near the high level of the day, it is an indication of higher prices and that the option is getting ready to turn up.

NOTE: All rules work best in active fast-moving markets and the big profits are made trading in active markets. If you follow these rules, you will make money. Make up your mind to follow the rules before you start and success is assured.

SPACE CHARTS
RULES FOR ACTIVE MARKETS AT HIGH LEVELS

Many times in history Wheat has sold at $1.75 to $3.50 per bushel. These high prices will recur some day, so you need to know how to trade in markets that move 10 to 20¢ per bushel per day and how to get out near tops and bottoms because the moves will be so fast that you cannot wait for Trend Line bottoms to be broken in every case, and cannot wait for daily bottoms to be broken or daily tops to be crossed, especially where the range is 15¢ per bushel a day, or even where it is 7 to 10¢ per day.

When a market is having a rapid advance or a rapid decline of this kind, you should keep a space chart of 3 points. By this I mean that during the day, when Wheat declines 3¢ per bushel from any top; then advances 3¢ per bushel from any bottom, you should record it. Then the first time that Wheat breaks under a bottom of a 3¢-move, consider that the trend has reversed temporarily. This may only be for one day or for one or two days, but it is a warning to get out.

You should also keep a chart of 1¢ movements if you are watching the tape. However, when the markets are very active at high prices, I consider that the best chart to keep is the 3¢ moves.

HOURLY CHART

In active, fast-moving markets, where you can get the prices every hour it is important to keep the Hourly high and low and also mark the opening of the hour and the closing of the hour.

Apply the same rules that you do to your Daily high and low chart. The first time that the market breaks a Trend Line bottom on the Hourly chart or crosses a Trend Line top, consider that the trend has changed temporarily.

If there are a series of hours with tops around the same level, or bottoms around the same level, for several hours, then when the market crosses 1¢ per bushel over an Hourly top, or breaks 1¢ under an Hourly bottom, consider that your trend has changed at least temporarily and trade accordingly.

Even in a narrow market or in a market that is moving 1 to 3¢ per day, if you keep an hourly high and low chart, you will see the value of it in getting a quick change in trend.

All of these rules are given you to protect your capital and protect your profits; to help you get out near the top as possible and as near the bottom as possible. Don't forget to always use stop loss orders. This is your "emergency brake" and your "safety valve" to protect you when the market reverses.

3-DAY CHART OR MAIN TREND INDICATOR

The 3-day Chart should be kept on a separate sheet of chart paper from the Daily high and low Chart and Trend Line. It is used in connection with the Minor Trend Indicator, or the Trend used with the Mechanical Method.

HOW TO MAKE UP 3-DAY CHART

For the 3-day Movement or Main Trend Indicator, the rules are as follows:

The 3-day Chart is made up of moves of 3 days or more. When an option starts to advance and makes higher bottoms and higher tops for 3 consecutive days, you move the line on the 3-day Chart up to the top of the 3rd day; then if it continues to move up, making higher tops without reacting as much as 3 days, you continue to move the line on the 3-day Chart up to the top of each day until the option reacts 3 days or makes lower bottoms for 3 consecutive days or more.

Then you move the line on the 3-day Chart down and continue to move it down to the lowest price as long as the option makes lower bottoms without rallying 3 days.

The first time that an option rallies 3 days from any bottom that is, making higher tops for 3 consecutive days or more, you move the line up.

This chart is based on higher tops and lower bottoms and not on closing prices. An option may close lower on the 3rd day, but not make a lower bottom, in which case you make no change on the 3-day Chart. An option may close higher on the 3rd day from the bottom but not make a higher top on the 3rd day and in that case, you do not move the line up on the 3-day Chart.

EXCEPTION TO RULE

There is an exception to the rule for making up the 3-day Chart. When an option is very active near the top or bottom, making a wide range, and crosses the top or bottom of a move made by the Trend Line Indicator in less time than 3 days, then you record the move on your 3-day Chart just the same as if there had been a move of 3 days in one direction.

INDICATIONS FOR CHANGE IN TREND

Rule 27 – CROSSING TOPS OR BREAKING BOTTOMS OF 3-DAY MOVES

The surest sign of a change in the main trend is when a move on the 3-day Chart is exceeded by 1 to 3¢. When an option breaks under a bottom made by the 3-day Chart, you consider that the main trend has turned down, and when a move crosses a top made by the 3-day Chart, consider that the main trend has turned up, at least temporarily.

Breaking 1¢ under the last 3-day bottom or crossing the last 3-day top by 1¢ in slow or semi-active markets is enough to show a change in the trend.

Rule 28 – FIRST 3-DAY REACTION OR RALLY

After a prolonged advance, watch the first time that there are 3-full days of lower prices or the first time that the 3-day Chart is moved down, as this will often be the first sign that the end of the move is near.

Next, watch the second move of 3 days down on the 3-day Chart and see if it is lower than the

Trend Line bottom or the minor Trend Indicator or under a 3-day bottom on the 3-day Chart. This will be a stronger indication of a reversal in trend.

Reverse this rule in a declining market. After a prolonged decline, watch the first time there is a rally of 3 days, as this will often be the first sign that a change in trend in near.

Rule 29 – *THE THIRD MOVE ON 3-DAY CHART*

The most important indication to watch is the third move down on the 3-day Chart after a prolonged advance or decline. For example: An option reacts 3 days; then advances to new high; then has a second 3-day reaction and advances to new high; then when the third reaction of 3 days comes from a new high, it is nearly always a signal that the move is over. If this move of 3 days the third time breaks a bottom on the 3-day Chart by 1, 2, or 3 points, depending on how high the option is and its activity, it is almost a sure sign that the main trend has turned down.

HOW TO COMBINE
TREND LINE INDICATOR AND 3-DAY CHART

The Trend Line Indicator always records the minor trend of the market, and when it reverses by breaking 1¢ under a previous Trend Line bottom or crossing 1¢ over a Trend Line top, it shows the minor trend, but the 3-day Chart always shows the main trend of the market.

It is never safe to trade against the main trend. In other words, if the 3-day Chart shows down trend, it is always better to sell short on rallies using the minor trend chart for placing stop loss orders. The same when the 3-day Chart shows up trend: It is always better to wait for reactions of 3 days and buy than it is to sell short, except in cases where there is a sharp advance.

When the minor Trend Indicator makes double or triple bottoms and double or triple tops and then breaks under these bottoms or crosses the tops, it will show a change in the major trend, but it is not safe to consider it a change in the main trend if the market is very low or narrow with small sales. Except on rapid advances, the 3-day moves will always show the main trend in plenty of time to get in and make money.

The big money is always made by going with the trend, and the 3-day Chart keeps you with the main trend.

RESISTANCE LEVELS

Every option makes a top or bottom on some exact mathematical point in proportion to some previous move. The movement of an option between extreme high and extreme low, either in a major or a minor move, is very important and by a proper division of this range of fluctuation, we determine the points where resistance or support will be met on a reverse move, either up or down. By carefully watching these Resistance levels in connection with your Trend Indicators, you can make a greater success and trade with closer stop loss orders.

RANGE OF FLUCTUATIONS

1/8 POINTS

Take the extreme low and extreme high of any important move; subtract the low from the high to get the range; then divide the range of fluctuation by 8 to get the 1/8 points, which are Resistance Levels or buying and selling points. When an option stops around these levels and makes bottom or top on or near them and shows a turn on the Trend Indicator, this is the place to buy or sell.

1/3 and 2/3 POINTS

After dividing an option by 8 to get the 1/8 points, the next important thing to do is to divide the range of fluctuation by 3 to get 1/3 and 2/3 points. These 1/3 and 2/3 points are very strong, especially if they fall near other Resistance Points of previous moves or when they are divisions of a very wide move.

HIGHEST SELLING PRICE

Next in importance is the division of the highest price at which Wheat, Corn, or Rye has ever sold and each lower top.

Divide the highest selling price by 8 to get the 1/8 points and also divide by 3 to get the 1/3 and 2/3 points.

This is very important: an option, after breaking the halfway point of the fluctuating range, will often decline to the halfway point of the highest selling price and will also work on the other Resistance Points in the same way.

When an option is advancing, it will often cross this halfway point of the highest selling point and then advance to the halfway point of the fluctuation and meet resistance.

MOST IMPORTANT GRAIN MOVEMENTS TO CONSIDER

The first and most important point: Consider the Resistance Levels between the extreme high and extreme low during the past 30, 20, 10, 5 and 3 years;

Next important point to consider: Resistance Points or divisions of the highest price at which an option of Wheat, Corn, or Rye has ever sold;

Then consider the fluctuation of each campaign which runs one year or more: Take the range between extreme high and extreme low and divide it into 8 equal parts to get the Resistance Points;

Then take a second top or a lower top than the extreme high and divide it by 8 to get the important Resistance Points;

Then take a third or fourth lower top and divide it by 8 to get the Resistance Points;

When you come to the last move, which may run several weeks or several months, that is the most important move to watch for your first Resistance Points.

ORDER OF RESISTANCE LEVELS

When an option is advancing and crosses the 1/4 point, the next most important point to watch is the halfway (1/2 point) or gravity center, or the average of the move or fluctuation.

Then the next point above the halfway point is the 5/8 point.

The next and strongest point after the halfway point is crossed is the 3/4 point.

Then if the range is very wide between these points, it is important to watch the 7/8 point of the move. This will often mark the top of an advance.

But in watching these Resistance Points, always watch your Trend Line Indicators, both on the Daily Chart and the 3-day Chart, and if they start making tops or bottoms around these Resistance points, it is safe to sell or buy.

THE AVERAGE OR HALFWAY POINT

Always remember that the 50% reaction or halfway point of the range of fluctuation or of the extreme highest point of an option of any particular move is the most important point for support on the down side or for meeting selling and resistance on the way up. This is the balancing point because it divides the range of fluctuation into two equal parts or divides the highest selling point into two equal parts.

When an option advances or declines to this halfway point, you should sell or buy with a stop loss order 1, 2, or 3¢ according to whether the option is selling at very high or very low levels.

The wider the range and the longer the time period, the more important is this halfway point when it is reached.

When an option advances to a halfway point and reacts several points from this level, then finally goes through it, you can expect it to make the next Resistance point indicated on your Resistance Level Card.

The same applies when an option declines and receives support several times on the halfway point, then breaks through it. It will then indicate the next Resistance Point on your Resistance Level Card or the next important bottom.

The greatest indication of strength is when an option holds one or more cents above the halfway point, which shows that buying or support orders were placed above this important Resistance Level.

A sign of weakness is when an option advances and fails to reach the halfway point by one or more cents; then declines and breaks the Trend Line or other Resistance Points.

NEXT RESISTANCE LEVELS
AFTER THE MAIN HALFWAY POINT HAS BEEN BROKEN

The next Resistance Level to watch after the main halfway point has been broken is the next halfway point of some previous move. By main halfway point I mean, the halfway point of the extreme fluctuating range of a grain option.

Another very important Resistance Level after the main halfway point is crossed is the halfway point of 1/2 of the highest selling price. This is a stronger support level than the halfway point of the minor fluctuating moves because it cuts the highest selling price in half, and is a strong buying or selling point until it is crossed by 1, 2, or 3 cents, according to the price of the option, whether it is very high-priced, medium or low-priced.

RESISTANCE POINTS NEAR SAME LEVELS

When two halfway points or any other two Resistance Points, either in the range of fluctuation or the division of the highest selling price, occur near the same level, you should add these two points together and divide by 2, as the halfway point between these two points will often be a support point on a decline or a selling point on a rally.

HOW TO LOOK UP RESISTANCE LEVELS

When you find an important Resistance Level or the strongest one – the halfway point – at a certain level, look to see if any other Resistance Level, whether it be 1/8, 1/4, 3/8, 5/8 or 2/3-point, falls around this same price.
You may find 3 or 4 Resistance Levels within a range around the same price. The more you find, the stronger resistance the option will meet when it reaches this level.
Then take the highest Resistance Level around this same price and the lowest, and add them together to get the average point of resistance.
Watch the activity of the option when it reaches these Resistance Levels. If it is advancing very fast or declining very fast on large volume, do not consider that it is going to stop around these Resistance Levels unless it stops or holds one or two days around these levels; then sell or buy, protected with stop loss orders.

MULTIPLES OF 12

You will also find this helpful in connection with your Trend Line Indicator: By going over past records you will find that May Wheat makes many tops and bottoms on multiples of 12 and on one-fourth of 12 and one-half of 12. For example: 48, 54, 60, 66, 72, 78, 84, 90, 96, 102, 108, 114, 120, 126, 132, 138, 144, 150, 156, 162, 168, 174, 180, etc.
Watch your daily highs and lows and when they hold for several days around an even price on multiples of 12 or the halfway points, you can buy or sell around these points with a stop loss order.
You will also find that Wheat often makes moves of 10 to 12¢ or 23 to 24¢ per bushel, 36¢ per bushel or 48¢ per bushel, that is, making its movements based on multiples of 12.

LOST MOTION

As there is lost motion in every kind of machinery, so there is lost motion in the grain market due to momentum, which drives an option slightly above or below a Resistance Level. The average lost motion is 1-7/8¢.

When an option is very active and advances or declines fast on heavy sales, it will often go from 1 to 1-7/8¢ above a halfway point or other strong Resistance Level and not go 3¢.

The same rule applies on a decline. It will often pass an important Resistance Point by 1-7/8¢ but not go 3 full points beyond it.

This is the same rule that applies to a gravity center in anything. If we could bore a hole through the earth and then drop a ball, momentum would carry it beyond the gravity center, but when it slowed down, it would finally settle on the exact center. This is the way grain options act around these important centers.

WEEKLY HIGH AND LOW CHART

The same rules may be applied to a Weekly high and low chart that we apply to the Trend Line Indicator and to the 3-day Chart.

As long as an option makes higher bottoms and higher tops each week on the Weekly Chart, you move the Trend Line up to the top of the week. Then the following week, if the option does not make a lower bottom or a lower top than the previous week, no change is made in the Trend Line, but the first week an option breaks a weekly bottom by 1/2¢ or more, you move the Trend Line down to the low of the week and continue to move it down to the low of each week as long as the option makes lower bottoms.

Then the first week that it makes a higher top than a previous week, move the Trend Line up to the top of that week and follow on, applying the same rules as applied to the other Trend Line Indicators.

For example: If an option declines for one or two weeks, making lower bottoms, then advances, making higher tops; then reacts for one week, making a lower bottom than a previous week; then moves up to a new high, and the following week or any week after extreme high has been made, it breaks the bottom of the reaction, you consider that the trend has turned down on the Weekly Chart.

These changes in trend on the Weekly Chart are stronger than changes in trend on the 3-day Chart.

The Weekly Chart often makes double and triple bottoms and double and triple tops just the same as the Daily Chart and the 3-day Chart. Therefore when the option makes a double or triple bottom on the Weekly Chart, you know that it is a strong indication for a change in the main trend to the up side. When an option makes a double or triple top on the Weekly Chart, it is a sign that it is meeting resistance and making final top.

3 WEEKS MOVES

The Rule of 3 may be applied to the Weekly Chart. An option will often react 3 weeks and not go lower the fourth week. If it does go slightly lower in the early part of the fourth week and at the end of the fourth week closes strong at or near the top of the week, it is an indication that the main trend has not changed and that the option is going higher. But any time an option does break under a bottom after having reacted 3 weeks and then rallies, it is in a very weak position and indicates much lower prices, especially if the option is at very high levels.

Reverse all of these rules in a declining market. If the option rallies 3 weeks from any bottom, then goes lower to a new low and later crosses the top that it made before 3 weeks' rally, it is a very important change in trend, which may last for some time.

7 TO 10 WEEKS' MOVES

After accumulation and distribution has been completed, Wheat will often advance or decline rapidly with only 2 to 3 days' reverse moves, running up or down 7 to 10 weeks. These are the moves in which you can pyramid and make big profits.

Watch for culmination around the 38th to 52nd day after a move starts, and if bottom or top is not made around this time, then watch for the next movement around the 66th to 70th day.

By going back over the charts and checking moves, you will see how important this rule is.

Many of my successful students use the 3-day Chart and the Weekly Chart for long pull trading and have made some very successful pyramids with these two charts alone.

This Mechanical Method, based on fixed rules, will overcome the human element, eliminating hope and fear as well as guesswork. Learn to stick to the rules and trade in active markets. Remember, practice makes perfect. The more work and study you do the greater success you will have. Apply all rules, keep your charts up to date at all times, and do no guesswork, and your success is sure.

HOW TO DETERMINE CULMINATIONS
AND CHANGES IN TREND

The big money is made in the Grain Market by following the main trend or big swings and not changing position or taking profits until the market shows by its own action that the trend has changed. If you will follow the rules, the market will tell you when the main or minor trend changes. Do not guess or trade on hope or fear. Give the market time to show a change in trend.

The activity and range in prices at high or low levels determine the change in trend according to whether the market is normal or abnormal. Abnormal prices and fluctuations occur during wars or after wars. The years when crops are very large or very small cause abnormal moves which run to extremes. You must never try to guess when tops or bottoms will be reached in abnormal markets as they will nearly always run longer than human reason or known facts would lead you to believe. That is why you must apply rules and wait for the market's action to show a definite change in trend.

FOUR RULES

Rule 1 – TIME RULE

The TIME FACTOR is the most important. When TIME is up, Time or Space movements will reverse.

Keep a record of the days that the market reacts, that is, actual trading days; also keep a record of the calendar days of each reaction or rally. When a reversal comes that exceeds the previous TIME movement, consider that the trend has changed, at least temporarily. After any important top or bottom is reached and the first reaction or rally comes, there is nearly always a secondary move which usually makes a slightly higher bottom or a lower top. The duration of this move may be 1, 2, 3 days or more, all depending upon the activity of the market and the duration of the advance or the decline. But your rule is to watch for an overbalancing of a previous TIME period before deciding that the trend has changed.

Rule 2 – SWING BOTTOMS AND TOPS

When a market advances, it continues to make higher bottoms and higher tops on the main swings. You must watch all of these reactions or bottoms; then the first time a SWING BOTTOM is broken, whether it be for 1, 2, 3 days or more, consider that the trend has changed and go with it.

When a market is declining, it continues to make lower bottoms and lower tops. Therefore, when the last SWING TOP is crossed, it indicates a change in trend.

Rule 3 – SPACE OR PRICE MOVEMENTS

By SPACE MOVEMENTS, I mean cents per bushel up or down from top to bottom. For example: Suppose Wheat starts to advance from 80¢ per bushel and reaches 90¢; reacts to 85¢; then advances to above $1.00 per bushel, reaching 112; then reacts to 107, which is again 5 cents' reversal in SPACE MOVEMENT. Then the advance is resumed and the price goes to 120; a quick reaction follows to 113, a decline of 7 cents per bushel, exceeding the two previous reactions of 5 cents per bushel. We call this *"overbalancing"* of a SPACE

MOVEMENT and an indication of a change in trend. But you must never depend upon the SPACE MOVEMENT alone to give a definite indication of a change in trend until it is confirmed by a reversal in TIME PERIOD and by the market breaking the last SWING BOTTOM.

Rule 4 – RESISTANCE LEVELS

When the price breaks back one-half or more of the previous SWING, this is also an indication of a change in trend. In a declining market, a rally of one-half or 50% or more of a SWING is the first indication of a change in trend. But these indications must be confirmed by the TIME RULE before you can be sure that there is a definite change in trend.

A review and study of past market movements will prove to you the accuracy and value of these rules.

Study the examples and comparisons of May Rye for 1924-1925 and 1945-1946.

AVERAGE SPACE MOVEMENT

As a general rule, Wheat or Rye will not react or decline more than 7 to 10 cents per bushel and in extreme cases not more than 12 cents per bushel before the advance is resumed. As a rule, breaking back or reversing more than 12 cents will show a change in trend when confirmed by the TIME RULE.

When a market is declining, the average rally is 7 to 10 cents and seldom more than 12 cents. In extremely weak markets, rallies may not run more than 3 to 5 cents per bushel, all depending upon whether prices are at normal or abnormal levels.

WHEN GRAIN IS IN THE STRONGEST OR WEAKEST POSITION

When Wheat, Rye or Corn is advancing and is in the last stages of a fast upswing, reactions will often last 2 days and then the advance will be resumed. An advance of this kind will sometimes run 42 to 49 days or 6 to 7 weeks and in extreme cases may run 3 to 4 months, but around 84 to 90 calendar days it is very important to watch for a change in trend.

Remember, the longer the duration in TIME a market has run up or down, the surer the indication of a change in the main trend when the TIME RULE shows a reversal. Also a very great range in fluctuations makes a change in trend more important when it comes.

Example – MAY RYE

1945

Jun   1   Low 131-3/8.

       19   High 146½, up 15 cents. No reaction lasted over 2 days and no one-cent break under a previous daily bottom.

       19   Was a signal day. Then followed a quick 2-day reaction.

       21   Low 138½. Then one-day rally to 142½. Then broke previous bottom.

       25   Low 135½, from which rally followed.

Jul   2   High 141¾. It failed to cross the last top of June 22. The downward trend was resumed, with the market making lower prices.

Jul   7   Low 130¼. A rally followed.

1945

13 High 138¼. This was a normal rally of 8 cents per bushel. The next decline ran to

18 Low 129, a signal day, when the minor trend turned up.

Aug 4 High 139¾, 2 cents under the top of July 2 and only 1½ cents above the top of July 13, making this a selling level with stop loss order above 142½. Then the main trend turned down again, with nothing more than one-day rallies.

21 Low 124, down 15 cents from the last top and 22½ cents from the top of June 19. This run lasted 13 market days and from the top of June 19 the decline was 51 market days and 60 calendar days – a place to watch for a change in trend. The market then rallied for 3 consecutive days, showing a change in trend, and started making higher tops and higher bottoms.

31 High 139-3/8, up near the last top. A 3-day reaction followed.

Sep 5 Low 133½. Note that this was less than a 6-cent decline. The advance was then resumed.

Oct 15 High 153½.

20 Low 148¼, the reaction lasting 5 market days and a decline of 5¼ cents per bushel. No indication either by TIME, SWING, or SPACE MOVEMENT that top had been reached, because no SWING BOTTOM had been broken, so this really was another 3-day reaction as there were 3 daily tops around 153½. A rapid advance followed.

Nov 13 High 182-1/8. A quick reaction followed.

16 Low 169¼. This was a 3-day reaction and a SPACE reaction of nearly 13 cents per bushel, exceeding the previous SPACE reaction. While SPACE movement indicated a change in trend, the previous TIME periods had not been exceeded and no SWING BOTTOM had been broken. Therefore, you could not decide that the minor or main trend had changed until there was a reversal in TIME or a SWING BOTTOM broken. A sharp 3-day rally followed.

20 High 187, up 63 cents from the low of August 21. By referring to 1924-1925 you would find that the advance at that time ran from 119 to 182¼, an advance of 63 cents. The SPACE MOVEMENT would make this a selling level with a stop loss order 3 cents away. November 20 was a signal day, the price closing at the low of the day's range. The decline continue to

23 Low 173½, a decline of 13½ cents. This exceeded the previous SPACE reaction but still the TIME period had not been exceeded nor had a SWING bottom been broken. A 3-day rally followed to

27 High 181¼, almost the same top as November 13, making this a selling level protected with a stop loss order 3 cents above. The decline was resumed and when prices broke 173½, they were under the first SWING bottom and the TIME period from the top exceeded the TIME period of all previous reactions since August 21.

Dec 5 Low 160, down 27 cents per bushel in 12 market days and 15 calendar days, which was a normal 2 weeks' reaction. The market rallied, making higher bottoms.

10 High 169.

15 Low of reaction 161½, a second higher bottom. The advance was resumed and prices crossed 169, the high of December 10, showing main trend up again.

For continuation of this advance, see analysis under
"May Rye Swing Comparison Chart."

MAY RYE

Comparison
of
Price and Time Moves

1924-1925   1945-1946
Market Days . . . . Calendar Days
3-day Market Moves

1924 - November 1, May Rye 119. Then a big upswing followed with no reaction of over 10 cents per bushel and no reaction lasting over 9 days.

1925 - January 28, high 182½, up 63½ cents in 88 days.

Notice on the Swing Chart that no SWING or reaction bottom was broken during this advance. The TIME of greatest reaction was 9 calendar days and the greatest price reaction 10 cents per bushel. This occurred December 27, 1924 to January 5-6, 1925. Therefore to change trend the market must decline more than 10 cents per bushel or more than 9 calendar days or break a Swing reaction bottom. Refer to Rules 1, 2, 3 and 4. By watching these 4 rules you could determine when the trend had changed and could sell out and go short.

1925

Jan 28 High 182½; Jan. 29 low 176½ – down 6 cents.

30 High 181½, up 5 cents, a lower top.

Feb 3 Low 169½, down 13 cents, and from Jan. 28 high the time was 6 calendar days. This gave two indications that top had been made: 2 Swing bottoms broken and price decline of more than 10 cents, which would indicate a short sale.

4 High 177½, up 8 cents from Feb. 3 low. This indicated a short sale with stop at 183½, which would be one cent above 182½ top. A decline followed that lasted more than 9 calendar days.

11 Low 154, down 28½ cents in 14 calendar days.

16 High 164, up 10 cents in 5 days, a normal rally.

17 Low 155, a higher bottom than Feb. 11, sign of support.

20 High 162, a lower top.

21 Low 157¼, a third higher bottom, sign of better support or buying. Stop should be placed on shorts at 165 or one cent above the top of Feb. 16. Stop was caught. You should buy for long account.

Mar 2 High 170¼, same high as Feb 9, a double top. Sell out and go short with stop at 172½. This top was not crossed and main trend continued down, breaking all lows of Feb. 11, 17, and 21 and showing great weakness. No rally lasted more than 3 or 4 days. Finally the low of 119, made on Nov. 1, 1924 was broken, a sign of greater weakness. You would stay short.

17 Low 110½, down 72½ cents from 182½, Time 48 days. Time Rule says to watch for change in trend 6 to 7 weeks or 42 to 49 days. Stop should be one cent above previous day's top after a decline of this much.

18 High 123½, up 13 cents, a sign of higher prices.

20 Low 113, down 10½ cents and a higher bottom than Mar. 17, which was 3 days apart. This would be a place to cover and buy when next it crossed the previous day's top.

Mar. 24 High 130; Mar. 25 low 124½; Mar. 26 high 130½, making Mar. 24-26 a double top. Then when prices broke under 124½, the low Mar. 25, you would sell out and go short. The decline continued.

Apr 16 Low 103, down 79½ cents from 182½ and nearing $1.00 per bushel, a natural support level – Time to watch for change in trend.

  22 High 112½, up 9½ cents.

  27 Low 102¼, only 3/4 cent under low of April 16, an indication of support, a double bottom and place to buy with stop at 99. The trend turned up and prices crossed the top of April 27 at 112½.

May 8 High 129. Note old tops of March 24-26 at 130 and 130½. You should sell out and go short against these old tops, placing stop at 132½. The trend turned down.

  22 Low 112; May 25 high 120½. When option expired, low 114½.

May Rye for Delivery May 1926

1925

Jul 16 Low 90½.

  31 High 105¾.

Aug 11 Low 93, a higher bottom than July 16 low of 90½ and a place to buy with stop at 89½.

Sep 2 High 100¼.

  3 Low 97¼.

  6 High 101¼, a higher top and sign of higher prices.

  8 Low 98¾, a third higher bottom – good sign of support. The prices crossed the tops of Sep. 2 and 6 and also tops of July 31 and Aug. 18. This indicated great strength and higher prices. A rapid advance followed.

Oct 6 High 140½, up 50 cents in 92 days. Our rule says to watch for change in trend in 3 months or 90 days. The greatest decline had been from August 18 to 26, from 107 to 93 or 14 cents per bushel, Time period 8 days. So you would raise stop one cent under previous day's low and watch for change in trend when a decline exceeded 8 days and 14 cents.

  11 Low 127, down 13½ cents in 5 days, a sign of change soon to come.

  16 High 137½, up 10 cents in 5 days, making a lower top – a place to sell short with stop at 141½. The next decline was over 8 days and more than 14 cents, showing main trend down.

––––––––––

1945 - 1946 was similar to 1924-1925, altho 1945-1946 made a greater range in price. Refer to analysis of May Rye on Page 20-21 and study the Comparison charts.

RYE AND WHEAT TRADING

1945 to 1947

Indicated Trades according to

MECHANICAL GRAIN METHOD

Pyramiding Plan ———— Initial Capital $3,000.00

Date	Bought	Price	Date	Sold	Price	Points Profit	Points Loss
DECEMBER RYE							
1945 Mch 28	5,000	108	'45 Jun 20	5,000	144	36	
Apr 5	5,000	113	" 20	5,000	144	31	
May 29	5,000	130	" 20	5,000	144	14	
			Total Points Profit			81 @ $50. ea.	$4,050.00
			Commission on 15,000 Bu.				37.50
			Net Profit				$4,012.50
MAY RYE							
1945 Aug 22	10,000	127	'45 Nov 14	10,000	174	43	
Oct 17	10,000	150	" 14	10,000	174	24	
Nov 2	10,000	158	" 14	10,000	174	16	
" 8	10,000	170	" 14	10,000	174	4	
			Total Points Profit			87 @ $100. ea.	$8,700.00
			Commission on 40,000 Bu.				100.00
			Net Profit				$8,600.00
MAY RYE							
1945 Dec 17	10,000	164	'46 Apr 26	10,000	258	94	
1946 Jan 16	10,000	189	" 26	10,000	258	69	
" 28	10,000	208	" 26	10,000	258	50	
Apr 5	10,000	225	" 26	10,000	258	33	
			Total Points Profit			252 @ $100. ea.	$25,200.00
			Commission on 40,000 Bu.				100.00
			Net Profit				$25,100.00
MAY WHEAT							
1947 Jan 23	15,000	193	'47 Mch 19	15,000	259	66	
Feb 8	15,000	205	" 19	15,000	259	54	
" 28	15,000	223	" 19	15,000	259	36	
Mch 5	15,000	241	" 19	15,000	259	18	
" 13	15,000	260	" 19	15,000	259	--	1
						174	1
			Total Points Profit			173 @ $150. ea.	$25,950.00
			Commission on 75,000 Bu.				187.50
			Net Profit				$25,762.50
MAY WHEAT							
1947 Jul 30	15,000	220	'47 Sep 13	15,000	274	54	
Aug 20	15,000	237	" 13	15,000	274	37	
Sep 3	15,000	254	" 13	15,000	274	20	
" 9	15,000	263	" 13	15,000	274	9	
			Total Points Profit			120 @ $100. ea.	$18,000.00
			Commission on 60,000 Bu.				150.00
			Net Profit				$17,850.00

TOTAL PROFIT OF FIVE PYRAMIDS IN PAST THREE YEARS $81,325.00

MAY WHEAT OPTION 18 YEARS   LOWEST RANGE....... 19¢ PER BUSHEL

GREATEST RANGE.....$1.05 "   "

AVERAGE PER YEAR 42¢ ON 10,000 BU—$4,200.00 PER YR.

LESSON 3

THE BASIS OF MY
FORECASTING METHOD FOR
GRAINS : GEOMETRIC ANGLES

THE BASIS OF MY FORCASTING METHOD FOR GRAINS

Mathematics is the only exact science. All power under heaven and on earth is given unto the man who masters the simple science of mathematics. Emerson said, "God does indeed geometricize." Another wise man said, "There is nothing in the universe but mathematical points." Pythagoras, one of the greatest mathematicians who ever lived, after experimenting with numbers and finding the proofs of all natural laws, said, "Before God, was numbers."
It has been said, "Figures don't lie."
Men have been convinced that numbers tell the truth and that all problems can be solved by them. The chemist, engineer and astronomer would be lost without the science of mathematics.

It is so simple and easy to solve problems and get correct answers and results with figures; it seems strange so few people rely upon them to forecast the future of business, stocks and commodity markets. The basic principles are easy to learn and understand. No matter whether you use geometry, trigonometry or calculus, you use the simple rules of arithmetic. You do only two things: increase or decrease.

There are two kinds of numbers, odd and even. We add numbers which is increasing; we multiply which is a shorter way to increase; we subtract which decreases; and we divide which also decreases. With the use of higher mathematics, we find a quicker and easier way to divide, subtract, add and multiply, yet very simple when you understand it.

Everything in nature is male or female, white or black, harmony or inharmony, right or left. The market moves only two ways: up or down. There are three dimensions which we know how to prove: width, length and height. We use three figures in geometry: the circle, the square and the triangle. We get the square and triangle points of a circle to determine points of time, price and space resistance; we use the circle of 360 degrees to measure time and price.

There are three kinds of angles: the VERTICAL, HORIZONTAL and DIAGONAL which we use for measuring Time and Price Movements. We use the square of odd and even numbers to get, not only the proof of market movements, but the cause.

HOW TO MAKE CHARTS

Charts are records of past market movements. The future is but a repetition of the past; there is nothing new. As the Bible says, "The thing that hath been, it is that which shall be." History repeats and with charts and rules we determine when and how it is going to repeat. Therefore, the first and most important point to learn is how to make charts correctly because, if you make an error on the chart, you will make an error in applying the rules to your trading.

SPACING: Use 1/8" for 1¢ per bushel on the daily, weekly or monthly charts except when the price is selling below $1 per bushel, then use 1/2¢ per bushel for each 1/8" space on the daily chart only.

No space is skipped on the daily chart for Sundays or holidays; therefore, the time period is for actual market days, but you should carry the calendar days across the top or bottom of the daily chart so that you will know when the price is 45, 60, 90, 120 or 180 days, etc., from an extreme low or high price.

WEEKLY CHART: When an option expires on May Wheat, or any other Grain, say, in the month of May for the May Option, and the new option does not start until August, you carry the time periods in weeks and begin the new option at the time period in the week in which it starts. This will enable you to always have the geometrical angles correct from any high or low, and to know the total time elapsed from any high or low price. This will make the geometrical angles correct for all past movements.

GEOMETRICAL ANGLES

After long years of practical experience, I have discovered that Geometrical Angles measure accurately Space, Time Volume and Price.

Mathematics is the only exact science, as I have said before. Every nation on the face of the earth agrees that 2 and 2 equals 4, no matter what language it speaks. Yet all other sciences are not in accord as mathematical science. We find different men in different professions along scientific lines disagreeing on problems, but there can be no disagreement in mathematical calculation.

There are 360 degrees in a circle, no matter how large or how small the circle may be. Certain numbers of these degrees and angles are of vast importance and indicate when important tops and bottoms occur in Grains, as well as denote important resistance levels. Once you have thoroughly mastered the geometrical angles, you will be able to solve any problem and determine the trend of any Grain.

After 50 years of research, tests and practical applications, I have perfected and proved the most important angles to be used in determining the trend of the Grain Market. Therefore, concentrate on those angles until you thoroughly understand them. Study and experiment with each rule I give, and you will make a success.

We use geometrical angles to measure space and time periods because it is a shorter and quicker method than addition or multiplication, provided you follow the rules and draw the angles or lines accurately from tops and bottoms, or extreme highs and lows. You may make a mistake in addition, or multiplication, but the geometrical angles accurately drawn will correct this mistake. Example: If you should count across the bottom of your chart 120 spaces, which represents 120 days, weeks or months then you begin at "0" and number vertically on your chart up to 120. From this top point at 120, draw a 45 degree angle moving down. This will come out at 0 on 120 points over from the beginning. If you have made a mistake in numbering, this will correct it.

Angles drawn on a chart always keep before you the position of the option and its trend, whereas, if you had a resistance point on time written down, you might mislay it, or forget it, but these angles are always on the chart in front of you.

These angles or moving-average trend lines, correctly drawn, will keep you from making mistakes, or misjudging the trend. If you wait and follow the rules, these angles will show you when trend changes.

The mean-average, as commonly used, is obtained by taking the extreme low price and the extreme high price of the calendar day, week or month, and dividing it by 2 to get the mean, or average price, for the day, week or month, and continuing this at the end of each time period. This is an irregular movement in spaces, or points, per week because at one time it may move up 2 points per week, and at another, 5 points per week, while the time period is a regular unit. Therefore, geometrical angles, which are really mean-averages, move up or down at a uniform rate from any bottom or top on daily, weekly or monthly chart.

HOW TO DRAW GEOMETRICAL ANGLES

There are three important points which we can prove with mathematics or geometry: the Circle, the Square and the Triangle. After I have made the square, I can draw a circle in it using the same diameter, and thereby produce the triangle, the square in the circle.

The angles, or moving trend line, measure and divide time and price into proportionate parts. Refer to Form 1, where I have drawn the square of 28. You will note that this is 28 high and 28 wide. In other words, 28 up and 28 across. It is the same as a square room which has a bottom or floor, a top or ceiling, and side walls. Everything has width, length and height. 28¢ was the low price for Cash Wheat in 1852.

To get the strongest and most important points in this square I divide it into 2 equal parts by drawing a horizontal and a vertical line. Note angle marked "A" which divides each of the smaller squares into 2 equal parts and runs from 0 to 28 diagonally. This is a diagonal line moving on a 45 degree angle and divides the large square into 2 equal parts. Then, note angle "B" at "14" running horizontally across. This divides the square into 2 equal parts. Note angle "C" which is a vertical line running up from 14, which is 1/2 of 28. This crosses at the center or 1/2 point at 14 where the other angles cross, dividing the square into 2 equal parts. Then, note angle "D" which forms another 45 degree angle moving from the N.W. corner to the S.E. corner, crossing 14 at the exact 1/2 point. You see by this that if we draw the first line through the center of the square, we divide it into 2 equal parts. When we draw the lines from the other directions, we divide it into 4 equal parts. Then, by drawing the 2 lines from each corner, we divide the square into 8 equal parts and produce 8 triangles. We use 28 because 28¢ was the lowest price Cash Wheat ever sold.

As you look at this square, it should be easy for you to tell with your eye where the strongest support point is, or resistance point. It is at the center where all the angles cross. 4 angles cross at this point so, naturally, this would be a stronger support point than a place where only 1 angle crosses. I could divide each one of these smaller squares into 4 or 8 equal parts by drawing angles in the same way. Later, when I give you the rules and examples, I will explain how to square the range of an option, that is, the difference between the extreme low and the extreme high prices, or the difference between any low point and any high point, and also how to square the bottom price.

Example: If the low of Wheat is 28, this square of 28 x 28 would represent squaring the Price by Time, because, if we have 28 points up in price, and we move over 28 spaces in time, we square the price with time. Therefore, when the option has moved over 28 days, 28 weeks or 28 months, it will be squaring its price range of 28.

PATTERN CHART FOR GEOMETRICAL ANGLES

The square of 90, or the Pattern Chart, shows all the measured angles that are important to use in determining the position of an option.

These angles are as follows: 3-3/4, 7-1/2, 15, 18-3/4, 26-1/4, 30, 33-3/4, 37-1/2, 45, 52-1/2, 56-1/4, 60, 63-3/4, 71-1/4, 75, 82-1/2, 86-1/4, and 90 degrees.

It is not necessary to measure these angles with a protractor. All you have to do to get the angles correct is count the spaces on the chart paper, using 8 x 8 to the inch, and draw the lines or angles accordingly.

On the square of 90, which you will receive with these instructions, note how equal angles drawn from the top and from the bottom prove themselves by the point at which they cross.

Example: The angles of 8x1 from "90" down both cross at 45, 5-5/8 points over from 0 counting to the right. Then, the angle of 4x1 from 0 and the angle of 4x1 down from 90, you will notice, cross at 11-1/4 on 45, equal distance from the other angle and twice the measure. The reason these angles prove this way is because the 45 degree angle, or 45 points or degrees from 0 to 45 is 1/2 of 90. Therefore, parallel angles, beginning at 0 going up and at 90 coming down, must cross on a 45 degree angle or at the gravity center.

HOW TO DRAW ANGLES FROM A LOW POINT RECORDED ON GRAIN OPTIONS

An example marked "Form 2" shows you the most important angles to use when Grain is working higher and advancing.

FIRST IMPORTANT GEOMETRICAL ANGLE (45 Degrees or 1 x 1)

The first and always most important angle to draw is a 45 degree angle or a moving trend line that moves up 1¢ per day, 1¢ per week or 1¢ per month. This is a 45 degree angle because it divides the space and time periods into 2 equal parts. As long as the market or an option stays above the 45 degree angle, it is in a strong position and indicates higher prices. You can buy every time it rests on the 45 degree angle with a stop-loss order 1¢, 2¢ or 3¢ under the 45 degree angle, but remember the rule: Never use a stop-loss order more than 3¢ away. Unless Grain options are near the low levels, or just starting in a bull market or selling at very low prices. I always use a stop-loss order 1¢ under the 45 degree angle. If this angle is broken by 1¢, you will usually find that the trend has changed, at least, temporarily and the option will go lower.

An easy way to calculate accurately how to put on this 45 degree angle is, for example: If the time is 28 days, 28 weeks or 28 months from the price where the option was bottom, then the angle of 45 degrees must be 28¢ up from the bottom and would cross at 28. This is one of the easiest angles to put on and one of the simplest to learn.

You can beat the market by trading against the 45 degree angle alone, if you stick to the rule: Wait to buy an option on the 45 degree angle or wait to sell it against the 45 degree angle.

SECOND IMPORTANT ANGLE (2 x 1)

This is the angle of 2 x 1, or the moving trend line which moves up at the rate of 2¢ per day, week or month. It divides the space between the 45 degree angle and the vertical angle into 2 equal parts and measures 63-3/4. That is why it is the next strongest and most important angle. As long as Grain holds above this angle, it is in a stronger position than when it is resting on a 45 degree angle because it is a more acute angle. When an option breaks under this angle of 2 x 1, or 2¢ for each time period, then it indicates that it will go lower and reach the 45 degree angle. Remember the rule of all angles: No matter what angle the option breaks under, it indicates a decline to the next angle below it.

THIRD IMPORTANT ANGLE (4 x 1)

Still stronger as long as an option holds above it; the angle which moves up 4¢ per day, week or month. This angle is 4 x 1 or 4 points of space or price, equals 1 period of time. It measures 75 degrees and divides the space between the angle of 2 x 1 and the 90 degree angle into 2 equal parts. Any option that continues to advance 4¢ per day, 4¢ per week or 4¢ per month, and remains above this angle, is in a very strong position as long as it stays above it, but when it breaks under, it indicates the next angle or next support point according to the position of the option on time and resistance levels.

FOURTH IMPORTANT ANGLE (8 x 1)

The angle of 8 x 1 or the one that moves up 8¢ per day, week or month. This angle measures 82-1/2 degrees. As long as the option can hold above this angle on daily, weekly or monthly charts, it is in the strongest position, but, when it reverses trend and declines below this angle, then it indicates a decline to the next angle.

FIFTH ANGLE (16 x 1)

It is possible to use an angle of 16 x 1, or 16¢ of price to 1 period of time, which measures 86-1/4 degrees, but this angle is only used in fast, advancing markets, like 1947-48, when Grains are moving up or down 16¢ or more per week, or month. There are very few options that will move up 16¢ per day, week or month, and very seldom.

You will note that with these 4 important angles we show the strong or bullish side of the market. All the time, by dividing the space with angles, we are getting the 1/2 point or the gravity center of time and price.

SIXTH ANGLE (3 x 1)

Note the angle drawn in green marked "3 x 1" which moves up at the rate of 3¢ per day, week or month measuring 71-1/4 degree. This angle is important at times, after markets have had a prolonged advance and are a long distance up from the bottom. It is an important angle to use on monthly and weekly charts.

These are all angles you need as long as an option continues to advance and work up and stays above the angle of 45 degrees, or the trend line of 1¢ per day, week or month.

While there are 360 degrees in a circle, and angles can form at any of these degrees. All of the important angles form between 0 and 90 because 90 is straight up and down and the most acute angle on which price can rise. Example: The 45 degree angle divides the space from 0 to 90 in half. The angle of 135 degrees is another angle of 45 degrees because it is 1/2 of the next quadrant between 90 and 180. 225 and 315 in a circle are also 45 degree angles. Therefore, all of the angles valuable in determining the trend of Grain are found between 0 and 90 degrees. When we divide 90 degrees by 8 we get the most important angles to use, then divide it by 3 and we get 30 or 60 degree angles, which are important to use for time and resistance points.

BOTTOMS FROM WHICH TO DRAW ANGLES OR MOVING TREND LINES

DAILY CHART: If Grains have been declining for some time, then start to rally by rallying from a bottom, it must make higher bottoms every day and higher tops. Then, after a 3 day rally on the daily high and low chart, you can put on the 45 degree angle and the angle of 2 x 1 from the bottom or low point. As a rule, it will only be necessary to put on these 2 angles, at first. If this bottom holds and is not broken, then you can put the other angles from the bottom.

WEEKLY CHART: If any option is declining and reacts for more than one week and continues down, for 3 weeks or more, then starts to rally and advances 2 weeks or more you would start to put the angles on from the low point of the decline, only using the angles above the 45 degree angle until the option again breaks under the 45 degree angle. After that, use the other angles on the lower or bearish side of the square.

WHAT TO DO AFTER THE 45 DEGREE ANGLE FROM BOTTOM IS BROKEN

After an option makes top, either temporary or otherwise, and breaks under the 45 degree angle, and starts moving down, then the first thing to do is draw angles below the 45 degree angle, starting from the bottom or low point. Note example marked "Form #3."

FIRST ANGLE ON BEAR SIDE OF THE SQUARE (2 x 1)

The first angle you draw on the Bear side of the square is 2x1 or 2¢ over and 1¢ up which moves at the rate of 1/2¢ per day, week or month, and measures 26-1/4 degrees. This is the first support angle the option should reach after it breaks under the 45 degree angle. As a general rule, when the price reaches this angle, it will receive support and rally. Sometimes it will rest on it for a long period of time, holding on this angle and making, higher bottoms; but when this angle of 2 x 1, or moving trend line of 1/2¢ per day, week or month is broken, then you must draw the next angle of 4 x 1.

SECOND IMPORTANT ANGLE (4 x 1)

The next important angle on the Bear side of the square, which moves up at the rate of 1/4¢ per day, is the angle of 4 x 1, measuring 15 degrees. It will be the next strong support angle from which the price should get support and rally.

THIRD ANGLE (8 x 1)

After the 4 x 1 angle is broken, the next important angle you will put on your chart is the angle of 8 x 1 which moves at the rate of 1/8¢ per day, week or month and measures 7-1/2 degrees. This is often a very strong support angle. After the option has had a big decline, it will rest on this angle several times or may make final bottom and start up from this angle crossing other angles and getting back into a strong position again. Therefore, this angle is important to use on a monthly or weekly chart after a prolonged decline.

FOURTH ANGLE (16 x 1)

This angle can be used on a monthly chart after a long period of time has elapsed from an important bottom. It moves at the rate of 1/16¢ per month and measures 3-3/4 degrees.

FIFTH ANGLE (3 x 1)

This angle, drawn in red ink, is a very important angle measuring 18-3/4 degrees. I strongly advise using it at all times and keeping it up on monthly charts from any important bottom. It can also be used to advantage at times on weekly charts, but is seldom of much value on a daily chart. It moves at the rate of 1/3¢ per day, week or month. By drawing this on the monthly chart for a long period of years, you will soon be convinced of its value and also by testing it on a weekly chart, you will find it valuable.

This completes all of the angles you will need to use from any bottom, at any time.

HOW TO DRAW ANGLES FROM TOPS ON DAILY, WEEKLY OR MONTHLY CHARTS

POSITION UNDER 45 DEGREE ANGLE DRAWN FROM TOP: After an option has made top and declined for a reasonable length of time, say, 3 days, 3 weeks or 3 months, breaking previous bottoms, then you start to draw angles down from the top. Note example marked "Form #4", which is the pattern for drawing angles from the top under the 45 degree angle.

45 DEGREE ANGLE FOR TOP: The first angle you draw is the angle of 45 degrees, or a moving trend line which indicates a decline of 1¢ per day, week or month. As long as the option is below this angle it is in the weakest position and in a Bear market.

OTHER ANGLES: In many cases an option will start declining an average of 8¢ per day, week or month; or 4¢ per day, week or month; 2¢ per day, week or month. Therefore, you should put on all of these angles from the top which moves faster than the angle of 45 degrees.

WEAKEST POSITION: The price of any Grain is in the weakest possible position when it declines and keeps under the angle of 8 x 1. It is in the next weakest position when it is dropping down at the rate of 4¢ per day, week or month, or under the angle of 4 x 1. It is in its next weakest position when it is dropping down under the angle of 2 x 1.

STRONGEST POSITION: The price is in a stronger position and indicates a better rally when it crosses the angle of 2 x 1, but this depends on how far it is down from the top and how far the angles are apart, as will be explained later under the rules.

CHANGING TREND: As long as the price is declining 1¢ per day, week or month, or falling below or under the 45 degree angle, it is still in a bear market and in a very weak position. When the option rallies and crosses the angle of 45 degrees after a prolonged decline, then you are ready to put on the angles on the other side of the 45 degree angle which shows that the price is in a stronger position in a Bear market, and may be getting ready to change into a Bull market.

POSITION ABOVE THE 45 DEGREE ANGLE DRAWN FROM TOP

(Refer to Form #5 which is the pattern for drawing angles above the 45 degree angle from the top.)

2 x 1 ANGLE FROM TOP: The first angle or moving trend line to draw, after the 45 degree angle from the top is crossed, and after the option indicates that it has made a temporary bottom, is the angle of 2 x 1 moving over 2¢ and down 1¢, or 1/2¢ per unit of time. This is moving down at the rate of 1/2¢ per month, week or day.

4 x 1 ANGLE: The next is the angle of 4 x 1 which moves down at the rate of 1/4¢ per day, week or month.

8 x 1 ANGLE: The next angle is the angle of 8x1 which moves down at the rate of 1¢ every 8 days, 8 weeks or 8 months; or 1/8 ¢ per time period.

STRONG POSITION: After the price has crossed the angle of 45 degrees and rallied up to the angle of 2 x 1, it will meet selling and react to some angle coming up from the bottom of the last move, but it is in a stronger position when it holds above this angle of 2 x 1 and is in the next strongest position when it crosses the angle of 4 x 1. Crossing the angle of 8 x 1, which is of least importance, it indicates it is in a very strong position again from the top. You must always consider a movement coming up from bottom and its position on angles from the bottom to determine its strength. It is important to consider the number of cents it has moved up from the bottom and how many cents it is down from the top.

3 x 1 ANGLE: The angle of 3 x 1, drawn in red ink on Form #5, moves down at the rate of 1¢ every 3 days, 3 weeks or 3 months, or 1/3¢ per day, week or month. This angle is important to use after prolonged declines.

This completes the forms of all the angles that you will need to use at any time from tops or bottoms. Practice putting these angles on tops and bottoms until you thoroughly understand how to do them, and know that you are getting them absolutely accurate. Then, you can begin to study the rules for determining the trend according to the position of the price on angles.

DOUBLE AND TRIPLE TOPS OR BOTTOMS

ANGLES CROSSING EACH OTHER: When there is a double bottom several days, weeks or months apart, you draw angles from these bottoms which are near the same price level. Example: From the first bottom draw a 45 degree angle and from the second bottom draw an angle of 2 x 1. When these angles cross each other it will be an important point for a change in trend. Note on chart marked "Form #6" that I have drawn the 45 degree angle from the first bottom "1B" and the angle of 2 x 1 on the right hand side of the 45 degree angle. Then, from the second bottom "2B", I have drawn a 45 degree angle and the angle of 2 x 1 which gains 2¢ per day, week or month, on the left hand side or Bull side of the 45 degree angle. You will note that the angle of 2 x 1 from the second bottom crosses the angle of 2 x 1 on the Bear side from the first bottom at 48, and that when price breaks under these angles, a change in trend takes place and it goes lower. Note that the angle of 2 x 1 from the third bottom "3B" crossed the angle of 2 x 1 on the Bear side from the first bottom at 53-1/2, and crosses the 45 degree angle from the second bottom at 8. This would be a point to watch for change in trend. I have placed a circle where these angles from the different bottoms come together.

Apply this rule to double tops and triple tops in the same way. It is not necessary for the tops or bottoms to be exactly at the same price level, but near the same level. Remember, always draw 45 degree angles from all important tops and bottoms.

PARALLEL ANGLES

Parallel angles or lines run from important tops and bottoms. As previously explained, the 45 degree angle is the most important and should be drawn from all important tops and bottoms. If an option starts advancing, we draw a 45 degree angle from the bottom. Then, if the option makes tops, declines and makes a higher bottom, advances and makes a higher top, draw a 45 degree angle from the first top, running the line up. This will give the oscillation or width of fluctuation in a parallel between the 45 degree angle from the bottom and the 45 degree angle running up from the top. Often an option will advance to the 45 degree angle from the first top, fail to cross it, then decline and rest on the 45 degree angle from the first bottom. Advance again working up for a prolonged Bull campaign between these parallel angles.

When the angles are very far apart, you can draw another 45 degree angle equal distance between them which is often a strong support angle from which the option will rally, but when it breaks under, it declines to the bottom parallel. Parallels can form between angles of 2 x 1 or 4 x 1 just the same as between 45 degree angles, which often occurs in a slow moving market.

GEOMETRICAL ANGLES OF MOVING TREND LINES DRAWN FROM "0"

When the price reaches bottom and starts up, you have been instructed to draw angles from this exact low point which shows the support in time periods, but there are other angles that later on will be just as important and sometimes more important than the angles drawn from the bottom. These are the angles that begin at "0" or zero, and move up at the rate they move up from the bottom. The starting point must be on the same line that the bottom is made on, as the time period begins from this bottom, but the angles move up from 0. These angles should be started every time an option makes a bottom especially on weekly and monthly charts, and should also be carried up on important movements on the daily chart.
Example: See chart marked "Form #7."

If an option makes low at 20, as shown on the chart, starting the 45 degree angle from 0, when will this angle reach 20? Answer: It will reach 20 in 20 days, 20 weeks or 20 months from the bottom or its starting point. In other words, in 20 days, 20 weeks or 20 months, it will be up 20 from 0, and at the price where the option made bottom. Then, the angle will continue on up at the same rate, and later, when the price breaks under the 45 degree angle from the actual bottom made at 20, and breaks the other support angles drawn from the actual bottom at 20, the next important point for support will be the angle of 45 degrees weakest possible position, and indicates much lower prices, but this depends on how high the option is selling and how much it has declined at the time it breaks the 45 degree angle from 0. These angles drawn from 0 especially the 45 degree angle, proves when price and time are balancing, or when the price is squaring out from its bottom.

"0" ANGLES STARTING AT THE TIME TOP IS MADE

When an option reaches extreme top on a daily, weekly or monthly chart, and the trend turns down, you should start an angle of 45 degrees from 0 moving up from the exact space and date that the top is made. This will prove the top is made. This will prove the square of the time period. It is very important when this angle is reached and indicates a change in trend. It is the last strong support and when broken, it will indicate much lower prices.

I have instructed you in each case to first draw the 45 degree angle from the bottom, top and 0 at bottom and top, but this does not mean that you must not use the other angles. All of the other angles can be used from 0, but the 45 degree ANGLE IS THE FIRST AND MOST IMPORTANT. After this angle is broken, you can use the other angles. It is not necessary to carry all of them along until you need them, but on the monthly chart, after a long series of years, these other angles should be carried along when price begins to approach the levels where they would be broken, or where the price would rest on them and receive support.

45 DEGREE ANGLE FROM "0" TO TOP AND BOTTOM: When a 45 degree angle moving up from 0 reaches the line or price of the bottom, it is very important. Then, again when it reaches the point of the extreme high price, it is very important for a change in trend.

You should carry the 45 degree angles and other angles up from 0 from all important 1st, 2nd and 3rd higher bottoms, especially those where very much time has elapsed between these bottoms. You should also start the angle of 45 degrees up from 0 from the 1st, 2nd and 3rd lower tops, especially those which show much time period elapsed. These angles are the most important to be carried on the weekly and monthly charts.

Never overlook keeping up the angles from 0 because they will tell you when time is squaring out with price from tops and bottoms, and will locate support angles or moving trend lines at a point on the Bear side, after the first 45 degree angle from a bottom is broken. You could not locate this support point in any other way except by the angles from 0.

You should go back over past records and bring up these angles and square out different tops and bottoms so that you can prove to yourself the great value of using these angles.

ANGLES FROM TOPS DOWN TO "0" AND UP AGAIN

A 45 degree angle starting down from any important top on a monthly or weekly chart should be continued down until it reaches 0, and then, started up again at the same rate. After a long number of years, between important tops and bottoms, this angle coming down and going up again is important. A 45 degree angle can also be continued down from any important bottom to 0, and then started up again. This will show the squaring of price with time from either top or bottom. Also, some angles can be moved to base on lowest price, and then up again.

TWO 45 DEGREE ANGLES FROM THE SAME BOTTOM

As we have previously explained, the 45 degree angle moves up at the rate of 1¢ per month and moves down at the rate of 1¢ per month. Refer to example on chart #8.

You will note that the low on this chart is shown as 52 and the price moves up to a high of 63. A 45 degree angle is drawn up from the bottom, and after the price reaches top and starts to work down, it breaks the 45 degree angle getting under it at a price of 59. You will note that I have drawn another 45 degree angle down from the bottom at 52. At the point where the price breaks under the 45 degree angle moving up from 52 to the 45 degree angle moving down from 52, the distance in points is 16. Therefore, the angles have widened until the price could decline 16¢, if it went straight down, before it reached the 45 degree angle moving down from the bottom.

Note that I have shown on the chart that the price continues down until it reaches 40, where it rests on the 45 degree angle from the bottom at 52. This would indicate the strongest support point and at least a temporary rally, especially as the price is down 23 points from the top. Later, you will find under "Resistance Levels," that 22-1/2¢ to 24¢ is a strong support point.

This shows that when an option gets into a very weak position by dropping under important angles moving down from bottoms, after having broken strong angles moving up from bottoms, it can decline to very low levels. These extreme fluctuations and declines have happened in the past and will happen again in the future. This proves the squaring out of time on the down side or the balancing up of Price and Time.

ANGLES OR MOVING TREND LINES FROM TOP TO THE NEXT TOP
(Refer to example on Form #9.)

You will see that we have started the bottom at 60. The option advances 6 months to 74, to a point marked "T" and makes top, reacts for 3 months to 64 breaking the 45 degree angle but resting on the angle of 2 x 1 from the bottom, then starts advancing and finally crosses again the 45 degree angle from 60, getting into a stronger position, having regained this angle. In order to determine where it might meet resistance, as it is in new high territory, we draw a 45 degree angle from the top at 74. The price advances to 90 on the 22nd month from the bottom, striking the 45 degree angle from the first top at 74, on the 16th month from the 1st top. Being 16 points up above the 1st top, the time equals the advance in the price above the 1st top. The 45 degree angle shows that this is a strong resistance point and a place to go short with stop 1 to 3 points above the 45 degree angle. A decline starts and in the 3rd month the price again breaks under the 45 degree angle from the bottom (at 60) at a very high level. In other words, it is 24¢ up from the bottom and is now in a much weaker position because it is so far from the base of support, and indicates a decline again to the angle of 2 x 1.

DON'T OVERLOOK THIS RULE: After an option has advanced to a new high level, then declines to the old top at 74, this may be a support point unless it breaks 3¢ under it. If it does, and also breaks the angle of 2 x 1, it will be in a weaker position and the next point to watch for support and a rally would be the next bottom at 64.

ANGLES FROM BOTTOM OF FIRST SHARP DECLINE

When an option that has been advancing for sometime makes top and holds for several days, several weeks or several months, then turns the trend down and has a sharp, severe decline, there is always a rally after this first decline. It usually makes a lower top on this secondary rally and then starts to work lower again. The bottom of the first decline is a very important point from which to draw angles especially the 45 degree angle moving down, as I have done on the chart marked "Form #10."

This chart shows the price rallying up to around 75, where the 45 degree angle coming up from the last bottom crosses the angle of 2 x 1 coming down from the top. Then the decline started and at 66 the price broke back under the angle of 45 degrees from the top, which put it in a very weak position. It declined to the angle of 45 degrees coming down from the bottom of the first sharp decline. This would be squaring out of time from the bottom and would be a place to buy for a rally. An option will often decline and drop a little below this angle from the bottom. Then, if it holds for several days or weeks under this angle, or on it, it is a place to buy for a rally.

On a monthly chart always carry this angle down from the bottom of the first sharp decline, as if often becomes very important later on in a campaign.

After an option has been advancing for some time and then has a sharp break lasting 2 to 3 days, 2 to 3 weeks or 2 to 3 months, then rallies and afterward breaks under the lows of this first sharp break, indicates that the main trend has turned and that it is going lower.

Apply the same rule when any Grain has been declining for a long time and then makes a sharp, quick recovery for 2 to 3 days, 2 to 3 weeks or 2 to 3 months, then reacts and crosses this first rally point that it made, an indication of higher prices.

It is important to draw angles from the price market starts up, and makes its last run, in a Bull market. Refer to Chart #11.

In this example note point marked "last bottom." In the last section of the Bull market a fast advance follows to a price of 84. We have drawn the angle of 2 x 1 (a gain of 2¢ per day, week or month) and the 45 degree angle from this bottom. When the angle of 2 x 1 was broken, it indicated the trend had turned down. The market declined and rested on the 45 degree angle, then rallied and made a second lower top, then broke the 45 degree angle, declined sharply and rested on the 45 degree angle drawn from the top at 84, which indicated that time and price had squared out or were equal. This would be a buying level with a stop-loss order 2¢ to 3¢ under this angle for a rally back to the angle of 2 x 1 from the top, as shown on the chart.

In a very active fast-moving market the price may stay above the angle of 4 x 1 or the angle of 8 x 1 from the "last bottom," but on the daily or weekly chart, after this first acute angle is broken, it indicates that the trend has turned down.

Always remember that after a prolonged advance, when the main trend turns down, it is safer to wait for rallies and sell short than to buy against the trend.

All of these rules are reversed at the end of a Bear market or sharp decline. It is important to note when the market starts down from the last top or rally, and makes its last run to bottom. Draw the angles from this last top and watch when the market reaches these important angles and crosses them.

After an option has been advancing for a long time, in the last run when there is a lot of momentum, it may cross angles from previous tops or bottoms, then fall back under them which is an indication of weakness. When an option has a sharp decline and is making bottom, it will drop under important angles and then recover quickly getting above them, which shows that it is getting into a strong position and changing trend.

ANGLES FROM HIGHER BOTTOMS AND LOWER TOPS

What rule should be followed when Grain makes higher bottoms and lower tops?

As prices advance and make higher bottoms on the monthly, weekly or daily chart, you should always draw angles from higher bottoms. Then, in the last section of a Bull market, if these important angles are broken from the last bottom, you know that the trend has turned down.

Apply this same rules as a market declines. Draw the angles from each lower top and watch the angles until the price again crosses the 45 degree angle from a 2nd, 3rd or 4th lower top. The 2nd lower top or 2nd higher bottom is always very important from which to draw angles and to measure time from as well.

SECTIONS OF MARKET CAMPAIGNS

All market campaigns, up or down, move in 3 to 4 sections. When an advance starts the market runs for several weeks or several months and then halts for several weeks or months, moving up and down over a range of 10¢ to 20¢ or more according to the price of the option, then the advance is resumed and the price crosses the high level of the 1st section, moves higher, halts again, and reacts for a period of time; then, crosses the top of the 2nd section and moves up again for another period of time and halts for the 3rd time, which is a very important point to watch as markets often culminate at the end of the 3rd section and a greater decline follows.

Most markets run out in 3 important sections or campaigns. However, after resting and reaction, if the price crosses the 3rd top, it will then move up to the top of the 4th section. This 4th advance may be a shorter period of time than the previous section, or, in some cases, may consume a greater period of time and halts for the 3rd time, which is a very important point to watch as markets often culminate at the end of the 3rd section and a greater decline follows.

Most markets run out in 3 important sections or campaigns. However, after resting and reacting, if the price crosses the 3rd top, it will then move up to the top of the 4th section. This 4th advance may be a shorter period of time than the previous section, or, in some cases, may consume a greater period of time especially if the option is very active and high priced. This 4th top is very important and generally marks a culmination and a reversal for a greater decline.

Reverse this rule in a Bear market. Watch the action of the market when it makes the 3rd and 4th decline. But, remember, in a Bear market, when rallies come, they make only 1 section or 1 move, or in extreme cases, only make the 2nd section, then reverse and follow the main trend down.

You will find it very helpful to study and watch these various sections of a campaign and, by applying the angles from tops and bottoms, you can detect the first minor and major changes in trend.

STRENGTH OR WEAKNESS DENOTED BY POSITION ON ANGLES

The angles on the monthly and weekly charts are of greater importance than those on the daily chart because the daily trend can change quite often, while only the major changes are shown according to the angles on the monthly and weekly charts.

Always consider the distance an option is from its beginning price when it breaks any important angle or crosses any important angle. The further away from the beginning price, the more important the change in trend, whether this is crossing angles from the top or breaking under an angle from the bottom.

WHEN AN OPTION IS IN THE WEAKEST POSITION

An option is in the weakest position when it has completed distribution and broken under a 45 degree angle from an important bottom on the weekly or monthly chart. It is also in the weakest position when it has broken under the 1/2 point between any important top or bottom. The longer the time period has run and the higher the price, the weaker the position. Example: (Refer to 2 day and weekly chart on May Beans, 1947-48).

If an option has advanced to 150 and has only moved down 25¢ when the 45 degree angle from an extreme low on a weekly or monthly chart is broken, then it is in a very weak position because it is so far above the 1/2 point on its price movement, already having squared out the time period with price.

Weakness in price develops when it breaks the 3/4 point, the 2/3 point, the 1/2 point, etc., but the position on the timing angles from the bottom tells you still more about the weak position.

An option shows its first weakness when it breaks the first important angle coming up from the last bottom in the final run in a Bull market.

WHEN AN OPTION IS IN THE STRONGEST POSITION

An option is always in the strongest position coming up from a bottom when it is holding above the very acute angles on the daily, weekly or monthly charts especially on monthly and weekly charts.

As long as the option holds above the angle of 2 x 1 (a gain of 2¢ per day) on the daily chart, it is in a very strong position, as far as the bottom is concerned. In fact, it is always in a strong position on the daily as long as it holds above the 45 degree angle. The same applies to weekly and monthly charts which are the most important trend indicators.

I have found that the Grains which have the greatest advances are those that always hold above the angle of 2 x 1 on the monthly chart, or gain 2¢ per month for a long period of time. I have seen prices rest 10 or 15 times on the angle of 2 x 1, and never break it until they have advanced 100¢ or more. In this way, the price stays ahead of time and stays within the square of time by being far above the angle of 45 degrees, and therefore is in a very strong position. But, the time must come when the cycle has run out and the main trend begins to change from a Bull market to a Bear market -- when the breaking of the angle from the last bottom shows a change in trend.

Another indication that an option is in a strong position is when it advances above it and then reacts and fails to break under. This is just the same as resting on a 45 degree angle and indicates a very strong position.

STRONGEST BUYING AND SELLING POINTS

The safest buying point is when the price rests on a 45 degree angle, placing a stop-loss order below it.

Another point to buy is on the 1/2 point of the price movement. Placing a stop-loss order under the 1/2 point.

When the main trend is up, it is also safe to buy, when the option reacts to the angle of 2 x 1 (a gain of 2¢ per time period) on the weekly or monthly chart.

REGAINING ANGLES OR CROSSING LINES

Remember, when any option breaks under the 45 degree angle from the extreme low price of a move on the daily, weekly or monthly chart, it is then in a very weak position and indicates a decline to the next angle. However, when an option can regain the 45 degree angle, it is in a stronger position.

The same rule applies to a 45 degree angle drawn up from any top. When the option crosses the angle on the daily, weekly or monthly, and stays above the 45 degree angle or any other angle to the left of the 45 degree angle, it is in a very strong position.

After the price once drops below or gets above any important angle, and then reverses its position by getting back above the angle or dropping back below it, it changes the trend again.

WHEN GRAIN IS IN A STRONG POSITION FROM BOTTOM AND IN A WEAK POSITION FROM TOP

An option is in a strong position from the bottom when it is keeping above the angle of 45 degrees, or the angle of 2 x 1, but at the same time it can be in a weak position when it rallies up and strikes against the 45 degree angle, or the angle of 2 x 1 coming down from the top, then it is a short sale until it can cross these angles or cross previous tops. When it breaks the angles from the bottom, it is in a weak position and indicates lower.

An option can be in a strong position from the top and in a weak position from the bottom, that is it may cross some important angles from the top after a long period of time, but at the same time may break under the 2 x 1 angle or 45 degree angle from the bottom, which would indicate that it is in a weak position and getting ready to go lower.

WHEN ANGLES FROM EXTREME TOP ARE CROSSED

The 45 degree angle, drawn from the extreme high price of an option is most important and when it is crossed, a major move may be expected.

QUICK CALCULATION OF ANGLES

It is not necessary to draw these angles from a price a long way back. You can make the calculations and determine where they cross. Example: Suppose, in January, 1951, you wish to get the 45 degree angle from June, 1930, when Soy Beans were high at 216. This will make 247 months to January, 1951, and the 45 degree angle, moving up from zero, will be at the price of 247; therefore, you start the 45 degree angle at 247 and move it up 1¢ per month until the price declines below it.

1920, February 15, Soy Beans high, 405. This was the highest in history until 1947. To get the angle and time period to February 15, 1951, will be 31 years or 372. The 45 degree angle moving down from 405 will cross at 33. February, 1953, will be 396 months from 1920, and November 14, 1953, will be 405 months, which equals the highest price; and the 45 degree angle moving down from the top will reach 0. Time and price will have squared out on the monthly chart making November, 1953, a very important period for a change in trend.

LATITUDE AND LONGITUDE

On all charts – daily, weekly or monthly – the price must move up or down on the vertical angles. Therefore, the price movement is the same as latitude. You should begin with 0 on any chart – daily, weekly or monthly – and draw the important angles and resistance levels across which measures latitude.

Next, number the time points in days, weeks or months across and draw the horizontal angle at each important natural angle, such as, 11¼, 22½, 33¾, 45, 67½, 78¾, 90, 101¼, 112½, 120, etc. Then, you will know when price reaches these important angles and meets resistance.

Longitude measures the time running across the chart, as it moves over each day, week or month. Therefore, you must keep you chart numbered from each important top and bottom in order to get the time measurements, according to angles. These important angles, such as, 11¼, 22½, 33¾, 45, 56¼, 60, 78¾, 90, etc., from each bottom and top will show you where the strongest resistance in price and time takes place. These angles prove the parallel or crossing point. Study past records and see what has happened when prices on monthly charts reached these important angles or time periods.

Example: 90 points up in price from 0, draw an angle horizontally across the chart. Then, 90 days, weeks or months, going to the right across the chart, draw a vertical angle up which will cross the horizontal angle at 90 and prove the square. By keeping all these angles up and understanding them on your charts, you will know when important time cycles are running out.

If the price of an option at 60 comes out on the 60th day, week or month, it will meet strong resistance because it has reached the square of price with time. It is at the same latitude or price, and the same longitude or time period. You can always put the square of 90 on a chart, either daily, weekly or monthly, and use the natural angles, but I advise only using this on the weekly and monthly. You can begin this square of 90 from any bottom or top, that is, going up 90 points or from the natural points which are 90, 135, and 180, but you must not fail to square the extreme low and high price, as well as the 2nd and 3rd lower tops and higher bottoms with time.

RULE FOR KEEPING TIME PERIODS ON CHARTS

It is very important that you keep the time periods on all of your charts, carrying them across from the bottom and top of each important move, in order to check up and know that you have you angles or moving trend lines at the correct point, and to see where major and minor cycles indicate changes in trend.

TIME PERIODS FROM BOTTOMS

When an option makes bottom one month and then the following month makes a higher bottom and a higher top, or anyway, after it makes a higher bottom and rallies for one month or more, you can start numbering from that bottom. The month that it makes the low belongs to the old downward movement and is the last move down. Count the first month up as 1, and then number across, on the ½" squares running them across, adding 4 each time.

Example: If an option has made bottom and advanced 50¢, and you look down at the bottom of the chart and find that the price is on the 25th month, then the angle of 2 x 1, moving up 2¢ per month would cross at 50, while the 45 degree angle moving up 1¢ per month would be at 25; and if the price broke back under 50 the following month, it would be falling under the angle of 2 x 1 and indicate a further decline. If you had an error on the chart in the timing or numbering across from the bottom, the moving trend line or angle would not come out correctly.

TIME PERIODS FROM TOPS

After an option has advanced and made an extreme high and reached for a few days, a few weeks or a few months, and you start putting on the angles from the top down, you must then begin to number the time periods across from the top. Apply the same rule for the top: The month, week or day that the option makes extreme high finishes the upward movement and is not to be counted. You can count the number of days, weeks or months moving across after that allowing the top month to be 0, the next month, week or day over to be 1, adding 4 across on the squares to get the correct position. If this time period is carried across on all the charts correctly, then you can always check up and find out if you have made any mistake in bringing down the angles or moving trend lines.

This is a simple way to always know when the angles or moving trend lines are correct because you simply add the movement to the bottom and subtract it from the top. Suppose the price referred to above, when the price has declined 75¢ was 150, then subtracting 80 from the top at 150, the angle would cross at 70 and the price of the option down 75¢ would be at 75. Therefore, it would be above the angle of 2 x 1 from the top and in position for a rally if the time cycle indicated it.

POINTS FROM WHICH TO NUMBER TIME PERIODS

The most important point on the monthly high and low chart to carry the time period is from the extreme low of the life of an option. From the extreme low price, the time period should always be carried across on the chart just the same as the important angles should be continued right along for years.

The next important point to number from is a 2nd or 3rd higher bottom, but you should not consider a bottom established until the market has held up or advanced 3 or 4 months, then commence numbering from that bottom, if it appears to be important.

Use this same rule at tops. After top is reached and the trend turns down, carry the time numbers across from the top; but after any top is crossed or bottom is broken, that you are numbering from, do not count that top or bottom of importance to number from except to determine a time period on another cycle 3, 5, 7, 10 or 20 years ahead. Tops that stay for a long time without being crossed are always the most important from which to carry the time periods. The extreme high reached by an option is always most important until that high is crossed. Then, the next high price made on a secondary rally, which is always a lower top, is the next most important top from which to number.

Always note the number of months between extreme high and between extreme low points, and note what angle the tops and bottoms come out on.

SQUARING THE PRICE RANGE WITH TIME

This is one of the most important and valuable discoveries I have ever made, and if you stick strictly to the rule, and always watch an option when Price is Squared by Time, or when Time and Price come together, you will be able to forecast the important changes in trend with greater accuracy.

The squaring of Price with Time means an equal number of points up or down balancing an equal number of time periods, either days, weeks or months. Example: If an option has advanced 24¢ in 24 days, then moving the 45 degree angle or moving trend line up at the rate of 1¢ per day, the timing line or time period and the price of the option are at the same level, and the price is resting on a 45 degree angle. You should watch for an important change in trend at this point.

If an option is to continue up-trend and remain in a strong position, it must continue to advance and keep above the angle of 45 degrees. If it breaks back under this angle, then it is out of its square on the Bear side of the 45 degree angle and in a weaker position. When you are squaring out time on a daily chart, look at the weekly high and low chart, and monthly high and low chart, and see if the option is in a strong position and has yet to run out the time periods because on a daily chart it has to react and then recover a position, squaring its price many times as long as the weekly and monthly charts point up. Market corrections or reactions are simply the squaring out of minor time periods and later the big declines or advances are the squaring out of major time periods.

SQUARING THE RANGE

Refer to Form #12, where a range of 12 points is shown from 48 low to 60 high. Now, suppose an option remains for several weeks or several months moving up or down in this range, never getting more than 12 points up from the bottom and not breaking the bottom, start the 45 degree angle from the bottom of 48 and move it up to the top of the range to 60, then when we see the option is holding this range and not going higher, move the 45 degree angle back to the bottom; then, back to the top of the range again moving it up or down over this range until the price breaks out into new low levels or new high levels. You will find that every time the 45 degree angle reaches the top of this range, or the bottom, there is some important change in the trend of the option.

1949, Feb. 9, May Soy Beans – low, 201½. To square this price with time on the weekly chart will require 201½ weeks, and the 45 degree angle moving up from 201½ will be at 403; but the 45 degree angle moving up from 0 will be at 201½ equalling the price.

The 1/8, 1/4, 1/3, 1/2 and other parts of 201½ must be watched in periods of time from 201½. 1/8 was 25¼ weeks or Aug. 6, 1949; 1/4 was Feb. 4, 1950; 1/2 was 101 weeks or Jan. 20, 1951. May and November Beans made high February 8, 1951, and the trend turned down.

1951, December 29, will be 150 weeks from February 9, 1949, and this is 3/4 of 201½, and is a very important date for a change in trend.

1952, January 15, will be 4 years from 1948, high 436-3/4, also important to watch for a change in trend.

1953, Dec. 29, will be 202 weeks from Feb. 9, 1949, and this will square the price of 201½ with time. Watch this date for an important change in trend.

You can also use the angles of 2 x 1 to the right of the 45 degree angle and the 2 x 1 to the left, as they again divide the time period into 2 equal parts and are of some value.

If an option finally moves out of this range on the up side, then the angles would begin at the new and higher bottom and move up, but from the point where the price went into new high, or any important bottom made while it was in the range especially the last bottom that it made, would be most important. You should then begin an angle at that bottom and continue on up again. Watch when this angle is broken or when time is squared out again with price which would be important for another change in trend, either major or minor.

THREE WAYS TO SQUARE TIME AND PRICE

We can square the range, that is, the number of cents from extreme low to extreme high with time; then square the extreme low price with time; and square the extreme high price with time. When the market passes out of these squares and breaks important angles, the trend changes up or down.

1.   The range that any option makes between extreme high and extreme low can be squared, so long as it remains in the same price range. If the range is 25¢, it squares with 25 periods of time--days, weeks or months. Continue to use this time period as long as it stays in the same range.

2.   Squaring Time with Bottom or Extreme Low Price – The next important price to square with time is the lowest price or bottom of any important decline. Example: If the bottom of an option is 25, then at the end of 25 days, 25 weeks or 25 months time and price are equal. Watch for a change in trend as based on its bottom or lowest selling price. As long as the option continues to

hold one bottom and advances, you can always use this time period running across and continuing the time period, noting every time it passes out of the square. Watch especially when the price reaches the 3rd square, the 4th square and again the 7th and 9th squares of its time period. These squares only occur frequently on the daily or weekly charts, as the monthly in most cases, would move out of a range, up or down, before it squared a bottom as many as 7 or 9 times. However, this does sometimes happen when an option is in a narrow range for many years.

Example: May Beans, 1939, July 27 – low 67. This would require 67 months or 67 weeks to square the lowest price. Note monthly chart marked "Squares of 44 and 67."

3. Squaring Time with Top or Extreme High Price – The other important price with which to square time is the extreme high price of an option. The time period must be carried across from the high of the daily, weekly or monthly, and the square of the top price in time must be noted and watched for a change in trend. If the top of an option is 50 then, when it has moved over 50 days, 50 weeks or 50 months, it has reached its square in time and an important change is indicated. This can be determined by the position of the angles from top and bottom. Example: May Soy Beans, 1948, Jan. 15 – high 436-3/4. This requires 436-3/4 weeks to Square Price with Time.

Both major and minor tops and bottoms on all time periods must be watched as they square out right along. Most important of all is the extreme high price on the monthly high and low chart. This may be very high and work out a long time period before it squares the top, in which case you have to divide the price into 8 equal time periods and watch the most important points like 1/4, 1/3, 1/2 and 3/4, but most important of all is when Time equals Price.

When you are watching the position of an option, after it has squared out from a bottom or a top, always look up the time period and the angles from the opposite direction. If the market is nearing a low price, squaring out a top, see how its relation is to the bottom as it might be in the 2nd or 3rd square period from the bottom which would be a double indication for a change in trend.

SQUARING WEEKLY TIME PERIODS

The year contains 52 weeks and the square of this in time is 52 by 52. Therefore, you can make up a square of 52 wide and 52 high: put on all of the angles from 0; then, chart weekly high and low prices of an option in this square. Example: If the low price of an option is 50, then the top of this weekly square would be 52 added to 50, which makes 102 as top of the square. As long as price stays above 50 and moves up, it will be working in the weekly square of 52. On the other hand, if the option makes top and works down, you would make up a weekly square 52¢ down from the top and 52 over to get the time period.

You can take the past movement of any option, put on a square of 52 x 52, and study the movement noting 13 weeks or 1/4, 26 weeks or 1/2, and 39 weeks or 3/4 points on time; and the changes in trend which take place when the price reaches these important resistance points in time and price. You would watch for a change in trend around these time periods.

SQUARING MONTHLY TIME PERIODS

At the time an option breaks a 45 degree angle, if it is selling at 135 on the 135th month, it is breaking a doubly strong resistance level – a strong angle and a natural resistance level. This would be time and space for balancing at resistance levels or geometrical angles and would indicate a big decline to follow. Reverse this rule at the end of a Bear campaign.

On a monthly chart, 12 months complete a year. Therefore, the square of 12 is very important for working out time periods on the monthly chart. The square of 12 is 144 and important changes often occur on even 12 months' periods from a bottom or top of an option, It will help, if you use the resistance levels on prices of the even 12's, noting 24, 36, 48, 60, 72, 84, 96, 108, etc. Watch how the option acts on angles when it reaches these important resistance points in price.

PRICE AHEAD OF TIME

Why do Grain options often cross the 45 degree angle on the daily, weekly or monthly chart, then have an advance for a short period of time, decline and rest on the same 45 degree angle? Because, when the price crosses the 45 degree angle the first time, it has not run out or overcome the square of time with price. Therefore, on the secondary reaction, when it rests on the 45 degree angle, it is at a time when price has reached the square of price in time. After that, a greater advance follows.

Reverse this rule at the top of a Bull Market. When an option breaks under the 45 degree angle, a long distance from the base or bottom, it is most important. Many times an option will rest on the 45 degree angle in the early stages of an advance, then later, on a reaction, rest on it again; then have a prolonged advance, react and rest on the 45 degree angle again, and then advance to a higher level; break the 45 degree angle the next time, which places it in an extremely weak position because it is so far away from the base and so much time has elapsed since the price made low. Don't forget: It is most important when angles are broken on the monthly and weekly charts.

This accounts for Grains that have a sharp, quick decline from the top and then advance and make a slightly higher top or a series of slightly lower tops, and work over until they overcome the square of the price range at a comparatively high level and break the 45 degree angle, then a fast decline follows.

STRONGEST ANGLES FOR MEASURING TIME AND PRICE

90 DEGREE ANGLE – Why is the 90 degree angle the strongest angle of all?
Because it is vertical or straight up and down.

180 DEGREE ANGLE – What is the next strongest angle to the 90 degree angle?
The 180 degree angle because it is square to the 90 degree angle being 90 degrees from the
90 degree angle.

270 DEGREE ANGLE – What is the next strongest angle to the 180 degree angle?
The 270 degree angle because it is in opposition to 90 degrees or 180 degrees, from the 90
degree angle which equals ½ of the circle, the strongest point.
270 months equals 22½ years, which is ½ of 45.

360 DEGREE ANGLE – What is the next strongest angle after 270 degrees?
It is 360 degrees because it ends the circle and returns to the beginning degree, and is
opposite 180 degrees, or the angle which equals ½ of the circle.

120 and 240 DEGREE ANGLES – What angles are next strongest to 90 degrees,
180 degrees, 270 degrees and 360 degrees?

120 degrees and 240 degrees angles because they are 1/3 and 2/3 of the circle.
120 degrees is 90 degrees plus 30, which is 1/3 of 90 degrees. 240 degrees is
180 degrees plus 1/3 or 60 which makes these strong angles, especially strong
for measurement of time.

45 and 135, 225 and 315 DEGREE ANGLES – What angles are next in strength?
45 degree angle because it is ½ of 90 degrees.
135 degree angle because it is 90 plus 45 degrees.
225 degree because it is 45 plus 180 degrees.
315 degree angle because it is 45 from 270 degrees.
The angle of 225 degrees is 180 degrees from 45 and the angle of 315 degrees
is 180 degrees from 135 degrees.

CARDINAL FIXED CROSS
The angles of 90 degrees, 180 degrees, 270 degrees and 360 degrees form the
first important cross, known as the Cardinal Cross. The angles of 45, 135, 225
and 315 degrees form the next important cross, which is known as the Fixed
Cross. These angles are very important for the measurements of time and
space, or price and volume.

22½, 67½, and 78¾ – Why is the angle of 22½ degrees stronger than 11¼° ?

Because it is twice as much – the same reason that a 45 degree angle is stronger than a 22½ degree angle. Again, the angle of 67½ degrees is 1½ x 45, therefore, quite strong when anything is moving up toward 90 degrees. 78¾ degrees is stronger than 67½ degrees because it is 7/8 of 90 degrees and, therefore, one of the strongest points before 90 is reached – important to watch on time, price and volume. Many Grains have important moves and make tops or bottoms around the 78th to 80th day, week or month, but don't overlook 84 months or 7 years – a strong time cycle.

DIVISION OF $1 - 1/8 POINTS – Why are the angles of 1/8 of a circle most important for time and space measurements?

Because we divide $1 into 1/2, 1/4 and 1/8 parts. We use 25¢ or 1 quarter, 50¢ or half dollar, and many years ago we had 12½¢ pieces.

While the most important figures of our basis of money are the 4 quarters, we do use the 1/8 part or 12½¢ in all calculations. Grain fluctuations are based on 1/8, 1/4, 3/8, 1/2, 5/8, 3/4, 7/8 and the whole figure. Therefore, any price measurement, as well as time, will work out closer to these figures when changed into angles of time rather than 1/2 or 2/3 points of price for the simple reason that the fluctuations moving in 1/8 proportions must come out closer to these figures. We use the denominations of 5¢ which equals 1/20 of a dollar, and 10¢ which equals 1/10 of a dollar.

Figuring $100, or par, as a basis for Grain prices and changing these prices to degrees, 12½ equals 45 degrees, 25 equals 90 degrees, 37½ equals 135 degrees, 50 equals 180 degrees, 62½ equals 225 degrees, 75 equals 270 degrees, 82½ equals 315 degrees and $100 equals 360 degrees.

Example: When an option sells at 50 on the 180th day, week or month, it is on the degree of its time angle.

Follow all the rules, study and experiment, and you will learn to do by doing, and make a success!

W.D. GANN

November 12, 1951

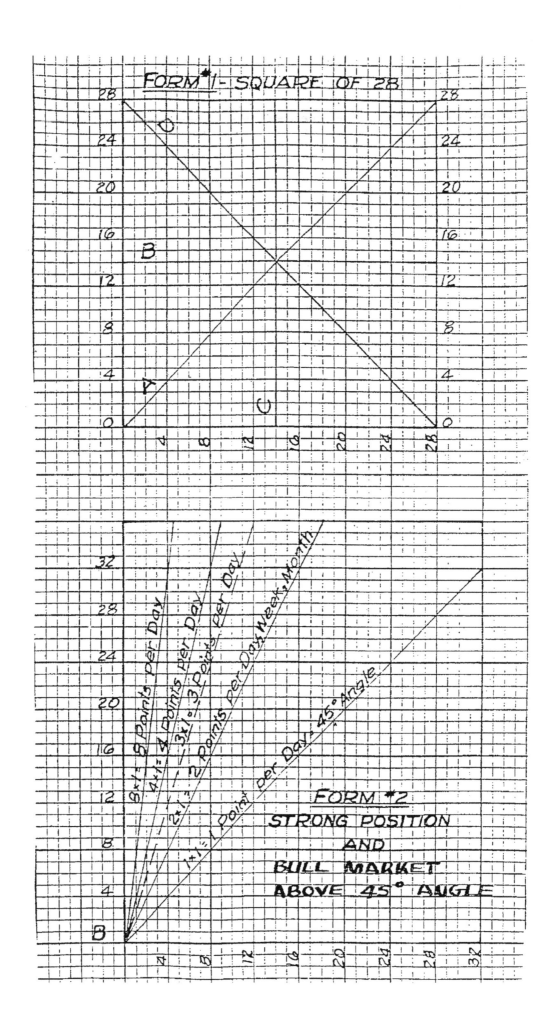

FORM #1 - SQUARE OF 28

FORM #2
STRONG POSITION
AND
BULL MARKET
ABOVE 45° ANGLE

8x1 = 8 Points per Day
4x1 = 4 Points per Day
3x1 = 3 Points per Day
2x1 = 2 Points per Day, Week, Month
1x1 = 1 Point per Day - 45° Angle

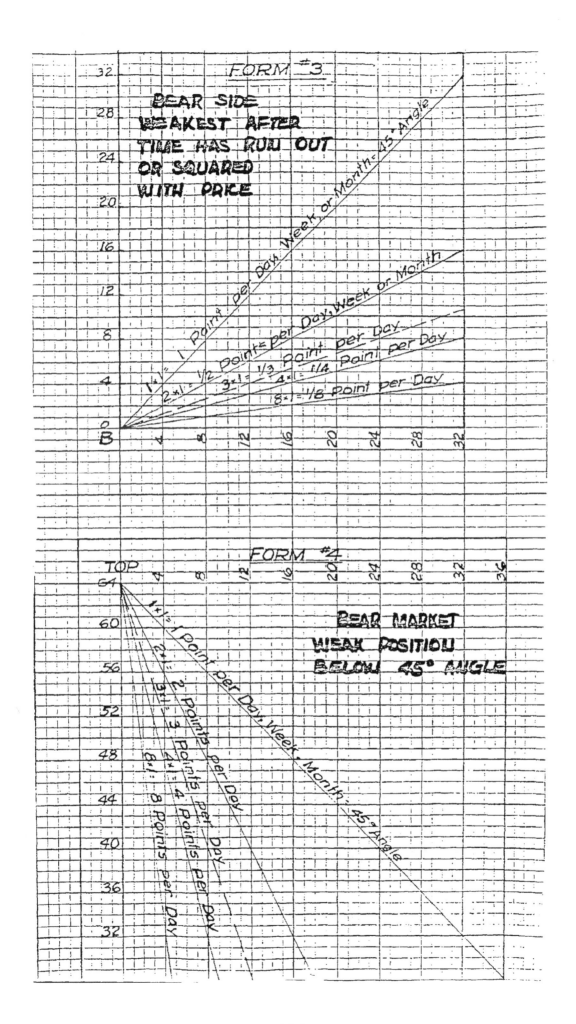

FORM #3

BEAR SIDE
WEAKEST AFTER
TIME HAS RUN OUT
OR SQUARED
WITH PRICE

1 Point per Day, Week or Month = 45° Angle
1x1 = 1 Point per Day
2x1 = 1/2 Point per Day, Week or Month
3x1 = 1/3 Point per Day
4x1 = 1/4 Point per Day
8x1 = 1/8 Point per Day

FORM #4

BEAR MARKET
WEAK POSITION
BELOW 45° ANGLE

TOP

1x1 = 1 Point per Day, Week, Month = 45° Angle
2x1 = 2 Points per Day
3x1 = 3 Points per Day
4x1 = 4 Points per Day
8x1 = 8 Points per Day

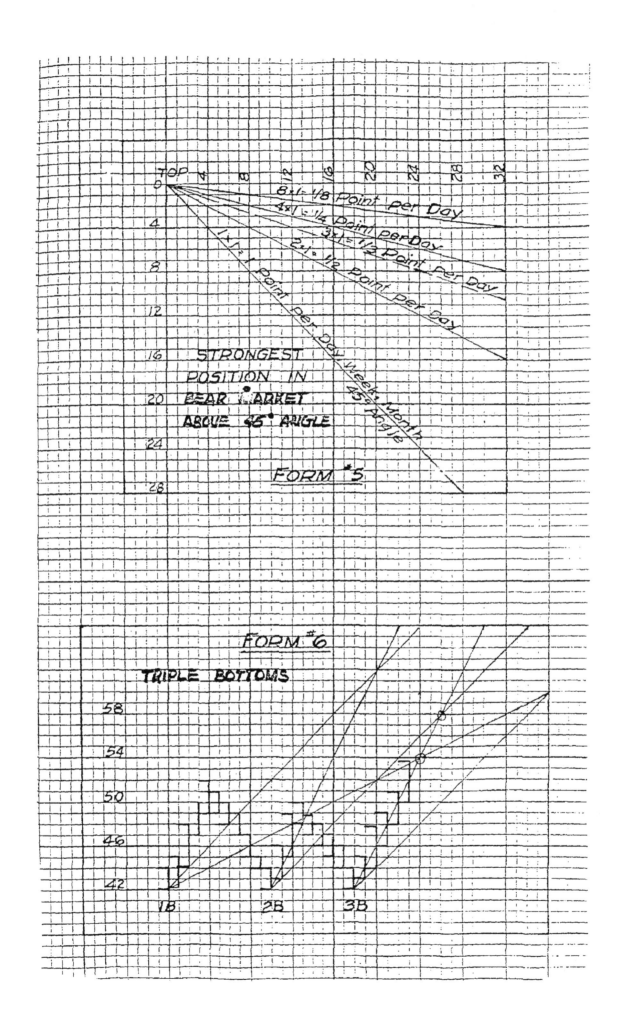

TOP 0

STRONGEST
POSITION IN
BEAR MARKET
ABOVE 45° ANGLE

8x1= 1/8 Point per Day
4x1= 1/4 Point per Day
3x1= 1/2 Point per Day
2x1= 1/2 Point per Day
1x1= 1 Point per Day week, month
45° Angle

FORM #5

FORM #6

TRIPLE BOTTOMS

1B   2B   3B

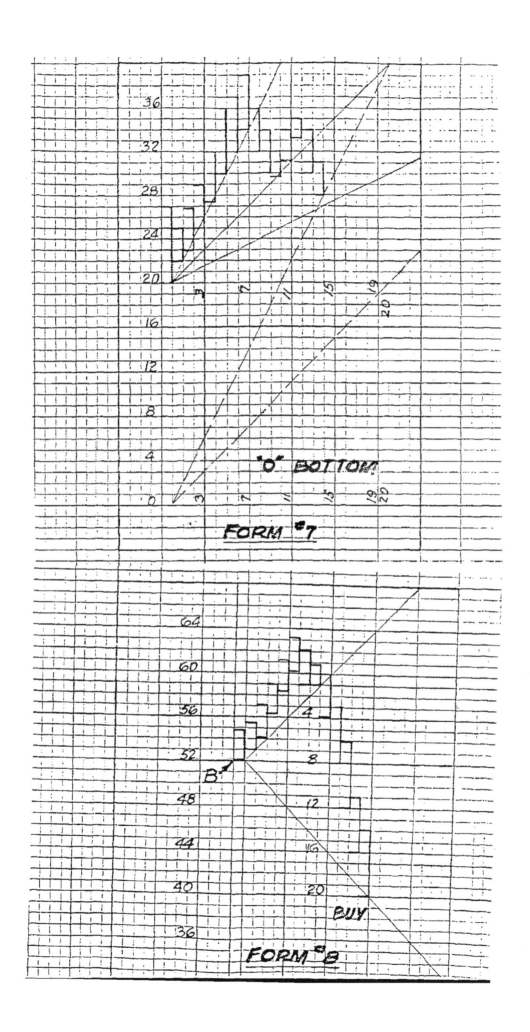

"O" BOTTOM

FORM #7

BUY

FORM #8

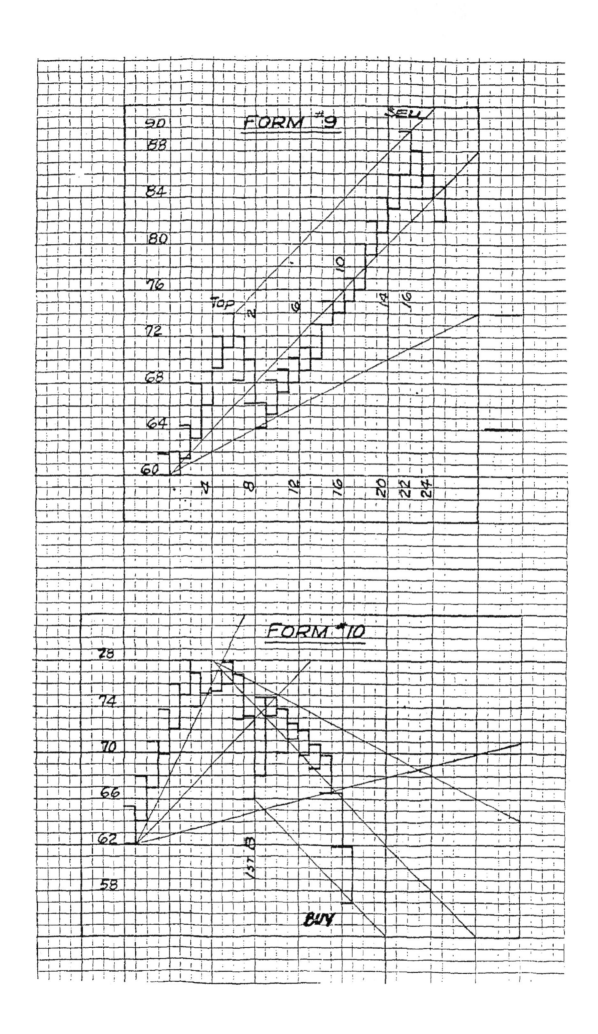

FORM #9

FORM #10

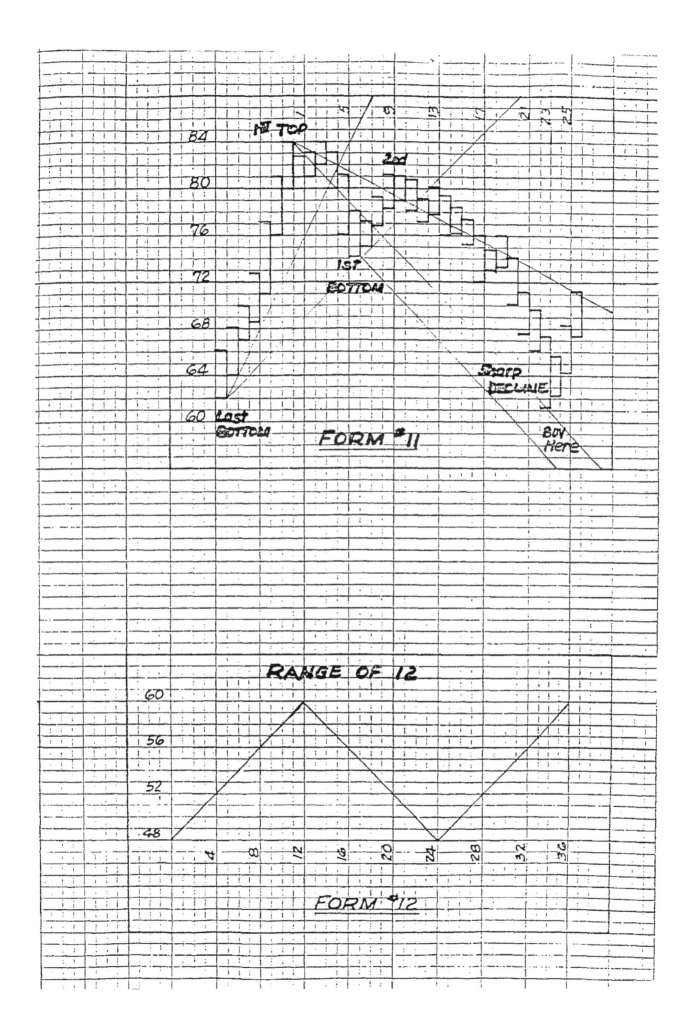

RANGE OF 12

FORM #11

FORM #12

LESSON 4

FORECASTING GRAINS
BY TIME CYCLES

AUTHOR OF
TRUTH OF THE STOCK TAPE
WALL STREET STOCK SELECTOR
NEW STOCK TREND DETECTOR
HOW TO MAKE PROFITS IN COMMODITIES

W. D. GANN

82 WALL STREET
NEW YORK 5. N.Y.

MEMBER
AMERICAN ECONOMIC ASS'N
ROYAL ECONOMIC SOCIETY

FORECASTING GRAINS BY TIME CYCLES

TIME RULES

TIME is the most important factor in forecasting market movements. While SPACE and VOLUME are important and momentum is also a factor to be considered, TIME will overbalance both SPACE and VOLUME and arrest momentum.

DAILY TIME RULE

A minor change occurs every 7, 10, 14, 20 and 21, 28 and 30 days. This time period is only a proportion of the major cycles.

MONTHLY TIME RULE

Changes in trend occur every 30, 60, 90, 120, 135, 180, 225, 270, 300, 315, and 360 days. The third and fourth months are the first of importance for a change in trend; the sixth next; then the ninth; and eleventh to twelfth most important.

The life of an option in Wheat or Corn can never be more than 12 months, therefore the important changes in trend occur in the 3rd, 6th, and 9th months, especially the 6th and 9th because they are one-half and three-fourths of the life of the Option.. The 4th or last quarter, or three months, nearly always marks a reversal in trend and a rapid move one way or the other.

RULES FOR FAST MOVES UP OR DOWN

The big market moves, like volcanic eruptions, are over very quickly because they are the result of weeks, months, or years of accumulation or distribution. When once angles or resistance are overcome and the accumulated forces are let loose, they move very rapidly until the energy is exhausted and the time is up. Check Wheat campaigns of 1917, 1924-25, 1933, 1945-46.

Seven weeks or 49 days usually marks the culmination of a rapid move up or down, especially if a major cycle is running out. Sometimes the top or bottom will be reached on the 52 day, but the change can start anytime between the 42nd and the 49th day, therefore begin to watch for tops and bottoms in the sixth week of a rapid move up or down. This change in trend may be only a minor one. 52 days is one-seventh of a year, which is a very important period. It is also one-seventh of 360° or 51-3/8°. The "seventh" period from the beginning of anything is the most fatal and often marks a rapid change in trend one way or the other.

TIME AND SPACE

SPACE movements are important, but can never overcome TIME. However, they are important to watch as they often give the first cue for a change in trend and the TIME change is shown later. For example:

If Wheat has been advancing for a long time and reactions of 5 to 7 cents have occurred several times; then a reverse move of 10 to 12 cents or more occurs, this is a sign that the opposing forces are staring to cause a change in trend and you should take warning.

If a market has been advancing for several months and has been reacting 3 weeks to one month according to our *Time Rule*, then a decline runs 5 weeks or into the second month, which exceeds the time of all previous reactions, it will mark the first important change in trend according to TIME. This rule can be applied to the minor daily moves as well as to the major yearly moves.

WHY BOTTOMS AND TOPS CHANGE

Bottoms and tops change over a period of years not only because Supply and Demand change, but because the forces or cause of price change and on account of longitude and latitude. The cycle that it is working in either forms squares or triangles which lowers or raises prices according to the forces which produce the energy that causes the moves.

WHY PRICES MOVE FASTER AT HIGH LEVELS THAN AT LOW LEVELS

The higher prices go the faster they move; the lower they go the slower they move and the smaller the fluctuations. Note the angles on the "Circle Chart" and "May Wheat Permanent Chart", which show that this is caused by the distance from the main center.

The big money is made in active markets when prices are at high levels and it is made in a short time. You can make plenty of money staying out of the market most of the time and waiting for these big moves.

HOW TO DETERMINE CHANGE IN TREND

1 - Change is indicated by position of the Daily Chart and by angles being broken or tops or bottoms being raised or lowered. Remember, a daily indication may only mean a move of 7 to 10 days.

2 - The Weekly Chart shows a more important change in trend, but judge according to the position on angles and whether the time cycle is running out or not. The Weekly Chart can reverse and only run down 3 to 4 weeks and sometimes only 2 weeks and a change occur in the 3rd week, then the trend continue up or down, as the case may be, but if it runs into the 5th week, expect the move to continue in that direction.

   Don't forget the Rule of Three. Remember that everything moves in threes. Watch the third day, week, and month. Daniel was 3 days in the lion's den, Jonah three days in the whale's belly. The 5th day was the Day of Ascension. Watch the 5th week, 5th month or 5th year in a market for a strong move up or down.

3 - The monthly change in trend is shown by broken angles, broken bottoms, etc. After a monthly change occurs, it may run 3 to 4 months and then reverse the trend, or may run 6 months to the next important time change, all depending upon the cycle it is in and how many months it has moved up or down from the base.

4 - Yearly changes are denoted by the cycles and by broken tops or bottoms of each Option. When the bottoms are broken or the tops are crossed after a long period, it means a big change, especially if a cycle has run out.

LOST MOTION IN SPACE

It is a well known fact in mechanics that it is impossible to make any kind of a machine that will run without lost motion. Markets have a period of lost motion which amounts to between 2 and 2½ cents, which is taking up the slack. In other words, they will exceed the angle or the main center at extreme points by 2 to 2½ cents; if they make 3 cents beyond the angle they will go higher or lower. When markets become extremely dull at low levels through lack of buying power, which is the same as lack of energy, they may fail to reach extreme points indicated, which would be an indication of strength. The same would apply if they failed to reach main centers, showing weakness.

LOST MOTION IN TIME

There is no such thing as slow motion in time, but there is a transition period which amounts to the same thing as lost motion in space movements. This varies according to the major and minor cycles from 1 to 3 cents above tops or bottoms, geometrical angles or price resistance levels.

WHEN THE MARKET IS WEAKEST OR STRONGEST

The market reaches its strongest or weakest point when the square of SPACE equals the square of TIME. In other words, when it is up or down 30 cents in 30 days, it will stand at the square of the base, and when it overcomes the square from the base at high or low levels, you can expect a big reverse move.

When a market hesitates at top or bottom and gets narrow and dull, watch the third to fourth day for a change in trend; next watch the 7th day; then 10, 14, 20, and 28 days.

When a market is advancing and the trend is up on the monthly, weekly and daily charts, it is in strong position as long as it stays above the angle of 78½° or 4 x 1 to the left of the 45° angle and should never be sold short in this position either on a weekly, monthly or daily chart.

It is still in a strong position when it is above the angle of 67½° or 2 x 1 to the left of the 45° angle, but breaking this angle a long distance from the base will indicate a decline to the angle of 45°. As I have said before, the angle of 45° is the "death" angle and when it is broken one way or the other, a big reverse move takes place.

When the angle of 22½° or 2 x 1 to the right of 45° is broken, it means complete destruction and return to the base or bottom.

But do not overlook the fact that lost positions can be regained on the daily, weekly, or monthly charts provided the main time cycle has not run out.

Note the position between bottom and top and whether it is above or below the main center or half-way point. One of the first indications of a reversal in trend will be the breaking of the 45° angle or the breaking of the half-way point in the last minor move.

DURATION OF MOVES

All market movements obey the law of "12" and its multiples.

Major changes occur in the 11th to 12th, 18th, 22nd to 24th, 34th to 36th, 42nd, 48th to 49th, 54th, 60th, 66th, 72nd, 78th, 84th, 90th, 96th, 102nd, 108th, 114th, 120th, 126th, 132nd and 144th months.

Wheat seldom moves more than 18 months in one direction without a big major reversal. The next important point for a top or bottom is the 28th to 30th month. It often culminates in the 27th or 28th month as there is a strong mathematical reason for this. Corn also follows this rule.

Remember, these numbers apply to weeks and days as well.

HOW TO DETERMINE DURATION OF MARKET MOVES

Besides the position of the cycle it is in and the position on angles, the height is determined by the width of the base. Reverse rule for bear market. If several weeks or months are taken up for distribution or accumulation, the greater the extent of the move up or down. The longer a market remains in a narrow range, the greater the move and the longer the duration when it starts.

The fastest moves occur in the 3rd or last stage of a cycle. Note end of 10, 20, 30, and 50-year Cycles on Wheat Chart. It is important to go over each 10-year Cycle and get the duration in Time of major moves and also the number of cents moved up or down.

SEASONAL TREND

The seasonal trend, or Nature's natural curve of Wheat, runs down from August to December or January, and runs up from February to June. Of course this varies according to crop conditions, Supply and Demand, and the cycle it is in. But if the curve of Supply and Demand remains smooth, Wheat would follow this natural trend.

TIME CYCLES

TIME is the most important factor in determining market movements because the future is a repetition of the past and each market movement is working out TIME in relation to some previous Time Cycle. A study of the various Time Periods and Cycles will convince you how the Grain Market repeats the same price levels under the same Time Periods of some previous cycle.

The Great Time Cycles are most important because they record the periods of extreme high or low prices. These cycles are: 90 years, 82 to 84 years, 60 years, 45 years, 30 years, and 20 years.

The Minor Time Cycles are: 13 years, 10 years, 7 years, 5 years, 3 years 2 years and one year.

GREAT TIME CYCLES

90-YEAR CYCLE

When we start from Sunrise or the Horizon and measure to Noon, we get an arc of 90 degrees, which is straight up and down staring from the bottom. 90 months or 90 years is a very important time period. The 90-year Time Cycle is one of the very important ones because it is two times 45. This time period must always be watched at the end of long time periods. For example:

1932 was 90 years from 1842. Study the Wheat prices around this time. 1850 and 1851 – add 90 years and we get 1940-41. Note low prices of Wheat around that time.

1855, June, high for Wheat 170. 90 years from this period gives 1945. Wheat reached high in June, selling at 170, some options at 168 and 169.

1850-51, extreme lows for Wheat. Add 45 years and we get 1895, when extreme low was reached.

From 1895, we again add 45 years, and get 1940.

84-YEAR CYCLE

This repeated 84 years from 1845 to 1852 and brought low prices in 1929 to 1933.

60-YEAR CYCLE

Compare 60 years from major tops and bottoms and see how this cycle works out.

49-YEAR CYCLE

The 49th Year ends a major cycle for Wheat and extreme high or extreme low prices occur 49 to 50 years apart. Note low 1845 and 1846: then 50 years later extreme low again. Note high 1867; and 50 years later, 1917 highest prices for over 100 years. Note 1932 and 1933 extreme lows were 80 years from 1852 lows.

The 49-year Cycle is 225° to 240° in the second circle of 360°, the period of 49 years being 588 months. Note that 576 is the end of the 4th square of 12, which is the fatal square or death point, representing the grave, the winter season, the end of life or anything, and the beginning over again.

45-YEAR CYCLE

The digits 1 to 9 when added up total 45. 45 is the most important angle. Therefore 45 years in time is a very important cycle. One-half of 45 is 22½ years or 270 months. One-fourth of 45 is 11¼ years or 135 months, which is three times 45. You will note how important these points are on the 360° Circle Chart.

One-eighth of 45 is 5-5/8 or 67½ months. One-sixteenth of 45 is 33¾ months.

30-YEAR CYCLE

Compare 1845-1867 with 1895-1897 and 1925-1927.

Compare 1914-1920 with 1944-1950.

20-YEAR CYCLE

This is a very important cycle because it is one-third of the 60-year Cycle. 20 years equals 240 months which is two-thirds of the Circle of 360°.

MINOR TIME CYCLES

13-YEAR CYCLE

In making up an Annual Forecast on Wheat, you consider the 49-year Cycle, the 30-year Cycle, the 20-year Cycle, the 10-year Cycle, and the 7-year Cycle, and in addition you must consider the 13-year Cycle because Wheat often works out this cycle from extreme high to extreme low and from extreme low to extreme high and the back to extreme low. Extremely large crops or extremely small or short crops often recur 13 years apart or 156 months apart.

Go over the Wheat chart from 1841 to date. Compare 1841 with 1854 or 13 years apart. Also note the 1842 low and 1852 high or 10 years apart. Then note 1855, or 13 years from 1842. Note extreme low in 1844 and extreme high in 1857; then 1854 to 1867; 1864 to 1877; 1867 to 1881; 1881 to 1894. Note extreme low was reached in 1894 in December and in January, 1895. 1888 to 1901; 1898, extreme high, to 1911; 1895, January, extreme low, to 1908 top, and higher prices in 1909. 1894 low to 1907 low, 13 years apart. 1904 low to 1917 high; 1907 to 1920; 1909 to 1922; 1914 to 1927; 1920 to 1933; 1921 to 1934; 1923, low in July, and 1936, low in June.

Note last low in 1924 in March; then 1937 was 13 years from 1924 and 20 years from 1917, and 30 years from 1907. Note lows were reached in March, 1907.

December, 1919: Wheat reached extreme high. 156 months later, in December, 1934, extreme low for May Wheat. Note the last extreme low before the lows of 1914, there were triple bottoms. In September and December, 1906 and a third bottom around the same level in March, 1907. 13 years later, in December, 1919, extreme high, and in May 1920, last high 13 years from these starting points. Then, as noted above, 13 years from extreme high in 1919 and 1920, the extreme lows were reached in 1932 and 1933.

It is important to note 13 years, 26 years, 39 years, and then 49 to 52 years from any extreme high or low point.

10-YEAR CYCLE

Wheat varies slightly at times from the 10-year Cycle, and tops come out between 10 years and six months and 11 years. This is due to the position of some previous tops or bottoms as Time and angles will show. But the main cause is that there are two crops of Wheat produced each year in this country and if the crop is extremely good or bad, high or low prices run over into the 11th year at extremes. Another thing is that there is a Wheat crop harvested almost every month in the year in some country.

Note top on Wheat in May, 1877. According to the 10-year Cycle there should be a top in May, 1887. The high of that year was reached in the month of May and a decline followed, but the extreme high prices for several years occurred in September, 1888, bringing the top out from 1877 in the 11th year.

The next top and extreme high prices would be due in 1898. The Leiter corner occurred in May, 1898, and the May Option sold at $1.85. According to the 10-year Cycle another top should come out in May, 1908. The high of the year 1908 was reached in May, but in the following May, 1909, extreme high prices were reached, coming out on the 11-year Cycle, which is due to 135 months or 11¼ years being 3/8 of 360°.

The next high point according to the 10-year Cycle would be due in 1918 or 1919. But note that the last extreme high for over 50 years occurred in 1867. Therefore extreme high prices on the 50-year Cycle would be due in 1917. May Wheat advanced to $3.25 in May, 1917, and the Government stopped trading in it, fixed the price at $2.50 per bushel and high prices prevailed until 1920.

For 1947, compare prices for 1847, 1907, 1917, 1927, and 1937.

7-YEAR CYCLE

This is a very important Cycle. You should check 7 years from any important top or bottom. Also watch 14 years, 21 years, 28 years and multiples of 7. Tops and bottoms often come out 7½ years apart or on the 90th month. It is very important to watch 90 months for minor as well as major top or bottom.

5-YEAR CYCLE

This period of 60 months is important because it is 1/4 of the 20-year Cycle and 1/2 of the 10-year Cycle, and 1/6 of the Circle of 360° or the 30-year Time Period.

3-YEAR CYCLE

Culminations of major and minor moves often occur in the 34th to 36th month from major and minor tops and bottoms. Always watch 3 years from any important top or bottom as a change in trend is likely to occur.

1-YEAR CYCLE

This is the smallest cycle but in view of the fact that there is a grain crop harvested in the United States every year and in fact a Spring and Winter crop of Wheat, important changes in trend often occur one year from previous tops and bottoms. This may not be a change in the main trend but a reaction can run one to three months at the end of a one-year period.

Whenever you start to make up a forecast one year or more in advance, always check back and see if the market is running out a major cycle or a minor cycle, especially when the market is nearing extreme high prices or extreme low prices. Study war periods and war cycles against war periods; normal cycles against normal time periods.

A careful review of all the major and minor cycles, when used in connection with the Geometrical Angles, will help you to determine which cycle is repeating the closest. By keeping up the months where extreme highs and lows in previous cycles were reached, you can rate the months when the market is making extreme lows or highs in the current cycle, which will give you a double check on your forecast.

December 4, 1946.

LESSON 5

MECHANICAL COTTON METHOD AND NEW TREND INDICATOR

CONTENTS

```
┌─────────────────────────────┐
│       W. D.  GANN           │
│                             │
│     820 S.W. 26TH ROAD      │
│                             │
│      MIAMI, FLORIDA         │
└─────────────────────────────┘
```

MECHANICAL COTTON METHOD
AND
NEW TREND INDICATOR

CAPITAL REQUIRED

The first point to consider when you start to operate with any Method on the Cotton Market is the amount of capital required, with which you can trade and never lose your capital and over a period of 5, 10 or 15 years be able to make profits, because a Method that will make profits and never lose your capital is the kind of a method that every man should follow to make a success.

As a general rule, I have always considered it advisable to use at least $1,500 capital for every 100 bales of Cotton traded in and to limit stop loss orders to not more than 30 points on every 100 bales. In this way you will be able to make 10 consecutive trades on your capital and the market would have to beat you 10 consecutive times to wipe out your capital, which it will not do. Whatever amount of capital you use to trade with, follow this rule: Divide your capital into 10 equal parts and never risk more than 10% of your capital on any one trade. Should you lose for 3 consecutive times, then reduce your trading unit and only risk 10% of your remaining capital. If you follow this rule your success is sure.

For the Mechanical Trend Indicator Method, you can start with capital of $1,000 when Cotton is selling under 10¢ per pound and begin trading in 100 bales, provided you make your first trade at a time when you can place a stop loss order not more than 30 points away, in fact, you should try to start when your risk will only be 20 points. In other words, with a capital of $1,000 you must figure that you would be able to make at least 7 to 10 trades with your capital and that the market would have to beat you 7 to 10 consecutive times to wipe out your trading capital. With this Method it is impossible for that to happen, *provided you follow the rules and trade on definite indications.*

Use a capital of $1,000 to trade in Cotton when it is selling under 30¢ per pound. From 12¢ to 20¢, use $1,500 for each 100 bales. From 20¢ to 30¢ use $2,000 for each 100 bales. From 30¢ to 40¢, use $3,000 capital.

If you want to start trading in a smaller unit on the New Orleans Cotton Exchange, use a capital of $500 for each 50 bales in normal markets and never risk more the 30 points on the initial trade. When markets are abnormal and at prices like 1946, 1947 and 1948, brokers require margin or $1,500 to $2,000 to trade in 50 bales. Under these conditions when there are wide fluctuations you can trade and risk 40 to 50 points on each trade, but try to keep your stop loss order 20 to 30 points above tops and below bottoms when possible. Then follow the same pyramiding plan as you would with a larger capital, never risking more than one-tenth of your capital on any one trade.

HOW TO KEEP THE CHART FOR THE TREND INDICATOR

Keep up daily high and low chart on each option and mark the opening and closing prices on the chart.

The Trend Indicator or Trend Line is obtained by following the daily moves. As long as an option is advancing and making higher bottoms and higher tops, the Indicator or Trend Line moves up each day to the highest price and continues to move up as long as the market makes higher tops and higher bottoms.

The first day that the option reverses and makes a lower bottom by 5 points or more, you move the Trend Line down to that bottom. Then, on the following day if the option moves down to a lower bottom, you move the Trend Line to the low of that day and continue to move it down as long as Cotton makes lower bottoms.

Then the first day that Cotton records a higher bottom and a higher top you move the Trend Line up again to the top of that day.

This Trend Line simply follows the swings of an option.

NEW HIGH AND NEW LOW THE SAME DAY

If an option makes a higher top in the early part of the day than the previous day, then before the market closes, goes down and makes a lower bottom than the previous day, you move the Trend Line up to the higher top reached in the early part of the day, then move it down to the bottom made later in the day.

The idea of the Trend Indicator is to show each higher top lower bottom so that you will always know where an option starts down from the last top or starts up from the last bottom.

WITHIN DAY

By a *"within day"* I mean a day when an option makes a higher bottom but does not make a higher top than a previous day; in other words, it remains within the range of the previous day.

If an option is declining and only rallies one day, making a higher bottom but not making a higher top, then breaks to new lows, I do not consider it important or advisable to move the Trend Line up; neither would I move the stop loss order down above this *"within day"* top unless it was after a prolonged decline in a fast-moving market.

Apply this same rule when an option is advancing and makes a lower top but not a lower bottom the same day, remaining within the range of the previous day; then if it advances to a higher level the following day, the Trend Line should not be moved down and stop loss orders should not be moved up under this bottom unless there has been a prolonged advance in a fast-moving market.

"Within moves" last sometimes as much as 2 or 3 days, that is remaining 2 or 3 days on a side move without breaking the bottom of a previous active day or crossing the top of that day. When a change occurs after a move of this kind, go with it. If it breaks the bottom after a series of *"within days"* go short. If it crosses the top after a series of *"within days"*, consider the trend up and go long.

HOW TO USE STOP LOSS ORDERS

With this Method you must always use a stop loss order, 10, 20, 30 or 40 points below the bottoms or above the tops made by the Trend Indicator.

Remember, stops are placed above or below the top or bottom of the Trend Indicator, and NOT placed above or below the high and low for the day, expect when you are applying the 7 to 10-day Rule and following a pyramiding move up or down, or where there is a Signal Top or Bottom Day, when you place stop loss orders above the top of the Signal Day or below the bottom of the Signal Day. The reason that it is called a Trend Line is because we do not record moves made during the day but only when an option makes a lower top and a lower bottom or a higher bottom and a higher top.

When Cotton is moving slowly, you can use 10-point stop loss orders with greater success and larger profits, but when it fluctuates rapidly the move will often go 15 points over a top or under a bottom and not go 20 points, therefore a 20-point stop loss order will not be caught as often. A stop loss order 30 points under a Trend Line bottom or over a Trend Line top will be caught less frequently than the 10 or 20-point stop loss orders. However, as a general rule, I only advocate using 30-point stop loss orders in very active markets.

SPACE CHARTS

You can keep charts of every 10, 20, or 30 point move up or down, but the most important in active markets is the 20-point chart. When Cotton breaks 10 points under a bottom on the 20-point chart or crosses a top on the 20-point chart by 10 points, it indicates a change in trend.

HOURLY CHARTS

In active, fast-moving markets, where you can get the prices every hour, it is important to keep the Hourly high and low and also mark the opening of the hour and the closing hour.

Apply the same rules that you do to your Daily high and low chart, and the first time that the market breaks a Trend Line bottom on the Hourly Chart or crosses a Trend Line top, consider that the trend has changed temporarily.

If there are several hours with tops around the same level or a series of bottoms around the same level, then when the market crosses 5 points over an Hourly top, or breaks 5 points under an Hourly bottom, consider that the trend has changed at least temporarily and trade accordingly.

Even in a narrow market or in a market that is moving 10 to 25 points per day, if you keep an Hourly high and low Chart, you will see the value of it in getting a quick change in trend.

TRADING INSTRUCTIONS

BUYING AND SELLING POINTS

RULE #1:   TRADING ON TREND LINE INDICATIONS ONLY

The simplest and easiest rule is to buy 100 bales, 50 bales or any other unit that you start trading in, and place a stop loss order 20 points under the last Trend Line bottom; then follow up with a stop loss order 20 points under the last Trend Line bottom and never use any other indication to sell out until the Trend Line breaks 20 points under a previous Trend Line bottom, where your stop is caught. Then reverse, selling 100 bales, or whatever your unit is and following that down with a stop loss order 20 points above each Trend Line top until your stop loss order is caught. Then reverse and go long again.

Remember, always allow your Trend Indicator to be your guide. When it turns down, follow it and do not expect a change until the Trend Indicator shows it. That is what your Trend Indicator is for – to keep you with the trend of the market. When it changes, you must change and reverse your position accordingly.

This rule will make the cautious investor or trader a very large percentage of profits each year if he trades when Cotton is active. The higher the price Cotton is selling at, the more money this rule will make.

RULE #2:   BUYING AT DOUBLE OR TRIPLE BOTTOMS

Buy against double or triple bottoms and protect with stop loss order 10, 20, or 30 points away according to the price and activity. When an option makes the same price level a few days apart, it makes what we call a double bottom on the Trend Indicator. A triple bottom is when an option makes bottom around the same level of prices the third time. A second or third bottom can be slightly higher or lower than the previous bottom, but remember this rule:

When you buy at the time an option reaches the third bottom, you should never risk more than 20 points, for when the third bottom is broken, especially if this bottom is around the same level, and your stop is caught, it will indicate that the main trend has changed and you should double up and go short.

Always reverse position when the trend changes. If you are long of the market and your stop is caught, you must go short. If you are short of the market and the trend changes and your stop is caught, you must go long or buy an equal amount.

The safest buying point is when an option makes a triple bottom near the same level, protecting with a stop loss order not more than 20 points under the lowest level of the triple bottom.

RULE #3: SELLING AT DOUBLE OR TRIPLE TOPS

This rule is just the reverse of Rule #2. Sell against double or triple tops with a stop loss order 10, 20, or 30 points above the top, but on a third top never use more than a 20-point stop loss order because, as a general rule, when an option reaches the same price level the fourth time, it goes through and moves higher. Therefore, it is always a sure indication that when Cotton goes above the third top, you can buy it for higher prices.

RULE #4: FOURTH TIME AT THE SAME LEVEL

Triple bottoms are the strongest and triple tops the strongest, but it is very important to watch an option when it reaches the same level the fourth time as it nearly always goes through. Therefore it is safe to reverse position and pyramid when an option goes through a triple top or crosses the same price level the fourth time.

Reverse the rule on the downside: Where triple bottoms are made close together and an option goes to this level the fourth time, it nearly always goes through. Therefore, when triple bottoms are broken, reverse position, sell out all longs and go short, always going with the trend and never against it.

RULE #5: ASCENDING OR RISING BOTTOMS AFTER A TRIPLE BOTTOM

After an option makes a third or triple bottom, then has a rally and from this rally reacts again, making a fourth bottom higher than the previous bottoms, it is a sign of strong support and indication of higher prices. Then, if the fifth bottom is higher, it is a still stronger indication that a greater advance will take place.

RULE #6: DESCENDING OR LOWER TOPS AFTER A TRIPLE TOP

After a triple top, watch the fourth top or the first rally after Cotton breaks away from the triple top. If this fourth top is lower than the previous tops, it is a sign of weakness and lower prices. Then after a decline, if the next top of a rally (which would be the fifth top counting from the first) is still lower, it is a sign of extreme weakness and indicates much lower prices.

RULE #7: 7 TO 10-DAY RULE FOR AN ACTIVE, FAST-MOVING MARKET

When Cotton is very active, declining fast and making lower tops and lower bottoms each day, after it has declined 7 days or more, you should make your stop loss order 20 points above each day's top, and when your stops are caught, reverse position and buy, placing stop loss order 20 points under the previous day's bottom.

When Cotton is very active and advancing fast, after it has advanced 7 to 10 days or more without breaking a previous day's bottom, you should follow your purchases up with a stop loss order 20 points under each day's low until the stop is caught. Then reverse and go short, placing a stop loss order 20 points above the previous day's top.

But do not consider that the main trend has changed up or down until Cotton crosses a Trend Line top or breaks under the last Trend Line bottom.

PYRAMIDING

RULE #8:   HOW TO PYRAMID

Much larger profits can be made pyramiding, and it is just as safe to pyramid if you adhere strictly to the rules.

If you are trading in 100 bales, then after you buy or sell the first 100 bales, when the market moves 40 to 50 points in your favor or when you have $200 to $250 profit, buy or sell 100 bales more so long as the Trend Indicator shows that the main trend is still up or down. Continue to buy or sell 100 bales more every time the market moves 40 to 50 points in your favor, always placing a stop loss order not more than 20 points below the Trend Line bottom or 20 points below each day's lowest, if you are long, and not more than 20 points bone the Trend Line top or 20 points above each day's highest, if you are short. If you have pyramided until you have 500 bales, then you should have an order in to sell 600 bales on stop, which would put you short 100 bales to start a new deal. Pyramid again in the same way or as long as the market moves in your favor.

But remember, when Cotton has moved 300 to 350 points in your favor, you must watch for a change in trend and be careful about buying or selling another lot on which you would have to take a loss. In active high-priced markets the move may run 500 to 720 points before an important change in trend.

RULE #9:   THE RUN OR PYRAMIDING MOVE

The big money in pyramiding is made in the run between accumulation and distribution. Pyramids should be started after double or triple bottoms. Then, when you get into this run, buy every 40 to 50 points up, protecting with a stop loss order 20 points under each day's bottom or 20 points under the last Trend Line bottom. By following up with a stop loss order 20 points under the Trend Line bottom, you will not get out until the main trend has changed. But in fast-moving markets, after you have bought the 5th and 6th lot, then it is safest to keep your stop loss orders 20 points under each day's bottom, because in active, fast-moving markets Cotton often declines 200 to 350 points in 2 days without breaking the Trend Line bottom or without declining and moving down on the 3-day Chart. If you use your rule for determining the top day, then you can get out before the trend changes or even before Cotton breaks the bottom of a previous day.

RULE #10: PYRAMIDING ON TREND LINE INDICATIONS ONLY

This pyramiding plan is simple and easy to use. You simply use Rule #1 to make your first trade, buying the first lot after the Trend Line Indicator shows uptrend by crossing a Trend Line top by 20 points; then use Rule #9 for buying the second lot after Cotton breaks out of a trading range, but remember, never buy the second lot until Cotton crosses the highest top of the trading range.

In a declining market, sell the first lot after the Trend Line shows down-trend by breaking a Trend Line bottom by 20 points; then use Rule #9 for selling the second lot after Cotton breaks out of a trading range, only selling the second lot when Cotton breaks the lowest bottom of the trading range.

RULE #11: SAFEST PYRAMIDING RULE

One of the safest rules to use for pyramiding when Cotton is at extremely high levels or extremely low levels is to start with 100 bales and when the market moves 50 points in your favor, buy or sell another 50 bales; then when it moves 50 points more, buy or sell 50 bales; then on the next 50-point move in your favor, buy or sell 50 bales. Continue to follow the market up or down with this amount until there is a change in trend.

RULE #12: FAST MARKETS AND WIDE FLUCTUATIONS

In fast-moving markets, like the years of 1923, 1927, 1929, and 1946, when you pyramid and have very large profits, you should follow down with a stop loss order about 50 points away from the market. Then, after a severe decline reduce stop loss orders, placing them about 40 to 50 points above the low level, because when a market is moving so fast as this, you should not wait for the Trend Indicator to show a change in trend by crossing a Trend Line top or even a previous day's top before changing position; also apply rules for determining bottom by Signal Day and Opening and Closing Prices.
Reverse this rule in an advancing market.

RULE #13: WHEN NOT TO PYRAMID

Never buy a second lot for a pyramid when Cotton is near a double top or sell a second lot when Cotton is near a double bottom.
Safety is the first consideration in starting or continuing a pyramiding campaign in Cotton.
Mistakes are made by buying or selling a second lot too near the accumulation or the distribution point. After a big run up or down, you must always wait for a definite change in trend before starting to pyramid.
Cotton often holds for several days or weeks in a range of 50 to 75 points moving up and down, not crossing the highest top or breaking the last bottom made. When it does get out of this range, crossing the highest top or breaking the lowest bottom, it indicates a bigger move and you should start to pyramid, buying the second lot after it makes a new high or selling when it breaks to a new low.

HOW TO DETERMINE CHANGE IN TREND

RULE #14: MINOR TREND INDICATOR

In a declining market, never consider that the minor trend has turned up until the trend changes on the Trend Line Chart or Trend Indicator. To change the trend on the Trend Indicator, Cotton must advance 20 or more points above the last top on the Trend indicator, according to the activity and price of Cotton, whether you are using 10, 20, or 30-point stop loss orders above the previous top.
In an advancing market, never consider that the minor trend has turned down until Cotton breaks 20 or more points under the last bottom on the Trend Indicator or Trend Line Chart.

Remember that breaking 10 points under a daily bottom or going 10 points over a daily top does not change the trend.

RULE #15: MAIN TREND INDICATOR

After a prolonged advance, never consider that the main trend has changed until a bottom made by the 3-day Chart has been broken.

After a prolonged decline, never consider that the main trend has turned up until a top made by the 3-day Chart has been crossed. It is very important to keep up a 3-day Chart.

RULE #16: BREAKAWAY POINTS

Watch the point and price from which the last move starts up and when that price is broken, consider that the main trend is changing to the downside.

When cotton is in strong position at high levels, watch the last bottom or starting point of the last move to new highs. When this level is broken, it is an indication that the main trend is turning down.

Watch the point and price from which the last move starts down and when that price is crossed, consider that the main trend is changing to the upside.

When Cotton is in a weak position at low levels and slowly working lower, making lower tops and lower bottoms, it is important to watch the last top or the point where Cotton breaks away from and makes new lows. Never decide that the main trend has turned up until Cotton begins to cross some of these levels that it broke away from.

RULE #17: SECOND AND THIRD HIGHER BOTTOMS AND LOWER TOPS

Watch the second and third higher bottoms. When Cotton breaks a second higher bottom, consider the main trend has changed to the downside.

Watch the second and third lower tops. When an option crosses the third lower top, consider the trend has turned up, at least temporarily, and go with it.

RULE #18: SECTIONS OF A MOVE

It is important to study the different sections or moves that Cotton makes between the first low level and the first, second, third, fourth, or fifth tops of a move. After Cotton has had several moves up and reacted, when it is near the end of the move, the gains over the last previous top will be less and the run from the last bottom to the last top will be less than in the early stages of the movement, an indication that the move has run out and that a culmination is near. Then apply your other rules and watch the Trend Indicator and 3-day Chart for a reversal in trend.

In a declining market, apply the same rule. When the declines or sections of a move become shorter, it indicates that the selling pressure is waning.

Watch the first rally, or first reaction after top or bottom has been made, and if Cotton runs 50 or 60 points, then watch the action of the next move of 50 to 60 points up or down. Cotton will often rally, or react about this same number of points three or four times but watch for a change for the fourth time.

Cotton will often react or rally 90 to 100 points several times in a big campaign. Watch the first time the reverse move is greater than 100 points as this will often mean a change in the main trend.

RULE #19: 30-FULL POINT INDICATION AT BOTTOM OR TOP

In very weak markets watch for the first advance of 30 full-points from any low level and in very strong markets for the first reaction of 30 full-points, which will indicate a change in the minor trend. By 30 full-points I mean, for example, from 630 low, a rally to 660 would be 30 full-points. If the low was 628, we would not count 30 full-points until the option rallied to 660.

Reverse this rule when Cotton is advancing. Suppose it advances to 668 and has not had a 30 full-point reaction for some time. Then if it declines to 630, I would consider it a 30 full-point reaction and an indication that the minor trend is reversing. In that case, if Cotton only declined to 638, or even to 631, we would not count it a full 30-point reaction, because full points are based on even figures.

RULE #20: SHARP 2-DAY SIGNAL MOVE

After a prolonged decline Cotton often has a sharp 2-day rally, making a very wide range in price, then moves in this same range for several days or weeks without getting higher than the top of the 2-day rally or without breaking the previous bottom. This shows support or accumulation. Then when the top of the 2-day rally is crossed, it is indication that you should buy a second lot to start a pyramid.

Apply the same rule after a sharp 2-day decline, which does not change the main trend because Cotton does not decline into the 3rd day, but later when the bottom of this sharp 2-day decline is broken, it is an indication that the main trend has turned down and you can start to pyramid again.

IMPORTANCE OF OPENING AND CLOSING PRICES

RULE #21: SIGNAL TOP DAY

The opening and closing prices are very important when Cotton is very active and reaches extreme high or low.

On the day that extreme high price of a move is reached after a big advance, if Cotton closes near the low of the day or closes below the halfway point of the day's range or closes below the opening, it indicates that the selling is better than the buying and that Cotton is getting ready to turn the trend down, at least temporarily. When there is a move of this kind, you should sell out and go short without waiting, placing a stop loss order on the shorts 20 points above the final day's high.

RULE #22: SIGNAL BOTTOM DAY

On the day that Cotton has a sharp break after a prolonged decline, if it closes higher than the opening or above halfway point or better still if it closes at the extreme high, after making a wide range and going lower than the previous day, it is an indication that the buying is better than the selling and that the trend is getting ready to turn up or that a bigger rally may be expected. Therefore you should cover shorts and buy without waiting for Cotton to make a higher top than a previous day or without waiting until the trend turns up by crossing a Trend Line top.

RULE #23: CLOSING NEAR THE TOP OR BOTTOM AND OPENING LOWER OR HIGHER

If Cotton has a big advance and closes near the top or at the exact top, then the next morning opens 10 to 20 points lower, it is a sign of weakness and an indication that Cotton is going lower, especially if it fails to cross the high of the previous day.

When Cotton is declining and closes near the lowest levels of the day, then next morning opens 10 to 20 points higher and never breaks the opening price and closes near the highest level of the day, it is a sure sign of good support and indicates that Cotton is going higher. If Cotton opens higher after closing weak and holds until 11 o'clock the same day without breaking the opening, it is a sign of higher prices and should buy.

RULE #24: A NARROW DAY AFTER A SHARP DECLINE OR A SHARP ADVANCE

After Cotton has been declining for some time and has a sharp break, closing weak or near the low level, if on the following day the range is very narrow and Cotton goes only slightly lower and closes about the same level, it is an indication that the move has run out and your stop loss order should be moved down 10 points above the top of the narrow day.

After Cotton has been advancing for some time and has a sharp advance, closing strong or near the high level, if on the following day the range is very narrow, it is an indication that a culmination is near and your stop loss order should be moved up 10 points under the bottom of the narrow day.

RULE #25: CLOSING AT THE SAME LEVELS FOR A SERIES OF DAYS

Watch the closing price of an option after a prolonged decline or a prolonged advance. If Cotton closes for a series of days around the same level, it is an indication that it is receiving support or meeting resistance around this level. Then the first day that it closes above or below this series of closings, it will be an indication of a change in trend and you should go with it.

RULE #26: THREE TOPS OR BOTTOMS NEAR THE SAME LEVEL AND CLOSING PRICE

Watch how Cotton closes when it has a sharp run up and makes a top. If it closes below the halfway point or near the low of the day, it is an indication that it is making top. Then, when it advances to the same level the second or third time, if it reacts the same day and closes near the low, it is a sure indication of good selling and that the trend is getting ready to turn down.

Reverse this rule in a declining market. If three bottoms occur around the same level and each time Cotton closes near the high level of the day, it is an indication of higher prices and that Cotton is getting ready to turn trend up.

NOTE: All rules work best in active fast-moving markets and the big profits are made trading in active markets. If you follow these rules, you will make money. Make up your mind to follow the rules before you start and success is assured.

3-DAY CHART
OR
MAIN TREND INDICATOR

The 3-day Chart should be kept on a separate sheet of chart paper from the Daily High and Low Chart and Trend Line. It is used in connection with the Minor Trend Indicator, or the Trend Line used with the Mechanical Method, which records every move where there is a higher top or a lower bottom.

HOW TO MAKE UP 3-DAY CHART

For the 3-day Movement or Main Trend Indicator, the rules are as follows:

The 3-day Chart is made up of moves of 3 days or more. When Cotton starts to advance and makes higher bottoms and higher tops for 3 consecutive days; you move the line on the 3-day Chart up to the top of the 3rd day; then if Cotton continues to move up, making higher tops without reacting as much as 3 days, you continue to move the line on the 3-day Chart up to the top of each day until Cotton reacts 3 days or makes lower bottoms for 3 consecutive days or more.

Then you move the line on the 3-day Chart down and continue to move it down to the lowest price as long as Cotton makes lower bottoms without rallying 3 days.

The first time that Cotton rallies 3 days from any bottom, that is, making higher tops for 3 consecutive days or more you move the line up.

This chart is based on higher tops and lower bottoms and not on closing prices. An option may close lower on the 3rd day, but not make a lower bottom, in which case you make no change on the 3-day Chart. An option may close higher on the 3rd day from the bottom but not make a higher top on the 3rd day, and in that case, you do not move the line up on the 3-day Chart.

EXCEPTION TO RULE

There is an exception to the rule for making up the 3-day Chart. When an option is very active near the top or bottom, making a wide range, and crosses the previous Trend Line top or bottom in less time than 3 days, then you record the move on your 3-day Chart just the same as if there had been a move of 3 days in one direction.

INDICATIONS FOR CHANGE IN TREND

RULE #27: CROSSING TOPS OR BREAKING BOTTOMS OF 3-DAY MOVES

The surest sign of a change in the main trend is when a move on the 3-day Chart is exceeded by 10 to 30 points. When an option breaks under a bottom made by the 3-day Chart, you consider that the main trend has turned down, and when a move crosses a top made by the 3-day Chart, consider the main trend has turned up, at least temporarily.

Breaking 10 points under the last 3-day bottom or crossing the last 3-day top by 10 points in slow or semi-active markets is enough to show a change in the trend.

In active markets, allow 30 full-points under the last 3-day bottom or 30 points above the last 3-day top before considering that the trend has reversed. For final top day use your Signal-Top-Day rule and 7 to 10-day Rule to catch the extreme in wild fluctuating markets at high levels.

When Cotton breaks 10 points under a double or triple bottom made by the 3-day Chart or advances 10 points above a double or triple top made by the 3-day Chart, it is important for a change in the main trend.

RULE #28: FIRST 3-DAY REACTION OR RALLY
After a prolonged advance, watch the first time there and 3-full days of lower prices or the first time the 3-day Chart is moved down, as this will often be the first sigh that the end of the move is near.

Next, watch the second move of 3 days down on the 3-day Chart and see if it is lower than the Trend Line bottom or the minor Trend Indicator or under a 3-day bottom on the 3-day Chart. This will be a stronger indication of a reversal in trend.

Reverse rule in declining market. After a prolonged decline, watch the first time there is a rally of 3 days, as this will often be the first sign that a change in trend is near.

RULE #29: THE THIRD MOVE ON 3-DAY CHART
The most important indication to watch is the third move down on the 3-day Chart after a prolonged advance or decline. For example: An option reacts 3 days; then advances to new high; then has a second 3-day reaction and advances to new high; then when the third reaction of 3 days comes from a new high, it is nearly always a signal that the move is over. If the third move of 3 days breaks a bottom on the 3-day Chart by 10, 20, or 30 points, depending on the price of Cotton and its activity, it is almost a sure sign that the main trend has turned down.

Reverse these rules in a declining market. Watch the first, second and third rally of 3 days. The first time a top is crossed on the 3-day Chart, consider the main trend has turned up. Also watch when the first 2-day sharp rally carries the price above the top made by the minor Trend Indicator and again apply the Closing Rule at low levels to determine the final low day for change in trend. When the move of 3 days, the third time crosses a top on the 3-day Chart, it is almost a sure sign that the main trend has turned up.

HOW TO COMBINE
NEW TREND INDICATOR AND 3-DAY CHART
The Trend Line always records the minor trend of the market, and when it reverses by breaking 10 points under a previous Trend Line bottom or crossing 10 points over the Trend Line top, it shows the minor trend, but the 3-day Chart always shows the main trend of the market.

It is never safe to trade against the main trend. In other words, if the 3-day Chart shows downtrend, it is always better to sell short on rallies, using the minor trend chart for placing stop loss orders. The same when the 3-day Chart shows uptrend. It is always better to wait for reactions of 3 days and buy than it is to sell short, except in cases where there is a sharp advance.

When the Trend Line or minor Trend Indicator makes double or triple bottoms and double or triple tops and then breaks under these bottoms or crosses the tops, it will show a change in the major trend, but it is not safe to consider it a change in the main trend if the market is very low or narrow with small sales. Except on rapid advances, the 3-day moves will always show the main trend in plenty of time to get in and make money.

The big money is always made by going with the trend, and the 3-day Chart keeps you with the main trend.

RESISTANCE LEVELS

Cotton makes top or bottom on some exact mathematical point in proportion to some previous move. The movement of an option between extreme high and extreme low, either in a major or a minor move, is very important and by a proper division of the range of fluctuation, we determine the points where resistance or support will be met on a reverse move, either up or down. By carefully watching these Resistance Levels in connection with your Trend Indicators, you can make a greater success and trade with closer stop loss orders.

RANGE OF FLUCTUATIONS

1/8 POINTS:

Take the extreme low and extreme high of any important move; subtract the low from the high to get the range; then divide the range of fluctuation by 8 to get the 1/8 points, which are Resistance Levels or buying and selling points. When an option stops around these levels and makes bottom or top on or near them and shows a turn on the Trend Indicator this is the place to buy or sell.

1/3 and 2/3 POINTS:

After dividing an option by 8 to get the 1/8 points, it is next important to divide the range of fluctuation by 3 to get the 1/3 and 2/3 points. These 1/3 and 2/3 points are very strong, especially if they fall near other Resistance Points of previous moves or when they are divisions of a very wide move.

HIGHEST SELLING POINTS

Next in importance is the division of the highest price at which an option has ever sold and each lower top:

Divide the highest selling price by 8 to get the 1/8 points and also divide by 3 to get the 1/3 and 2/3 points.

This is very important as an option, after breaking the halfway point of fluctuation range, will often decline to the halfway point of the highest selling price, and will also work on the other Resistance Points in the same way.

When an option is advancing, it will often cross the halfway point of the highest selling point and the advance to the halfway point of the fluctuation and meet resistance.

MOST IMPORTANT COTTON MOVEMENTS TO CONSIDER

The first and most important point: Consider the Resistance Levels between the extreme high and extreme low during the past 30, 20, 10, 5, 3 and 1 years;

Next important point to consider: Resistance Points or divisions of the highest price at which an option has ever sold;

Then consider the fluctuation of each campaign which runs one year or more; Take the range between extreme high and extreme low and divide by 8 to get the Resistance Points;

Then take a second top or a lower top than the extreme high and divide it by 8 to get the important Resistance Points;

Then take a third or fourth lower top and divide it by 8 to get the Resistance Points;

When you come to the last move, which may run several weeks or several months, that is the most important move to watch for your first Resistance Points.

ORDER OF RESISTANCE POINTS

When an option is advancing and crosses the 1/4 point, the next most important point to watch is the halfway point (1/2 point) or gravity center, or the average of the move or fluctuation.

Then the next point above the halfway point is the 5/8 point.

The next and strongest point after the halfway point is crossed is the 3/4 point.

Then, if the range is very wide between these points, it is important to watch the 7/8 point of the move. This will often mark the top of an advance.

But in watching these Resistance Points, always watch your Trend Line Indicators, both the Trend Line on the Daily Chart and the Trend Line on the 3-day Chart, and if they start making tops or bottoms around these Resistance Points, it is safe to sell or buy.

THE AVERAGE OR HALFWAY POINT

Always remember that the 50% reaction or halfway point of the range of fluctuation or of the extreme highest point of an option of any particular move is the most important point for support on the downside or for meeting selling and resistance on the way up. This is the balancing point because it divides the range of fluctuation into two equal parts or divides the highest selling point into two equal parts.

To get this point, add the extreme low of any move to the extreme high of that move and divide by 2.

When an option advances or declines to this halfway point, you should sell or buy with a stop loss order 10, 20, or 30 points away depending on whether Cotton is selling at very high or very low levels. It requires 30 points below a main halfway point, or 30 points above a main halfway point to show change in trend.

The wider the range and the longer the time period, the more important is the halfway point when it is reached.

When an option advances to a halfway point and reacts several points from this level, then finally goes through it, you can expect it to make the next Resistance Point indicated on your Resistance Level Card.

The greatest indication of strength is when an option holds ten or more points above the halfway point, which shows that buying or support orders were placed above this important Resistance Level.

A sign of weakness is when an option advances and fails to reach the halfway point by 10 or more point; then declines and breaks the Trend Line or other Resistance Points.

NEXT RESISTANCE LEVELS
AFTER THE MAIN HALFWAY POINT HAS BEEN BROKEN

The next Resistance Level to watch after the main halfway point has been broken is the next halfway point of some previous move. By main halfway point I mean, the halfway point of the extreme fluctuating range of an option.

Another very important Resistance Level after the main halfway point is crossed is the halfway point of 1/2 of the highest selling price. This is a stronger support level than the halfway point of minor fluctuating moves because it cuts the highest selling price in half, and is a strong buying or selling point until it is crossed by 10, 20, or 30 points, according to the price of an option, whether it is very high, medium or low in price.

RESISTANCE POINTS NEAR SAME LEVEL

When two halfway points or any other two Resistance Points either in the range of fluctuations or the division of the highest selling price, occur near the same level, you should add these two points together and divide by 2, as the halfway point between these two points will often be a support point on a decline or a selling point on a rally.

HOW TO LOOK UP RESISTANCE LEVELS

When you find an important Resistance Level or the strongest one – the halfway point – at a certain level, look to see if any other Resistance Level, whether it be 1/8, 1/4, 3/8, 5/8, or 2/3 point falls around the same price. You may find 3 or 4 Resistance Levels within a range around the same price. The more you find, the stronger resistance the option will meet when it reaches this level. Then take the highest Resistance Level around this same price and the lowest, and add them together to get the average point of resistance.

Watch the activity of the option when it reaches these Resistance Levels. If it is advancing very fast or declining very fast on large volume, do not consider that it is going to stop around these Resistance Levels unless it stops or holds one or two days around these levels; then sell or buy with stop loss orders.

OTHER RESISTANCE POINTS

Cotton will often react 1/4 to 1/3 of the last move and continue to rally or react 1/4 to 1/3 for a long time; then the first time it reacts more than 1/3 or breaks the 1/2 point, consider the trend has changed.

LOST MOTION

As there is lost motion in every kind of machinery, so there is lost motion in the Cotton Market due to momentum, which drives an option slightly above or below a Resistance Level. The average lost motion is about 15 points above or below important points, but 20 to 30 points means a change in trend.

When an option is very active and advances or declines fast on heavy volume, it will often go 10 to 15 points above a halfway point or other strong Resistance Level and not go 30 Points. The same rule applies on a decline. It will often pass an important Resistance Point by 15 points but not go 30 full points beyond it.

This is the same rule that applies to a gravity center in anything. If we could bore a hole through the earth and then drop a ball, momentum would carry it beyond the gravity center, but when it slowed down, it would finally settle on the exact center. This is the way Cotton acts around those important centers.

WEEKLY HIGH LOW CHART

The same rules may be applied to a Weekly high and low Chart that we apply to the Trend Line Indicator and to the 3-day Chart.

As long as an option makes higher bottoms and higher tops each week on the weekly chart, you move the Trend Line up to the top of the week. Then the following week, if the option does not make a lower bottom or a lower top than the previous week, no change is made in the Trend Line, but the first week the option breaks a weekly bottom by 5 points or more, you move the Trend Line down to the low of the week and continue to move it down to the low of each week as long as the option makes lower bottoms. Then the first week that it makes a higher top than a previous week, move the Trend Line up to the top of that week and follow on, applying the same rules as applied to the other Trend Line Indicators.

For Example: If an option declines for one or two weeks, making lower bottoms, then advances, making higher tops; then reacts for one week, making a lower bottom than a previous week; then moves up to a new high and the following week, or any week after extreme high has been made, it breaks the bottom of the reaction, you consider that the trend has turned down on the Weekly Chart.

These changes in trend on the Weekly Chart are stronger than changes in trend on the 3-day Chart.

The Weekly Chart often makes double and triple bottoms and double or triple tops just the same as the Trend Line on the Daily Chart and the 4-day Chart. Therefore when the option makes a double or triple bottom on the Weekly Chart, you know that it is a strong indication for a change in the main trend to the upside. When an option makes a double or triple top on the Weekly Chart, it is a sign that it is meeting resistance and making final top.

The Rule of 3 may be applied to the Weekly Chart. An option will often react 3 weeks and not go lower the 4th week. If it does go slightly lower in the early part of the 4th week and at the end of the 4th week closes strong at or near the top of the week, it is an indication that the main trend has not changed and that the option is going higher. But any time an option does break under a bottom after having reacted 3 weeks and then rallies, it is in a very weak position and indicates much lower prices, especially if the option is at very high levels.

Reverse all of these rules in a declining market. If an option rallies 3 weeks from the bottom, then goes lower to a new low and later crosses the top that it made before the 3 weeks' rally, it is a very important change in trend, which may last for some time.

7 TO 10 WEEKS' MOVES

After accumulation and distribution has been completed, Cotton will often advance or decline rapidly with only 2 to 3 days' reverse moves, running up or down 7 to 10 weeks. On these moves you can pyramid and make big profits.

Watch for culmination around the 49th to 52nd day after a move starts, and if bottom or top is not made around this time, then watch for the next move around the 66th to 70th day.

By going back over the charts and checking the moves, you will see how important this rule is.

Many of my successful students use the 3-day Chart and the Weekly Chart for long pull trading and have made some very successful pyramids with these two charts alone.

HOW TO DETERMINE CULMINATIONS
AND CHANGES IN TREND

The big money is made in the Cotton Market by following the main trend or big swings and not changing position or taking profits until the market shows by its own action that the trend has changed. If you will follow the rules, the market will tell you when the main or minor trend changes. Do not guess or trade on hope or fear. Give the market time to show a change in trend.

The activity and range in prices at high or low levels determine the change in trend according to whether the market is normal or abnormal. Abnormal prices and fluctuations occur during wars or after wars. The years when crops are very large or very small cause abnormal moves which run to extremes. You must never try to guess when tops or bottoms will be reached in abnormal markets as they will nearly always run longer than human reason or known facts would lend you to believe. That is why you must apply rules and wait for the market's action to show a definite change in trend.

FOUR RULES

Rule 1 – TIME RULE
The TIME FACTOR is most important. When TIME is up, Time or Space movements will reverse.

Keep a record of the days that the market reacts, that is, actual trading days; also keep a record of the calendar days of each reaction or rally. When a reversal comes that exceeds the previous TIME movement, consider that the trend has changed, at least temporarily. After any important top or bottom is reached and the first reaction or rally comes, there is nearly always a secondary move which usually makes a slightly higher bottom or a lower top. The duration of this move may be 1, 2, 3 days or more, all depending upon the activity of the market and the duration of the advance or decline. But your rule is to watch for an overbalancing of a previous TIME period before deciding that the trend has changed.

Rule 2 – SWING BOTTOMS AND TOPS
When a market advances, it continues to make higher bottoms and higher tops on the main swings. You must watch all of these reactions or bottoms; then the first time a SWING BOTTOM is broken, whether it be for 1, 2, 3 days or more, consider that the trend has changed and go with it.

When a market is declining, it continues to make lower bottoms and lower tops on the main swings. Therefore, when the last SWING TOP is crossed, it indicates a change in trend.

Rule 3 – SPACE OR PRICE MOVEMENTS
By SPACE MOVEMENTS, I mean points up or down from top to bottom. For example: Suppose Cotton starts to advance from 20¢ per pound and advances to 25¢ per pound and makes top; then reacts to 24 cents, advances to 26¢ and reacts to 25¢, a reaction of 100 points; later it again advances (as it did in 1946 to 3685 for March Cotton) and reverses, breaking back more than 100 points or a greater movement than a previous space reversal, this would

indicate that the main trend had turned because the SPACE MOVEMENT had *"overbalanced"* the previous moves indicating a change in trend. But you must never depend upon the SPACE MOVEMENT alone to give a definite indication of a change in trend until it is confirmed by the reversal in TIME PERIOD and by the market breaking the last SWING BOTTOM.

Rule 4 – *RESISTANCE LEVELS*
When the price breaks back one-half or more of the previous SWING, this is also an indication of a change in trend. In a declining market, a rally of one-half or 50% or more of a SWING is the first indication of a change in trend. But these indications must be confirmed by the TIME RULE before you can be sure that there is a definite change in trend.
A review and study of past market movements will prove to you the accuracy and value of these rules.
Study the movement of October, March, and July Cotton from August 1945 to October 8, 1946.

AVERAGE SPACE MOVEMENT
As a general rule, Cotton will react in normal markets more than 100 points before the main trend is resumed, but when it is selling above 30¢ per pound reverses can run anywhere from 175 to 400 points or whatever SPACE MOVEMENT the market has previously made. When this is reversed and exceeded, it will show a change in trend, especially when confirmed by the Time Rule.

WHEN COTTON IS IN THE STRONGEST OR WEAKEST POSITION
When Cotton is advancing and is in the last stages of a fast up-swing, reactions will often last only 2 days and then the advance will be resumed. An advance of this kind will sometimes run 42 to 49 days or 6 to 7 weeks and in extreme cases may run 3 to 4 months, but around 84 to 90 calendar days it is very important to watch for a change in trend.

Example – OCTOBER COTTON – 1946 Delivery
1945
May   31 Opened at 2150

Jun   11 High 2220
       18 Low 2150, buying level – same bottom as May 31.

Jul   10 High 2237, selling level. Did not go 30 points above top of June 11.
       16 Low 2195
       18 High 2220, lower top. When it broke the last SWING BOTTOM at 2195 it showed
          downtrend and never had more than a 2-day rally.

Aug 20 Low 2063, down 174 points in 41 days from July 10 top.
(Note low of previous option was 2034 on Dec. 14 and 29, 1944, making 2063 a higher SWING BOTTOM.)

       22 High 2105, a 2-day rally.

       24 Low 2077, a 2-day reaction. Then moved up more than 3 days and crossed SWING TOP at 2105, showing main trend up and time to buy.

Sep 13 High 2182.

Sep 15 Low 2150, a 2-day reaction.

19 High 2185.

26 Low 2156, above low of Sept. 15, the last SWING BOTTOM – a buying level with stop at 2130. Main trend continued up and prices crossed 2237, the high of July 10, in the month of October, showing uptrend. You should buy more.

Nov 13 High 2371.

17 Low 2275, down 96 points in 4 market days. Last SWING BOTTOM was 2243, made in October. Failing to break it showed main trend up. It started making higher bottoms.

Dec 27 High 2388.

1946

Jan 7 Low 2328, down 60 points in 7 market days.

Main trend continued up and prices crossed previous tops with no 3-day reaction.

Feb 16 High 2637.

20 Low 2569, down 68 points in 3 days.

Mar 4 High 2716.

6 Low 2628, down 88 points in 2 days.

Note Nov. 16 to 20 it declined 96 points but this time did not decline as much. Trend still up.

11 High 2687, up 4 days.

16 Low 2640, down 5 days, a higher SWING BOTTOM than Mar 6. Trend still up. Prices moved up and crossed Mar. 4 high.

25 High 2722, a new high.

26 Low 2688, only one day reaction. Main trend up.

Apr 6 High 2845. From Mar, 26 this was 10 market days with no day's low below the previous day's lowest.

9 Low 2782, down 63 points in 2 days. This was not as much as the reaction from Mar, 4 to 6, when it declined 88 points in 2 days.

10 High 2834, up 52 points in 1 day. Main trend still up. Last SWING BOTTOM made April 9 at 2782. When this bottom was broken, it indicated lower prices because no SWING BOTTOM had been broken since Aug 20, 1945.

12 Low 2706. This low level was not broken and the market moved in a narrow trading range making higher support levels until June 3 when the market advanced to new high levels, crossing the highs of April 6, which was a signal for very much higher prices.

Jul 19 High 3665. There were never more than 2-day reactions, and no reaction of more than 120 points from the low of April 12. The market made a Signal Day which indicated top for a greater reaction. On the 3rd day from the top the market had declined over 200 points which exceeded all reactions from August 20, 1945 to date.

Jul 30 Low 3145, a decline of 500 points in 8 market days. This was the greatest decline since the lows were reached Dec. 10, 1938. The decline from the high of 1937 was 670 points. This sharp decline from July 19 to 30 indicated a reversal in trend and that the Bull Market was nearing its final top.

Aug 8 High 3652, a sharp advance from the low of July 30.

Aug 20 Low 3525. Prices down a little over 100 points from the high of Aug. 8.

After this decline there was no reaction that lasted more than 2 days and no decline of more than 160 points until October 8.

Oct   8   High 3928, the highest in the history of this option. The previous high on October Cotton was 3725 in April, 1920.

From the high of October 8 the market broke back 3 days, then rallied making a lower top, then declined and broke the TREND LINE BOTTOM giving a definite indication that the main trend had turned down. This decline exceeded 500 points, which was the decline from July 19 to 30, and also indicated, according to SPACE MOVEMENT, that the main trend had turned down. The most important indication of a change in the major trend was when the market declined more than 7 market days from the high of October 8 exceeding the TIME PERIOD from July 19 to July 30, and indicated by TIME and PRICE or SPACE MOVEMENT that the main trend had turned down. From that time on Cotton was a sale on all rallies, as indicated by the Trend Line Indications and other rules.

Remember that the *"overbalancing"* of TIME is the most important indication of a change in trend.

Study the March, July and October options in future years and apply these rules and you will see how well they work out.

———————

This Mechanical Method is based on fixed rules which will overcome the human element, eliminating hope and fear as well as guesswork. Learn to stick to the rules, trade in active markets and your success is sure.

June 2, 1948.

LESSON 6:

THE BASIS OF MY

FORESCASTING

METHOD FOR COTTON

THE BASIS OF MY FORECASTING METHOD FOR COTTON

Mathematics is the only exact science. All power under heaven and on earth is given unto the man who masters the simple science of mathematics. Emerson said: "God does indeed geometrize." Another wise man said: "There is nothing in the universe but mathematical points." Pythagoras, one of the greatest mathematicians that ever lived, after experimenting with numbers and finding the proofs of all natural laws, said: "Before God was numbers." He believed that the vibration of numbers created God and the Deity. It has been said, "Figures don't lie." Men have been convinced that numbers tell the truth and that all problems can be solved by them. The chemist, engineer and astronomer would be lost without the science of mathematics.

It is so simple and easy to solve problems and get correct answers and results with figures that it seems strange so few people rely on them to forecast the future of business, stocks and commodity markets. The basic principles are easy to learn and understand. No matter whether you use geometry, trigonometry, or calculus, you use the simple rules of arithmetic. You do only two things: You increase or decrease.

There are two kinds of numbers, odd and even. We add numbers together, which is increasing. We multiply, which is a shorter way to increase. We subtract, which decreases, and we divide, which also decreases. With the use of higher mathematics, we find a quicker and easier way to divide, subtract, add and multiply, yet it is very simple when you understand it.

Everything in nature is male and female, white and black, harmony or inharmony, right and left. The market moves only two ways, up and down. There are three dimensions, which we know how to prove – width, length and height. We use three figures in geometry – the circle, the square, and the triangle. We get the square and triangle points of a circle to determine points of time, price and space resistance. We use the circle of 360 degrees to measure Time and Price.

There are three kinds of angles – the vertical, the horizontal, and the diagonal, which we use for measuring time and price movements. We use the square of odd and even numbers to get not only the proof of market movements, but the cause.

HOW TO MAKE CHARTS

Charts are records of past market movements. The future is but a repetition of the past. There is nothing new. As the Bible says – "The thing that hath been, it is that which shall be." History repeats and with charts and rules we determine when and how it is going to repeat. Therefore, the first and most important point to learn is how to make charts correctly because if you make an error in the chart, you will make an error in applying the rules to your trading.

YEARLY CHART

You should keep a yearly high and low chart, that is, recording the extreme high and the extreme low price made during the calendar year, or the life of an option, on one line. The spacing for the price can be 25 points to each 1/8 inch or 50 points.

MONTHLY CHART

You must always keep up a monthly high and low chart, which is the most important chart of all in determining the main trend. This chart records the extreme high and the extreme low price for the calendar month on one line and each space or 1/8 inch on the cross – section chart paper should represent 20 points or 1/5 cent per pound. When prices are very high use 30 points to 1/8 inch.

WEEKLY CHART

The next and one of the very important charts to keep is a weekly high and low chart. For Cotton you should use 1/8 inch to represent 15 points, 30 points represent 2 weeks of time periods, and 60 points represent 4 weeks of time.

WEEKLY MOVING-AVERAGE OR MEAN POINT

To get a weekly moving-average, we take the extreme low for the week and the extreme high for the week and divide by 2, getting the half-way or mean point for the week. This can be recorded on the weekly high and low chart or on a separate chart, recording the weekly-moving-average with a dot and using one line on the chart for each week. Importance of this Weekly Mean Point will be explained later.

THREE TO SEVEN WEEKS' MOVES

In Bull Markets, Cotton usually runs three to seven weeks with higher closings on Saturdays. After the first Saturday that prices close lower than on Monday (which would indicate that the trend is down), if it is only a reaction in a Bull Market which is to be continued, there will be only two Saturdays that the market will close lower and on the third Saturday the market will close higher (which would indicate that the trend is still up). Reverse this rule in a Bear Market. But always judge the strength or weakness by position on angles.

In rapid markets a move will run 6 to 7 weeks and have some kind of a minor reversal in trend, but often markets will continue for several months only reacting two weeks, then resting possibly two or three weeks and resuming the main trend. Often they move right on up or down in the third week. This same rule applies to daily movements. Fast markets will only move 2 days in the opposite direction to the main trend and on the third day will resume the upward or downward course in harmony with the main trend. Watch for a change in trend 84 to 90 calendar days from any important top or bottom. Also watch 84 to 90 market days from any important top or bottom. The next important time period to watch for an important change in trend is 120 days or 4 months. Use this both for calendar days and market days.

DAILY CHART

When you are trading in Cotton you should keep up a daily high and low chart, but for study purposes it is enough to keep up the weekly and monthly charts, which give you the main trend. The daily chart shows the minor trend and shows the change in trend more often than the charts of a longer time period. The indications on the daily chart do not last as long and a change in trend may only run for 3 to 7 days. The scale for the daily chart is 10 points for each 1/8 inch.

No spaces are skipped on the daily chart for holidays or Sundays. Therefore, the time period is for <u>actual market days and not calendar days</u>. However, you should carry the <u>calendar days</u> along at least every 2 weeks, as later, under rules for Time Periods for a change in trend, you will find that it is necessary to check up and know when the market is 30, 60, 80, 120, 135, etc., days from a top or a bottom, which means calendar days, the exact measurement of time for the daily chart. Often the daily chart on actual daily movements comes out on an exact mathematical angle of time measurement at the same time the calendar days come out on exact time measurement, making it a doubly important point for change in trend.

RULES FOR TIME

2-DAY REACTION

The opening and closing prices are very important for determining a weak or strong position as they show where the balance of power rests – whether on the up or down side, according to Space and Time.

SIGNAL DAY

In judging the trend with the daily chart, one of the most important rules to use in a fast advancing or declining market, there will only be 2-day reactions, that is, when the market is advancing and reacts 3 full days and closes weak, it will be a signal that the minor trend has changed. Reverse this rule in a declining market. When a market reaches top, opens strong, advances to new highs in the forenoon, then declines and breaks the lows made of the opening and closes near low levels for the day, it is a signal that temporary top has been made.

A single signal day is when the market opens strong, advances to a higher level than the previous day, making a new high for the move, then sells off and closes weak near the low levels for the day, or below the low of the previous day, it is a Signal Day and indicates that the trend has reversed at least temporarily. Making a new high and closing below the half-way point of the day is also a sign of weakness.

GEOMETRICAL ANGLES

After long years of practical experience, I have discovered that Geometrical Angles measure accurately Space, Time, Volume and Price.

Mathematics is the only exact science, as I have said before. Every nation on the face of the earth agrees that 2 and 2 make 4, no matter what language it speaks. Yet all other sciences are not in accord as mathematical science. We find different men in different professions along scientific lines, disagreeing on problems, but there can be no disagreement in mathematical calculation.

There are 360 degrees in a circle, no matter how large or how small the circle may be. Certain numbers of these degrees and angles are of vast importance and indicate when important tops and bottoms occur on Cotton as well as denote important Resistance Levels. When once you have thoroughly mastered the Geometrical Angles, you will be able to solve any problem and determine the trend of Cotton.

After more than 45 years of research, tests and practical applications, I have perfected and proved the most important angles to be used in determining the trend of the Cotton Market. Therefore, concentrate on those angles until you thoroughly understand them. Study and experiment with each rule I give you, and you will make a success.

We use geometrical angles to measure Space and Time Periods because it is a shorter and quicker method than addition or multiplication, provided you follow the rules and draw the angles or lines accurately from tops and bottoms or extreme highs and lows. You may make a mistake in addition or multiplication, but the geometrical angles accurately drawn will correct this mistake. For example: If you should count across the bottom of your chart 120 spaces, which represents 120 days, weeks or months, then you begin at "0" and number vertically on your chart up to 120, then from this top point draw a 45-degree angle moving down, this will come out at "0" on 120 points over from the beginning. If you have made a mistake in numbering, this will correct it.

Angles drawn on a chart always keep before you the position of the option and its trend, whereas, if you had a resistance point on time written down, you might mislay it or forget it but these angles are always on the chart in front of you.

The moving – average as commonly used is obtained by taking the extreme low price and the extreme high price of the <u>calendar day</u>, week or month, and dividing it by 2 to get the mean or average price for the day, week or month, and continuing this at the end of each time period. This is an irregular movement in spaces or points per week because at one time it may move up 5 cents per week and at another 10 cents per week, while the time period is a regular unit. Therefore, geometrical angles, which are really moving averages, move up or down at a uniform rate from any bottom or top on a daily, weekly or monthly chart.

HOW TO DRAW GEOMETRICAL ANGLES

There are three important points that we can prove with mathematics or geometry: the Circle, the Square, and the Triangle. After I have made the Square, I can draw a Circle in it using the same diameter, and with the different Squares produce the Triangle and the Square in the Circle.

The angles or moving-trend – line averages measure and divide Time and Price into proportionate parts. Refer to Form "I" where I have drawn the square of 90. You will note that this is 90 high and 90 wide – in other words, 90 up and 90 across. It is the same as a square room, which has a bottom or floor, a top or ceiling, and side walls. Everything has width, length and height.

To get the strongest and most important points in this Square, I divide it into 2 equal parts by drawing a horizontal and a vertical line. Note angle marked "A", which divides each of the smaller squares into 2 equal parts and runs from "0" to "90" diagonally. This is a diagonal line moving on a 45-degree angle and divides the large square into 2 equal parts. Then note angle "B" at "45" running horizontally across. This divides the Square into 2 equal parts. Note angle "C", which is a vertical line, running up from "45" which is one-half of "90". This crosses at the center or half-way point at "45", where the other angles cross, dividing the Square into 2 equal parts. Then note angle "D", which forms another 45-degree angle moving from the N.W. corner to the S.E. corner, crossing "45" at the exact half-way point. You see by this that if we draw the first line through the center of the square, we divide it into 2 equal parts – then when we draw lines from the other directions, we divide it into four equal parts – then by drawing the two lines from each corner, we divide the square into 8 equal parts and produce 8 triangles.

As you look at this Square, it should be easy for you to tell with your eye where the strongest support point is, or resistance point. It is at the center where all the angles cross. Four angles cross at this point, so naturally this would be a stronger support point than a place where only 1 angle crosses. I could divide each one of these smaller squares into 4 or 8 equal parts by drawing angles in the same way. Later, when I give you the rules and examples, I will explain how to square the Range of option, that is, the difference between the extreme low and the extreme high prices, or the difference between any low point and any highpoint, and also how to square the bottom price. For example: If the top is 90, the square of 90 x 90 would represent squaring the Price by Time, because if we have 90 points up in Price, and we move over 90 spaces in Time, we square the Price and Time. Therefore, when the option has moved over 90 days, 90 weeks, or 90 months, it will be squaring its price range of 90.

PATTERN CHART FOR GEOMETRICAL ANGLES

The square of 90, or the Pattern Chart, shows all the measured angles that are important to use in determining the position of an option. These angles are as follows: 3-3/4, 7-1/2, 15, 18-3/4, 26-1/4, 30, 33-3/4, 37-1/2, 45, 52-1/2, 60, 63-3/4, 71-1/4, 75, 82-1/2, 86-1/4, and 90 degrees.

It is not necessary to measure these angles with a protractor. All you have to do to get the angles is to count the spaces on the chart paper, using 8 x 8 to the inch, and draw the lines or angles accordingly.

On the square of 90, which you will receive with these instructions, note how equal angles drawn from the top and from the bottom prove themselves by the point at which they cross. For example:

The angle of 8 x 1 drawn from "0" and the angle of 8 x 1 drawn from "90" down both cross at 45, 5-5/8 points over from "0" counting to the right. Then, the angle of 4 x 1 from "0" and the angle of 4 x 1 down from 90, you will notice, cross at 11-1/4 on 45, equal distance from the other angle and twice the measure. The reason these angles prove this way is because the 45-degree angle or 45 periods of time from "0" to 45 is one-half of 90. Therefore, parallel angles beginning at "0" going up and at 90 coming down must cross on a 45-degree angle or at the gravity center.

HOW TO DRAW ANGLES FROM A LOW POINT RECORDED BY COTTON

FIRST IMPORTANT GEOMETRICAL ANGLE

The first, and always the most important, angle to draw is a 45-degree angle or a moving-average that moves up 10 points per day, 15 points per week, or 20 points per month. This is a 45-degree angle because it divides the Space and Time Periods into two equal parts. As long as the market or option stays above the 45-degree angle, it is in a strong position and indicates higher prices. You can buy every time it rests on the 45-degree angle with a stop-loss order 10, 20 or 30 points under the 45-degree angle, but remember the rule: <u>Never use a stop-loss order more than 50 points away</u>. Unless Cotton is near the low levels or just starting in a Bull Market or selling at a very low price, I always use a stop-loss order 10 points under the 45-degree angle. If this angle is broken by 10 points, you will usually find that the trend has changed at least temporarily and the option will go lower.

An easy way to calculate accurately how to put on this 45-degree angle is: For Example: If the time is 30 days, 30 weeks or 30 months from the point where the option was bottom, the angle or 45 degrees must be 300 points up from the bottom and would cross at 30/8. This is one of the easiest angles to put on and one of the simplest to learn. You can beat the market by trading against the 45-degree angle alone if you stick to the rule: Wait to buy on the 45-degree angle or wait to sell it against the 45-degree angle.

SECOND IMPORTANT ANGLE – 2 x 1

This angle moves up at the rate of 20 points per day or 2 spaces of price for 1 period of time. On the monthly chart it would move up 40 points per month and on the weekly chart it would move up at the rate of 30 points per week. The Space between the 45-degree angle and the vertical angle divided into 2 parts makes the angle of 2 x 1 measure 63-3/4 degrees. That is why it is the next strongest angle above the 45-degree angle. As long as an option holds above this angle it is in a very strong position because this angle is more acute than the 45-degree angle.

When an option breaks under this angle it is in a weaker position and indicates that it will go lower and the next support angle is the 45-degree angle. The longer period of time which has elapsed from the low level to the high level, the greater the decline will be because the angles have spread further apart.

Remember the rule of all angles: No matter what angle the option breaks under, it indicates a decline to the next angle below it.

THIRD IMPORTANT ANGLE – 4 x 1

This angle – which is still stronger as long as the price of Cotton holds above it – is the angle, which moves up 40 points per day, week or month. This angle is 4 x 1, or 4 points of Space equal 1 period of Time. It measures 75 degrees and divides the space between the angle of 2 x 1 and the 90-degree angle into two equal parts.

Any option that continues to advance 40 points per day, 60 points per week, or 80 points per month, and remains above this angle is in a very strong position as long as it stays above it, but when it breaks under, it indicates the next angle or next support point according to the position of the option in Time.

FOURTH IMPORTANT ANGLE – 8 x 1

The angle of 8 x 1 or the one that moves up 8 spaces per day, week or month, measures 82-1/2 degrees. As long as an option can hold above this angle on daily, weekly or monthly charts, it is in the strongest possible position, but when it reverses trend and declines below this angle, then it indicates a decline to the next angle.

You will note that with these four important angles we show the strong or bullish side of the market. All the Time by dividing the Space with angles we are getting the half-way point or the gravity center of Time and Price.

These are all the angles you need as long as an option continues to advance and work up and holds above the angle of 45 degrees or the moving-average of 10 points per day, 15 points per week or 20 points per month.

While there are 360 degrees in a circle and angles can form at any of these degrees, all of the important angles form between "0" and "90" because 90 is straight up and down and the most acute angle on which an option can rise. For Example: The 45-degree angle divides the space from "0" to "90" in half. The angle of 135 degrees is simply another angle of 45 degrees because it is one-half of the next quadrant between 90 and 180. 225 and 315 in a circle are also 45-degree angles. Therefore, all of the angles valuable in determining the trend of an option are found between "0" and "90" degrees. When we divide 90 degrees by 8 we get 11-1/4, the next important angle to use – then divide it by 3 and we get 30 degree and 60 degree angles, which are important to use for Time and Resistance Points.

KIND OF BOTTOMS FROM WHICH ANGLES OR MOVING-AVERAGE LINES ARE TO BE DRAWN

DAILY CHART

If an option has been declining for some time – then starts to rally (by rallying from a bottom it must make higher bottoms every day and higher tops) – then after a 3-day rally on the daily high and low chart, you can put on the 45-degree angle and the angle of 2 x 1 from the bottom or low point. As a rule, it will be necessary to put on these two angles at first. If this bottom holds and is not broken, then you can put on the other angles from the bottom.

WEEKLY CHART

If an option is declining and reacts for more than one week and continues down, we will say, for three weeks or more, then starts to rally and advances two weeks or more, you would start to put the angles on from the low point of the decline, only using the angles above the 45-degree angle until the option again breaks under the 45-degree angle – after that you would use the other angles on the lower or bearish side of the Square.

WHAT TO DO AFTER THE 45-DEGREE ANGLE FROM BOTTOM IS BROKEN

After an option makes top, either temporary or otherwise, and breaks under the 45-degree angle and starts moving down, then, the first thing you do is draw angles below the 45-degree angle, starting from the bottom or low point. Note example: Angles Drawn on Monthly, Weekly and Daily Charts.

FIRST ANGLE ON BEAR SIDE OF THE SQUARE – 2 x 1

The first angle that you draw on the bear side of the Square is the angle of 2 x 1 or 2 points over and 1 point up, on a daily chart this would be moving up at the rate of 5 points per day or 1/2 the rate of the 45-degree angle. This angle measures 26-1/4 degrees. This same angle on a weekly chart would move up at the rate of 7-1/2 points per week, and on a monthly high and low chart, based on the scale of 1/8 inch to 20 points, this angle would be moving up at the rate of 10 points per month. This is the support angle which the option should reach after it breaks under the 45-degree angle. As a general rule when the option reaches this angle it will receive support and rally but you should always consider the time period and the main cycle the market is working in and, also, see if there are resistance levels crossing at the same price level where the angle is. Some time it will rest on this angle for a long period of time that is holding the angle and making higher bottoms, but when this angle of 2 x 1 is broken on a daily, weekly or monthly chart the next angle to watch is the angle of 4 x 1.

SECOND IMPORTANT ANGLE – 4 x 1

The next important angle on the bear side of the Square, which moves up at the rate of 2-1/2 points on the daily chart, is the angle of 4 x 1 measuring 15 degrees. It will be the next strong support angle which the option should get support and rally from.

THIRD ANGLE – 8 x 1

Then, after the 4 x 1 angle is broken, the next important angle you will place on your chart is the angle of 8 x 1, which moves at the rate of 1-1/4 points per day, 3-3/4 points per week, or 5 points per month, and measures 7-1/2 degrees. This is often a very strong support angle. After an option has had a big decline, it will often rest on this angle several times or may make final bottom and start up from this angle, crossing other angles and getting back into a strong position again. Therefore, this angle is important to use on a monthly or weekly chart after a prolonged decline.

This completes all of the angles that you will need to use from any bottom at any time.

HOW TO DRAW ANGLES FROM TOPS ON DAILY, WEEKLY OR MONTHLY CHARTS

POSITION UNDER 45-DEGREE ANGLE DRAWN FROM TOP

After an option has made top and declined for a reasonable length of time, say, three days, three weeks or three months, breaking previous bottoms, then you start to draw angles from the top. Note Example: Angles on Monthly Charts.

45-DEGREE ANGLE FROM TOP

The first angle you draw is the angle of 45 degrees or a moving-average, which indicates a decline of 10 points per day, 15 points per week, or 20 points per month. As long as the option is below this angle it is in the weakest position and in a Bear Market.

OTHER ANGLES

In many cases an option will start declining on an average of 10 to 40 points per day and sometimes will decline the limit of 200 points per day. In cases of this kind, when the market is very active you should put on all of the other angles from the top which move down faster than the angle of 45 degrees.

WEAKEST POSITION

The option is in the weakest possible position when it declines and keeps under the angle of 8 x 1. It is in the next weakest position when it is dropping down at the rate of 40 points per day, 60 points per week, or 80 points per month, or under the angle of 4 x 1. It is in its next weakest position when it is dropping down under the angle of 2 x 1.

STRONGEST POSITION

The option is in a stronger position and indicates a better rally when it crosses the angle of 2 x 1, but this depends on how far it is down from the top and how far the angles are apart, as will be explained later under the rules.

CHANGING TREND

As long as an option is declining 10 points per day, 15 points per week, or 20 points per month, or falling below or under the 45-degree angle, it is still in a Bear Market and in a very weak position. When an option rallies and crosses the angle of 45 degrees after a prolonged decline, you are ready to put on the angles on the other side of the 45-degree angle, which shows that the option is in a stronger position in a Bear Market and may be getting ready to change into a Bull Market.

POSITION ABOVE 45-DEGREE ANGLE DRAWN FROM TOP

2 x 1 ANGLE FROM TOP

The first angle or moving-average you draw after the 45-degree angle from the top is crossed and after the option indicates it has made a temporary bottom that is the angle of 2 x 1, moving over 5 points and down 1 point, or 5 points per unit of Time. This is moving down at the rate of 5 points per day, 7-1/2 points per week, or 10 points per month.

4 x 1 ANGLE

The next is the angle of 4 x 1, which moves down at the rate of 2-1/2 points per day, 3-3/4 points per week, or 5 points per month.

8 x 1 ANGLE

The next angle is the angle of 8 x 1 which moves down at the rate of 1 point every 8 days, 8 weeks or 8 months, or 1/8 point per Time Period.

STRONG POSITION

After the option has crossed the angle of 45 degrees and rallied up to the angle of 2 x 1, it will meet selling and react to some angle coming up from the bottom of the last move, but it is in a stronger position when it holds above this angle of 2 x 1, and it is in the next strongest position when it crosses the angle of 4 x 1. Crossing the angle of 8 x 1, which is of least importance, it indicates that it is in a very strong position again from the top. You must always consider a movement coming up from the bottom and its position on angles from the bottom to determine its strength. It is important to consider the number of points it has moved up from the bottom and how many points it is down from the top.

This completes the forms of all the angles that you will need to use at any time from tops or bottoms. Practice putting these angles on tops and bottoms until you are thoroughly familiar with them and know that you are getting them absolutely accurate. Then, you can begin to study the rules for determining the trend according to the position of the option on angles.

DOUBLE AND TRIPLE TOPS OR BOTTOMS

ANGLES CROSSING EACH OTHER

When there is a double bottom several days, weeks or months apart, you draw angles from these bottoms, which are near the same price levels. For Example: From the first bottom, draw a 45-degree angle and from the second bottom, draw an angle of 2 x 1 – then, when these angles cross each other, it will be an important point for a change in trend.

Apply this rule to double tops and triple tops in the same way. It is not necessary for the tops or bottoms to be exactly at the same price level, but near the same price level. For Example: If an option makes one top and the next top is 30 points lower, you would consider it a double top in the same way, if bottoms are 20 or 30 points apart, you would consider them double bottoms.

Angles coming down from tops and crossing angles coming up from bottom are very important for a change in trend when they cross each other.

Always watch the 45-degree angle from any important top and bottom and from the last swing top and bottom from which the market starts up or down. Breaking of the first important angle indicates the first change in trend. Breaking the last 45-degree angle from the last extreme low level, from which a 45-degree angle is drawn, is most important and crossing the 45-degree level in the last high level is very important for a major change in trend, especially on the monthly chart.

GEOMETRICAL ANGLES OR MOVING-AVERAGE LINES DRAWN FROM ZERO

When an option reaches bottom and starts up, you have been instructed to draw angles from this exact low point, which shows the support in Time Periods, but there are other angles which, later on, will be just as important and sometimes more important than the angles drawn from the bottom of an option. These are the angles that begin at "0" or zero, and move up at the same rate that they move up from the bottom. The starting point must be on the same line that the bottom is made on as the Time Period begins from this bottom, but the angles move up from "0". These angles should be started every time an option makes a bottom, especially on weekly and monthly charts, and should also be carried up on important movements on the daily chart.

If an option makes low at 515, which was the low on October Cotton, June 9, 1932, as shown on the chart, starting the 45-degree angle from "0", when will this angle reach 515? Answer: It will reach 515 in 51-1/2 days, 34-1/3 weeks, or 25-3/4 months from the bottom or its starting point. In other words, in 51-1/2 days, 34-1/2 weeks, or 25-3/4 months, it will be up to 515 from "0" and at the price where the option made bottom. Then, the angle will continue on up at the same rate and later, when the option breaks under the 45-degree angle from the actual bottom made at 515 and breaks the other support angles drawn from the actual bottom at 515, the next important point for support will be the angle of 45 degrees moving up from "0". When this angle is broken, it is in the weakest possible position and indicates much lower prices, but this depends on how high the option is selling and how much it has declined at the time it breaks the 45-degree angle from "0". These angles drawn from "0", especially the 45-degree angle, prove when Price and Time are balancing, or when the option is squaring out Time from its bottom.

SQUARING TOPS AND BOTTOMS OR EXTREME HIGH AND LOW LEVELS

From each high price or low price the market squares out in Time and balances price and time, as shown by the geometrical angles.

Example: 1932, June 9, October Cotton low was 515. To square this on the daily chart would mean 51-1/2 days at 10 points per day. This can be used as market days and also as calendar days. The squares can be carried across the chart so you will know when each Time Period runs out and each square ends and a new square begins.

Each important higher bottom should be used for squaring out with Time. December 10, 1938, October Cotton low 728. November 29, 1943, October Cotton low 1812. November 7, 1946, October Cotton low 2307.

The highest levels or tops must also be squared out on weekly or monthly charts, which are more important Time Periods. October 3 and 9, 1946, October Cotton reached the extreme high price of 3928. This is the most important high level to use for squaring out time on the weekly and monthly charts.

To get the time required to square any low point on a weekly chart, divide by 15. Dividing 515 by 15 gives 34-1/3 weeks to square out this low level. This Time Period, for the end of each square, should be placed on your chart all the way across so that you will know at the present time what square in time the market is working.

To get the resistance levels in price for the top of the square, first, add 515 to 515 which gives 1030. This would be the end of the first square in price. The second square in price would end at 1545 and the fourth square at 2060. Continue these squares up from the low level until the price reaches the high of 3928.

To square 515 on a monthly chart, divide 515 by 20, which gives 25-3/4 months, the time required on the monthly chart to square the extreme low price. You can use 26 months or the even figure and carry this across on your charts to see what square the price is working in at any future date. Also, carry across the square of 728, 1812 and 2307, the important low levels. The next in importance is to square out the extreme high price of 3928. You divide this by 20. This would give 196 months, with 8 points over, which would equal approximately 196-1/2 months, to complete the square of 3928. Divide 196-1/2 by 2 to get 1/2 of the square in Time. This would give 98-1/4 months. Divide by 4 to get 1/4 of the Time Period. Next, divide by 8 to get 1/8 of the Time Period. This would give 24-1/2 months, making this Time Period important because it is the end of two years where important changes take place.

Also divide the time period of 196-1/2 months by 3, which would give 65-1/3 months and an important time period. Another reason why this would be important is that 5-1/2 years equals 66 months. Next, 2/3 of the Time Period would give approximately 131 months. Another reason why this is an important Time Period for a change in trend is that 132 months is 11 years.

THREE IMPORTANT TIME PERIODS FROM WHICH TO SQUARE TIME

We have already referred to squaring the extreme low levels and extreme high levels with Time. The third is the squaring of the range between extreme high and extreme low prices. Example: October Cotton 3928 high and 515 extreme low gives a range of 3413. To square this price range on the monthly chart, divide 3413 by 20. This gives 170-1/2 months. Then, divide 170-1/2 by 2, 3, 4 and 8 to get the 1/2, 1/4, 1/8 and 2/3 points. Watch these periods for important changes in trend, applying the seasonal trend, and major and minor time cycles, as well as the geometrical angle, and watch for important change in trend. Example: 1/2 of 170-1/2 is 85-1/4 months. There is another reason why this would be important for a change in trend, that is, the 7-year cycle or 84 months.

It is also important to square the range between 728, the low on October Cotton in 1938, and 1812 the low in 1943, and 2307 the low in November 1946.

These squares should be marked on the bottom of your chart, when the time period is squaring out low levels, and mark across the top of the chart, when the time period is squaring out the extreme high levels.

The calendar year can be divided into 8 equal time periods and into 1/3 and 2/3 time periods. But, you must remember that in using time periods to forecast the Cotton market the time must start from the exact dates of high and low prices. Starting with the extreme low, June 9, 1932, you add 45 days, 90 days, 120 days, 135 days, and 180 days to get the important Time Period, or the proportionate part of one year's time from the extreme low. From the extreme high of October 3 and 9, 1946, you would add the time periods in weeks to see when the time was running out from this top, and watch for important changes in trend.

ZERO ANGLES STARTING AT THE TIME TOP IS MADE

When an option reaches extreme top on a daily, weekly or monthly chart, and the trend turns down, you should start an angle of 45 degrees from "0", moving up from the exact date that the top is made. This will prove the square of the Time Period. It is very important when this angle is reached and it indicates a change in trend. It is the last strong support and when broken, it will indicate much lower prices.

I have instructed you in each case to first draw the 45-degree angle from bottom, top, and from "0" at bottom and top, but this does not mean that you must not use the other angles.

All of the other angles can be used from "0", but the 45-degree angle is the first and most important. After this angle is broken, you can use the other angles. It is not necessary to carry all of them along until you need them, but on the monthly chart, after a long series of years, these other angles should be carried along when the option begins to approach the levels where they would be broken, or where the option would rest on them and receive support.

OUTSIDE OR EXTREME LOW 45-DEGREE ANGLE

This angle is of great importance because it is the last support from the last starting point, beginning with the low in 1932, the 45-degree angle was broken and prices went lower. January 1936, low for October Cotton was 980. The advance started and reached high March 10, 1937, at 3395. The 45-degree angle drawn from 980 was broken and the trend continued down until December 10, 1938, when the low was reached at 727. From this low level the main trend turned up. The important 45-degree angle moving up was drawn from this bottom. In 1939, between July and November, there was a series of lows at 900. A 45-degree angle starts at 9 cents in November 1939, which was a higher bottom than December 1938.

1940, May low for October Cotton, 840. A 45-degree angle starts from this low, which was higher than the previous bottom.

1940, October low on the option for delivery in 1941 was 870. A 45-degree angle was drawn from this low. The advance started and continued on the up-trend making higher bottoms and higher tops until October, 1946, when extreme high was reached at 3928, just below the 45-degree angle from 515, which meant that price and time had balanced on the monthly high and low chart. After extreme high was reached and the big smash took place, when Jordan of New Orleans was in trouble, and prices were declining the limit of 200 points per day, and 45-degree angles were broken, you would look to see where the last support was on an outside 45-degree angle. The angle of 45 degrees, moving up at the rate of 20 points per month from October 1940, crossed at 2340 in November 1946.

Next, the important half-way point must be considered. From the low of 727, in 1938, to the high of 3928, in October 1946, the half-way point is 2328. From this you can see that the 45-degree angle crossed at 2340 and the half-way point was 2328. Our rule is that lost motions and momentum can carry prices to about 30 points below a 45-degree angle, or below the main half-way point.

November 7, 1946, October Cotton sold at 2307, just 20 points below the half-way point and 33 points under the 45-degree angle, but it closed the same day very much above the half-way point and the 45-degree angle.

This writer, with the knowledge that the 45-degree angle and the half-way point should be bottom and a strong support point, bought several thousand bales of Cotton, some of it at the extreme low level, and made substantial profits on the rise. This proves to you the value of having the angles on from all important tops and bottoms.

After the 45-degree angle from the outside low level is broken the next important support angle is the 45-degree angle moving up from zero. Starting a 45-degree angle from 0, December 1938, when October Cotton was low at 728, this angle crossed or reached a price of 2520 in June 1949, making this a strong support and buying point. June 7, 1949, October Cotton sold at 2485 and closed the month far above this angle. The advance continued reaching 2982 in February 1950, the time of this writing. If you did not know how to use this 45-degree angle from "0" you would not know that there was a support point around 2520 to 2480. Note that the low in May 1947, was 2450, and that the option for delivery in the year 1950 made a higher bottom than the option for delivery in 1948.

By looking at the Time Periods you will note that June 9, 1949, was 17 years from June 9, 1932. Therefore, you would watch for a change in trend on June 9, 1947, and the low was reached 2 days before this date and by June 9, 1949, the price had moved up to 2510, and continued to advance.

I wish to emphasize the fact that keeping up all the Resistance Levels, and having all the Time Periods on your chart, and the geometrical angles from all important tops and bottoms brought up to date, will enable you to determine these safe buying and selling points from which you can make a fortune in a short period of time by sticking strictly to the rules and eliminating all guess work and trading on mathematical science, and not on hope.

45-DEGREE ANGLE FROM ZERO TO TOP AND BOTTOM

When a 45-degree angle, moving up from "0" reaches the line or price of the bottom, it is very important -- then, again when it reaches the point of the extreme high price, it is very important for a change in trend.

You should carry 45-degree angles and other angles up from "0" from all-important first, second and third higher bottoms, especially those where very much time has elapsed between these bottoms. You should also start the angle of 45 degrees up from "0" from the first, second and third lower tops, especially those which show much time period elapsed. These angles are the most important to be carried on the weekly and monthly charts.

Never overlook keeping up the angles from "0" because they will tell you when Time is squaring out with Price from tops and bottoms and will locate support angles or moving-average lines at a point on the bear side after the first 45-degree angle from a bottom is broken. You could not locate this support point in any other way except by the angles from "0".

You should go back over past records and bring up these angles and square out different tops and bottoms so that you can prove to yourself the great value of using these angles.

W.D. GANN

February 18, 1950

RESISTANCE LEVELS

If we wish to avert failure in speculation we must deal with causes. Everything in existence is based on exact proportion and perfect relation. There is no chance in nature because mathematical principles of the highest order lie at the foundation of all things. Faraday said: "There is nothing in the Universe but mathematical points of force."

Every Cotton option makes a top or bottom on some exact mathematical point in proportion to some previous high or low level.

The movement of an option between extreme high and extreme low, either in a major or a minor move, is very important and by a proper division of this range of fluctuation, we determine the points where resistance or support will be met on a reverse move, either up or down. By carefully watching these Resistance Levels in connection with your Trend Lines, you can make a greater success and trade with closer stop-loss orders. You can tell by the Resistance Points why Cotton should receive support or meet selling at old tops or bottoms.

RANGE OF FLUCTUATIONS

1/8 POINTS

Take the extreme low and extreme high of any important move; subtract the low from the high to get the range; then, divide the range of fluctuation by 8 to get the 1/8 points, which are Resistance Levels or buying and selling points. When an option stops around these levels and makes bottom or top on or near them and shows a turn on the Trend Line, this is the place to buy or sell. Sometimes the market will hold for 3 to 7 days, making bottom or top around these important Resistance Levels, and, at other times, may hold for several weeks around them.

1/8 AND 2/3 POINTS

After dividing an option by 8 to get the 1/8 points, the next important thing to do is to divide the range of fluctuation by 3 to get the 1/3 and 2/3 points. These 1/3 and 2/3 points are very strong, especially if they fall near other Resistance Points of previous moves or when they are divisions of a very wide move.

HIGHEST SELLING PRICE

Next in importance is the division of the highest price at which any option of Cotton ever sold and each lower top.

Divide the highest selling price by 8 to get the 1/8 points and, also, divide by 3 to get the 1/3 and 2/3 points.

This is very important as an option, after breaking the half-way point of the fluctuating range, will often decline to the half-way point of the highest selling price, and will also work on the other Resistance Points in the same way.

When the market is advancing it will often cross the half-way point of the highest selling point, and then advance to the half-way point of the fluctuation and meet resistance.

MOST IMPORTANT COTTON MOVEMENTS TO CONSIDER

The first and most important point: Consider the Resistance Levels between the extreme high and extreme low of the life of an option.

Next, Resistance Points or divisions of the highest price at which the option has ever sold.

Then, consider the fluctuation of each campaign, which runs one year or more. Take the range between extreme high and extreme low and divide into 8 equal parts to get the Resistance Points.

Lastly, take a third or fourth lower top and divide it by 8 to get the Resistance Points.

Example:

October Cotton –	515	to	3725	high	1920,		low	1932	
	727	"	3928	"	1946,		"	1938	
	1812	"	3928	"	1946,		"	1943	
	2307	"	3928	"	1946,		"	1946	(Nov.)
	2307	"	3560	"	July 16, '47,		low	Nov. '46	
	2307	"	3490	"	May 17, '48,		"	Nov. '46	
	2460	"	3560	"	July 16, '47,		"	May '47	

ORDER OF RESISTANCE LEVELS

When an option is advancing and crosses the 1/4 point, the next important point to watch is the half-way point (1/2 point) or gravity center, or the average of the move or fluctuation.

The next point above the half-way point is the 5/8 point.

The next and strongest point after the half-way point is crossed is the 3/4 point.

Then, if the range is very wide, it is important to watch the 7/8 point of the move. This will often mark the top of an advance.

But in watching these Resistance Points, always watch your Trend Lines on the Weekly Chart and follow rules given on Formations. If the option starts making tops or bottoms around these Resistance Points, it is safe to sell or buy.

THE AVERAGE OR HALF-WAY POINT

Always remember that the 50% reaction or half-way point of the range of fluctuation, or of the extreme highest point of an option, or any particular move, is the most important point for support on the down side or for meeting selling and resistance on the way up. This is the balancing point because it divides the range of fluctuation into two equal parts.

To get this point, add the extreme low of any move to the extreme high of that move and divide by 2.

When an option advances or declines to this half-way point, you should sell or buy with a stop-loss order 10, 20, or 30 points according to whether the option is selling at very high or very low levels.

The wider the range and the longer the time period, the more important is this half-way point when it is reached.

You can make a fortune by following this one rule alone.

A careful study and review of past movements in any option will prove to you beyond doubt that this rule works and that you can make profits following it.

Buy or sell at the most important half-way point of the major move and place stop-loss orders 10 to 30 points under the half-way point or 10 to 30 points above the half-way point. By major moves we mean the half-way point between the extreme low and extreme high, when the range runs 250 to 300 points or more. A minor half-way point would be the 1/2 point between a minor top and a minor bottom. Reactions usually run back half of the last move or to the half-way point.

When the range between the 1/2 point and the 5/8 point is 150 to 200 points or more, and the option crosses the half-way point, it will go to the 5/8 point and meet resistance and then react or decline. The 5/8 point is a very important point to watch for top or reaction. An option will often react from the 5/8 point back to the half-way point and be a buy again.

The same rule applies when an option is declining. If the range is 100 to 200 points or more between the 1/2 point and the 3/8 point, then the option breaks the half-way point, and it will decline to the 3/8 point and make bottom and rally to the 1/2 point, or higher.

When an option advances to a half-way point and reacts several points from this level, then finally goes through it, you can expect it to make the next resistance point indicated on your Resistance Level card, or the next old top.

The same applies when Cotton declines and receives support several times on a half-way point, then breaks through it. It will then indicate the next resistance point on your Resistance Level card, or the next important bottom.

The greatest indication of strength is when a Cotton option moves 20 or more points above the half-way point, which shows that buying or support orders were placed above this important Resistance Level.

A sign of weakness is when an option advances and fails to reach the halfway point by 20 or more points, then declines and breaks the Trend Line, or other Resistance Points.

NEXT RESISTANCE LEVELS

AFTER THE MAIN HALF-WAY POINT HAS BEEN BROKEN

The next Resistance Level to watch after the main half-way point has been broken is the next half-way point of some previous move. By main half-way point I mean, the half-way point of the extreme fluctuation range of the life of an option.

Another very important Resistance Level after the main half-way point is crossed is the half-way point or 1/2 of the highest selling price. This is a stronger support level than the half-way point of minor fluctuating moves because it cuts the highest selling price in half, and is a strong buying or selling point, until it is crossed by 10, 20 or 30 points according to the price of the option, whether it is very high-priced, medium or low-priced.

In the last stages of Bull or Bear Campaigns use only the half-way point of short or minor moves. It is most important to watch the Resistance Levels of the final move, which may run several weeks or months, particularly the half-way point.

When it is exceeded by 30 full points, the trend usually reverses.

LOST MOTION

As there is lost motion in every kind of machinery, so there is lost motion in the Cotton market due to momentum, which drives an option slightly above or below a Resistance Level. The average lost motion is 30 to 40 points, depending upon the activity of the market.

When Cotton is very active and advances or declines fast on heavy volume, it will often go from 20 to 40 points above a half-way point or other strong Resistance Level and not go 50 points. The same rule applies on a decline. It will often pass an important Resistance Point by 20 to 40 points but not go 50 full points beyond it.

This is the same rule that applies to a gravity center in anything. If we could bore a hole through the earth and then drop a ball, momentum would carry it beyond the gravity center, but when it slowed down, it would finally settle on the exact center. This is the way Cotton acts around these important centers.

A study of the Resistance Levels between bottoms and tops of individual options will prove how accurate the market works out to these important points.

W.D. GANN

February 18, 1950

FORECASTING COTTON BY TIME CYCLES

TIME CYCLES

Every movement in the market is the result of a natural law and of a cause which exists long before the effect takes place and can be determined years in advance. The future is but a repetition of the past, as the Bible plainly states: "The thing that hath been, it is that which shall be; and that which is done, is that which shall be done, and there is no new thing under the sun." – Eccl. 1:9.

Everything has a major and a minor, and in order to be accurate in forecasting the future, you must know the major cycle, as the most money is made when extreme fluctuations occur.

GREAT CYCLES

Never overlook the great cycles, which mark extreme high and low prices which occur over a long period of time.

82 to 84 years. This is one of the great cycles in Cotton and it is running out 82 years from 1864; the extreme high point, and Cotton should be high between July 9, 1946, and October 5 to 8, 1946, according to this cycle and the main trend run down for several years following these extreme high prices. This is what the cycle indicated.

90-YEAR CYCLE

This is three times the 30-year cycle and two times the 45-year cycle, and is important to watch for extremes. 1954 will be 90 years from 1864. You can also check back against extreme low points, and see how the cycle works out 90 years later.

60-YEAR CYCLE

The circle equals 360 degrees and the main Cotton cycle is 360 months or 30 years. You should always use this cycle of 30 years and proportionate parts of it. The 60-year cycle is twice the 30-year cycle. Example: High on Cotton 1864; low 1894; high 1923-24, 30 years from the bottom, completing the 60-year cycle.

49-50 YEAR CYCLE

A major cycle in Cotton occurs every 49 to 50 years. A period of "jubilee" years of extreme high or low prices, lasting from 5 to 7 years, occurs at the end of the 50-year cycle. "7" is a fatal number referred to many times in the Bible, which brings about contraction, depression and panics. Seven times seven equals 49, which is known as the fatal evil year, causing extreme fluctuations.

30-YEAR CYCLE

This is the main cycle, as stated above, and the minor cycles are proportionate parts of the 30-year cycle or circle:

30	years			or	360	months
22-1/2	"	is	3/4	or	270	"
20	"	"	2/3	"	240	"
15	"	"	1/2	"	180	"
13	"	"		"	156	"
10	"	is	1/3	"	120	"
9	"	"		"	108	"
7-1/2	"	is	1/4	"	90	"
5	"	"	1/6	"	60	"
3-3/4	"	"	1/8	"	45	"
1-7/8	"	"	1/16	"	22-1/2	"
2-1/2	"	"	1/12	"	30	"
			1/32	"	11-1/4	"

20-YEAR CYCLE

The next important cycle is the 20-year cycle, which is 2/3 of the 30-year cycle.

15-YEAR CYCLE

This is the next in importance because it is 1/2 of the 30-year cycle.

13-YEAR CYCLE

This cycle is very important as you can see later by the examples against previous years. You can prove for yourself by checking and adding 13 years to any important top or bottom.

10-YEAR CYCLE

The next important major cycle is the 10-year cycle, which is 1/3 of the 30-year cycle and 1/2 of the 20-year cycle. This produces fluctuations of the same nature and extreme high or low every 10 years.

ODD CYCLES

These are the 9 and 13-year cycles. The market often makes important tops and bottoms on these cycles, as the record will show. For 9 years, check 1918 to 1927, 1923 to 1932, 1932 to 1941, 1937 to 1946, 1934 to 1943, 1941 to 1950, 1920 to 1929, 1938 to 1947, and 1945 to 1956.

MINOR CYCLES

These are the 5, 3, 2 and 1-year cycles. The smallest cycle – 1-year – will often show a change in the 10th or 11th month. Cycles do not always come out in even months. Follow swings on daily, weekly and monthly angles.

Example: Note on the swing chart that in 1824 Cotton sold at 30 cents a pound; then followed a long decline, reaching 7 cents a pound in 1831 and 1832. It advanced to 20 cents a pound in 1835 and 1836. In 1843, 1844, 1845 and again in 1848, it sold at 5 cents a pound. Fifty years later, in 1893 to 1898, it sold at 5 cents a pound.

The extreme high price for Cotton was reached August 23, 1864, when it sold at $1.89 a pound. Thirty years later, in 1893 and 1894, it reached the extreme low price of 5 cents. Fifty years from the extreme high, or 1914, prices were around 6-1/2 cents per pound, from which the great "jubilee" period with seven years of high prices followed at which time Cotton advanced to 43.75 cents a pound in 1919 and 1920. Note that from 1864 to 1872 extreme high prices for Cotton prevailed.

You can easily see the working out of the 30, 20 and 10-year cycles from the swing chart, which gives you over 140 years of prices. The July chart on Futures from 1869 to date will show you the 60, 30, 20, 15, 10 and minor cycles.

Regardless of whether the market is running out a 5, 10, 20, or 30, 60, 82, 84 or 90-year cycle, it seldom moves more than three years in either direction without a reverse movement. Campaigns often end in the 18th month. The 22nd and the 23rd months are important for culminations, as you can see by going back over the charts. Also watch 27, 28, 30 and 36 months for culminations.

WAR MARKETS

Study all movements after a war starts until 1 or 2 years after the war is over, and compare one war period against another war period or cycle. Example: 1861 to 1865, 1914 to 1920, 1939 to 1945.

During the war periods watch for an important change in trend to occur near the 10th and 12th months, from tops and bottoms.

Each cycle – either major or minor – should be divided by 1/8, 1/4, 1/2, 3/4, 1/3 and 2/3 to determine important dates for change in trend. Also, divide prices from high to low for space movements.

13-YEAR CYCLE

In making up a forecast on Cotton, consider all the major and minor cycles but do not overlook the fact that there is an 82-84-90-year extreme cycle in Cotton, which you must consider from any extreme high or low point, such as the extreme high in September, 1864, and the extreme lows in 1844, 1848, 1894, 1932 and 1933. In addition, the 13-year cycle must be considered. Cotton works out remarkably accurate on the 13-year cycle because around the 13 years there is an extremely large, or an extremely short crop. This causes extreme fluctuations in Cotton. Go back over the past record of prices and you will see how extremes have occurred 13 years apart, as follows:

1804	low	to	1817	high	(13 years later)
1817	high	"	1829-31	low	
1822	low	"	1835	high	(extreme high)
1825	high	"	1838	low	
1835	high	"	1838	low	
1844-45	low	"	1857	high	
1848	low	"	1861	high	(began the big advance due to beginning of Civil War)

1851-52   last lows before big advance started; then in 1864 – 13 years later – extreme high of history was reached. Cotton sold at $1.89 a pound.

1852	low	to	1865	high	(last extreme high point)
1856	high	"	1879	high	
1858	low	"	1871	low	
1865	high	"	1878	low	
1869	high	"	1882	low	(new low)
1871	low	"	1884	low	
1891	low	"	1904	high	
1894	low	"	1907	high	
1896	low	"	1909	high	(Note: in 1909 and 1910 there were extreme high prices)
1898	low	"	1911,	May,	last high from which a big decline followed. Large crops both years.

1902	high	to	1916	high	
1903	high	"	1916		(13 years later, a big Bull Market)
1904	high	"	1917	low	(Feb. extreme High – 13 years later – extreme low from which a big Bull Market started.)
1908	low	"	1921	low	(low of a big decline)
1910	high	"	1923	high	(another big Bull campaign and extreme high)
1914	low	"	1927	high	(extreme high for that period with a short crop)
1918	high	"	1931	low	(first year of extreme low)
1919	high	"	1932	low	(extreme low)
1920	high	"	1933	low	(March. Last extreme low before big advance. 1933, July 17 high, 1946, July high.)
1921 (June & July)	low	"	1934	high	(August)
1922 (February)	low	"	1935	low	(March, 1948 should be low prices)
1923	high	"	1936) 1937)	high	
1937	high	to	1938	low	(add 13, gives 1950-51 for low prices)

When the time of a cycle is up and the monthly trend reverses, look to see if vital angles have been broken; if they have, you can expect a big move.

GEOMETRICAL ANGLES

Remember that the geometrical angles from previous tops or bottoms will show you what cycle the market is following, and when the trend changes. The squaring out of tops and bottoms is just as important as time cycles and it shows when the trend is changing and time and space have balanced out. Therefore, consider these points in working out your forecast of Cotton for future years, as outlined above. Never overlook considering the month when the seasonal changes are due, that is, the months of March and May, August and September, and December and February.

PREVIOUS OPTIONS

It is important to note when an option crosses the high point of the previous option, or breaks the low point of the previous option, that is, the high and low of the option in the previous year. Each option will work against its own previous tops and bottoms. Always consider October against its bottoms; July and the other options against their bottoms and tops. When the tops made several years back are crossed or bottoms made several years back are broken, it is very important for a change in trend.

In a Bull Market, there will not be more than two months with prices closing lower than the opening; and if it is a strong Bull Market, there will not be more than one month with lower closing, and the third month must always be higher than the opening.

Reverse this rule in a Bear Market. If a market is extremely weak or extremely strong, there is not likely to be more than three weeks or one month in which the trend will be reversed.

YEARLY TIME RULE

Watch prices between January 2 and 7. If prices start up and are higher on the 10th, they are likely to continue on up and the change in trend will not take place until about March or April, depending upon the cycle in which the market is moving.

If prices show downward trend by January 10, they are likely to continue on down until March or April, but you should follow the trend as indicated by Time Cycles and Angles.

It is very important, when the high or low prices made in January are broken by 30 points, especially in an active market, which would show an important change in trend. Remember, all rules work best in active markets.

EXAMPLES FOR MAKING FORECASTS:

Judge the position on angles and the time in the cycle before deciding that an important change in trend is due.

1941 – To forecast this year check:

1881, the 60-Year Cycle

January	1290	high
May	1050	low
August	1300	high for year
September	1160	low
December	1280	high

1911, the 30-Year Cycle

January	1380	
March	1250	
June	1380	high, same as January
July	....	trend turned down
October	880	low for the year

1921, the 20-Year Cycle

February	1310	low
May	1520	high
June	1130	low
October	2180	high
November	1500	low

1926, the 15-Year Cycle

January	1850	high for year
April	1700	low of reaction
May	1770	high
June	1600	low of reaction
August	1810	high, last before sharp decline in Sept. as crop was one of largest on record.
December	1250	low of year

1928, the 13-Year Cycle

February	2170	low, sharp advance followed.
June	2285	high, sharp decline followed.
September	1750	low
October	2010	high of rally
November	1800	low

1931, the 10-Year Cycle

(February		
(March	1225	high, a Bear Market balance of the year.
October	540	low (13 years from 1918 top and 15 years or 180 months from 1916 top)

1932 - 1923 - 1914, 9-Year Cycle

December	(1914)	750	low
November	(1923)	3720	high
June	(1932)	515	low
July	(1941)	1745	high

Note: In the 9th year from any top or bottom big advances or declines take place.

Check the 7-Year Cycle or 84 months back; also the 14-year Cycle or 168 months back. 90 months or 7-1/2 years back are also important.

1942 – To forecast this year check:

1882, 1892, 1912, 1922, 1932 and all other cycles.

Check future years in like manner.

YEARS OF EXTREME HIGH PRICES

The government control of crops during the last few years has interfered with the law of supply and demand, yet the market has followed the time cycles closely and the trend has changed when tops and bottoms have squared out. Time squares out all things and the New Deal will square out and bust between 1950 and 1954. After that the law of supply and demand will govern prices.

Going back five 20-Year Cycles or 100 years, the price of Cotton was 5 cents a pound in 1844-48 and 50 years later, in 1894-96, it again sold at 5 cents. From 1915 to 1920 high prices were recorded – 50 to 60 years from Civil War prices.

1946 – Because this was a year of extreme high prices you should check back the master time periods or major time cycles which would run 90, 82-84, 60, 50, 40, 30, 20, 15, 13, 10, 9, and 7.

The extreme high price on Cotton was reached August 23, 1864, when it sold at $1.89 a pound, the highest price in history. If we add 82 years to this price we get 1946, and by adding 84 years, we get 1948. Add 90 years to 1864 and you get 1954. Study the price of Cotton from 1850 to 1854 and you will find extreme low levels.

YEARS OF EXTREME LOW PRICES

Study 1894 to 1898, when Cotton sold at 5 cents a pound, which was 30 years from 1864. Add 90 years to 1864, and you get 1954. Therefore, the cycles indicate some extreme low prices for Cotton and, going back 20 years to 1932 and 1934, we again find extremely low prices. By checking back on the various cycles you will be able to determine when extreme high or low prices can be expected, near what months they should occur, based on previous cycles.

1943-44 to 1948 will be 50 years from 1894-1898, 30 years from 1914 and 20 years from 1934, the extreme high price years. Therefore, very low prises for Cotton will occur from 1946 to 1948, but in 1945-46 there was a big advance in Cotton, which was 13 years from 1933, 9 years from 1937, and 18 years from 1928. The extreme high price was reached in October 1946.

SECTIONS OF THE MARKET

Most all markets move in about three sections in a Bull or Bear Campaign, and they are:

1st – Accumulation or distribution.

2nd – A halting period.

3rd – Final rush to top or bottom, where distribution or accumulation takes place.

1925 Extreme low of the year was reached in December; then a rally to January and February, and then down again.

1926 Recorded the largest Cotton crop in the history of the United States. Extreme low was reached in December.

1927 There was a short crop. Extreme high was reached September 6 and the trend turned down.

1928 February was low after the high of the previous September. Then, from the low in February the market advanced, making high on June 29 to July 5, from which the trend turned down again after the government report in July 1928. The low was reached in September; then the trend turned up and continued up the remainder of the year.

1929 Extreme high in the month of March; declined to July; then rallied to September, where the trend turned down again.

1930 Extreme low in March; then a big rally in April; then down, with extreme low for the year in December.

1931 February high for the year; low was reached in the latter part of May and early June; then a big rally to June 27; followed by a sharp decline, reaching bottom October 5 and 8, which was the extreme low for the year.

1932 June 9, extreme low for the year, from which a sharp advance followed, making top on August 28 and 29. The trend turned down in September shortly after the government report. December 8, extreme low for the year with prices around the same low as in June 1932, some options being 20 to 30 points higher.

1933 The market rallied in January; made extreme low for the year in February; reached extreme high for the year on July 18. Important to note: August 18, September 9, and October 16, if bottoms are made around the same levels. A change in trend started on September 9, which was the low, with prices not quite as low as August 16; then a double bottom on October 16, very important, indicating that the trend would be up for the rest of the year, which it was.

1934 February 13, extreme high, with prices of the October option higher than in July 1933. From February the trend turned down, running to May 1, when extreme low was reached. Then followed a rally to August, as you can see by your chart. This was extreme high for the year – the October option selling at 1390. In September the main trend turned down. November, low of reaction.

1935 January, high of rally and high for the year.
March, sharp decline, low of the year.
May and July, high of rally.
September, low of reaction.
November, high of rally.

1936 January, last low, slow market until May; then Bull Market started in June.
July, high for the year; trend turned down.
November, low of reaction.

1937 April, high for the year, October option 1395, the same top as August 1934, 32 months apart and 58 months from June, 1932 low – two months short of 5-year cycle. Note angle from 515 at 15 points per month called top at 1380. A sharp decline followed from April 1937, with no rallies of importance. November, low 780.

1938 March, high of rally and high for the year.
December, low of year at 725, 20 years from 1918 and 15 years from November 1923. Note 700 was 1/2 of top 1400, held above and showed strong. Reason for bottom at 725 was two times 360 equals 720.

1939 September, high 10¢. Note 20 years from 1919 top in October. November, low of reaction.

1940 April, high 1020, same as August 1939, and 20 years from April 1920.
May, low of sharp reaction.
October, high of small rally.
November, low 870 on 1941, October option.

1941 Was slow and narrow until April; then sharp advance to July 28. October high 1746.

IMPORTANT POINTS TO WATCH

LONG, DULL PERIODS

The market will often narrow down and hold in a narrow range for several weeks or months. This is when accumulation or distribution is taking place. Time is required to complete accumulation or distribution and for prices to square out in time from previous tops or bottoms. When the market becomes slow and dull, wait until activity starts and a definite trend is indicated; then follow it. Watch the market when any option goes 20 to 30 points under a bottom or over a top as this usually marks a change in trend. Twenty points in Cotton equals $1.00 per bale; therefore, after the market is in a previous top trading range for a period of weeks or months, when Cotton advances 20 points above, it will be a signal for further advance. Reverse this on the downside.

SHARP TOPS OR BOTTOMS

When the range is wide, as a rule on rapid advances or declines, Cotton makes sharp tops or bottoms; then reverses quickly. See September, 1869; June, 1872; May, 1884; May 1889; December 1889; February 1904; December 1905; December, 1909; April, 1920; November, 1923; September, 1927; July, 1933; August, 1934; April, 1937; and, April and October, 1946.

In a fast advance Cotton will invariably make a sharp top and not make a double or triple top; therefore, you should use a space chart of 20-point moves up or down, or 30-point moves up or down to determine the first change in trend.

Note the sharp top of July 18, 1933, and no double top, from which a sharp decline of nearly 400 points followed. Also, note top of July 28, 1941, and sharp sell-off, July, 1946, and October, 1946.

In a very active, fast market, sharp bottoms will often be made, but as a general rule Cotton will make double bottoms or triple bottoms more often than it will make double tops.

DOUBLE TOPS OR BOTTOMS

The same levels of prices are often made many times and sometimes occur weeks, months or years apart. Watch these old Resistance Levels for change in trend and note position on Master Chart Squares.

1871 – April 1350 Low
1873 – Nov. 10 1365 Low
1878 – Oct. & Dec. 970 Low
1879 – Sept. & Oct. 990 Low
1880 – Sept. & Oct. 1050 Low
1881 – April & May 1040 Low
1883 – July 970 Low
1884 – Oct. 970 Low
1894 – Nov. 535 Low
1898 – Nov. 520 Low

1900 – July 1020 High
1900 – Oct. 1020 High
1908 – May 820 Low
1908 – Oct. 830 Low
1909 – Dec. 1645 High
1910 – July 1655 High
1912 – July 1300 High
1912 – Dec. 1295 High
1916 – Aug. 1290 Low
1917 – Feb. 1395 Low
1918 – Sept. 3725 High
1919 – July 3590 High

TRIPLE BOTTOMS OR TOPS

The greatest advances or declines start where three tops or bottoms are made around the same level.
Note: 1873 –January, February and April, same tops.
1875 –August, October and December, same tops.
1876 –February and March – same level – 1480.
1877 –January 1465.
1879 –December 1480.

These same levels were made from August 1876, to December 1879, and never reached again until February, 1904, or 30 years from the 1874 tops.

1885 –January, February and March 1150 high.
1890 –April 1140 high. Not reached again until 1903.
In a long, Bull or Bear Cycle, important tops or bottoms continue to be made at lower or higher levels.
1907 –July, August and September – same levels – 1300.
1909 –December 1645 –1910, July 1655,
1911, May 1615, – triple tops.
Triple tops years apart always mean a very rapid decline to follow. Note the fast decline from May 1911.

The last important triple top occurred on October Cotton in September 1918, October 1919, and April 1920, when it sold at the same price – 3725. After that it declined to around 11 cents in a little less than a year.

Triple tops – whether Daily, Weekly or Monthly – work the same. When prices reach the same level the fourth time, they nearly always continue on, but failing to get above the old tops, or to break old bottoms the fourth time is a very strong indication for a reverse move. The Master Chart shows why tops and bottoms occur at the same level.

OLD TOPS AND BOTTOMS

You should watch the last high for one, two or even three years or longer. When the market crosses these highs of previous years, it generally indicates much higher prices. In the same way watch the yearly bottoms and, then, when they are broken by 20 or 30 points, it generally means a change in the major trend and much lower prices.

The greater the time period between old tops and old bottoms the greater the decline or advance will be when bottoms are broken, and tops are crossed. Remember, for a market to give a definite indication it must not only go below old bottoms or above old tops, but IT MUST CLOSE ABOVE or BELOW these OLD LEVELS at the end of the day, week or month. CLOSING PRICES ARE VERY IMPORTANT TO WATCH!

Tops often become bottoms and bottoms become tops. When old tops – which have been resistance levels for some time – are crossed, they will then be support and buying points on reactions. When old bottoms are broken by 30 points, it shows a reversal in trend and they become resistance levels or selling points on rallies.

CLOSING LEVELS

In a very fast, active market, when prices are at extremely high levels around 30 to 40 cents per pound, the market will have to advance or decline 50 or 60 points, and close this much above or below old tops or bottoms to indicate a change in trend.

CHANGES IN SEASONAL TREND

Cotton has important seasonal trends, which occur at about three different periods in the year, and they are:

1. The first important period for a seasonal change in trend is the planting season, which begins in March and runs to the end of May.

2. The next important seasonal change is the maturity season, which is August and September.

3. The third important season is the harvesting season, which runs from August to December. The heaviest ginning is usually during the months of October and November, with the final weight of the crop culminating in the first half of December.

APRIL 6 to 17 AND MAY 5 to 10

This is a very important period for a change in trend and very often important for a bottom from which the main trend turns up because by this time professional traders are able to determine something about the number of acres that have been or will be planted. Consider the time from last top or bottom.

JULY AND AUGUST

These are the most important months when crop scares develop and the market becomes very active. The government reports, which occur around the 8th of the month, often start an important change in trend. It is always very important to study your charts carefully just before a government report, as they will indicate whether accumulation or distribution is taking place, and the change will come after or just before the government report. As a rule, the change in trend comes after the report is out.

SEPTEMBER 6 to 20

The most important change of trend in the year and the one that you can always make a lot of money on. The change usually occurs between September 6 and 20. If the market is low at this time and the trend turns up, it runs up until the latter part of November or December. If the market has been advancing and the trend turns down in September, it will generally run until October and possible into December.

A man who sticks to this rule and watches the change in trend in September, can make a fortune. Then, watch the next change in December, when Cotton as a rule is bottom. Selling short in September and buying in December for the Spring rise will average out a large profit. September crop reports usually come around the 8th to 10th, and at this time of the year it is generally well known about what size the crop will be, although there are years when damage occurs in September and October, or the crop improves in September and October.

OCTOBER 10 TO 20 AND NOVEMBER 15 TO 30
Always watch these periods for changes in trend.

DECEMBER 10 TO 15 MOST IMPORTANT
Around this time the final crop estimate is made by the government and the heavy movement of Cotton to the market is about over. Therefore, if the crop has been large, prices will reach bottom around December 10 to 15, when you can cover shorts and buy for a substantial rally. If you will go over a long number of years, you will find that the average lows have been made in December, although lows do occur in some years in October or November.

When the crop is extremely short, the trend will often turn up in September and prices go against the seasonal trend and make top in late November or early December. Example:

1923 – The crop was extremely short. Last low level was reached on July 30 and the extreme high of the year on November 30. The market advanced 1700 points or 17 cents a pound in four months. After this the trend turned down on December 1 and prices were down 10 cents a pound in 60 days.

STUDY and COMPARE all years of extreme high prices and years of extreme low prices. In this way you will learn how prices move at extreme levels.

WHAT YOU NEED TO LEARN
TO BE SURE OF TOPS AND BOTTOMS

1. RESISTANCE LEVELS and PRICE BUYING POINTS from all the major tops and bottoms and minor tops and bottoms as well. Never overlook the last move up from the minor low and the last move down from the minor top.

2. MINOR TREND INDICATOR on DAILY CHART should be kept up.

3. MAIN TREND INDICATOR.

4. BREAKAWAY POINT.

5. HIGHER BOTTOMS and LOWER TOPS. Also 1st, 2nd and 3rd higher bottoms, and 1st, 2nd and 3rd lower tops.

6. SECTIONS OF MOVE in TIME from MAIN TOP or BOTTOM.

7. SIGNAL DAY AT TOP OR BOTTOM on DAILY CHART, ALSO SIGNAL WEEK.

8. SINGLE, DOUBLE, TRIPLE TOPS or BOTTOMS.

9. RULES for ACTIVE MARKET.

10. NATURAL RESISTANCE LEVELS and TIME PERIODS from Master 360 Degree Circle.

11. FAST MARKETS and WIDE FLUCTUATIONS at the end of Bull or Bear Campaigns. Study these culminations in the past, then you will know what to do in the future.

12. GEOMETRICAL ANGLES – These are the most important of all rules for determining both PRICE and TIME culminations. ALL TIME PERIODS from major tops and bottoms and ALL ANGLES from major and minor tops and bottoms, as well as ANGLES from ZERO at tops and bottoms must be kept up on your charts in order to be accurate.

13. First, change in the minor trend on the Daily Chart.
Second, important change in the minor trend on the Weekly Chart – More important than the Daily.
Third, change in trend on the Monthly is still of greater importance.
Fourth, change on the Quarterly Chart is a greater change in main trend.
Fifth, Change in trend on the Yearly Chart is still a greater change in main trend.

14. SQUARING TIME with PRICE on major and minor movements. Learn to use squares of all numbers both for Time Periods, Resistance Levels and Prices.

> Example: The square of 2 is 4
>   "   "   " 3 is 9
>   "   "   " 4 is 16
>   "   "   " 5 is 25
>   "   "   " 6 is 36
>   "   "   " 7 is 49
>   "   "   " 8 is 64
>   "   "   " 9 is 81

Consider all half-points between the squares, both odd and even. See Tables of Squares and Half-way Points.

15. SEASONAL TREND – Always consider whether the trend is running with the seasonal trend or opposite; then follow markets until change in trend is shown by Daily or other charts.

16. Last but not least of all: NEVER GUESS or TRADE ON HOPE OR FEAR. When in doubt, get out. When you do not know the trend, stay out! Buy with a reason and sell on a rule or for a good reason. Learn to watch and wait. Take care of your health. Obedience to all these rules will bring success.

W.D. GANN

February 20, 1950

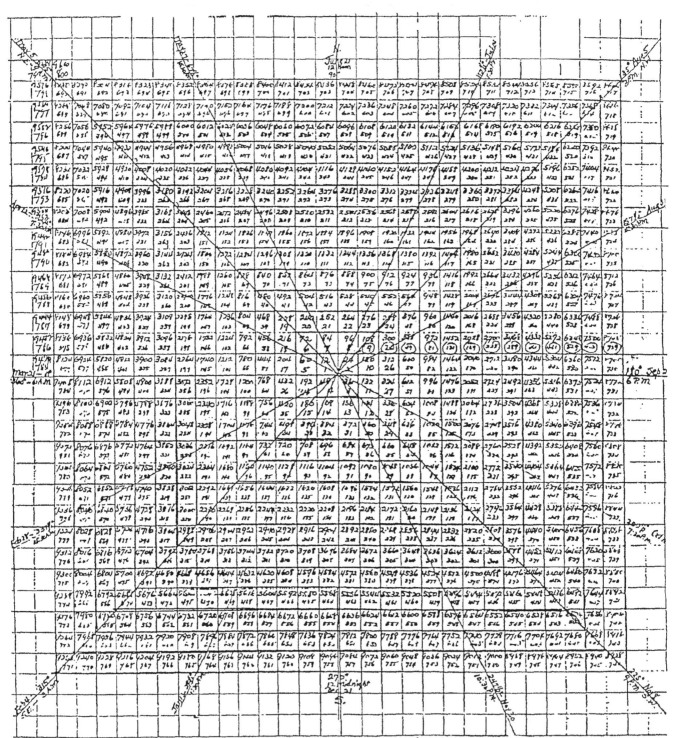

Master Price & Time Chart
for
Cotton, Coffee, Cocoa, Wool,
and Grain

LESSON 7

CASH AND MAY

SOY BEAN FUTURES

CASH AND MAY SOY BEAN FUTURES
by
W. D. GANN

TIME PERIODS FROM FEBRUARY 15, 1920 TO NOVEMBER 4, 1954

These periods run from 1 to 38. Suppose you want to get the 1/2 points or 26 weeks from any of these important highs and lows, you move down to the column marked "1/2" and run across to get all the time periods which are 1/2 year or 26 weeks from any important high or low. Running from 1 to 38, these are:

Aug 19,	Jun 29,	Apr 2,	Oct 14,	Apr 17,	Jan 25,	Jun 19,	Feb 8,
Mar 11,	Apr 14,	Jul 31,	Apr 25,	Apr 25,	Jul 19,	Aug 18,	Nov 22,
Apr 9,	May 24,	Aug 13,	Sep 26,	Feb 20,	May 24,	Jun 29,	Nov 10,
Apr 13,	Aug 12,	Jan 7,	Jun 7,	Oct 25,	Feb 12,	Aug 17,	Oct 20,
Feb 18,	Oct 31,	Nov 20,	Jan 25,	Mar 25,	May 2,		

All of these dates are 1/2 of the yearly time periods.

MOST IMPORTANT TIME PERIODS FROM ANNIVERSARY DATES

These are the actual dates of extreme highs and lows from 1 to 38 on the Time Table and are as follows:

Feb 15,	Dec 28,	Oct 5,	Apr 10,	Oct 20,	Jul 27,	Dec 20,	Aug 10,
Sep 13,	Oct 17,	Jan 27,	Oct 28,	Oct 28,	Jan 15,	Feb 14,	May 20,
Oct 9,	Nov 26,	Feb 9,	Mar 24,	Aug 24,	Nov 16,	Dec 28,	May 8,
Oct 16,	Feb 8,	Jul 9,	Dec 10,	Apr 21,	Aug 14,	Feb 13,	Apr 16,
Aug 20,	Apr 27,	May 18,	Jul 27,	Sep 27,	Nov 4.		

Study these periods in years that follow to see when high and low prices repeat around these dates. Example.

Suppose you want to look up November, 1954 for May Soy Beans; first you look for the actual dates of highs or lows. You find November 26, 1948, high 276-3/4 and November 16, 1949, low 220 ½. Next you look for the 1/2 point and find November 22, 1948, November 10, 1950, and November 20, 1954. Then you would look through the column of 1/8 points in time and find November 19, November 23, November 30, and November 12. Next, the 1/4 points in time periods are: November 11, November 23, November 15, and November 21. Next, 1/3 points are: November 27, November 9, and November 27. Next, the 3/8 points are: November 8, November 24, November 6. Then, the 5/8 points are: November 28, November 12. Next the 2/3 points are: November 26. The 3/4 points are: November 18, November 17, November 12, November 11, November 16, Next, the 7/8 points are: November 14, November 5, November 14.

WEEKLY TIME PERIODS FOR SOY BEANS
FEBRUARY 15, 1920 TO NOVEMBER 4, 1954

All of these Time Periods from different highs and lows are shown on the column running down from November 4, 1954. The high on November 4 was 299. Run down the column to 18; then look at the top at the date and you will see that 18 is February 9, 1949, low 201½. Therefore, 299 was the 45° angle moving up from "0" from 201½.

To get the present position up to the week ending January 22, 1955, you add 11 weeks. Add 11 to 299 gives 310. In the same way, add 11 to all the other figures in the same column and it brings them all up to date. Look in column 21 and you will see the time is 253 weeks to November 4, 1954. This 253 weeks is from December 28, 1949, when the last low was made at 224.

For the week ending January 22, 1955, you add 11 weeks, which gives 264, which means that the 45° angle from "0" on the Weekly Chart crosses at 264. Each week this angle moves up 1¢. Therefore, when the price closes below this angle, it will be in a weaker position and indicate lower prices.

The most important time cycle is from July 27, 1939, low 67. This is under column 6. You move over on column 6 to the line under November 4 and you find the time 797 weeks. Add 11 to this to bring it to January 22, 1955, gives 808 weeks. This can be divided by 2, 3 and 4 to get the angles up to date.

Check all of the other time periods in the same way. Check the Price and Time resistance levels with the Time Table which runs from 1 to 40 years. Example: The last high on May Beans, December 29, 1954, was 285¼. 286¼ is 1/2 the range of the option. Look at the table under 1/2 points and you see that 286 is in the 1/2 zone and is 5½ years in time. 266½ in the same zone is 5-1/8 years. You will find all of these shown in the instructions and the resistance levels from Time and Price.

Study this Price and Time Resistance Table in connection with the Master Square of 52 and you will see that it is the most important Price and Time Trend Indicator that I have ever discovered.

MAY SOY BEANS: NOVEMBER 1954 - JANUARY 1955

November 4 – High 299, a Signal Day on the daily high and low chart. Look at 299 on the Price Scale and you will find that it comes out at 5-3/4 years, an exact resistance level, and also 299 weeks from February 9, 1949, therefore, Time and Price balanced on 45° angle from "0", making this a selling level.

Why did May Bans make high on November 4? Look at the Table and you will see that the 5/8 point or Midseason comes out on November 8, which is important for a change in trend. Then, if you lay the bottom of the Calculator at "0" on 201½, the last extreme low for May Beans on February 14, 1949, you find that this angle crossed at 299 in the week ending November 6, 1954, which was why the price made top and turned down.

November 15 – Low 282. 282 is 17¢ down from 299, which is 1/3 of a year and an exact resistance level.

August 20, 1953, May Beans low 239½. Note 240-3/8 is 1/2 of the range from 44 to 436-3/4. Place "0" of the Calculator at 239½ on this date. Adding 52 to this price gives 281½, which is the top of the time period for the first year. The week ending November 20, 1954, was 65 weeks or 1¼ years from the extreme low and the price made 282 in this week and the minor trend turned up.

April 27, 1954, May Beans extreme high 422. This was an advance of $1.82½ per bushel from the low of August 20, 1953. 182 equals 3½ years in time and is at the exact resistance level of 3½. The reason for the high on April 27 was: 1/3 of the year from December 28, 1932, the extreme low of 44¢ per bushel and 3/4 year from July 27, 1939, low 67¢. Therefore, both time periods and the price came out on exact resistance levels. If we use the exact high price of 422, it equals 8 years, which is 416 plus 6½ = 422½ as the 1/8 point and natural resistance. From April 27, 1954 to the week ending November 6, 1954, the time was 26 weeks or 1/2 year, which was the reason for the top at 299.

From the low of 265-3/4 on September 27, 1954, the week ending December 30, 1954 was 13 weeks or 1/4 of a year, and December 28 was the anniversary date or 22 years from December 28, 1932, making this very important for a change in trend. On December 29, 1954 May Beans made last high of rally at 285¼ and trend turned down again.

January 15 –The next or most important point to consider is January 15 1948, the extreme high. Therefore, January 15, 1955 ends 7 years or 364 weeks. Prices can go straight up or straight down at the end of the 7-year period. On January 17, 1955 May Beans sold down to 268½, and made bottom for a rally.

HOW TO DETERMINE CHANGE IN TREND

Calculate the total cents per bushel that the price is up from extreme low levels and minor low levels. Calculate how much the actual high or low price is up from "0". Calculate how many cents per bushel the price is down from any extreme high level or minor tops. Then calculate the range between extreme high and low and you will find that the price will come out on the Resistance Level that is in exact agreement with the Calculator and the Tables for the Price and Time.

Example: February 9, 1949, low 201½. This was down 215¼ from 435-3/4. If you will look at the Table, you will see that 4 years equals 216 weeks, making this an exact resistance or support level. Next, consider the price 201½. 182 is 3½ years; add 19½ to 182, which is 3/8 year, gives exactly 201½ as a resistance and buying level. Then consider the circle of 360°. 1/2 is 180; add 22½ to 180 gives 202½. 22½ is 1/6 of the circle and 1/2 of 45°. The high in 1920 was 405, 1/2 of this is 202½. All of this indicated a support and buying level at 202½ to 201½. Refer to the high of April 10, 1937 and you will find it was 202½. Therefore, the price at that time was exactly on a selling level which later became a buying level.

down from November 4, 1954. The high on November 4 was 299. Run down the column to 18; then look at the top at the date and you will see that 18 is February 9, 1949, low 201½. Therefore, 299 was the 45° angle moving up from "0" from 201½.

To get the present position up to the week ending January 22, 1955, you add 11 weeks. Add 11 to 299 gives 310. In the same way, add 11 to all the other figures in the same column and it brings them all up to date. Look in column 21 and you will see the time is 253 weeks to November 4, 1954. This 253 weeks is from December 28, 1949, when the last low was made at 224.

For the week ending January 22, 1955, you add 11 weeks, which gives 264, which means that the 45° angle from "0" on the Weekly Chart crosses at 264. Each week this angle moves up 1¢. Therefore, when the price closes below this angle, it will be in a weaker position and indicate lower prices.

The most important time cycle is from July 27, 1939, low 67. This is under column 6. You move over on column 6 to the line under November 4 and you find the time 797 weeks. Add 11 to this to bring it to January 22, 1955, gives 808 weeks. This can be divided by 2, 3 and 4 to get the angles up to date.

Check all of the other time periods in the same way. Check the Price and Time resistance levels with the Time Table which runs from 1 to 40 years. Example: The last high on May Beans, December 29, 1954, was 285¼. 286¼ is 1/2 the range of the option. Look at the table under 1/2 points and you see that 286 is in the 1/2 zone and is 5½ years in time. 266½ in the same zone is 5-1/8 years. You will find all of these shown in the instructions and the resistance levels from Time and Price.

Study this Price and Time Resistance Table in connection with the Master Square of 52 and you will see that it is the most important Price and Time Trend Indicator that I have ever discovered.

MAY SOY BEANS: NOVEMBER 1954 - JANUARY 1955

November 4 – High 299, a Signal Day on the daily high and low chart. Look at 299 on the Price Scale and you will find that it comes out at 5-3/4 years, an exact resistance level, and also 299 weeks from February 9, 1949, therefore, Time and Price balanced on 45° angle from "0", making this a selling level.

Why did May Bans make high on November 4? Look at the Table and you will see that the 5/8 point or Midseason comes out on November 8, which is important for a change in trend. Then, if you lay the bottom of the Calculator at "0" on 201½, the last extreme low for May Beans on February 14, 1949, you find that this angle crossed at 299 in the week ending November 6, 1954, which was why the price made top and turned down.

November 15 – Low 282. 282 is 17¢ down from 299, which is 1/3 of a year and an exact resistance level.

August 20, 1953, May Beans low 239½. Note 240-3/8 is 1/2 of the range from 44 to 436-3/4. Place "0" of the Calculator at 239½ on this date. Adding 52 to this price gives 281½, which is the top of the time period for the first year. The week ending November 20, 1954, was 65 weeks or 1¼ years from the extreme low and the price made 282 in this week and the minor trend turned up.

April 27, 1954, May Beans extreme high 422. This was an advance of $1.82½ per bushel from the low of August 20, 1953. 182 equals 3½ years in time and is at the exact resistance level of 3½. The reason for the high on April 27 was: 1/3 of the year from December 28, 1932, the extreme low of 44¢ per bushel and 3/4 year from July 27, 1939, low 67¢. Therefore, both time periods and the price came out on exact resistance levels. If we use the exact high price of 422, it equals 8 years, which is 416 plus 6½ = 422½ as the 1/8 point and natural resistance. From April 27, 1954 to the week ending November 6, 1954, the time was 26 weeks or 1/2 year, which was the reason for the top at 299.

From the low of 265-3/4 on September 27, 1954, the week ending December 30, 1954 was 13 weeks or 1/4 of a year, and December 28 was the anniversary date or 22 years from December 28, 1932, making this very important for a change in trend. On December 29, 1954 May Beans made last high of rally at 285¼ and trend turned down again.

January 15 –The next or most important point to consider is January 15 1948, the extreme high. Therefore, January 15, 1955 ends 7 years or 364 weeks. Prices can go straight up or straight down at the end of the 7-year period. On January 17, 1955 May Beans sold down to 268½, and made bottom for a rally.

HOW TO DETERMINE CHANGE IN TREND

Calculate the total cents per bushel that the price is up from extreme low levels and minor low levels. Calculate how much the actual high or low price is up from "0". Calculate how many cents per bushel the price is down from any extreme high level or minor tops. Then calculate the range between extreme high and low and you will find that the price will come out on the Resistance Level that is in exact agreement with the Calculator and the Tables for the Price and Time.

Example: February 9, 1949, low 201½. This was down 215¼ from 435-3/4. If you will look at the Table, you will see that 4 years equals 216 weeks, making this an exact resistance or support level. Next, consider the price 201½. 182 is 3½ years; add 19½ to 182, which is 3/8 year, gives exactly 201½ as a resistance and buying level. Then consider the circle of 360°. 1/2 is 180; add 22½ to 180 gives 202½. 22½ is 1/6 of the circle and 1/2 of 45°. The high in 1920 was 405, 1/2 of this is 202½. All of this indicated a support and buying level at 202½ to 201½. Refer to the high of April 10, 1937 and you will find it was 202½. Therefore, the price at that time was exactly on a selling level which later became a buying level.

HIGH AND LOW PRICES FOR
CASH AND MAY BEAN FUTURES

We are giving these prices as far back as there are any records of Cash Soy Beans so that you can check them in working out future yearly and monthly cycles.

1913 Nov 15 low	154	1923 Feb 15 high	214	1930 Jun 15 high	216
1915 Jan 15 high	235	1923 Oct 15 low	209	1931 Jan 15 high	146
1915 Oct 15 low	188	1924 Oct 15 low	216	1931 Nov 15 low	152
1916 Oct 15 low	210	1925 Feb 15 high	264	1932 Mar 15 high	66
1917 Oct 15 high	257	1925 Dec 15 low	216	1932 Dec 28 low	44
1918 Feb 15 high	382	1926 Jan 15 high	238	1933 Jul 18 high	104
1919 Mar 15 low	292	1926 Dec 15 low	182	1933 Oct 15 low	68
1920 Feb 15 high	405	1927 Jun 15 high	220	1934 Jul 20 high	154
1921 Feb 15 low	217	1927 Dec 15 low	160	1934 Nov 15 low	89½
1921 Nov 15 high	222	1928 Jun 15 high	213	1935 Feb 10 high	126
1921 Dec 15 low	218	1928 Nov 15 low	189	1935 Oct 15 low	68
1922 Feb 15 high	216	1929 Jul 15 high	246	1936 Aug 15 high	119
1922 Oct 15 low	189	1929 Nov 15 low	168	1936 Sep 20 low	110

The above figures are taken from Government records. They only reported cash prices on the 15th day of each month.

Futures trading started October 5, 1936. The low of May Beans on that day was 120. From this date on, all of the future high and low prices are given in the printed Time Tables. You can check any time period in weeks from these Tables but use these Cash Prices to get future cycles. Example: 1915, January 15, a 40-year cycle terminates January 15, 1955. From February 1925, a 30-year cycle ends in February 1955, and the low of a 30-year cycle ends in December 1955.

PRICE RESISTANCE LEVELS FOR
CASH AND MAY SOY BEAN FUTURES

When any extreme high or low price is reached, look up the position on the Table for Weekly Periods and Prices; then when the price is down or up from an important level, look to see what resistance level it is on.

The Table below gives (1) the advance or decline from a low or a high price and (2) the position of the high or low price. All of these are covered from 1920 through November 1954. In future, when high or low prices are reached, look up the price resistance in the same way and look up at the same time the Time Periods and Time Resistance Levels, the same as we have shown in the examples. In this way you get the position for Time and Price Resistance and changes in trend which will be shown on the Master Calculator and the Tables for Time and Price Periods.

				cents		
1920	high	405				on 7-3/4 years
1932	low	44	down	361		on 7/8 year and 7 years
1933	high	104	up	60		on 2 years and 1-1/8 year
1933	low	68	down	36		on 1½ years and 2/3 year
1934	high	154	up	86		on 3 years and 5/8 year
1934	low	89½	down	64½		on 3/4 year and 1¼ years
1935	high	126	up	36½		on 2½ years and 2/3 year
1935	low	68	down	58		on 1½ years and 1-7/8 years
1936	high	119	up	51		on 2-1/3 years and 1 year

Year	Month		Price		Change	Note
1936		low	110	down	10	on 2-1/8 years and 1/4 year
1937		high	202½	up	92½	on 3-7/8 years and 3/4 year
		from	68	up	134½	on 2-5/8 years
		from	44	up	158½	on 3 years
1939		low	67	down	135½	on 1½ years and 2-5/8 years
1939		high	131½	up	64½	on 2½ years and 1¼ years
1940		low	69	down	62½	on 1-1/3 years and 1¼ years
1941	Sep	high	202	up	133	on 3-7/8 years abs 2½ years
1941	Oct	low	154½	down	47½	on 3 years and 7/8 year
1942	Jan	high	203½	up	49½	on 3-7/8 years and 1 year
1942	Oct	low	164	down	39½	on 3-1/8 years and 3/4 year
1947	Oct	low	334	up	170	on 6-2/3 years and 3¼ years
1948	Jan	high	436-3/4	up	102-3/4	on 8-3/8 years and 2 years
		from	164	up	272-3/4	on 5¼ years
		from	44	up	392-3/4	on 7½ years
		from	67	up	369-3/4	on 7-1/8 years
1948	Feb	low	320½	down	116¼	on 3-1/3 years
1948	May	high	425	up	104½	on 2 years
1948	Oct	low	239	down	186	on 4-5/8 years and 3-5/8 years
		from	436-3/4	down	197-3/4	on 8-3/4 years and 3-3/4 years
1948	Nov	high	276-3/4	up	37-3/4	on 5-1/3 years and 3/4 year
1949	Feb	low	201½	down	75½	on 3-7/8 years and 1½ years
		from	436-3/4	down	235½	on 5½ years
		from	44	up	157½	on 3 years
		from	67	up	134½	on 2-5/8 years
1949	Aug	high	243½	up	42	on 4-2/3 years and 3/4 year
1949	Dec	low	224	down	19½	on 4-1/3 years and 3/8 year
1950	May	high	323½	down	99½	on 7-1/8 years and 1-7/8 years
		from	201½	up	122	on 2-1/3 years
1950	Oct 16	low	232½	down	91	on 4½ years and 1-3/4 years
1951	Feb	high	344½	up	112	on 6-5/8 years and 2-1/8 years
		from	201½	up	143	on 2-3/4 years
1951	Jul	low	258½	down	76	on 5-1/8 years and 1½ years
1951	Dec	high	309-3/4	up	41¼	on 6 years and 3/4 year
1952	Apr	low	281	down	28-3/4	on 5-3/8 years and 1/2 year
1952	Aug	high	314-3/4	up	33-3/4	on 6 years and 5/8 year
1953	Feb	low	279-3/4	down	35	on 5-3/8 years and 2/3 year
	Apr	high	309	up	29¼	on 6 years and 5/8 year
	Aug	low	239½	down	69½	on 4-5/8 years and 1-1/3 year
	from		201½ to 239½ up		38	on 3/4 year
	from		436¾ to 239½ down		197¼	on 3-3/4 years
1954	Apr. 27	high	422	up	182½	on 8-1/8 years and 3½ years
	from		44	up	378	on 7¼ years
	from		67	up	355	on 6-7/8 years
1954	May	low	361	down	61	on 7 years and 1-1/8 years
	Jul 22	low	284½	down	137½	on 5½ Years and 2-5/8 years
	Jul 27	high	306-3/4	up	22¼	on 5-7/8 years and 1/2 year
	from		422	down	115¼	on 2-1/3 years
	Sep 27	low	265-3/4	down	41	on 5-1/8 years and 3/4 year
	Nov 4	high	299	up	33¼	on 5-3/4 years and 5/8 year
	from		239½	up	59½	on 1-1/8 years

CASH AND MAY SOY BEAN FUTURES
TIME PERIODS FROM IMPORTANT HIGHS AND LOWS

You will receive a printed Table showing the important highs and lows with prices. These Time Periods are marked from 1 to 38. The first time period starts February 15, 1920, high 405, and the next time period starts December 28, 1932, low 44¢. These are two of the most important time periods to measure future time periods from.

1936 Oct. 5 – Trading in Soy Bean Futures started. These time periods are brought up to the week ending October 10, 1936.

From   Feb. 15, 1920 to the week of Dec. 28, 1932, the time is 672 weeks.
       Feb. 15, 1920 to the week of Oct. 10, 1936, the time is 869 weeks.
       Dec. 28, 1932 to the week of Oct. 10, 1936, the time is 197 weeks.

The following is what you add to the above figures to get the time for the dates below:

1937	Apr. 10,	add	26	weeks	1949 Feb. 9,	add	11 weeks
1938	Oct. 20,	add	80	weeks	Mar. 24,	add	6 weeks
1939	Jul. 27,	add	40	weeks	Aug. 24,	add	21 weeks
	Dec. 20,	add	21	weeks	Nov. 16,	add	13 weeks
1940	Aug. 10,	add	33	weeks	Dec. 26,	add	6 weeks
1941	Sep. 13,	add	57	weeks	1950 May 8,	add	19 weeks
	Oct. 17,	add	5	weeks	Oct. 16,	add	23 weeks
1942	Jan. 27,	add	15	weeks	1951 Feb. 8,	add	16 weeks
	Oct. 28,	add	39	weeks	Jul. 9,	add	22 weeks
					Dec. 10,	add	22 weeks

The Soy Bean Market was closed from Jan. 1943 to July 1947. Trading in May Soy Beans started again October, 1947.

					1952 Apr. 21,	add	19 weeks
					Aug. 14,	add	16 weeks
1947	Oct. 28,	add	261	weeks	1953 Feb. 13,	add	26 weeks
1948	Jan. 15,	add	11	weeks	Apr. 16,	add	9 weeks
	Feb. 14,	add	4	weeks	Aug. 20,	add	18 weeks
	May 20,	add	14	weeks	1954 Apr. 27,	add	36 weeks
	Oct. 9,	add	20	weeks	May 18,	add	3 weeks
	Nov. 26,	add	7	weeks	Jul, 27,	add	10 weeks
					Sep. 27,	add	9 weeks
					Nov. 4,	add	5 weeks

This brings the calculations up to the 38th column. The above time period given as November 4 is, of course, for the calendar week ending November 6, 1954.

It is most important that you carry and consider the total Time Periods up to date from February 15, 1920, December 28, 1932, July 27, 1939, January 15, 1948, February 14, 1948, and February 9, 1949, extreme low 201½. Next in importance are: Oct. 16, 1950, Feb. 8, 1951, February 15, 1953, Aug. 20, 1953, Apr. 27, 1954, and July 27, 1954. All Time Periods should be brought up to date on the Weekly Chart but the above are the most important. You can then look at the Time Table and see whether the time is on 1/4, 1/2, 2/3, 3/4, or a yearly period.

You must also carry the total advance or decline from these highs and lows in order to determine the resistance levels on your Time Tables. Then by placing the Calculator over your Weekly Chart, you can see the trend changes and the resistance levels.

EXAMPLE:

1939 July 27, low 67¢, the lowest price which May Futures ever sold
1948 Jan. 15, high 436-3/4, highest price at which May Bean Futures ever sold.

From July 27, 1939 to January 15, 1948, the total time period was 3094 days or 442 weeks. The 45° angle moving up from "0" on the Weekly Chart crossed at 442, and the price reached 436-3/4, just below this angle. This was a balancing of Time and Price.

From July 27, 1939 to December 23, 1954, 5628 days or 804 weeks. This was 84 squares of 67 based on days. It was 12 squares of 67 based on weeks.

To get the angle moving up from "0" at the rate of 1/4¢ per week, we divide 804 by 4. This gives 201; add 67 gives 268, where the angle of 4x1 crossed on December 23, 1954. If we add 1/4 of 67, which is 16-3/4, it gives a resistance point of 284-3/4. Divide 804 weeks by 1/3 and we get 258. If we add 22 to this, we get 290, 22 being 1/2 of 44, the extreme low for Cash Beans.

MAY SOY BEANS
DAILY, WEEKLY AND MONTHLY

Before you make a trade, analyze the position on the daily, weekly and monthly high and low charts.

MAY BEANS DAILY HIGH AND LOW –

1954

Nov. 4, high 299, a Signal Day. Then the trend turned down.

Nov.15, the price was on the angle of 2x1 from 265-3/4, a support level and the market rallied.

Nov.30, high 292¼, closed below the 2x1 from 295. Minor trend still down.

Dec. 7, low 277, on the 45° angle from 299 and the 4x1 from 265-3/4. Time and Price had balanced and the market was due for a rally.

Dec.10, high 283½, a lower top and below the 45° angle from 292½. Trend still down.

Dec.14, low 274½. Had a wide opening with a gap. Never sold below the opening and closed at the top, a Signal Day and an indication that the market was ready to rally. Note the low on October 6 was 274, making this a double bottom.

Dec.17, high 280¼ and closed below the 45° from 292¼.

Dec.20, low 276½ on the 2x1 from 274½ low, a support and buying level.

Dec.21, high 281.

Dec.23, low 277-3/4, on the 2x1 from 274½, a support level.

Dec.27, opened at 278½, never sold below the opening. High 281½, closed 281¼, a SIGNAL DAY, indicating higher prices. For the first time the price closed above the 2x1 from 299 and above the 4x1 from 265-3/4, indicating uptrend.

Because April 27, 1954 was high for May Beans and July 27, 1954 was high for the present option and September 27 was low for the present option, made December 27 important for a change in trend. The Daily Chart indicated that the trend was turning up on that date.

Dec.28, opened at 282½, leaving a gap. At 12 o'clock had not sold below the opening or filled the gap, indicating higher.

Dec.29, opened at 285, high 285¼, low 282½, closed 283, – a SIGNAL DAY, indicating lower prices. After this there was a Time Turn from December 31 to January 5, 1955, and the main trend continued down.

When important time periods are running out and prices are reaching resistance levels, watch the Daily high and low Chart for the first indication of a change in trend. Use the Master Square of 90 on the Daily Chart to get trend indications.

WEEKLY HIGH AND LOW CHART

1953, Aug. 20, low 239½. The 2x1 angle moving up 1/2¢ per week crossed at 274½ for the week ending December 18, 1954. The price received support on this angle and closed above the 45° angle from 265-3/4, indicating minor trend up.

1954, Dec. 28, the price crossed the top of the two previous weeks and advanced to 45° angle from 306-3/4 which crossed at 284½ on Dec. 29, and the 1x2 moving down 2¢ per week from 299 crossed at 283. The price closed at 282 fro the week below these angles and below the 1/2 point of the option at 288¼, indicating a selling level and lower prices. The decline continued to January 17, 1955.

MONTHLY HIGH AND LOW CHARTS

From August 20, 1953, low 239½, the angle of 1x2 moving up 2¢ per week crossed at 267½ in October, 1954, and the price declined slightly below this level but closed above it, indicating higher.

Dec. 28, 1954 was 264 months from December 28, 1932, therefore, the 45° angle from "0" crossed at 264. Add 22, which is 1/2 of 44, the extreme low, and this gives another 45° angle at 285, a resistance and selling level.

December 29, 1954 was important for a change in trend because it started a new monthly cycle. January 15, 1955 is the next important change in trend, which is 7 years from January 15, 1948.

The 1x4 moving down from 306-3/4 crosses at 287 for the monthly period ending January 20, 1955. This indicates that the main trend from the top is down, but the main trend from the bottom is up.

From the above figures, you can see that if May Soy Beans break 268 and 264, they will be in a very weak position and indicate much lower prices, especially as it is near 7 years from the top and 35 years from February 15, 1920, high 405.

1955, January 6, was 806 weeks from July 27, 1939. This is 15½ years, as you can see on your table for Weekly Price Periods. The time periods running from January 6 up to February 15, 1955 are all of great importance for change in trend.

When you get ready to make a trade in May Soy Beans or any commodity, be sure you have all angles up to date and all time periods on your Daily, Weekly, and Monthly Charts in order that you do not overlook anything or make a mistake.

W. D. GANN

January 24, 1955.

LESSON 8

RULES FOR TRADING IN SOY BEANS, CORN, WHEAT, OATS AND RYE

RULES FOR TRADING
IN
SOY BEANS, CORN, WHEAT, OATS AND RYE

(These instructions are new discoveries and rules made since 1946 and cover Soy Beans as well as other Grains – Soy Beans being more profitable to trade in than most of the other Grains. Most of the rules and examples are applied to Soy Beans but can be used on any other Grains.)

RULES FOR 2-DAY CHART MOVES

The 2-Day Chart moves start from any low level when the market is advancing and move up 2 days or more. The line on the chart moves up to the highest price of the day and continues to move up as long as prices make higher bottoms and higher tops. The first time prices reverse and make lower bottoms for two consecutive days the chart moves down on the line to the extreme low and continues to move down as long as prices move down without a rally of two days or more.

When a top on the 2-Day Chart is crossed it is an indication of higher prices. When the bottom is broken on a 2-Day Chart it indicates a change in trend and lower prices.

RULE 1-A: TREND INDICATIONS
The Main Trend is up as long as no bottom on the 2-Day Chart is broken. The Main Trend is down as long as no 2-Day top is crossed. You should always trade with the Main Trend; buy when the Trend is up and sell when the Trend is down, following all the rules given.

RULE 2-A: THE TIME TURN IN TREND
Nearly always, there are exceptions to rules and these exceptions occur when markets are very active and prices are moving fast, making a wide range in

fluctuations of 7 to 10¢ per bushel a day. In cases of this kind the Turn or Change in Trend can take place on a 1-day Trend, as you will see from examples given. When prices are near extreme highs or extreme lows you can record the 1-day move instead of 2-days, and when the first swing or move is broken, or prices go below a 1-day reaction, consider that the Trend has changed, at least temporarily. When prices are very active and fluctuate over a wide range near a low level, use the same rule and consider that the Trend has changed when prices have crossed a 1-day top, then go with it.

Use the rules for SIGNAL DAY, GAPS, DAILY LIMITS AND IMPORTANT RESISTANCE LEVELS to enable you to determine the top and bottom when there is no reversal on the Trend Line at extreme highs or lows.

RULE 3-A: STOP-LOSS ORDERS

Because markets make false moves at times and the Trend changes suddenly, you must always use a Stop-Loss Order for your protection. When the 2-day chart is making higher bottoms and higher tops, follow up with a Stop-Loss Order 1 to 2¢ per bushel below the bottoms on the 2-day chart. A series of tops and bottoms around the same level are of greater importance when prices exceed the top or break the bottom levels. By trading with the main trend, Stop-Loss Orders are not very often caught and you make greater profits. NEVER GUESS – LET THE MARKET TELL ITS OWN STORY! Buy or sell only on rules and definite indications.

When Prices are Declining and the Trend is down, based on the 2-day chart, continue to sell short and follow the market down with Stop-Loss Orders 1 to 2¢ above the tops on the 2-day chart. As a general rule, a Stop-Loss Order 1¢ above is seldom caught.

RULE 4-A: HOW TO DETERMINE EXTREME HIGH OR EXTREME LOW PRICES

In using the 2-day chart always refer to and use the rules mentioned above, and throughout this lesson.

In trading with the 2-day chart, it is necessary to have rules which are exceptions to the regular rules because at times, when there is a prolonged advance which winds up with a fast move, a Turn is not made on the 2-day chart or the 1-day chart. Therefore, it is necessary to know what rules to use to catch the Turn and protect your profits. The same applies after there has been a prolonged decline which winds up with a fast decline with rallies which are very small and prices making lower tops and lower bottoms each day for a period of 7 days or more. Then there is a quick reversal without a Turn on the 1-day or the 2-day chart, or without a 1 or 2-day Trend Line being broken on the advance, or a 1 or 2-day Trend Line being crossed on a rally. In cases of this kind, apply the 7 to 10-day rule and when the market is advancing, follow up with a stop-loss order 1¢ under each day's low, and watch for a SIGNAL DAY which will indicate that the advance is over. After there has been a SIGNAL DAY, either sell out before the close of that day or on any rally the following day. If you do not sell out, be sure and place a stop-loss order 1¢ below the low of the SIGNAL DAY.

Read the rules on GAPS carefully and if a GAP occurs on a SIGNAL DAY, it is a more definite indication that the Trend is changing because it is likely to be an Exhaust Gap. You should also apply Rule 28.

Examples: Some of the most important Signal Top Days on November Beans occurred in 1950: May 3 and 25th, June 15, and 16th, July 17 and 26th (the final high). August 15 and 30th, September 25 and October 16 (low for the greatest decline since July 26).

When the market has declined for a considerable time and then makes lower tops and lower bottoms for a period of 7 days or more, watch for a SIGNAL DAY and for an EXHAUST GAP for a change in Trend when you should cover short sales and buy for a rally.

1950, July 26, Soy Beans made Extreme High, which was also a GAP DAY and a SIGNAL DAY. By following these two rules on SIGNAL DAY and GAP DAY you would sell out at the top at the Time when the Turn on the 1 or 2-day chart did not come. Again, on October 16 at the low, which was a SIGNAL DAY, there was no Trend Line Turn on the 1 or 2-day charts, but the SIGNAL DAY and the 7 to 10-day Rule would get you out of shorts and long near low levels.

EXCEPTIONS TO THE RULES
When prices have advanced 10 to 14 days, without breaking the low of the previous day, moving straight up on the 2-day chart, and if prices at the end of the move are making a range of 5 to 10¢ per bushel, daily, you follow up your trades with stop-loss order 1¢ below each day's bottom, or on the last day there is a break back of 5¢ or more below the top, sell out. You can also use the rule for SIGNAL DAYS in moves of this kind. These will be referred to under "Examples".

RULE 5-A: 10 TO 14 DAY MOVES
When the main trend is up and prices are advancing, reactions seldom last more

than 10 to 14 days before the main trend is resumed. It is generally safe to buy on 10 to 14 Day reactions, as long as the 2-day chart shows the main trend up. Buy when the top of the 2-day chart is crossed or when there is a series of tops and prices move into new high levels. Reverse this rule in a declining market; sell on 10 to 14 Day rallies as long as the 2-day chart shows main trend down; sell when 2-day bottoms are broken or when a series of days around the same low level are broken. Average reaction in an advancing market runs 3 to 4 weeks. Average declines in a Bear Market, when the rallies come, average 3 to 4 weeks then continue the main trend down.

Remember, when a market is advancing very rapidly in the last stages of a Bull Market, reactions seldom last more than 2 to 3 days. Therefore, it is safe to buy on 2 to 3 day reactions, and place a stop-loss order 1¢ below the last 2-day bottom. Reverse this rule in a Bear Market. When the decline is running fast in the last stages of a Bear Market, rallies seldom last longer than 2 days and sometimes only 1 day. Therefore, it is safe to sell on rallies of 1 to 3 days and place a stop-loss order 1 to 2¢ above the top on the 2-day chart. Always try to buy or sell so you can place a stop-loss order below a 2-day bottom or above a 2-day top.

RULE FOR TRADING ON TREND LINE INDICATIONS BASED ON 2-DAY CHART

You either buy on reactions on the 2-day chart, or buy when the top of the 2-day chart is crossed and follow up with a stop-loss order 1 to 2¢ below the last bottom on the 2-day chart. When the 2-day bottom is broken, you reverse positions; sell out longs and go short.

TIME AND PRICE BALANCE

By recording the greatest reaction in Price, when the market is advancing and the greatest Time Period of reaction occurs, you will be able to tell when the market is over-balanced.

Examples: November Beans, May 25, high 230. June 16, low 208, a Price decline of 22¢ per bushel, time 22 calendar days and 18 market days. June 21 to 24th, the market declined 3 days and the Price decline was 5-½¢. July 17, high 257½. July 19, low 240, a decline of 17½¢ per bushel in 2 days. Price had overbalanced the previous reaction, but Time had not over balanced.

July 26, extreme high 272. This was a SIGNAL DAY and a GAP DAY which was an EXHAUST GAP, and you would have gotten out of the market and been short on these rules. July 29, low 259½, a decline of 12½¢ in 3 days. This had exceeded the Time Period of the reaction on June 19 and had over balanced the Time. The decline continued to August 2, low 256, down 16¢ time 7 days. A 1-day rally followed to August 3, high 261½ , up 5½¢, the same as the decline from June 21 to 24th. After August 3, the decline continued and when prices were down more than 17½¢, they over balanced the Price decline from July 17 to 19th. After this, the decline was faster to August 15, low 236¼, a decline of 35-3/4¢ from 272. August 15 was a SIGNAL DAY and was also 60 days from June 16, low. This was a buying indication where you would cover shorts and buy.

From July 26 to August 15, the greatest rally was 2 days, and when Prices advanced for 3 days they had over balanced the Time Period and indicated higher prices; and when Prices advanced more than 5½ ¢ per bushel they had over balanced the Price rally.

From August 15 to 30 there was only one 2-day reaction. On August 30 the high on November Beans was 254¼ , which was ½ point between 272 and 236¼. This ½ point was the selling level where you would sell out long Beans and sell short. After Prices declined for 3 days they had over balanced the Time Period. The Price advance from August 18 to 22nd was 5¢ per bushel; therefore, when Prices declined more than 5¢ they had over balanced the Price move of the previous rally.

October 7 to 16 Prices made lower tops and lower bottoms each day and were down 7 days. You would apply the 7 to 10-DAY RULE and follow the market down with stop loss order 1¢ above each day's high. On October 16 the high was 229-3/4. This would make the stop loss order 230-3/4. However, after the SIGNAL DAY, on October 16, you should have covered shorts and bought November Beans because this SIGNAL DAY occurred on an exact Time Period 1/3 of a year from the low of June 16.

From October 16, low, a sharp advance followed and when Prices crossed 231½ , on October 18, which was the ½ point of the life of the option, you had another SIGNAL TO BUY, and could expect the advance to Balance the move between August 15 to 30th which was 18¢ per bushel. October 23, November Beans advanced to 245-3/4 which was slightly more than 18¢ per bushel and then reacted slightly, indicating higher Prices.

By watching the Balancing of Time and Price, together with the other rules, it will help you to determine when Prices are reaching Extreme Highs or Extreme Lows.

PRICE RESISTANCE LEVELS

Read all of the rules covering Resistance Levels. You will note on your Resistance Cards that the Resistance Levels are figured in 1/8 of the range, and 1/8 of extreme high or low prices. When 1/8 of the range is 10¢ or more per bushel, you can use ½ of 1/8, or 1/16 of the range, especially after an advance of 40¢ to $1 per bushel or a decline of 40¢ to $1. A reverse move or a reaction, or a rally of 1/16 of the total range is an important Resistance point in making the first indication of a change in trend and this 1/16 point will become a support or buying point for a ceiling or selling point.

Examples: 1950, February 2, November Beans, low 191¼; July 26, high 272; range 80-3/4¢. 1/8 of this would be 10¢ per bushel; 1/16 would be 5¢ per bushel. If you add 7/16 of this range to 191¼ it gives 226½ which was the extreme low on October 16, 1950, giving another reason to expect support and a buying level, and the day this price was reached was a SIGNAL DAY, which confirmed that good buying orders were in the market around this Level. Divide the extreme low of 191¼ by 1/8 and add it to 191¼ and it gives 215-1/8. By adding 3/16 to the low price, it gives 227, a Resistance or buying Level.

If you add 7/16 of 191¼ to 191¼, it gives 274.47, and the high on July 26 was 272. If you subtract 1/16 of 272 from 272, it gives 255 and the first important rally came from 256.

You can always figure the percentage of extreme high and extreme low prices to get Resistance Levels. Also watch and consider the Natural Resistance Levels.

NATURAL PRICE RESISTANCE LEVELS

Our unit of money is $1 or 10¢, therefore, we divide 100 x 1/8, 1/3, 10 and 16 which gives the Natural Price Resistance Levels as follows:

6¼, 12½, 18-3/4, 25, 31¼, 33-1/3, 37½, 43-3/4, 50, 56¼, 62½, 66-2/3, 68-3/4, 75, 81¼, 87½, 93-3/4, and 100.

Continue these Resistance Levels for 200, 300, etc. and consider always that the most important are 150, 175, 187½, etc., but any of these Natural Resistance Levels are important and extreme high or low prices can be made around these levels when the time periods indicate a change in trend. There is usually a variation of 2 to 3¢ per bushel around any Resistance Level which is caused by momentum or lost motion.

IMPORTANCE OF TIME PERIODS

Time Periods from high or low levels are of greater importance than price resistance levels, but they must be considered together with SIGNAL DAYS, 7 to 10 Day Rule, GAPS, and Daily Price Limits. Balancing of Time and Price, all of which will help you to determine a change in trend, close to extreme high or extreme low level.

YEARLY TIME PERIODS

The year should be divided by eight (8) to get the important periods for changes in trend.

 1/8 of a year equals 6½ weeks, or 45 days

 3/4 of a year equals 13 weeks, or 91 days

 3/8 of a year equals 19½ weeks, or 135 to 138 days

 1/2 of a year equals 26 weeks, or approximately 182 days

 5/8 of a year equals 32½ weeks, or 225 to 227 days

 3/4 of a year equals 39 weeks, or approximately 273 days

 7/8 of a year equals 45½ weeks, or 318 days

 52 weeks equals 1 year, or 264 seven-day periods

All of these periods are important to watch for a change in trend, but the most important are 13, 17, 26, 35, 39, and 52 weeks, and the same proportionate periods in the 2nd year, 3rd year, etc.

The year can also be divided by 3 to get 1/3 which is 17-1/3 weeks and 2/3 of a year which is 34-2/3 weeks. These periods are also important to watch for a change in trend from any important high or low level.

Remember, you do not begin to count time from January 1. Start to count the Time Periods from extreme low and extreme high dates.

All Time Periods, from major and minor tops and bottoms, should be kept up. When you find several Time Periods coming out, based on previous tops and bottoms around the same time, it means a greater change in trend.

NATURAL SEASONAL TIME CHANGES

While we do not use the calendar months for time periods, unless an extreme high or low should occur around January 2 or 3rd, we do use the Seasonal Time Periods which are more important and many of the important highs and lows have occurred around these Seasonal Time Periods.

These periods are as follows:

December	21, any year
February	5
March	21
May	5
June	21
August	5
September	21
November	8

Then repeat, December 21, etc., for the 2nd and third years.

These Seasonal Time Periods divide the year into 8 equal parts of approximately 45 days each. You can divide these time periods into 2 equal parts which are approximately 22½ days. Example: December 21 to February 5 gives January 13 as the ½ period, and between June 21 to August 5 is July 14.

The variation from these Time Periods is usually 3 to 4 days before or after the actual dates. The most important changes in Grains occur during FEBRUARY, MAY, AUGUST and NOVEMBER, therefore, these dates and months are the most important to watch for major changes in trend, but always keep in mind the dates of the previous highs and lows of past years and watch for the change in trend around these dates. Also, look at your 2-day chart on each different options and get the dates when the important highs and lows have been made and then watch the Time Periods based on 1/8, 1/4, 1/3, 1/2, etc. of each yearly period from a high or low price.

RECORD OF HIGH AND LOW DATES

It is important to keep a record of the dates when the extreme high and low prices were made on the different options in order to watch these dates in the same months each year for a change in trend.

	1920,	February	15,	high	405	
	1930,	June	15,	high	216	
	1932,	December	28,	low	44	
	1936,	October	5,	low	120	(this was when future trading started)
May Beans,	1939,	July	15,	low	67¢	(lowest of the op)
	1941,	September	14,	high	202½	
	1941,	October	17,	low	154½	
	1942,	January	10,	high	203½	(highest future sold up to that time)
	1947,	October	28,	low	334	

May Beans, 1947, November 29, highs were made on Wheat and the first top was made on May Beans

1948, January 15, high 436-3/4
February 14, low 320½

Nov. Beans, June 15, high 347½

May Beans October 15, low 240
November 23, high 276-3/4

1949, February 9, low 201½

Note that the old top on September 14, 1941, was 202½ which was ½ of the 1920 high of 405, making 201½ a support point and buying level in February 1949.

May Beans 1949, August 26, high 243½
November 16, low 220½

Nov Beans 1950, January 31
February 2, low 191¼
February 6
April 14, low 203
May 3
May 25, high 230
May 13, low 212½
June 16, low 208
July 26, high 272
August 30, high 254¼
October 16, low 226½

You can see that most of the highs and lows occur between the 13th and 17th of the different months and around the 23rd to the 29th of the different months each year.
Therefore these dates, each month, are the most important to watch for a change in trend.

The government report is issued around the 10th of each month each year, therefore sometimes highs and lows occur around the 9th and 10th of the month.

The most important changes in trend occur at the end of 3 months or 13 weeks, which is ¼ of a year; around 120 days, which is 1/3 of a year; and 26 weeks or 182 days, which is ½ of a year.

Note that the last low on November Beans, June 16, 1950, was 208 and that a low occurred August 15, which was 60 days. The next extreme low, October 16, which was 1/3 of a year from June 16, and 1/2 of a year from April 14, 1950.

November Beans made a high of 230, May 25, 1950, and the extreme high was made July 26, and the next secondary high, August 30.

1950, October 26, will be 92 days or ¼ of a year from July 26, high; therefore, this will be an important date to watch for a change in trend. You will note also that the last low on June 24, 1950, was 209½. This was just before the war broke out, therefore, October 24, 1950, will be ½ of a year from this date.

GAPS AND WHAT THEY INDICATE ON GRAINS

GAPS on an advancing market are made when the opening price is above the closing price of the previous day, and the low [of] the day the gap is made [is] higher than the highest price of the previous day. When a market is declining, a GAP occurs at the opening price which is below the low of the previous day, and the price declines and the high the day the GAP is made is lower than the low price of the previous day.

The cause of GAPS in an advancing market is that there is a large amount of buying orders which is usually caused by some sensational news, and the market closes strong near the highest price of the day. Over night a large amount of buying orders accumulate, both by traders who are short of the market and wish to cover and by buyers for long account, who have missed the market and decide to buy, regardless of the price. This accumulation of buying orders often causes a wide opening at higher levels above the high of the previous day, leaving a GAP. GAPS can be in a series of several days, that is, GAPS can occur from 3 to 5 times without being filled. The last day a GAP occurs, and the price declines 1¢ below the lowest price on the day the GAP was made, is an indication that the market has reached top, at least temporarily, and you should sell out Grains and go short.

EXHAUST GAPS

After there has been a prolonged advance in any Grain, there often occurs just 1 day with a GAP and this often is a SIGNAL DAY and many times it occurs near some important ½ point. When a GAP of this kind occurs, and the price declines the following day and fills the GAP, your stop-loss order at this time should be 1¢ below the lowest price on the day the GAP is made, or if it is a SIGNAL DAY you can sell out at the opening of the following day, or on any small rally. However, as a rule you should place a stop-loss order 1¢ below the low on the day the gap was made, and then reverse position.

Examples: NOVEMBER BEANS – July 15, 1950, high 250½, closed 249 July 17, which was Monday, a large accumulation of buying orders buying orders came in and the opening price was 254. The low of the day was 253. The high 257½, closed 255. This was not a SIGNAL DAY but it was a GAP DAY because the lowest price was 2½, above the high of the previous day. Therefore, you would place a stop-loss order at 252 which was 1¢ below the low of July 17. This would put you out of long Beans and put you short at 252. A sharp decline followed to July 19 when low was made at 240. This was a buying level because it was at the ½ point of 44¢ to 436-3/4.

July 21, high 253, low 249, closed at 253 on the top and left a GAP at 247½. This would make the stop-loss order at 246½ or 1¢ below the day of the GAP.

July 22, low 248, did not catch stop-loss order because it did not go 1¢ below the GAP.

July 25, low 253½, high 263, closed at 263.

July 26, prices opened strong at 266 which was 3¢ above the closing price, leaving a GAP 3¢ wide. The low was 266, the high was 272, closing price 268. This was a SIGNAL DAY and 269-3/8 was ½ between 191¼ and 347½. These were two reasons why you would sell out November Beans on July 26 and go short because it was a SIGNAL DAY and at an important ½ point. Prices had had a sensational advance and if you did not sell out you would raise your stop-loss order to 265, 1¢ below the low level of July 26, when the GAP was made. On July 27 your stop would have been caught and you would be out of longs and short of November Beans at 265.

July 27, the GAP was filled. The price closed at 264 and continued on down.

EXHAUST GAPS IN A DECLINING MARKET
When a market has been declining for a considerable period of time and the range of decline is quite large, GAPS are of greater importance. GAPS can occur at the extreme low day, the same as they can occur at an extreme high. When a market has been declining for a considerable length of time, people hold on and hope for a rally. Finally, the market closes weak and at the lowest prices of the day; traders make up their minds to sell out longs and take a loss, they place the selling orders at the market at the opening the following day. There may also be a large amount

of orders to sell for short accounts. This accumulation of selling orders exceeds the demand and prices open below the low of the previous day, leaving a GAP which may be filled the following day, or there might be several GAPS occur before there is a SIGNAL DAY at or near an important ½ point. When you are short of the market and a GAP occurs, you pull the stop-loss order down 1¢ above the highest price made on the day the GAP occurred.

Examples: September 16, 1950, November Beans, high 241½, low 239¼, closed at 240. Note that 240 is the important ½ point. Therefore, large buying or selling orders often occur around these important points. The market had declined at this time from the high of 254 and from extreme of $2.72.

September 18, high 238, low 233½, closed at 236 leaving a GAP from 238 to 239¼ which was the low of the previous day. This GAP was not filled for some time, but your stop-loss order on short Beans would have been pulled down to 239 or 1¢ above the high of September 18.

September 25, prices declined to 231¼ which was the ½ point between 191¼ and 272. This was the natural support or Buying Level for at least a moderate rally.

October 4, high 239¼ which filled the GAP and advanced to the low of September 16, but failed to reach the closing price. And, of course, the reason it failed to go through this level was because 240-3/8 is the important ½ point. Therefore, you could have sold short at this level and placed a stop-loss order at 241-3/8.

October 16, November Beans, low 226½. This was a SIGNAL DAY. Prices declined at the opening only ½¢ per bushel below the low of September 14, then rallied and closed above the close of September 15, and near the high price of the day. This was a SIGNAL DAY and the time to cover shorts and buy, even though there was no GAP at this time. If you did not cover shorts when you saw near the closing of the market that it was a SIGNAL DAY, you would have placed a stop-loss order at 230-3/4, 1¢ above the high of September 16.

Always watch for GAPS after a prolonged advance, or a prolonged decline, and then follow the rules. Also, watch for SIGNAL DAYS when there has been a prolonged advance or a prolonged decline. Apply the 7 to 10 Day Rule when prices have been advancing and making higher bottoms each day, or when they have been declining and making lower bottoms each day.

DAILY PRICE LIMITS AND WHAT THEY INDICATE

At the present time, the limit of fluctuations on Soy Beans on any one day is 10¢ per bushel, which means that the price can advance or decline 10¢ from the closing price of the previous day. The limit on Wheat is 8¢ per bushel each day.

When prices move up or down, the limit in one day is usually the result of increased demand and heavy buying or selling, both for the long and short accounts. Often when prices move the limit in one day, there is a GAP and when prices are at the extreme it is often a SIGNAL DAY and at the same time prices are often near some important resistance level. When markets are very active and prices are moving rapidly, they sometimes go the limit for 3 to 4 consecutive days. In September, 1939, when Hitler started the war, Wheat prices moved up the limit for 4 consecutive days and made top at the opening on the morning of the 5th day and a sharp decline followed. Under normal conditions prices seldom go up or down the limit for more than 2 to 3 days. When they go up or down the limit for 2 consecutive days and close on the extreme high or low for the day, it is generally safe to buy or sell at the opening the following day and place a stop-loss order 2 to 3¢ away.

1950, July 25, November Soy Beans advanced the limit and closed at the extreme high of the day. This was after an advance of 32¢ per bushel in 6 market days, and leaving a GAP and also a SIGNAL DAY. The 7 to 10 DAY Rule could be applied as well as the weekly time rule which was 30 days from June 24, low; 60 days from May 25; and 4 months or 1/3 of a year from the high of March 27, making this a time to sell out longs and go short because it was an EXHAUST GAP, a SIGNAL DAY and prices had gone up the LIMIT and were at an important ½ point.

1950, October 16, November Soy Beans, low 226½, a SIGNAL DAY and a day to cover shorts and buy, based on the 7 to 10 Day Rule and resistance level.

1950, October 18, prices opened higher, leaving a small GAP and advanced the limit, closing at the high price of the day, and after this time did not give a signal for lower prices. Reactions were very small.

1950, October 25, November Beans opened sharply higher, leaving a GAP and advanced the limit of 10¢ per bushel, closing only 1¢ below the high of the day. This was the second time since October 16 that prices had advanced the limit. The advance continued through October 26, and 27th, making new high levels with May Beans up 2/3 of the range of the life of the option to October 27. Still there was no SIGNAL DAY and prices had not broken 1¢ per bushel below the low of any previous day since the bottom on October 16. From this level, you would watch October 30 for a change in trend or a SIGNAL DAY against the August 30 top, and because December 28, 1932, was a low date and November 29, 1947, was a high date.

At this writing, there have been two GAPS which have not been filled since October 16. You would now watch for a SIGNAL DAY, a GAP, or for prices to break 1¢ below the previous day's bottom to indicate a change in trend and, at least, a fair sized reaction.

1950, October 26, 92 days, or ¼ of a year from July 26, high. Therefore, November 26 will be 1/3 of a year from July 26, high, and this will be important to watch for a change in trend on May Soy Beans which are now the main trend indicator.

WEEKLY HIGH AND LOW CHART

The Weekly High and Low Charts are very important and you measure time periods in 1/8, 1/4, 1/3, 3/8, 1/2, 5/8, 2/3, 3/4, 7/8 of a year, and 52 weeks or 1 year. These time periods are calculated from the extreme low or the extreme high and from minor tops and bottoms. You do not start to count time periods based on the calendar year starting January 1, unless there was an extreme low or an extreme high on January 2 or 3rd any year. The extreme lows and extreme highs are the most important to count and measure time periods from.

Examples: 1932, December 28, Cash Soy Beans, extreme low 44¢. This means that you should always watch around the 28th day of the month for an important change and watch for SIGNAL DAYS, GAPS or ½ points which might occur around this time.

1948, January 15, May Beans highest price in history, 436-3/4. Therefore, you should watch the 15th to 17th day of each month for a change in trend and when these time periods come out on 13 weeks, which is ¼ of a year; 17 weeks, which is 1/3 of a year; 26 weeks, which is ½ of a year; 35 weeks, which is 2/3 of a year; 39 weeks, which is 3/4 of a year; and 52 weeks which is 1 year, from an extreme high or low, it is more important for a change in trend. ½ of a year is just as important as the ½ between high and low prices. All time periods should be carried across the chart from important bottoms and tops and moved consecutively across as the years go by. When a new high or a new low is made, time periods should be carried from these levels.

Suppose you are watching a time when the price is nearing an important ½ point. Look across the top and you might find 156 weeks, which would be 3 years; another time period, 104 weeks or 2 years; another time period 52 weeks, or 1 year; and, another time period 65 weeks, or 1¼ years. If several of these time periods were coming out around the same time, and a SIGNAL DAY occurred and a GAP occurred at the same time, near an important ½ point, it would be a sure indication for an important change in trend.

You learn to do by doing! You will learn how well these time periods work by checking time from each top and bottom and finding the time period that a following top or bottom came out on, and also by checking at the same time to find what important resistance level was reached around this time. Never overlook the fact to compare previous tops and bottoms and see if a high or low price is reaching some previous low level, or some previous high level of a previous campaign, even though it might have been years ago.

Example: February 9, 1949 May Soy Beans, low 201½. Suppose that in February, May, August or November, May Beans break this low level, it would be very important for lower prices, if it occurred on an exact time period from a previous high or low. Suppose that on February 9, 1951, or 3 years, or 156 weeks, May Beans are selling below 201½, it would be a very important indication for a very much lower level. You would watch the next extreme which was 154½ made on October 17, 1941, in a war period. Suppose, in 1951, we are in a period of peace and there is a large crop of Beans in prospect, you would figure that prices could go to 154½ or lower, and you would apply all of the rules to get an indication when prices might reach low for a minor rally, but you would follow, at all times, the main trend. As long as the main trend is down, it is safe to sell on rallies, and when the main trend is up, it is safe to buy on reactions or to buy when important tops are crossed.

NOVEMBER BEANS WEEKLY CHART

Trading started in November Soy Beans on July 7, 1947, therefore, it is important for you to study the time periods on the Weekly Chart from each important high and low level. These time periods, in weeks, are marked across from the bottom and from the tops, and arrows point to the important periods, such as, 1/8, 1/4, 1/3, 1/2, etc., of a year from each extreme high or low.

1947, November 22, high 383. This was the highest in history for November Beans.

1948, October 3, low 232. This was 65 weeks or 1¼ years from July 7, 1947; 45 weeks, or 7/8 of a year from November, 1947, high; and 16 weeks from June, 1948, high.

1949, June low 193. This was 36 weeks, or 2/3 of a year from October, 1948; 52 weeks, or 1 year from June, 1948; and 81 weeks from November, 1947.

1949, August, high 249½. This was 39 weeks or 3/4 of a year from November, 1948, high; 91 weeks, or 1-3/4 years from 1947, high; and 63 weeks from June, 1948, high.

1950, February 6, low 191¼, which was ½ of the highest selling price, 383, and a safe place to buy, protected with a stop-loss order. This was 35 weeks, or 2/3 of a year from June, 1938, low; 71 weeks from October 1948, low, which was 1-3/8 years; and, 26 weeks, or ½ of a year from August, 1949, high; 65 weeks, or 1¼ years from November, 1948, high; 117 weeks, or 2¼ years from the extreme high in November, 1947; 88 weeks from 1948, high – this was close to 1-3/4 years. These exact time periods coming out close to February 5, a NATURAL TIME PERIOD, and the fact that the price was at the most important ½ point, made it a sure, safe time to buy.

Check all other weekly high and low time periods for all important tops and bottoms. Keep these time periods marked on the chart ahead of time in order that you can see what the future indications are for a change in trend.

Do not guess. Follow definite rules. LET THE MARKET TELL ITS OWN STORY and trade only on definite indications and place stop-loss orders to protect your principal and your profits! The more time you put in studying, the more apt you are to make a success. You will continue to learn more every year if you study the market and apply the rules. Great opportunities are sure to come every year for making profits. You must be prepared for them by a thorough understanding of the rules and in this way you will not miss the opportunities.

When prices are in a narrow trading range, which they often are at extreme low levels, WAIT! Allow the market plenty of time to give a DEFINITE INDICATION which way it is going. You can make plenty of profits after the market has broken out of a trading range, either up or down.

                                                        W.D. GANN

October 28, 1950

By going over the May, July and November Soy Beans' Chart, both daily and 2-day charts, you can see how profitable it is to trade on the 2-day chart. The buying and selling points are marked on the 2-day chart and also the place for stop-loss order is marked. Note X below bottoms and above tops.

EXAMPLES:

July Soy Beans advanced from November 16, 1949, to December 5, 1949 until February 2 and 6th, 1950, each move on the 2-day chart was a lower top, showing that the main trend was down. On February 6, the price declined to 219. You would buy at this level because it was a double bottom, and if you look at your resistance card, you will find that 218-3/8 is ½ of the highest prices at which May Beans ever sold. Therefore, you would buy May or July Beans against this important ½ point and place a stop-loss order at 217. If you waited for the 2-day chart to show a change in trend you would buy when July Beans crossed 225, which was above the last top on the 2-day chart. From this time on there were 6 moves or swings up on the 2-day chart making higher bottoms and higher tops, and if you kept a stop-loss order 1¢ below the bottom on the 2-day chart, you would have gotten the benefit of the complete move of a profit of nearly $1 per bushel.

May Beans. From the high of 436-3/4, on January 15, 1948, which was the highest price on record that May Beans ever sold, to the low of 201½, which May Beans reached in February, 1949, gives a ½ point of 319-1/8. July Beans advanced to 320-3/4 on May 8, 1950, and May Beans sold at 323-3/4. If you had sold out and gone short around 319, you would have made big profits in a few days. Note that from March 27 to March 30, 1950, July Beans declined 16¢ per bushel in 3 days. This was the greatest reaction in price and time. The next reaction, from April 25 to 27th, was a 2-day reaction with a decline of 11¢ per bushel. A smaller decline than the previous reaction, both in time and price, and showing no indication that the main trend had turned down.

July Beans. May 3, high 317. May 5, Low 298-1/8 – a decline of 19¢ per bushel which was 3¢ greater than the previous decline when low was made on March 30. This had over-balanced the price reaction but had not over-balanced the time period of 3 days. A 2-day rally followed to May 8, making high at 320-3/4. A very small gain the last day and failing to go 4¢ per bushel above the previous tops was a sign of weakness.

This is where the 2-day chart at this extreme shows a reversal which a 3-day chart would not show. This was a TIME TURN on the 2-day chart, and, if you had waited for lower prices a second day, you would still have been able to sell at high levels. When the price declined to 297½ on May 12, it was below the bottom of May 5 and the first time that a 2-day bottom had been broken since February 6.

Remember, we have a rule which says that fast moves last about three months, and that FEBRUARY, MAY AUGUST and NOVEMBER are important months for changes in trend for Soy Beans and other Grains.

The decline which started from May 8 continued to May 17. July Beans declined to 284½. Note that the last bottom on the 2-day chart made April 27 was 284, making this a double bottom and buying level. Every day's top on the daily chart had been lower and the price had declined 1/3 from the high of 320¾ to the low of 219, making this a support level.

NOVEMBER BEANS - 1950:

January 3, high 207½. This is where the option started.

January 4, low 204½

January 5, high 207, This was a turn on the 1-day chart

January 9, when prices broke below 204 we sell short and protect with stop-loss order at 208 which is 1¢ above the high of January 5. The decline continues to January 31, making low at 191½ without ever making a 2-day rally. We know that 383 was the highest price at which November Beans ever sold.

Using the rule of ½ of the highest selling price would make 192 to 191½ a sure safe buying point protected with stop-loss orders at 189. If you waited for the 2-day chart to show the turn, it advanced to 195½ on February 3; declined to 191¼ Feb. 6 making a double bottom. On February 18, for the first time crossed a 2-day trend line top, making it a buy based on the 2-day chart rules.

The advance continued making higher bottoms and higher tops. March 27, high 210. This was above the opening price of the option of 207½ on January 3 and indicated higher prices. A 2-day reaction followed from March 29, low $2. Note that the last bottom on March 23 was 199¼. You would buy more and protect with stop-loss order at 198¼. When the price crossed 210 you would buy more. The advance continued until May 3, high 230. This was up 38-3/4¢ per bushel from low of Feb. 6.

Note: from April 14, low 203, to the high of 230 on May 3, there had not been a 2-day bottom broken. In fact, no bottom was broken on the daily chart. This is where you would apply EXCEPTION TO THE RULES to protect your profits, by selling out on the first 5¢ decline from a high level.

Note: May 1, high 229½, May 2, low 224½; and May 3, high 230, the price opening at 226 and closing at 225. This was a SIGNAL DAY and you should sell out longs and go short. Price declined to 215 on May 5 which was back to the same low levels made May 25 to 26, which was a series of bottoms and a buying level because this was only a 2-day reaction. A quick 2-day rally followed to May 8, making a lower top and closing near the low making another SIGNAL DAY, indicating a short sale.

May 13, low 212½. Note that 211-3/4 was ½ between 191½ and 230, making this a buying level. Prices advanced to May 25 reaching 230, making this a double top and a place to sell out and go short.

May 26 prices react to 221½, a 1-day reaction. The market rallied to 228 on June 1, making higher bottoms for 3 consecutive days. This is where we use the EXCEPTION and record this move on the 2-day chart. You would stay short and reduce stop-loss orders to 229 on shorts.

June 6, low 216½.

June 10, high 223½. This was a top on the 2-day chart and the stop-loss order should be moved down to 224½.

June 16, low 208. Note this was just above the opening price of the option at 207½ on January 3 and there was also a 2-day top at 208½ on April 10, making this a buying level. However, if you waited for the turn on the 2-day chart, you would have bought at 216 on June 26 when prices crossed the last 2-day top at 215 made on June 21.

June 24 low 209½, a higher bottom than June 16. When prices crossed 215 on June 26 they were above the 2-day top and indicated higher prices. After prices crossed 230, the double top, you would figure from 191¼ to 230 was 38-3/4 cents. You would add 38-3/4 to 230, which would indicate 268-3/4. The high on July 26 was 272. War had started and war is always Bullish and causes advances in Grains. The market advanced rapidly and when prices crossed the double tops at 230 you would buy more.

July 3, high 242-3/4, a 1-day reaction to July 5 to 234. A 1-day rally to July 6, a 1-day reaction to 234¼ on July 7. We record this move on the 2-day chart. You would raise stop-loss orders to 233 and buy more, when the price crossed 243, because it was above ½ between 44¢ and 436-3/4.

July 17, high 257½, up 49½ cents from the low of June 16. Here you would apply the Exception to the Rule and place stop-loss order at 252, 1 cent under the low of July 17 which would close out your longs and you would go short one contract at 252. July 19, low 240, a 2-day reaction and a buying level because it was at the ½ point and only 1¼ cent below the low of July 12. A rapid advance followed reaching 272 on July 26. This was up 80-3/4 cents from the extreme low and 64 cents from 208. There had only been one 2-day reaction since June 24 low.

July 26 was an EXHAUST GAP and SIGNAL DAY because prices closed 4¢ below the top. They did break back 5¢ from the high. You would either sell out on July 27 and go short, or place a stop-loss order at 265, which was 1¢ below the low of July 26. This is where the Exception to the Rule got you out at the right time. The market declined for 3 days to July 29 which was a greater decline in time than any since June 16 and indication prices were going lower.

August 2, low 256.

August 3, high 261½, a 1-day rally which would show on the 2-day chart as an exception, as this made the TIME TURN.

The extreme high is always the most important to figure resistance levels from. The secondary high on any option is also important to figure resistance levels from to the extreme low. The extreme high on November Beans was 383 on November 22, 1947. The secondary high was 347½ on June 12, 1948. The extreme low was 191¼ in February, 1950. The ½ point between 347½ and 191¼ was 269-3/8 which is very important, making this a selling level on July 26, 1950, and prices never went 3¢ above it before the big break. Always have these important resistance points marked on your daily chart as well as your 2-day chart so you will know when they are reached.

August 4 you would sell more November Beans at 255, 1¢ under the low of August 2. Stop loss order would be 262½.

August 5, low 245¼.

August 8, high 253½.   This was a 2-day rally as shown on the 2-day chart.

August 10, low 238-3/4.

August 11, 248.   We show this on the 2-day chart because it was a rally of 9¢ per bushel in one day.

August 15, low 236¼.   Note that the lows made on July 5 and 7th were 234 and 234¼, making this a buying level with stop-loss order at 233 because the market had declined 36¢ per bushel from July 26 and 240½ between 208 and 272.

At no time did the prices close 1¢ under 240, another indication that this was a buying level. August 16, 17 and 18, each day the low prices were higher. On August 18 the high was 244-3/4 and the market closed at 244¼. This was a move up on the 2-day chart. However, the last actual high on the 2-day chart was made on August 8 at 253½. Based on this, we would hold November Soy Beans bought with a stop at 238½ which would be 1¢ under the lows of August 17 and 18.

August 18, November Beans advanced to 247-3/4.

August 22, declined to 241½, a 2-day reaction. Stop-loss order could be moved up [to] 240½.

August 30, high 254. Note that between 272 and 236¼ this was the ½ point and a selling level. Also, the last high on August 8 was 253½ which was a trend line top, making 254 a price at which to sell out longs and go short.

September 2, low 245½. This was the ½ point between 236¼ and 254 and indicated a minor rally.

September 5, high 250-3/4.

September 7, low 242-3/4. This was below the ½ point of the last move and a SIGNAL for low prices after a rally.

September 9, high 248¼, a 2-day rally and the first 2-day rally since August 30. November Beans were a short sale with a stop at 252½ which is above the September 5 high but prices will have to cross 254 to indicate up trend and higher prices. When they closed below 245½, which is the ½ point between 254 and 236¼, they indicated lower.

LESSON 9

MASTER EGG COURSE

W. D. GANN   -   MASTER EGG COURSE

I am sending one copy of the Master Even Square Chart for Eggs showing the squares from 2 to 16 at 30 points per unit. One Daily high and low chart on October Eggs for 1949 delivery beginning November 1, 1948 up to date.

Please note the Master Square Chart which starts at 30 and moves on around to where the square ends at 7680. You will find a green ring around 6000 or 60 cents, the extreme high price of December 28, 1920. A ring around 1050 which is closest to the extreme low price of 1037. You will find 15 cents circled, this is 1/4 of 60. 20 cents circled in green; this is 1/3 of 60. 30 cents circled in green; this is 1/2 of 60. 45 cents circled in green which is 3/4 of 60. Please note that the small figures beginning at 1 move around the squares, ending at 256 which is the square of 16. These are the figures for timing either in days, weeks or months.

Example: May 3, 1949, October Eggs high 5025. This was on the timing angle of 168, which is 14 years and 169 is the square of 13. Note that the price of 5010 hits the 7/16 point of the circle at 5010, which would make this a resistance and selling level based on the Master Square Chart. See notes and time periods on the right hand of this Master Chart.

I wired Chicago last night that October Eggs was a sure sale today. The reasons were as follows: Based on the angles on the daily high and low chart the angle of 4 x 1, which moves 2-1/2 points per day from the first top at 4760 made December 6, 1948 crossed at 5020. The 45 degree angle moving up, from the low of 4685 on March 16, 1949 crossed at 5020. The angle of 67-1/2 degrees, which moves up 20 points per day from the low of 4785 on April 18, crossed at 5020 and the angle moving up from 4735 on Feb. 14 crossed at 5005, making 5 important angles coming out at this high point. A sure point for great resistance because the time from the starting of the option was over six months. The time from the first important top on December 6, 1948, was close to 5 months and the angle from this top called the top exactly.

Since receiving   [blank]   letter stating that the contracts for Eggs were changed on Feb. 1 and that 1 point now equals $1.44, I did some experimenting to adjust angles to the money value because that is very important. I wanted to get something that would work to an angle of 11-1/4 degrees and by multiplying 144 x 8 it gave 1152 or $11.52 profit on 8 points. This would give an angle of 5 x 4 or about 39 degrees, moving up at the rate of 8 points per day, instead of the 45° angle which moves 10 points per day.

Years of this research and experience have proved that the first advance from which a reaction runs more than three days will set an angle for an important top later. This rule works on weekly and monthly charts also. After there is a second or third top and when there is a greater decline from the third top an angle from that bottom must call bottoms and tops of the next advance. You will note that on the greatest decline from Jan. 24 to Feb. 8 the price declined to the angle of 8 x 1 from the extreme low of 4485, and the angle of 2 x 1 from the third top called the second and also the last bottom at 4560. From this low of 4560 we start the angle moving up at the rate of 8 points per day. It calls the low for March 2 next it called the top at 4850 on March 30 from which a two day reaction followed, and finally on May 3 this angle in green crossed the first top angle at 5020, on May 3, 1949.

The market closed at the half-way at the range of the day on May 3. May 4 was a signal day. The opening was at 50 cents; the high was 5005; the low for the day was 4980. The market closed at 4985. This was the first day since April 18 that the market had broken the low of the previous day and closed under. The total time from 4560 to 5025, was 58 market days and in view of the fact that the option is over 6 months old a greater reaction can be expected. The 45 degree angle from the last low of 4795 is the most important one to watch for support and a secondary rally. The decline should run at least five days with not more than one-day rally.

Other reasons for the top on May 3 were as follows:

First move up from 4485 to 4760 -- total gain 275 points.

First move down 215 points.

Second move up from 4560 to 4850 -- total gain 290 points.

Second move down 4850 to 4775 -- loss 75 points.

Third move up 4775 to 5025 -- total gain 250 points. This was 25 points less than the first gain and 40 points less than the second gain up.

The greatest time period from Jan. 24 to Feb. 8 was 11 market days. And the last advance from April 18 was 11 market days, therefore, when the market declines more than 11 days it will over balance the greatest time period. When it declines more than 75 points it will over balance the last price declines or space reversal, and indicate lower prices.

Study the Master Chart against previous tops and bottoms and you will see how it confirms the geometrical angles on other charts. Example:

5010 is opposite 180 degrees from 60 cents. 4890 is on a 45 degree angle from 1050 the extreme low price. 4950 is 180 degrees from 45 cents.

From 30 cents, which is half of 60, the 45 degree angle crosses at 48 cents. This is why the market made three bottoms around 48 cents on April 13 to 18. The Master Chart shows the same resistance levels and by using the time period with it you will learn the basic mathematical and geometrical law for market movement.

May 4, 1949

By going over back records and carefully studying all the important tops and bottoms you will see the working of the law.

Since the fluctuation of Eggs on the minimum of 5 points, now equals $7.20 which is two circles of 360 degrees, one-half of this is 360 and makes an angle moving at the rate of 2-1/2 points per day very important. The fluctuations will now work better to the circle of 360 degrees. In a few days I will send you another Master Chart showing each 15 degree angle and the resistance levels which will help you to determine resistance and turning points.

Example: The range in fluctuations and the life of the present option of October Eggs is 4485 low and 5025 high, making a range of 540 points. Subtract 360 from 540 and we have the balance of 180. This means that the market had advanced 1-1/2 circles or cycles and was at 180 degree angle on May 3, 1949. The writer sold October Eggs at 5015 on May 3, 1949.

Even Squares for Cotton & Eggs
Time and Price

DEC 28-1920
DEC-28 1948 = 336 Months
APRIL 28-1949 - 4 "
344 0 "
JULY 28-1949 = 343 "
7 X 49 = 343 "

DEC 28-1920 - High 60¢
MAY 2. 1949 = 1481 weeks

Square 2538 = 44444
44444/125 = 83 "
1400/= 40 "

From ☐ 38 to 39
1/4 = 19 1/4 weeks
1/2 = 38 1/2 "
1481 + 38 1/2 = 1482 1/2
MAY 13-1949 = 1482 1/2

1440 = 4 X 360
MAY 30, 1949 = 45 weeks
In new 360 cycle.

NE 45°   1/8   1/16   0° EAST 360°   15/16   SE 315°
3/16   North 90°   13/16   3/4   1/2   5/16   5/8   135° NW   7/16   180° WEST   9/16   SW 225°

MASTER 360° SQUARE OF 12 CHART FOR EGGS

This chart is the square of 360 beginning at 15 and ending at 4320. It represents 288 spaces of 15° each. In time this would be 288 days, 288 months or 288 weeks.

The earth makes one revolution on its axis every 24 hours and moves one cycle of 360°. We divide the circle up into 15° angles and show the most important angle such as 90, 120, 180, 270, 315 and 360. There are 12 months in the year and 365-1/4 days. The sun moves 360° in 365-1/4 days. Therefore, this chart would represent in time 12 months for each line of 360°, and would represent 360 points for the price of Eggs. The angles show the important resistance angle for Eggs when prices reach these angles and makes tops or bottoms on them and later work to 90°, 180°, 270° and 360° to these extreme high and low levels. The most important being the ones outlined above. The next are 120° and 240° or 1/3 and 2/3 of the circle. Next in importance are 45, 135, 225 and 315.

The next in importance are 60° and 300°.

Any of the angles or degrees that a high or low price forms on becomes important when the degrees or cycles as outlined above forms to the high or low prices. You should study the time periods from each low point to the next low point and from a low point to a high point and from a high point down to a low point, always giving the most weight to the record high and record low level.

Example: 1920 December 28 Eggs high 60 cents per dozen. Note that this was in the 5th cycle of a second square of 12 x 360 and on the 270° or 3/4 of the circle, and where a 45° angle moving up from the 9 cycle crossed at a 45° angle moving down from the end of the first square of from 4320 crossed at 60 cents, making this a strong natural resistance level. To get the cycles of 360° back from this price you move back on the same line, or on the 270° line. This gives the resistance levels at 5640, 5280, 4920, 4560, 4200, 3840, 3480, 3120, 2760, 2400, 2040, 1680, 1320, 960, 600 and 240 which represents the degree of the highest price.

Moving back on a 45° angle from 60 cents the resistance levels are: 5625, 5235, 4845, 4455, 4065, 3675, 3285 and 2895.

Moving down on a 45° angle the resistance levels are: 5670, 5340, 5010 and 4680.

1947 September 10, high 5855. This was a lower top than the extreme high and is next in importance to figure time periods from and to measure resistance levels. This price occurs in the fifth cycle of the second square of 360° and on the 90° angle. The resistance levels on the 90° angle are as follow:

5490, 5130, 4770, 4410, 4050, 3690, 3330, 2970, 2610, 2250, 1890, 1530, 1170, 810, 450 and 90 in the first cycle which represents the 90° angle or 1/4 of a circle.

Moving back to the left from 5855 on a 45° angle the resistance levels are as follows:
5520, 5190, 4860, 4530, 4200, 3870, 3540, 3210 and 2880.

Following a 45° angle down to the left from 5855 the resistance levels are:
5475, 5085 and 4695.

1948 June high 5370. This was a second lower top and is important for resistance levels and time period.

5370 is in the second square in the third cycle on 330°. The resistance level moving back or 5010, 4650, 4290, 3930, 3570, 3210, 2850, 2490, 2130, 1770, 1410, 1050, 690 and 330 which represents the degree of 5370. Moving ahead to the right the next resistance level would be 5730 and 6090. Following the 45° angle down the resistance levels are: 4980, 4590, 4200, 3810, 3420, 3045, 2655, 2265, 1875, 1485 and 1095. A 45° angle moving to the right gives resistance levels 5700 and 6045. Minor tops can be checked in the same way for resistance levels and the time period carried forth from all other high levels.
The extreme low level is always important for resistance levels and for time periods. The minor low levels in the same way.
1930 extreme low for Eggs 10-3/8. This occurs in the first square of 360 in the third cycle and on an angle of 315°. The resistance of 360 to this price are: 1395, 1755, 2115, 2475, 2835, 3195, 3555, 3915, 4275, 4635, 4995, 5355, 5715 and 6075, all of which are on the 315° angle.
Moving down on a 45° angle from 1055 the resistance levels are: 1355, 1695, 2020, 2355, 2685, 3015, 3345, 3675, 6005, 4335.
Moving up on a 45° angle the resistance levels are: 1410, 1785 and 2160.
In order that you may check the resistance levels and time periods we are giving high and low prices for each year.
1918, September low 34 cents. October high 47 cents.
1919, June and September high 47 cents and 4750.
December low 3150.
1920, December 28 high 60 cents.
1921, April low 2425.
December high 50 cents.
1930 low 10-3/8.
1932 June low 15 cents. October high 2425.

1933, March low 15 cents. This was the same low as June 1932 and was 1/4 of 60 cents making it an important support level and buying level.

1935, May high 2675.

1936, January low 2050. August high 2750.

1937, October low 1750.

1938, September high 2550.

1939, April low 16 cents, holding one cent above 15 cents the double bottoms made this a strong support and buying levels.

1941, June to September high 3050 and 3060. Note this was just above 30 cents which is 1/2 of 60 and in natural resistance level.

1942, January high 3425, is well above the 1/2 way point of 60 cents. February low 3090, still holding above 30 cents and in a strong position indicating higher prices.

1943, July 4450 (high). This was on the 270th month from 60 cents to high level and 45 cents is 3/4 of 60, making this a resistance level on time and prices, and a place to sell short; failing to reach 45 cents showed that the market was weaker.

1944, October low 3350.

1945, May to July high 4540. This was getting through 45 cents, 3/4 of 60 but could not hold it and a reaction followed because time was running against the market.

1945, September low 34 cents. Just 25 points below the low of January of 1942 and a support level, on the 73rd month from the low of August 1939, and 159 months from the 1932 low.

1946, April, June and September high 4625 and 4650.
       October low 3875 on the 89 to 90th month from August 1939 and on the 172nd to 174th month from the 1932 low.

1947, September 10 high 5855, 321 months from the high of 60 cents. November low 45 cents. This was at the end of the Square of 360 which ends 12 x 360 at 4320. Failing to break 30 points back into this square indicated support and higher prices and was 101 month from 1939 low and 185 month from 1932 low.

1948, June high 5370. November 1 low 4385.

1949, May 3, high 5025 up to this writing. On the 341st month from 60 cents July will be 343 months which is 7 x 49 and important for big break. August will be 120 months from 1939 low. Also important.

June 1940 will be 203 months from 1932 low. Note 202-1/2 is 180 plus 22-1/2 making this very important for a change in trend.

1940 December. The 45° angle moving up from zero crosses at 5050 in May 1949 and, of course, hits this angle. 4850 in May 1949 will be on the 45° angle from 4855 high making 4850 a resistance point.

1949 October Eggs for delivery in 1949. The low of this option was 4485 on November 1, 1948. In the first cycle of the second square on 165°. This gives 4845 at the same degree or 360 points added to 4485. Next we had 180 or half the cycle and this gives 5025 as a strong resistance level. Note that 5040 is 14 x 360 or 2 cycles in the second square of 360, and that 5010 is on the 45° angle from 60 cents, and the price of 4995 is on the same angle of 315° from 1035, the extreme low or 11 cycles over.

When using these Master Charts always consider the time periods from minor tops and bottoms and the geometrical angles on the daily high and low chart. In this way you will get many resistance levels at the same price which will indicate the culmination at extreme high and extreme low prices. You will benefit by going over previous high and low prices and checking them in connection with the Master Chart.

W. D. GANN

OCTOBER EGGS

TREND INDICATIONS ON DAILY HIGH AND LOW CHART

From April 18, when the low was 4795, the trend has been up. The 45 degree angle and the 4 by I January 24 top crossed at 4960 on May 10, a support point. We covered shorts and bought at 4990 on May 11 because the market did not go down the third day.

May 16, the 45 degree angle from April 18 crosses at 4995. On May 17 it crosses at 5005, May 18 5015, May 19 5025, and May 20 5035.

While the main trend is up we advise selling short Monday, May 16, for the following reasons: The last extreme high was 5855, and the last extreme low 43 cents. One-half of this is 5077, making this a selling point for reaction. The last extreme low in 1932 was 1275. Four times this is 51 cents, and the fourth time is always important. October eggs should not close above 51 cents before having a greater reaction than they have had for some time.

From 4795 on April 18 to May 13 high of 5065 is an advance of 270 points, which equals 270 degrees or 3/4 of a circle.

From the last low on March 16 there have been four two-day reactions, and the market is up nearly 400 points. This is another reason for selling. The time the market makes lower bottoms for the second consecutive day, it will indicate a minor change in trend.

From February 8 low 4560, not one two-day or more reaction bottom has been broken. Every one has been higher. Therefore, the first time the low of a two-day swing reaction has been broken, it will indicate lower prices and a change in trend.

Starting from 0, 5040 is the end of the 14th cycle of 360 degrees and should prices decline to 5010 they will be 30 points back into the cycle which will be an indication for lower prices, especially if prices close under this level, or near it.

The angle of 1 by 2 moving up from the low of May 10 will be at 5040 on May 16, and the angle of 1 by 4 from December 6 will cross at 5040 on May 16. Should the market close under 5040 on May 16, it will be another indication for lower prices.

From the low of March 16 to May 16 will be 61 calendar days, and May 16 will be 67 market days from February 8. The angle of 2 by 1 which moves up 5 points a day will reach 4920 on May 20. This is the last support angle which the price has rested on two times in the past.

May 19 will be 45 market days from March 16 and 70 market days from February 8, making these periods important for change in trend.

OCTOBER EGGS

WEEKLY HIGH AND LOW CHART

The main trend is up. The 45 degree angle from February 8 will cross at 4980 on May 17, which is 14 weeks or 7 day periods from February 8. As long as the market holds above this angle it is in position to rally. Breaking it and closing under it will turn the minor trend down.

The low of the past two weeks was 4955 and 4960. Breaking these lows will indicate much lower.

MONTHLY HIGH AND LOW CHART

The main trend is up on the Monthly Chart. The 45 degree angle will be down from 5855 and 5370 has been crossed by the price showing up trend. The 45 degree angle moving up from 0 in December 1940, which is the end of a cycle, reaches 5050 in May, making this a resistance level and selling level. The 45 degree angle from 60 cents, the extreme high, to where the 45 degree from August 1939, the last low at 13 cents, moves up to 60 cents and then moves down, crossing at 5050 in May 1949. The fact that two angles cross at 5050 and at 5077 is the average half way point or gravity centre between 5855 and 43 cents makes October eggs a short sale not to close at 51 cents before a reaction.

The supporting angle on the Monthly Chart moving up from 4385, the low in 1948, crosses at 4800 in May 1949, and the 45 degree angle moving down from 5855 crosses at 4850 in May, making this a support level.

In 1941, February, low 1860. The 45 degree angle moving up from 0 crosses at 4950 in May 1949. Breaking this angle indicates 4850 to 4800.

1949, June 4 and 11 will be 90-91 weeks from September 10, 1947. This 1-3/4 years or 270 degrees and is a resistance level.

From December 28, 1920, high 60 cents, to December 28, 1947, was 324 months, the square of 18. 342½ months is one-half between the square of 18 and the square of 19. July 13, 1949 will be 342½ months from December 28, 1920. July 28, 1949 will be 343 months from December 28, 1920. 343 is 7 times 49. This indicates that the market can break fast in the month of July.

1949, July 10, is 22 months from September 10, 1947 and July 25 will be 22½ months from September 10, 1947.

1948, June 17, high 5370. 1949, June 17, will be 12 months or 1 year, important for a change in trend.

1936, November, high. May, 1949, 150 months, or 12½ years.

1945, October and November high since May 1949, 42 months, or one-half of 84 months, a 7 year cycle.

OCTOBER EGGS

1946, November, low. May, 1949, 30 months, or 2½ years.

1947, November, low 43 cents, to May, 1949, 18 months, or 1½ years. All of these time periods indicate October Eggs are reaching time cycles for an important change in trend.

W.D. GANN

NINE MATHEMATICAL POINTS FOR PRICE CULMINATIONS

1. Resistance levels made by market fluctuations.

2. Natural resistance levels in the squares and 360 degree circle.

3. Geometrical angles.

4. Time cycles and time periods.

5. Squaring out price with time from tops and bottoms.

6. Odd and even squares and the half-way points between both odd and even squares.

7. Weekly high and low charts, angles that form on it.

8. Monthly high and low charts, angles that form from tops and bottoms.

9. Natural time cycles based on the 360 degree master chart.

Of the above the most important is the geometrical angle, because they measure time with price, and show when the market is overbalanced on the up or down side.

There are 9 digits which equal 45, another reason why the 45 degree angle is so important.

We use 9 angles to measure time. The 45 degree angle is the balance, or gravity center (See chart enclosed). There are three important angles to the left of the 45 degree angle and three to the right. The 1 by 3 angle to the left and the 3 by 1 to the right.

SQUARE OF 45

Study this chart. Note A, B, C, D, E, F, G, H and I are the strongest resistance points as proven by the angles which measure price and time.

MEASURING TIME

Man first learned to record and measure time by the use of the sun dial, and by dividing the day into 24 hours of 15 degrees in longitude. The reflection of the geometrical angle on the sun dial indicated the time of day. Since all time is measured by the sun, we must use the 360 degree circle to measure time periods for the market, but remember you must always begin to count time in days, weeks and months from the extreme high and extreme low levels, and not from exact seasonal or calendar time periods. 45 days is 1/8 of a year. 90 degrees is 1/4 of a year, or a square, 112½ days is 90 plus 22½, 120 is 1/3 of a circle and a triangle. 135 is 90 plus 45, and 150 is 90 plus 60, 157½ is 135 plus 22½, 165 is 120 plus 45. 180 is 1/2 of a circle, or opposite to 0, the starting point. Very important for change in trend. 202½ is 180 plus

22½. 225, a 45 degree angle is 180 plus 45. 240 a triangle, is 2 times 120. 247½ is 225 plus 22½. 270 is 3/4 of a circle and 3 squares of 90. 292½ is 270 plus 22½. 315 is 270 plus 45. 337½ is 315 plus 22½ and 360 degrees is the complete circle. You measure weekly and monthly time periods in the same way as you do the days and watch all of these important time angles for changes in trend.

You can make up a square of 52 for time and price. If you want to use eggs at 10 points per day, the top of the first line would be 520 price, the second 1040, the third 1560, and the top of the 10th line would be 5200, the top of the 11th line would be 5720.

Because 1 year, or 365¼ days, represents one round trip or cycle in which the sun covers 360 degrees, makes it very important to watch for change in trend at the end of each 12 months period from any important top and bottom.

The year must be divided by 8, which gives 6½ weeks, 13 weeks, 18½ weeks, 26 weeks, 32½ weeks, 39 weeks, 45½ weeks and 52 weeks. Divide the year by 3 gives 17 weeks and 35 weeks.

May 14, 1949   W.D. GANN

RESISTANCE LEVELS FOR PRICE

This chart shows a circle of 360 degrees and a price of 60 cents for eggs divided into 8 equal parts, marked in red. 7½ cents is a 45 degree angle, or 1/8. 15 cents is a 90 degree angle, or ¼. 22½ cents is 135 degree angle, or 3/8. 30 cents is 180 degree angle, or ½. 3750 is a 225 degree angle, or 5/8. 45 cents is 270 degree angle, or 3/4. 5250 is a 315 degree angle, or 7/8 of a circle. 60 cents represents the complete circle. We next take 1275 from 60 cents and get a range of 4725. This is marked in green in the same way as the resistance levels for 60 cents in price.

You will note that 1/3, or 120 degrees is 20 cents and 2/3 or 240 degrees is 40 cents. The range between 43 cents and 5855 is also marked on this chart. This will help you to understand how resistance levels and price work out together. You will note the time periods required to square the high and low prices.

At 50 points per month it requires 120 months to square the high price of 60 cents per dozen.

From December 28,1920 to December 28, 1930 is the end of the first square, or cycle, on the monthly chart. The second square in time ends December 28, 1940, and the third square ends December 28, 1950, making 1950 the year for a big decline in eggs.

From the low of 1275 it requires 25½ months to square the price. These periods run out as follows:

1935,   March 15, end of first square.

1937,   April 30, end of second square.

1939,   June 15, end of third square.

1941,   July 30, end of fourth square.

1943,   September 15, end of fifth square.

1945,   October 30, end of sixth square.

1947,   December 15, end of seventh square.

Remember that 7 is always fatal, and that extreme highs and extreme lows in rapid advances and declines occur in this time period. 1947, September 10, high, 5855. This was 90 days before the end of the square. In November the price of eggs declined to 43 cents, the lowest they have sold up to this writing.

1950,   January 30, 8th square of 1275. The 8th square is also important for smashes and declines.

1920,   December 28, high 60 cents, to January 30, 1933, low, 1275, time 157 months. 157½, is the half way point between 135 and 180. Therefore, this low level occurred on an exact angle and mathematical point.

The range of 4725 between extreme high and extreme low at 50 points per month requires 94½ months to square the price range.

1933,   January 30 to December 15, 1940, first square of the range when the cycle ended and prices started up.

1948,   October 30, second square of range in time.

1949,   May 30, is 7 months in the third square of the range.

1949,   May 30 is 340 months from December 28, 1920 and July 28, will be 341 months, or 7 times 49.

1933,   January 30 to May 30, 1949, 196 months. This is the square of 14.

1949,   May 15 is 5964 days. Divide this by 7 to get 7 day periods. This gives 852 weeks to May 15, 1949.

Note that 851 is the square of 29. Therefore this time period is 11 weeks in the square of 30. 1/8 of 59, the difference between the square of 29 and the square of 30, is 7-3/8. Therefore, 82 weeks is moving into the 90 degree period, or 1/4 of the square between 29 and 30.

EXTREME LOW PRICES

Time required to square this at 30 points per week is 42½ weeks. Twenty times 42½ weeks gives 850 weeks.

May 1st, 1949 was 850 weeks, or the 20th square of 1275. May 15, 1949 will be two weeks of the 7 day period from the 21st square of 1275.

(See Resistance Card on October Eggs).

360 DEGREE MASTER CIRCLE CHART FOR EGGS

This chart shows every 5 degrees starting with 0 degrees and moving to 360. 12 cycles end at 4320, 13 cycles at 4680, 14 cycles at 5040, 15 cycles at 5400, 16 cycles at 5760, 17 cycles at 6120. The minimum fluctuation on eggs is 5 points. Use this chart to get the exact number of degrees from any bottom to another bottom, or from any top to another top and from any top to a bottom. Study the outlines and study all past market movements based on price and time as indicated by these charts and the rules, and you will soon learn the working of the mathematical law that determines market movements.

May 14, 1949   W.D. GANN

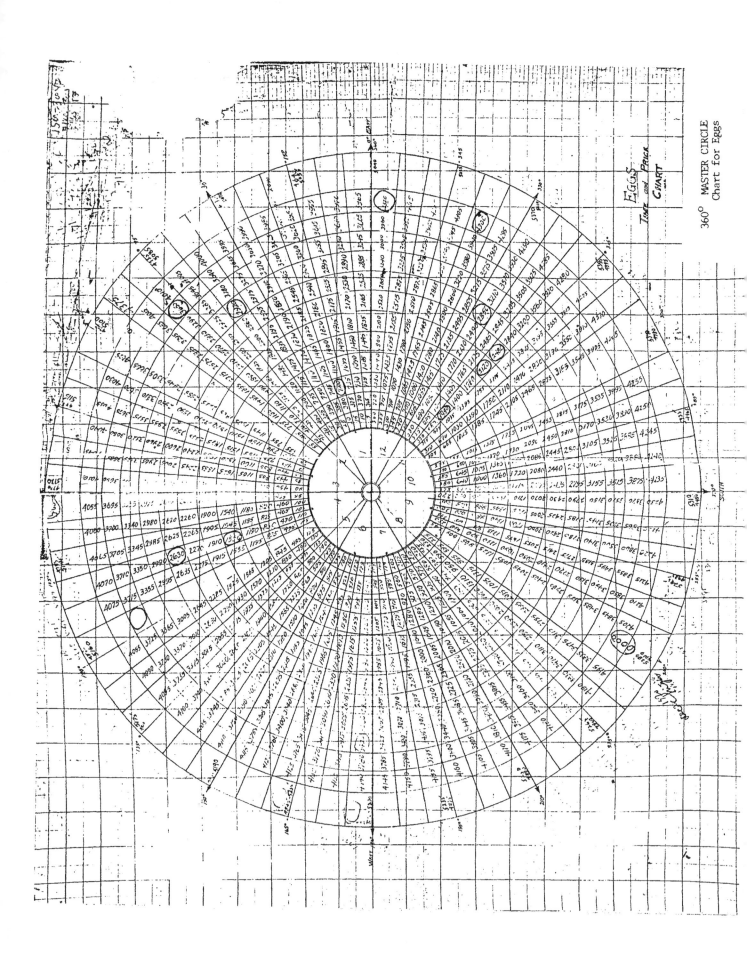

EGGS

360° MASTER CIRCLE
Chart for Eggs

TIME and PRICE CHART

—250—

EGGS

HOW TO DETERMINE CULMINATIONS
AND CHANGES IN TREND

The big money is made in Eggs by following the main trend or big swings and not changing position or taking profits until the market shows by its own action that the trend has changed. If you will follow the rules, the market will tell you when the main or minor trend changes. Do not guess or trade on hope or fear. Give the market time to show a change in trend.

The activity and range in prices at high or low levels determine the change in trend according to whether the market is normal or abnormal. Abnormal prices and fluctuations occur during wars or after wars. The years when supply is very large or very small cause abnormal moves which run to extremes. You must never try to guess when tops or bottoms will be reached in abnormal markets as they will nearly always run longer than human reason or known facts would lead you to believe. That is why you must apply rules and wait for the market's action to show a definite change in trend.

FIVE RULES

RULE 1 – TRADING ON TREND LINE INDICATIONS ONLY

You will make the most money by following Trend Line indications and by buying and selling on Trend Line indications and placing stop loss orders below Trend Line bottoms or above Trend Line tops and not taking profits until your stops are caught or the Trend Line reverses.

How to Keep the Trend Line on your charts: When the market starts advancing, making higher bottoms and higher tops, you move the Green Trend Line up to each day's high. As long as the market continues to make higher bottoms and higher tops, the Trend Line moves on up. The first day that the market reverses and makes a lower bottom than a previous day by 10 to 20 points, you move the Trend Line down to the low of that day; then as long as the market makes lower bottoms, the Trend Line continues to move down to the low of each day. After that, when the market makes a higher bottom by 10 to 20 points, you start moving the Trend Line up to the top of each day again.

When the market makes double or triple tops according to Trend Line movements, you can sell against the double tops with a stop 20 to 50 points above the top, but reverse position and go long when the price crosses double or triple Trend Line tops. Reverse this rule in a Bear Market - buy against double or triple Trend Line bottoms with a stop 20 to 50 points under the Trend Line bottoms. If stop is caught, reverse position and go short.

You can make more money with this rule than in any other way because you will always be with the trend. However, applying other rules will of course help you to determine objectives or resistance levels.

Never consider that the main trend has changed to the downside as long as Trend Line bottoms are higher. Never consider that the market has changed to uptrend until Trend Line tops are crossed and of course Trend Line bottoms are higher.

Study and apply Rule 1 and prove to yourself its value and follow it and you will make success.

RULE 2 – TIME RULE

The TIME FACTOR is the most important. When TIME is up. Time and Space movements will reverse.

Keep a record of the days that the market reacts, that is, actual trading days; also keep a record of the calendar days of each reaction or rally. When a reversal comes that exceeds the previous TIME movement, consider that the trend has changed, at least temporarily. After any important top or bottom is reached and the first reaction or rally comes, there is nearly always a secondary move which usually makes a slightly higher bottom or a lower top. The duration of this move may be 1, 2, 3 days or more, all depending upon the activity of the market and the duration of the advance or the decline. But your rule is to watch for an overbalancing of a previous TIME period before deciding that the trend has changed.

RULE 3 – SWING BOTTOMS AND TOPS

When a market advances, it continues to make higher bottoms and higher tops on the main swings. You must watch all of these reactions or bottoms, then the first time a SWING BOTTOM is broken, whether it be for 1, 2, 3 days or more, consider that the trend has changed and go with it.

When a market is declining, it continues to make lower bottoms and lower tops. Therefore, when the last SWING TOP is crossed, it indicates a change in trend.

RULE 4 – SPACE OR PRICE MOVEMENTS

By SPACE MOVEMENTS, I mean price movements up or down from top to bottom. For example: Suppose Eggs start to advance for 20¢, reach 22¢, then react to 21.50, advance to 23.50, react to 23¢, making several moves of 50 points, then react 75 to 100 points, they have exceeded the previous PRICE reaction. We call this "overbalancing" of SPACE or PRICE movement and an indication of a change in trend. But you must never depend upon a reversal in PRICE MOVEMENT alone to give a definite indication of a change in trend but depend upon overbalancing of a previous TIME PERIOD, the breaking of a 3-day bottom or of the last SWING BOTTOM. TIME is always most important and when the main trend is ready to change, a reversal in TIME gives a definite indication of a change in the main trend.

RULE 5 – RESISTANCE LEVELS

When the price breaks back one-half or more of the previous SWING, this is also an indication of a change in trend. In a declining market, a rally of one-half or 50% or more of a SWING is the first indication of a change in trend. But these indications must be confirmed by the TIME RULE before you can be sure that there is a definite change in trend.

A review and study of past market movements will prove to you the accuracy and value of these rules.

Study the examples and comparisons of the various campaigns.

AVERAGE SPACE MOVEMENT

As a general rule, Eggs will not react or decline more than 30 to 50 points and in extreme cases not more than 100 points before the advance is resumed. As a rule, after a prolonged advance or decline, a reverse move of 100 points or more will show a charge in trend when confirmed by the TIME RULE.

When a market is declining and very weak, the average rally is 30 to 50 points, and seldom more than 100 points. In extremely weak markets, rallies may not run more than 20 to 30 points, all depending upon whether prices are at normal or abnormal levels.

April 23, 1947

W. D. GANN

RULES FOR EGGS

RULE 1 - BUYING AT DOUBLE OR TRIPLE BOTTOMS

Buy against double or triple bottoms and protect with stop loss order 10, 20, or 30 points away according to the price and activity. When an option makes the same price level a few days apart, it makes what we call a double bottom on the Trend indicator. A triple bottom is when an option makes bottom around the same level of prices the third time. A second or third bottom can be slightly higher or lower than the previous bottom, but remember this rule:

When you buy at the time an option reaches the third bottom, you should never risk more than 10 points, for when the third bottom is broken, especially if this bottom is around the same level, and your stop is caught, it will indicate that the main trend has changed and you should double up and go short.

Always reverse position when the trend changes. If you are long of the market and your stop is caught, you must go short. If you are short of the market and the trend changes and your stop is caught, you must go long or buy an equal amount.

The safest buying point is when an option makes a triple bottom near the same level, protected with a stop loss order not more than 10 points under the lowest level of the triple bottom.

RULE 2 - SELLING AT DOUBLE OR TRIPLE TOPS

This rule is just the reverse of Rule 1. Sell against double or triple tops with stop loss order 10, 20, or 30 points above the top, but on a third top never use more than a 10 point stop loss order because, as a general rule, when an option reaches the same price level the fourth time, it goes thru and goes higher. Therefore, it is always a sure indication when it goes above the third top, you can buy it for higher prices.

The safest selling point is when an option makes a triple top near the same level, protected with a stop loss order not more than 10 points above the highest level of the triple top.

RULE 3 - 7 TO 10 DAY RULE FOR AN ACTIVE, FAST-MOVING MARKET

When an option of eggs is very active, declining fast and making lower tops and lower bottoms each day, after it has declined 7 days or more, you should make your stop loss orders 10 points above each day's top, and when your stops are caught, reverse position and buy, placing stop loss order 10 points under the previous day's bottom.

When an option is very active and advancing fast, after it has advanced 7 to 10 days or more without breaking a previous day's bottom, you should follow your purchase up with a stop loss order 10 points under each day's low until the stop is caught. Then reverse and go short, placing a stop loss order 10 points above the previous day's top.

But do not consider that the main trend has changed up or down until an option crosses a Trend Line top or breaks under the last Trend Line bottom.

RULE 4 - SIGNAL BOTTOM DAY
On the day that an option has a sharp break after a prolonged decline, it closes higher than the opening or above the halfway point or better still if it closes at the extreme high, after making a wide range and going lower than the previous day, it is an indication that the buying is better than the selling and that the trend is getting ready to turn up or that a bigger rally may be expected. Therefore, you should cover shorts and buy without waiting for the option to make a higher top than a previous day or without waiting until the trend turns up by crossing a Trend Line top.

TABLES FOR SQUARES 144
FOR EGG PRICES

In using the square of 12 and its multiples time and prices come out accurately because the multiples of 9, the highest digit, work in harmony with 12's. These are the two most important figures for measuring time and price and for getting the natural squares and resistance levels. There are 12 months in a year and 12 signs which makes the combination of 9 and 12 work to precision when you use the proper time periods from high and low prices.

The table below gives the number of times 144 but you can use 1/2 of 144 which is 72, 1/4 which is 36, 1/8 which is 18, and 1/16 which is 9, added to any of these figures or subtracted from them. You can also add or subtract these proportionate units of time and price to any price or to any time period. All of which is shown on the MASTER SQUARE of 144.

1	x	144	=	144		24	x	144	=	3456
2	x	"	=	288		25	x	"	=	3600
3	x	"	=	432		26	x	"	=	3744
4	x	"	=	576		27	x	"	=	3888
5	x	"	=	720		28	x	"	=	4032
6	x	"	=	864		29	x	"	=	4176
7	x	"	=	1008		30	x	"	=	4320
8	x	"	=	1152		31	x	"	=	4464
9	x	"	=	1296		32	x	"	=	4608
10	x	"	=	1440		33	x	"	=	4752
11	x	"	=	1584		34	x	"	=	4896
12	x	"	=	1728		35	x	"	=	5040
13	x	"	=	1872		36	x	"	=	5184
14	x	"	=	2016		37	x	"	=	5328
15	x	"	=	2160		38	x	"	=	5472
16	x	"	=	2304		39	x	"	=	5616
17	x	"	=	2488		40	x	"	=	5760
18	x	"	=	2592		41	x	"	=	5904
19	x	"	=	2736		42	x	"	=	6048
20	x	"	=	2880		43	x	"	=	6192
21	x	"	=	3024		44	x	"	=	6336
22	x	"	=	3168		45	x	"	=	6408
23	x	"	=	3312		46	x	"	=	6480

Twenty-four times 144 is 3456 and 25 x 144 is 3600. One-half between these is 3528. If you add 18 you get 3546. Add another 18 gives 3564. Add 18 again gives 3582. This is the way you get the different resistance points for price levels of eggs.

January 19, 1952

THE MASTER SQUARE FOR PRICE AND TIME TRENDS ON EGGS

The proper relation of time with price in the squares from highs and lows is very important for determining buying and selling levels. This Master Square begins at 0 where the heavy red line runs straight across and each square ends at 360 where it is marked EAST and MARCH 20 on the chart. This price and time scale starts with the even squares. The first square of 2 is 4 and the square of 4 equals 16, and so on through. Each square is in a different color so that you can see where one square ends and the next one starts from 360. We use March 20, the beginning of the spring season for a starting point instead of January 1, the starting of the calendar year, because prices and time work out more accurately to the seasonal trend.

The price on eggs is in units of 5 points which is the minimum fluctuation. At the end of the square of 4, the price is 80. At the end of the square of 14, which equals 196, the price is 980. For the lowest price on eggs, 10-3/8, we use 1040 as closest even figure. This is in the square of 15, at 208 time period, which is 12 spaces or periods in the square of 15, but because we use the even squares the price is working around to the square of 16, which ends at 256, on time.

The odd squares end 5 points above 180 degrees, and they are marked in circles with different colors. In order that you see the ending of the odd squares. The square of 3 is 9 and the ending of the square of 35 is 1225. All prices from 180 to 380 are in the even squares and all prices from zero to 180 are in the odd squares.

During the past 33 years there has been 49 important high and low levels. 21 of these have occurred in the odd squares, and 28 in the even squares.

The small figures below the price in the square are the time periods in days, weeks and months running from zero and show the total number of fluctuations from zero to any price.

Example: 1040 is 208 spaces from zero, and 5 x 208 is 1040.

October eggs, lowest price 1500, time period 300. Highest price 5855, Time period 1171 or a gain of 871 price periods of 5 points each, and 871 Time periods from 1500. 871 is in the square of 30 and is on a 90 degree angle at 270, December 21, making this a resistance level because 871 is 3/4 of the square of 30, the same as 270 is 3/4 of 360.

Beginning with the square at 1500, the lowest price for October eggs, the highest price of 5855 comes out in the square of 30 at 871, but starting the square at zero, 5855 comes out in the square of 36, which ends at 1296, and 5855 is at 1161 in the square of 35, and 15 points below the 45 degree angle at May 5.

The important angles used are 22½ degrees, 45 degrees, 90 degrees and 180. There are 8, 45 degree angles in the complete circle or square, and 16 angles of 22½ degrees. The most important angles are 45 degrees, 90 and 180. These are natural angles in the circle of 360 degrees and show the natural time and price resistance levels in the natural squares starting from zero.

The time periods used are the seasonal periods starting with the spring season, March 20, and the mid-spring season ends May 5, where the 45 degree angle in red is shown. April 22 is 22½ degrees or 1/2 of a 45 degree angle and comes on the time period from March 20. May 27, is 67½ degrees and is nearest to the beginning to the summer season. June 21 starts summer where 90 degrees is shown and July 14 is at 112½ degrees or 22½ degrees from June 21.

August 5 is mid-summer and this is a 45 degree angle. 135 degrees from March 20. This is 3/8 of the year and 3/8 of a circle. August 31 is 157½ degrees and is an angle of 22½ degrees and is 1/2 from August 5, to September 21.

September 21 starts the fall season and is 180 degrees from March 20. This is 1/2 of the year and 1/2 of a circle, and square.

October 16 is at 202½ degrees which is an angle of 22½ degrees and is 1/2 from September 21.

November 8 is 225 degrees, a 45 degree angle and the middle of the fall season which is 5/8 of a year and 5/8 of a circle.

November 30, is 247½ degrees which is an angle of 22½ degrees and is 180 degrees from May 27.

December 21 is 270 where the winter season begins. This is 3/4 of the year and 3/4 of a circle.

January 13 is 292½ degrees, a 22½ degree angle and is 1/2 from December 21 to February 4.

February 4 is at 315 degrees, a 45 degree angle and is mid-winter season and 7/8 of a year.

February 28 is 337½ degrees and an angle of 22½ degrees and is 1/2 from February 4 to March 20 and March 20 completes the circle of 360 degrees and 365 calendar days.

BASIC PRICE FOR EGGS

Before future trading started in 1920, the price for case eggs in New York and Chicago, was a base price of 12¢ a dozen which was the lowest price over a long period of years. In 1880, low 14½¢, 1888 high 32½¢. 1896 low 12¢, 1897 low 7¢, 1899 high 20¢. 1900 low 12¢, 1919 high 73¢.

The low price of 7¢ was in the square of 12 at 45, within 3 of 144 and within 70 points of 72, which is the end of the square of 12 and at the angle of 270, 3/4 of the square of 16 and in time 3/4 of a year. This was a natural resistance level. In 1921, in the month of January, the January option sold at 64¢, the highest price any future ever sold. This was in the square of 36, and just 5 points above the 45 degree angle at February 4, which is 7/8 of a circle and square and a natural resistance level.

1931, in the month of January, the January option of eggs sold at 10-3/8, the lowest price in history. The price of 1040 is on an angle of 67½ degrees at the date, May 27. The price was at 208 time period from zero in the odd square of 15 and 15 points from the 90 degree angle.

The October option on May 28, 1932 sold at 1500 which was its lowest price. This was 5 points above the 45 degree angle at 225, November 8. This was 5/8 of a circle and square and a natural resistance level.

1947, September 10, October eggs highest 5855. This was in the square of 36 but the price was in the square of 15 at 1171, and 15 points from 45 degree angle, May 5, and only 10 points from the 45 degree angle from the low of 1500. This was 180 degrees or opposite a natural selling level.

After the high of 5855, the next extreme low of 3225. On October 2, 3225 was within 25 points of 1/2 of 64¢, the highest level, and 3225 is on the angle of 247½ degrees at November 30. This is a 22½ degree angle and the price of 3225 was on the 45 degree angle from 1200. Note that 3225 is in the square of 26 at 685, and this is 75 less than 2 square of 380. Also, 3225 is on the 45 degree angle from 10-3/8, making this a strong support and buying level.

The time periods must be kept up for days weeks and months from each high and low price in order to determine future buying and selling levels. Below are the high and low levels and the position in the squares showing why prices stopped at these levels.

1037 is in the square of 15, at 208 on the angle of 67½ degrees.

1200 is in the square of 16, at 240 and 5 points from the 90 degree angle.

1275 is in the square of 16, 5 points from the end of the square of 16 and is on 250 time period.

1300 is on the 22½ degree angle, April 13.

1500 is in the square of 18 on the 45 degree angle.

1600 is in the square of 18 at 320 at 347½ degree angle, February 28.

1750 is in the square of 19 at 350 and 10 points from the angle of 112 degrees.

1875 is in the square of 20 at 375 and 10 points from 247½ degrees.

1950 is in the square of 20 at 390 on the 45 degree angle which is 315, February 4.

2100 is in the square of 22 at 420, 5 points from the 90 degree angle.

2300 is in the square of 22, at 460, 10 points from 247½ degrees.

2385 is in the square of 22 at 476, 10 points above the 45 degree angle at 315.

2425 is in the square of 24, at 485, and is 5 points from zero, March 2.

2550 is in the square of 24 at 510, 15 points from 112½ degrees July 1.

2625 is in the square of 24, at 525, on 157½ degrees.

2700 is in the square of 24, at 540, 10 points from the 45 degree angle November 8.

2750 is in the square of 24, at 550, 10 points from 247½ degrees.

2950 is in the square of 26, at 590, 5 points from 45 degree angle, May.

3075 is in the square of 26, at 615, 5 points from 45 degree angle, August.

3160 is in the square of 26, at 632, 5 points from 202½ degrees.

3225 is in the square of 26, at 645, 6 points from 247½ degrees, November 30.

3350 is in the square of 26, at 670 on 337½ degrees at Feb. 28.

3400 is in the square of 28, at 680 at 1/2 between the zero angle and 22½ degrees, April 12.

3700 is in the square of 28, at 740, 1/2 between 202½ and the 45 degree angle, November 8.

3860 is in the square of 28, at 772, and 5 points above the 45 degree angle, February 4.

4125 is in the square of 30 at 825, and 1/2 between 112½ degrees and 45 degrees, August 5.

4225 is in the square of 30 at 845, 15 points from 180 degrees, Sept. 21.

4300 is in the square of 30 at 860, 15 points from 45 degree angle, November.

4375 is in the square of 30 at 875 and 1/2 between the 90 degree angle and 292½, January 13.

4400 is in the square of 30, at 880, and 5 points from 222½.

4450 is in the square of 30, at 690, 15 points from 337½, February 28.

4550 is in the square of 32, at 910, and 10 points from 22½ degree angle, April 12.

4600 is in the square of 32, at 920, 1/2 between the 45 degree angle and 67½ degrees May 27, and on the 45 degree angle from 1040 low.

4650 is in the square of 32 at 930, 5 points from the 90 degree angle, June 21.

4675 is in the square of 32 at 935, 5 points from 45 degree angle from 104 and 1/2 between 90 degrees and 112½ degrees.

4700 is in the square of 32 at 940, on 112½ degrees, July 14.

4720 is in the square of 32, at 944, 15 points from 45 degree angle, August. 5.

4760 is the square of 32, at 950, 15 points from 45 degree angle.

5000 in the square of 32, at 1,000, 5 points from 292½ degrees, Jan. 12.

5065 in the square of 32, at 1015, and 1/2 from 45 degrees and 337½, Feb. 23.

5170 in the-square of 34, at 1035, 10 points from 22½ degrees, April 12, and on the 45 degree angle, from 3225.

5375 is in the square of 34, at 1075, 5 points from 45 degree angle, Aug. 8.

5440 is in the square of 34, at 1088, 10 points from 180 degrees, Sept 21, and 5 points from the square of 33.

5475 is in the square of 34, at 1095, 10 points from 45 degree angle, from 3225.

5600 is in the square of 34 at 1120, 5 points from 45 degree angle and on the 45 degree angle from 1600.

5675 is in the square of 34 at 1135, and 15 points from 292½, Jan. 13.

5865 is in the square of 36 at 1171, and 15 points from 45 degree angle, May 5.

6400 is in the square of 36, at 1280, and 5 points from 45 degree angle, February 4.

1921 January 14, high 6600 in square 37 at 1/2 between 45 at 67½ degrees, Time 1320.

From 1920 to 1953 a period of 33 years, there was a total of 49 important tops and bottoms. 21, of these occurred on the 45 degree angle and 24 on the angles of 22½ degrees, and 4 on the angles of 90 and 180 degrees, and at no time did the price vary more than 15 points from an actual, natural angle.

This is the proof of what can be done working with mathematics.

WHY PRICES MOVE FASTER AT HIGH LEVELS

Prices move faster at high levels because the squares are greater and the distance between the angles are wider and prices move a greater distance in the shorter period of time.

Example: 1040 low, 1 square, or round trip to 1350 is 310 points, and from 90 degrees to a 45 degree angle is 35 points. From 1600 to 1950 a complete square is 350 points. From 3075 to 3595 the square or round trip is 520 points, and 45 degrees equals 60 points, between the angle.

From 3225 to 3755 a complete square is 530 points.

From 3720 to 4280 is a gain of 560 points to complete a round trip.

From 4550 to 5170 is 620 points. This makes 85 points between zero and the 45 degree angle and shows why prices can move so fast.

From 5780 which is the end of the square of 34 to the next 45 degree angle is 90 points.

From 5700 to 6400, a round trip is 700 points and to move 45 degrees requires 80 points.
1952, Dec. 9, October eggs low 4375. To complete the square or round trip, ends at 4985, a gain of 620 points, which equals 360 degrees, and 4375 to 5190 is a gain of 795 points and at 1 degree for 5 points equals a gain of 159 degrees, and from 4955 to 5170 is 185 points more than the square and 5140 is 90 above the end of the square and 5170 is 105 more than a round trip.

Also, 5170 is 25 points less than a round trip or complete square from 5855.
From 5855 high to 3225 low was a decline of 4½ squares and 3225 was exactly on the 22½ degree angle from 247½, November 30.

WHY WAS OCTOBER EGGS HIGH AT 5065 JULY 12, 1952?
5065 is just 5 points above 180 degree angle from 3225, and exactly 180 degrees from 2750 low. When October eggs sold at 3960, Oct. 15, 1952, they were on the angle of 180 degrees at 3225, and on the 45 degree angle from 5065 the highest price. At 3860 it was on the 90 degree angle from 3400 and just above the 45 degree angle from 5675.
1952, Dec. 9, October eggs low, 4375 on the 90 degree angle from 1040 and on the 45 degree angle from 1950. Also, on the 45 degree angle from 270, this was on the inner square and in the square of 36.

HIGH AND LOW PRICES ON THE INNER SQUARE
1050, 4375, 3350, 3400, 4650, 4625, 2625, 3160, 3225.
From 3360 to 5170 was a gain of 1310 points. This was 2 squares and 56½ degrees over.

1920	September	21	high	5175	to	March	21, 1953.	Time	390	months
1921	January	17	high	6400	to	March	17, 1953.	"	386	"
1931	January	30	low	1040	to	March	30, 1953.	"	266	"
1932	May	28	low	1500	to	March	28, 1953.	"	250	"
1933	March	2	low	1512	to	April	2, 1953.	"	241	"
1933	December	21	low	1300	to	March	21, 1953.	"	231	"

YEARS	MONTHS	WEEKS	DAYS	HIGH	LOW	1953
1939, Nov. 6	76	330	2112		3675	Mar. 8
1947, Sept. 10	66	222	2008	5855		Mar. 10
1947, Nov. 1	64	279	1957	4300		Mar. 1
1948, June 14	57	248	1734	5375		Mar. 14
1948, Sept. 20	54	233	1642		4390	Mar. 30
1949, Sept. 10	66	182	1276	6576		Mar. 10
1950, Oct. 2	29	126	885		3225	Mar. 2
1951, Mar. 4	22	96	670	5475		Mar. 4
1951, July 10	20	87	609		4760	Mar. 10
1951, Sept. 4	18	78	547	5470		Mar. 4
1951, Dec. 27	15	65	456	4560		Mar. 27
1952, Feb. 14	13	56	396		4125	Mar. 14
1952, Mar. 31	12	52	366	4400		Mar. 31
1952, May 16	10	43	304		4195	Mar. 16
1952, July 21	8	35	243	5065		Mar. 21
1952, Oct. 16	3	13	90		3860	Mar. 16
1952, Dec. 9	3	13	90		4375	Mar. 9

After you have the time periods, and the high and low dates, you can then get the angles from the time periods and tell when high and low prices will be reached. The following indications are figured from March 10, 1953 when October eggs sold at 5170. For 386 months the time period is on the 45 degree angle at 5135. 266 months is the 90 degree angle 5165. 250 months is the 45 degree angle at 5136. 341 months the 45 degree angle crosses at 5165. For 231 months the 90 degree angle crosses at 5100. For 76 months the 90 degree angle crosses at 5145. For 66 months the 45 degree angle crosses at 5180. For 64 months the 45 degree angle crosses at 5185. For 57 months 45 degree angle crosses at 5180. For 54 months the 45 degree angle crosses at 5150. For 29 months the 45 degree angle crosses at 5110. For 22 months the 45 degree angle crosses at 5135. For 20 months the 90 degree angle crosses at 5135. For 18 months the 22½ degree angle crosses at 5160. For 15 months the 45 degree angle crosses at 8190. For 13 months the 90 degree angle crosses at 5115. For 12 months the 90 degree angle crosses at 5115. For 10 months the 90 degree angle crosses at 5125. For 8 months the 90 degree angle crosses at 5130. For 5 months the 45 degree angle crosses at 5200 and 5125. For 3 months the 90 degree angle crosses at 5120. These angles from the monthly time periods show why the price stops at 5170.

For March 10, 1953.

Below are the angles from the time periods in months, weeks and days.

From Sept. 10, 1947 the 66 months, the 45 deg. angles crosses at 5180 and 5135, and 222 weeks the 90 degree angle crosses at 5145.

From Oct. 2, 1950, the 29th month, the 90 deg. angle crosses at 5110, and from 126 weeks the 22½ deg. angle crosses at 5165, and from 885 days the 90 deg. angle crosses at 5035.

On Feb. 15, 1952, the 12th month, the 90 deg. angle crosses at 5115, and from 56 weeks the 45 deg. angle crosses at 5190, and from 395 days the 45 degree angle crosses at 5130.

May 16, 1952, from 10 months, the 90 deg. angle crosses at 5125, from 43 weeks the 90 deg. angle crosses 5140. From 304 days the 45 deg. angle crosses at 5175.

July 21, 1952, from 5 months the 90 deg. angle crosses at 5125. From 17 weeks the 90 degree angle crosses 5125, and from 121 days 90 degree angle crosses at 5130.

Dec. 9, 1952, from 3 months, 90 deg. angle crosses at 5120 for 13 weeks the 90 deg. angle crosses at 5115 and from 90 days the 45 deg. angle crosses at 5139.

To get future indications, carry forward the dates in months, weeks and days, and analyze the position in the same way outlined above. The more you study and practice with this Master Chart the greater accuracy you will develop and you will appreciate its great value.

March 13, 1953   W. D. GANN

PRICE AND TIME CHART FOR EGGS FUTURES

This chart shows each five points fluctuation which is the minimum for Eggs. Each circle 360 degrees, contains 72 period of 5 degrees, each, or five points on Eggs and Cotton.

The chart is based on the Seasonal Trend, and begins at Mar. 21 any year at zero. And each 15° in longitude is marked and the calendar date shown. There are 24 hours of longitude in each circle of 360°, which represents one revolution of the earth on its axis. This is used on the hourly chart, where we keep the high and low during the day.

It requires 365-1/4 days for the earth to make one complete revolution around the sun and move 360° -- These natural angles and Time periods are based on the earth and Sun's natural position.

In connection with the circle of 360° you should never overlook the fact of the natural squares of numbers. Example: For the first 30 degrees, one degree is the square of one, four is the square of two, nine is the square of three, 16 is the square of 4 and 25 is the square of 5.

From 30 degrees to 60 degrees, the natural squares are: 36 the square of 6, 49 the square of 7.

From 60 degrees to 90 degrees, the natural squares are: 64, the square of 8 and 81 the square of 9.

From 90 degrees to 120, which is from the natural square, to the triangle in the circle, the natural of numbers are: 100, the square of 10.

From 120 to 150, are the following squares: 121, the square of 11, and 144, the square of 12.

From 150 to 180, the squares are as follows: 169, the square of 13.

From 180 to 210, the squares are: 196, the square of 14.

From 210 to 240, the squares are: 225, the square of 15.

From 240 to 270, the squares are: 256, the square of 16, and always very important, for a Time change and price resistance.

From 270 to 300, the squares are: 289, the square of 17.

From 300 to 330, the squares are: 324, the square of 18.

From 330 to 360, the squares are: 2500, which is the square of 50. Also, in this 30 degree zone, the square of 60 is 3600, and is 30°, or at the end of the sign, and at the end of the circle of 360°.

You can carry the natural squares on around the circle. For example: The square of 20 is 400, which is 40 more than 360. Therefore, it would be at 40 degrees from zero.

The 45, 90, 135, 180, 225, 270, 315 and 360 degree angles

The triangles of 120° and 240° are shown.

Also the 60° and 300°. And, the other angles of 15° and 30° and their multiples are shown in black lines or angles. All time periods are shown in black ink.

Most all the important highs and lows on Eggs, are shown on this chart. The low prices have a red circle around them. The high prices have a green circle around them.

This will enable you to see when the price is at the same longitude of the previous high and low price, or when the price is 90, 120, 180 and so forth, from the previous high and low price.

Example: 1,500 was the lowest price October Eggs ever sold. This was May 28, 1932, and the longitude of the price was 60° – and the date was May 21st. This means that the price occurred 7 days from the natural angle. Follow the line out and you can see when the price is in this same zone and on the same angle. 4740, 5100, 5460, 5820, 6180 and 6540 are on this same angle. When October Eggs sold at 4375 on Dec. 9th, 1952 they were within 5 points, or 5° of 1500, and in the 9th circle or zone from 1500.

When October Eggs sold at 5275, on April 13th and April 17th 1953, they were 180° from 4375, and within 5 points or 5° of 180° from 1500. Compare the high prices and other low prices in the same way against previous high and low prices.

1/4 of the circle is 90° – 1/3 is 120° and 1/2 is 180°. When Oct. Eggs sold at 5275, on April 17th, they were 2 circles of 360° and 1/2 or 180 over, from the low of 4375. The opposition of the 180° is the strongest resistance points, and that is why heavy selling took place at 5275 and caused prices to react. Note the 5275 is within 5° of November 22nd, the triangle point of 240, therefore, the price was ahead of time. To be on Time, any around April 30th, 1953, the price would have to be at 5075. Refer to your chart for the weekly high and low, which starts at 1500 and shows each 25 points in the square. This chart starts at zero, May 28th, 1932. And, 5275 is at the 45° angle, and the date is July 14th. Therefore, from May 28th, 1932, in the 21st year, the price is ahead of time, and should the price decline below 5160 it will be below the time period of May 28th. And, to be on Time, around April 20th, price would have to be 50¢ per dozen.

On the 360° circle chart, on April 17, 1953, the price declined from 5275 to 5190 and closed at this level, which on Time was August 23rd, and to be back at the calendar date, the price would, of course, have to decline to around 5065 on April 21st to 23rd.

Work out all future time periods and resistance levels in this same way, and study the past records and you will see how well prices obey the natural law.

You should make up a chart of this kind in the same way for Cotton, Cocoa, Lard and Rubber when you are trading in these commodities.

Always figure how many points, and how many degrees, prices are up from the last low level, and how many points, and how many degrees they are down from the last high level. And, of course, keep up all time periods, daily, weekly and monthly so that you can see how the price is conforming to the time periods.

Example: October Eggs – On April 21st, will be 90 market days from December 9th, low, and the price to be above the square, would have to be above 5275. And, it is almost a sure thing that the price will be much lower, because price closed on April 17th, below the 45° angle from January 2nd low, 4475.

REFER TO THE WEEKLY CHART

April 18th 1953 is 1½ squares of 5855, based on the scale of 30 points to 1/8 of an inch, or 30 points equal 1 week in time. The fact that this square ended April 18th, is one of the reasons why prices broke so fast on April 17th. You should always watch the ending of the squares, based on the 30 point scale for Eggs, and the 25 point scale on the weekly chart, and note the position on the geometric angles, at the time the squares of the high, low and range end. Also, never overlook the fact, of how the price and time stands on the natural squares.

The more you study this chart, in fact the more you study and practice any chart, the more knowledge you will gain, and the greater accuracy you will obtain on future trends.

April 17, 1953   W. D. GANN

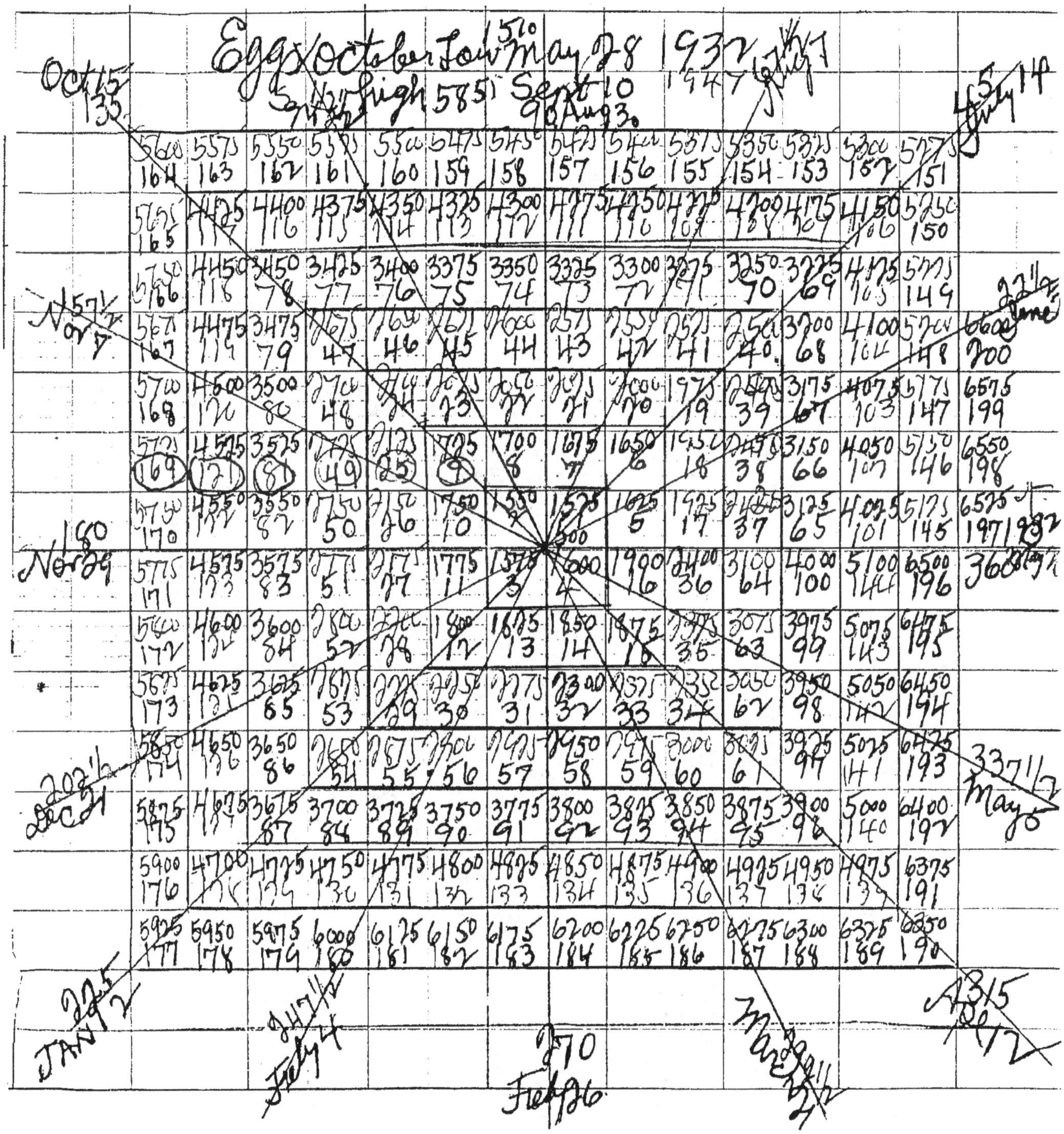

Eggs October Low May 28 1932

$5\frac{1}{0}$

Low high 585 Sept 10

98 Aug 3.

Oct 15 133

Nov 57½ or 7

160 Nov 29

203½ Dec 24

335 Jan 2 ½

JAN 2

Feb 26 270

March 2

May 6 337½ 7

45 July 14

22½ June

360

A315 Dec 12

100 to 6460 → $1008.00 = 9.216.00 → Gain $8.208.00

1500 → $2.160.00 to 5855 — Gain $6,783.60

Eggs 70 Points to 1 Month

70 Points = $100.80/100

5855 = $8.446.60

6400 = $9.216.00 — 70 → $1008.00

5460	5390	5320	5250	5180	5110	5040	4970	4900	4830
78	77	76	75	74	73	72	71	70	69
5530	3360	3220	3150	3080	3010	2940	2870	2800	4760
79	47	46	45	44	43	42	41	40	68
5660	3360	1680	1610	1540	1470	1400	1330	2730	4690
77	48	24	23	22	21	20	19	39	67
5670	3430	1750	630	560	490	420	1260	2460	4620
71	49	25	9	8	7	6	18	38	66
5740	3500	1820	700	140	70	350	1190	2590	4550
47	50	26	10	2	1	5	17	37	65
5810	3570	1890	770	210	280	1120	2520	4480	7000
73	51	27	11	3	4	16	36	64	100
5880	3640	1960	840	910	980	1050	2450	4410	6930
84	52	84	12	13	14	15	35	63	99
5950	3710	2030	2100	2170	2240	2310	2380	4340	6860
85	53	29	30	31	32	33	34	62	98
6020	3780	3850	3520	3590	4060	4130	4200	4270	6790
86	54	55	56	57	58	59	60	61	97
6090	6160	6230	6300	6370	6440	6510	6580	6650	6720
87	88	89	90	91	92	93	94	95	96

LESSON 10

MASTER CHARTS

W. D. GANN

82 WALL STREET
NEW YORK 5

MASTER CHARTS

****

The Master Charts are permanent and represent natural angles and permanent resistance points for either price, time or volume. These points do not change and you should study them carefully on each different Master Chart and learn how to apply them.

MASTER "12" CHART

The MASTER CHART is the Square of "12 " or 12 x 12, making the first square end at 144. The Second Square of "12" ends at 288, the Third Square of "12" at 432; and the Fourth Square at 576, which will cover most anything that you want, but you can make up as many more squares as you need.

This chart may be used and applied to anything -- TIME, SPACE, PRICE OR VOLUME, the number of points up or down; days, weeks, months and years.

On Square No. 1, which runs from 1 to 144, I have drawn the finer angles to show the grand-center or strongest resistance point in each minor square. The minor centers, which are the strongest for minor tops and bottoms are 14, 17, 20, 23, 50, 53, 56, 59, 86, 89, 92, 95, 122, 125, 128, 131.

The major center is where the strongest resistance is met. These numbers are 66, 67, 78 and 79. Stocks going up or coming down to these prices will meet with stubborn resistance. The next strong angle is the 45°, and the numbers of greatest resistance on it are 14, 27, 40, 53, 66, 79, 92, 105, 118, 151, and 144. The other diagonal 45° angle from 12 is equally strong. The numbers are 12, 23, 34, 45, 56, 67, 78, 89, 100, 111, 122, and 133.

The numbers which are cut by the 45° angles through the center of each of the one 1/4 squares are next in strength. These numbers are 7, 20, 33, 46, 59, 72, 61, 50, 39, 28, 17, and 6, and on the other side of the Square, after you pass the half-way point, these numbers are 73, 96, 99, 112, 125, 138, 139, 128, 117, 106, 95 and 84.

The numbers at the tops and bottoms of the squares are important prices for important tops and bottoms to be made because they are opposition numbers and are equal to the half-way point. These numbers for Square No. 1 are 1, 13, 25, 37, 49, 61, 73, 85, 97, 109, 121, 133. The top numbers are 12, 24, 36, 48, 60, 72, 84, 96, 108, 120, 132, and 144. These are very important to measure time in days, weeks, months and years.

The opposition angle, which runs through the center of the Square, from east to west, equally dividing it, is one of the very strong angles because it equals one-half. Any stock moving up or down and reaching these prices will meet with any resistance and make tops or bottoms. These numbers are 6, 7, 18, 19, 30, 31, 42, 43, 54, 55, 66, 67, 78, 79, 90, 91, 102, 103, 114, 115, 126, 127, 138, 139.

Remember, when anything has moved three sections over from the beginning, it reaches the square of its own place, which is the first strong resistance. When it has moved six sections over it reaches the opposition, or what equals the half-way point of its own place and meets still stronger resistance. Moving over nine places or sections from its own place, it reaches the 3/4 point, another square. The 8th and 9th sections are the strongest and hardest points to pass because this is the "death" zone. The next and still stronger is the 12th section or column which ends at 144. Anything getting into this section meets the strongest resistance but once it moves out of the square and gets as much as 3 points into Square #2, that is, making 147, will indicate much higher. But after reaching this, it should not drop back to 141 or 3 points into Square #1.

When a stock gets into the Second Square of "12", it has faster moves, and when the time or number of months from any bottom or top moves into the Second Square, it is an indication of faster moves, both up and down.

Apply the same rule to the 3rd, 4th, 5th and 6th Squares. In the 3rd and 4th squares of the Master "12", you will find that most of the big bull and bear campaigns culminate, when measured by months, which determines the division, according to time. All of the other rules given you to apply to Space movements, angles and time, can be used with the Master "12" tables.

SQUARE OF NINE

You have already had the MASTER SQUARE OF TWELVE explained, which represents days, weeks, months and years, and the measurements of TIME in the Square of Twelve or the square of the Circle; also used to measure price movements and resistance levels.

The SQUARE OF NINE is very important because nine digits are used in reassuring everything. We cannot go beyond nine without starting to repeat and using the 0. If we divide 360° by 9, we get 40, which measures 40°, 40 months, 40 days, 40 weeks, or 40 months, and shows why bottoms and tops often come out on these angles measured by one-ninth of the circle. This is why the children of Israel were 40 years in the wilderness.

If we divide our 20-year period, or 240 months, by 9, we get 26-2/3 months, making an important angle of 26-2/3°, months, days, or weeks. Nine times 9 equals 81, which completes the First Square of Nine. Note the angles and how they run from the main center. The Second Square of Nine is completed at 162. Note how this is in opposition to the main center. The Third Square of Nine is completed at 243, which would equal 243 months or three months over our 20-year period and accounts for the time which often elapses before the change in the Cycle, sometimes running over 3 months or more. The Fourth Square of Nine ends at 324. Note the angles of 45° cross at 325, indicating a change in cycles here. To complete the 360° requires Four Squares of Nine and 36 over. Note that 361 equals a Square of 19 times 19, thus proving the great value of the Square of Nine in working out the important angles and proving up discrepancies.

Beginning with "1" at the center, note how 7, 21, 43, 73, 111, 157, 211, 273, and 343 all fall on a 45° angle. Going the other way, note that 3, 13, 31, 57, 91, 133, 183, 241, and 307 fall on an angle of 45°. Remember there are always four ways that you can travel from the center following an angle of 45°, or an angle of 180° or an angle of 90°, which all equal about the same when measured on a flat surface. Note that 8, 23, 46, 77, 116, 163, 218, 281 and 352 are all on an angle from the main center; also note that 4, 15, 34, 61, 96, 139, 190, 249, and 316 are on an angle from the main center, all of these being great resistance points and measuring out important time factors and angles.

Study the SQUARE OF NINE very carefully in connection with the MASTER TWELVE and 360° CIRCLE CHART.

SIX SQUARES OF NINE

You will receive six Permanent Charts, each containing 81 numbers. The First Square of Nine runs from 1 to 81. Everything must have a bottom, top, and four sides to be a square or cube. The first Square running up to 81 is the bottom, base, floor or beginning point. Squares #2, 3, 4, and 5 are the four sides, which are equal in containing 81 numbers. The Sixth Square of Nine is the top and means that it is times times as referred to in the Bible, or a thing reproducing itself by being multiplied by itself. Nine times nine equals 81 and six times 81 equals 486. We can also use nine times 81, which would equal 729.

The number 5 is the most important number of the digits because it is the balance or main center. There are four numbers on each side of it. Note how it is shown as the balancing or center number in the Square of Nine.

We square the Circle by beginning at 1 in the center and going around until we reached 360. Note that the Square of Nine comes out at 361. The reason for this is: it is 19 times 19, and the 1 to begin with, and 1 over 360 represents the beginning and ending points. 361 is a transition point and begins the next Circle. Should we leave the first space blank or make it "0", then we would come out at 360. Everything in mathematics must prove. You can begin at the center and work out, or begin at the outer rim and work into the center. Begin at the left and work right to the center or to the outer rim or square.

Note the Square of Nine or the Square of the Circle, where we begin with 1 and run up the side of the column to 19, then continue to go cross until we have made 19 columns, again, the square of 19 by 19. Note how this proves up the circle. One-half of the circle is 180°. Note that in the grand-center, where all angles from the four corners and from the East, West, North and South reach gravity center, number 181 appears, showing that at this point we are crossing the Equator or Gravity center and are starting on the other half of the circle.

We have astronomical and mathematical proof of the whys and wherefores and the cause of the workings of geometrical angles. When you have made progress, proved yourself worthy, I will give you the Master Number and also the Master Word.

THE HEXAGON CHART

Since everything moves in a circle and nothing moves in straight lines, this chart is to show you how the angles influence stocks at very low levels and very high levels and why stocks move faster the higher they get, because they have moved out to where the distance between the angles of 45° are so far apart that there is nothing to stop them and their moves are naturally rapid up and down.

We begin with a circle of "1" in the center and while this only contains 1, yet the circle is 360° just the same. We then place a circle of circles around this circle and 6 circles complete the second circle, making a gain of 6 over the first one, ending the second circle at 7, making 7 on this angle a very important month, year, and week as well as day, the seventh day being sacred and a day of rest. The third circle is completed at 19. The fourth circle around is completed at 37, a gain of 18 over the previous circle. The fifth circle is completed at 61, a gain of 24 over the previous circle. The sixth circle is completed at 91, a gain of 30 over the previous circle, and the seventh circle at 127, a gain of 36 over the last circle. Note that from the first the gain is 6 each time we go around. In other words, when we have traveled six times around we have gained 36. Note that this completes the first Hexagon and as this equals 127 months, shows why some campaigns will run 10 years and seven months, or until they reach a Square of the Hexagon, or the important last angle of 45°.

The eighth circle around is completed at 169, a gain of 42 over the first. This is a very important angle and an important time factor for more reasons than one. It is 14 years and one month, or double our cycle of seven years. Important tops and bottoms culminate at this angle as you will see by going over your charts.

The ninth circle is completed at 217, a gain of 48 over the previous circle. The tenth circle is completed at 271, a gain of 54. Note that 271 is the 9th circle from the first, or is the third 90° angle or 270°, three-fourths of a Circle, a very strong point. All this is confirmed by the Master Twelve Chart, by the four seasons and by the Square of Nine Chart, and also confirmed by the Hexagon Chart, showing that mathematical proof is always exact no matter how many ways or from what directions you figure it.

The eleventh circle is completed at 331, a gain of 60 over the last circle. The 12th circle is completed at 397, which completes the Hexagon, making a gain in 11 circles of 66 from the beginning. 66 months, or five years and six months, marks the culmination of a major campaign in stocks. Note how often they culminate on the 60th month, then have a reaction, and make a second top or bottom in the 66th month. Note the number 66 on the Master Twelve Chart. Note it on the Square of Nine and see that 66 occurs on an angle of 180° on the Hexagon Chart, all of which confirms the strong angle at this point.

We have an angle of 66°, one of 67½, and one of 68, confirming this point to be doubly strong for tops and bottoms or space movements up or down.

Note the number 360 on the Hexagon Chart. It completes a circle of 360°. From our beginning point this occurs at an angle of 150° on the Hexagon Chart going around, but measuring from the center, it would equal an angle of 90° or 180°, making this a strong point, hard and difficult to pass, and the ending of one campaign and the beginning of another.

Again with the center of the Hexagon Chart at "1" notice that 7, 9 [19?], 37, 61, 91, 127, 169, 217, 271, 331, and 397 are all on this direct angle and are important points in time measurement. Beginning with "1" and following the other angle, note that 2, 9, 22, 41, 66, 97, 134, 177, 226, 281, and 342 are all on the same angle of 90°, or an angle of 60° and 240° as measured by the Hexagon Chart.

Go over this chart and the important angles each way and you will see why resistance is met either on days, weeks, months, or years, and why stocks stop and make tops and bottoms at these strong important points, according to time and price.

When any stock has passed out above 120° or especially above 127° or 127 points and gone out of the Square of the first Hexagon, its fluctuations will be more rapid, and it will move faster up and down. Notice near the center that in travelling from 6 to 7 it strikes the angle of 180° or 90°, but when the stock gets out to 162, it can travel up to 169 before striking another strong angle. That is why fast moves occur up and down as stocks get higher and as they move from a center in time.

Remember that everything seeks the center of gravity and important tops and bottoms are formed according to centers and measurements of time from a center, base or beginning point, either top or bottom. The angles formed going straight up and across, may form just the same going across as the stock travels over for days, weeks, months or years. Thus, a stock going up to 22½ would strike an angle of 22½°. If it moves over 22½ days, 22½ weeks, or 22½ months, it would also strike an angle of 22½°, and the higher it is when these angles are struck and the angle it hits going up, the greater the resistance to be met. Reverse the rule going down.

Market movements are made just the same as any other thing, which is constructed. It is just the same as constructing a building. First, the foundation has to be laid and then the four sides have to be completed and last, but not least of all, the top has to be put on. The cube or hexagon proves exactly the law, which works because of time and space in the market. When a building is put up it is built according to a square or hexagon. It has four walls or four sides, a bottom and a top; therefore, it is a cube.

In working out the 20-year Cycle in the stock market, the first 60°, or 5 years, from the beginning forms the bottom of the cube. The second 60°, running to 120, completes the first angle or the first side and runs out the 10-year Cycle. The third 60°, or the second side, ends 15 years or 180°. It is very important because we have the building half completed and must meet the strong resistance at this point. The fourth 60°, or the end of 20 years or 240 months, completes the third side. We are now two-thirds around the building, a very strong point which culminates and completes our 20-year cycle. The fifth 60°, or 300° point, days, weeks, or months, completes 25 years, a repetition of the first 5 years, but it completes the fourth side of our building and is a very important angle. The sixth 60° or 360°, completing the circle and ending 30 years as measured by our Time Factor, which runs 1° per month on an angle of 45°, completes the top. This is a complete cube and we begin over again.

Study this in connection with the Hexagon Chart. It will help you.

W. D. GANN

W. D. GANN

82 WALL STREET
NEW YORK 5

MASTER CHARTS (Continued)

THE MASTER CHART OF 360°

This chart begins at "0" and runs around the circle to "360". We first divide by two and get 180°; then divide 180 by 2 and we get 90°; then divide 90 by 2 and the get 45°; then divide 45 by 2 and we get 22½°; then divide 22½ by 2 and we get 11¼°; then divide 11¼ by 2 and we get 5-5/8° – all of which form the important angles around the circle.

I have only shown all the important angles from 3-3/4 to 360°. All the angles drawn in red, because they are the important square angles.

After dividing the circle by 2, the next important number to divide by is 3. Dividing by 3, we get 120°, 240° and 360°, making the important triangle points. We then divide 120 by 2 and get the angles of 60°, 150°, 210°, 300° and 330°. We divide 60 by 2 and get the angles of 30° and their proportionate parts around. Then divide 30 by 2 and get the angles of 15° and their proportionate angles around the circle. Then divide 15 by 2 and we get the angles at 7½° around the circle.

24 hours in a day divided into the circle equals 15° for each hour. There are 48 divisions of the circle of 7½°, which are important in measuring day, weekly and monthly time periods.

Study the Major Chart of 360° carefully and you will see why cycles repeat. When anything has traveled up 180°, it starts to go down to the opposite point and each angle up to 180° is the opposite on the other side of the circle. That is why tops and bottoms come out at each one of these degrees. For instance, top coming out at 90° or 90 months at one time will occur 90° or 90 months apart, and there will be similar tops causing rapid fluctuations and fast moves up and down because this angle is so acute that stocks can not remain long before starting in the opposite direction.

Note the culminations that occur every 14 and 15 years, 180 months, or when an 180° angle or an angle straight up and down is reached. How rapid the moves are when they near this angle and how fast they move up and down and how quickly reverse. It is the same with the 45°, the 135°, the 225° and the 315° angle. Note how this proves the important campaigns, when tops and bottoms workout in regularity and equal number of months apart. Note the 22½°, and then follow the next important angle, the 30° angle, then the 45°, then note the 60° and 67½° are close together, but both very strong angles. Note also 112½° and 120°, both strong angles and close together, indicating important tops and bottoms. Also note 150° and 157½°, strong angles close together, indicating important tops and bottoms, and so on all the way around.

When the circle is divided by 2 and 3 and redivided, we get the following important angles and measurements of time, space and volume around the circle of 360°:-

5-5/8, 7-1/2, 11-1/4, 15, 16-7/8, 22-1/2, 27-7/8, 30, 33-3/4, 37-1/2, 39-3/8, 45, 50-5/8, 56-1/4, 60, 61-7/8, 67-1/2, 73-1/8, 75, 78-3/4, 82-1/2, 84-3/8, 90, 95-5/8, 101-1/4, 105, 106-7/8, 112-1/2, 118-1/8, 120, 123-3/4, 129-3/8, 135, 140-5/8, 146-1/4, 150, 152-7/8, 157-1/2, 163-1/8, 168-3/4, 174-3/8, 180, 185-5/8, 191-1/4, 196-7/8, 202-1/2, 208-1/8, 210, 213-3/4, 219-3/8, 225, 230-5/8, 236-1/4, 240, 241-7/8, 247-1/2, 253-1/8, 258-3/4, 264-3/8, 270, 275-5/8, 281-1/4, 286-7/8, 292-1/2, 298-1/8, 300, 303-3/4, 309-3/8, 315, 320-5/8, 326-1/4, 330, 331-7/8, 337-1/2, 343-1/8, 348-3/4, 354-3/8, 360, which completes the circle.

These points are all made by a division of angles and are measurements of one-half, one-third, one-fourth, one-eight, one-sixteenth, one-thirty-second and one-sixty-fourth.

Compare these points with your Master Twelve Chart, your Square of Nine Chart, your Hexagon Chart and your Major Chart of 360°. You will see how they all confirm the important angles and time factors.

The number "7" being so important in determining the culmination in weeks, days, months and years, we must divide the circle by 7 to get the important points, or the one-seventh points in the circle, which are vital and important angles.

The first one-seventh of 360 equals 51-3/7, the second equals 102-6/7, the third equals 154-2/7, the fourth equals 205-5/7, the fifth equals 257-1/7, the sixth equals 308-4/7, and the seventh completes the circle, equalling 360°, days, weeks, months or years. If you divide each of these points by 2, you'll also get other important and valuable angles which will confirm and correspond to the other angles in the other charts.

One-seventh of a year or one-seventh of the circle shows why so many fast market movements culminate in the 49th day or the 52nd day and why the 7th week is so very important in culminations and also the 7th month as well as the 7th year.

1½ times 51-3/7 equals 77-1/8 and shows why the angles are so very strong around that point, and why the 77th day, 77th week and 77th month are so important for culminations.

MASTER 360° CIRCLE CHART SQUARED

The Master 360 Circle Chart when squared is 90 x 90, and contains 8,100 cells, zones or spaces. Therefore, the Square of 360 will contain 32,400 spaces. This shows why a stock fluctuates up and down so many times over the same territory, because it is working out the number of cells or vibrations of each space in a square. For example:

> 1/8 of 90 equals 1,012-1/2.
> 1/4 of 90 equals 2,025
> 1/2 of 90 equals 4,050
> 3/4 of 90 equals 6,075
> 1/3 of 90 equals 2,700
> 2/3 of 90 equals 5,400

The Square of 360, or 360 times 360 equals 32,400.

1/4 of 360 equals 8,100
1/3 of 360 equals 10,860
1/2 of 360 equals 16,200
2/3 of 360 equals 21,600
3/4 of 360 equals 24,300
7/8 of 360 equals 28,350

These points are very important to use for volume of sales as well as time and price measurements.

Suppose you want to know the number of days required to fill or work out the Square of 90. There are 365 days in a year. 20 years will give you 7,300 days, and in counting the leap years will run a little over this. Therefore, about 22 years, 2 months and 10 days are required to work out each vibration in the Square of 90.

THE SPIRAL CHART

The Spiral Chart represents the correct position, time and space of anything that begins at zero and begins to move round and round. It shows just exactly how the numbers increase as the spiral moves round and round and why stocks move faster as they grow older, or swing so much more rapidly as the price reaches higher levels. At center, beginning point or zero, it requires 45° to represent 1 point. When the stock traveled seven times around from the center, it then required seven points to strike a 45° angle. When it has traveled around the spiral twelve times, it will then require a space of 10 points before striking a 45° angle. It would also mean that the stock could move in one direction ten months without striking anything to cause any very great reaction. On this chart, we have only shown the 45, 60, 90, 120, 135, 180, 225, 240, 270, 300, 315 and 360 degree angles. This shows the division of the circle by 2, 4 and 8, and also shows the one-third point and the two-thirds point; being the vital and most important angles, we placed them so you can see how space or time makes rapid fluctuations.

NEW YORK STOCK EXCHANGE PERMANENT CHART

This Chart is a Square of 20, or 20 up and 20 over, making a total of 400, which can be used to measure days, weeks, months or years, and to determine when tops and bottoms will be made against strong angles, as indicated on this Permanent Chart.

For example: the New York Stock Exchange was incorporated May 17th, 1792. Therefore, we began at "0" on May 17, 1792. 1793 ends on a 1, when the Stock Exchange was 1 year old. 1812 will come out on 20;

1832 on 40   1892 on 100
1852 on 60   1912 on 120
1872 on 80   1932 on 140

Note that 139, or 1931, strikes the 45° angle, running from 20 down, and that this is in the 7th zone, or the 7th space over, which indicates that 1931 is the ending of a bear campaign, and the starting of a bull market. But we must watch out for a break around May and June, 1931, when this angle is hit at the end of the 139th year.

You will notice that the numbers which divide the square into equal parts, run across 10, 30, 50, 70, 90, 110, etc., and that the year 1802 comes out on 10, the year 1822 on 30, the year 1842 on 50, the year 1862 on 70. Note that the year 1861, when the Civil War broke out, was on the number 69, which is a 45° angle. Then note that 1882 ended in May on a 90° angle, and at the 1/2 point, 180° angle, running horizontally across.

Again in 1902, it was at 110; the 1/2 point, and in 1903 and 1904, hit the 45° angle.

Note that the years 1920 and 1921 hit the 45° angle on No. 129 and 1922, the first year of the bull market, was at 130 at the 1/2 point.

Note that 1929 was on the 137th number, or 137th month, and hit an angle of 45°, and that the year 1930 was at the 1/2 point on the 4th square, a strong Resistance Point, which indicated a sharp, severe decline.

Again, 138 is at the 1/2 point on the Master 12 Chart.

1933 will be on 141, in the 8th zone, and at the center or 1/2 point of the 2nd quarter of the Square of 20.

The years 1934 and 1935, ending in May, will be on 142 and 143, and 1935 will come out on the 45° angle at the grand center in the 8th zone and at the 1/2 point of the 2nd square, going to 1/2 of the total square, which will indicate a decline and bottom for an advance to run up in 1936, with 1937 striking at 145, which is 1/4th of the column on the way up in the square.

If you will study the weeks, months, as well as the years, and apply them to these important points and angles, you will see how they have determined the important tops and bottoms in the past campaigns.

MASTER CALCULATOR FOR WEEKLY PERIODS
TO DETERMINE THE TREND OF STOCKS AND COMMODITIES

by W.D. GANN

This Master Calculator shows Weekly Time Periods of 7 days each or a total of 52 weeks in one year. This represents 364 calendar days, therefore at the end of each year there is a gain of one day and at the end of 7 years, a gain of 7 days, the time period coming out one week before the date of the important high and low prices. You must also add one day for each leap year. Suppose you want to get the time period for 15 years, you multiply 365 by 15, add the number of leap years and then divide the total days by 7 to get the weekly periods of 7 days each in order to use the Calculator. (See Tables for Price and Time Periods).

The total square of 52 is 2704, which we can use to measure weeks, days, months, years or hours. In using days, it would, of course, require 2704 days to pass through the square of 52. This would give 386 weeks and 2 days or approximately 7 years and 5 months, very close to the important cycle of $7\frac{1}{2}$ years, which is 90 months.

If we used hours to balance or square 2704, we get 112-2/3 days by dividing 2704 by 24, the total number of hours in a day during which time the earth makes one complete revolution on its axis.

The Square of 52, which is composed of 7-day periods, is one of the most important for measuring Price and Time. The number 7 is referred to in the Bible more times than any other number, except the number 3. Both of these numbers are very important to use in connection with price and time changes.

You start Time periods from the actual dates of important high and important low prices and not from the first day of each month or the first day of each year.

The Calculator is 104 weeks wide, which equals 2 years. The time periods run across the bottom of the Calculator, from left to right to 104, which completes 2 years, and to 208, which completes 4 years. At the top of the Calculator, running across to the left, the time periods run to 312, which ends 6 years, and to 416, which ends 8 years, and to 520, which completes a 10-year cycle.

DIVISIONS OF TIME PERIODS

The year is divided by 1/8, which equals $6\frac{1}{2}$ weeks

1/4,	"	"	13	"	
1/3,	"	"	17	"	
3/8,	"	"	$19\frac{1}{2}$	"	
1/2,	"	"	26	"	a most important time and resistance level
5/8,	"	"	$32\frac{1}{2}$	"	
2/3,	"	"	35	"	
3/4,	"	"	39	"	very important for a change in trend
7/8,	"	"	$45\frac{1}{2}$	"	

1 year, which is 52 weeks.

The angles run from each of the time periods for Price and Time in order to balance the Square and show resistance levels where price and time periods indicate a change in trend.

THIRD AND FOURTH DIMENSIONS OF TIME AND PRICE

We know of three dimensions – height , width and length – but there is a fourth dimensions or element in market movements. We prove the fourth dimension with the Master Calculator or Square of 52 in Time Periods of 7 days each for 7 weeks or more, and the same price relation. 7 x 52 equals 364 or 7 years.

THE CIRCLE, TRIANGLE AND SQUARE

The circle of 360° and the nine digits are the basis of all mathematical calculations. The Square and the Triangle form within the circle, but there is an inner circle and an inner square, as well as an outer square and an outer circle, which prove the fourth dimension in working out market movements.

PRICE

The most important points to consider are:

1. Lowest price.
2. Highest price.
3. The 1/2 point, mean or average between the extreme high and the extreme low. We get the fourth dimension, as shown on the Master Calculator, by drawing 45° angles from the 1/2 point or gravity center, which is the most important for price resistance.
4. Volume of Sales. This is the power which drives the market up or down but remember that TIME is the most essential element and when Time is completed, the volume of sales starts to move the market up or down.

TIME

Time is divided into sections or cycles by which we determine the change in trend.

1. Daily high and low prices
2. Weekly high and low prices
3. Monthly high and low prices
4. Yearly high and low prices

The Weekly and the Yearly Time Periods are most important for trend indications and for changes in trend.

The day is divided into hours, minutes and seconds. The four divisions of the day are: Sunrise, Noon, Sunset and Midnight. Of these the most important are: Noon, when the Sun is straight overhead or on a 90° angle, and Midnight, the opposite point or 180° from Noon and 90° from Sunset.

Because we are using 7-day Time Periods with the Calculator, 1/2 of 7 days or 3½ days is important to watch for a change in trend. Always watch the 3rd and 4th day from any important high or low level for a minor change in trend, which later may become a major change.

7-DAY PERIODS: The time periods of 7 calendar days from any important high or low level is of great importance. 14 days is the most important and 21 days or three weeks is next in importance. Reactions will often run 2 weeks, and sometimes 3 weeks and then resume the main trend. Rallies in a Bear Market often run 14 days, and sometimes 21 days and then resume the downward or main trend.

MULTIPLES OF 7 DAYS: The square of 7 or 49 days is very important for change in trend. You can start to watch for this change after the 42nd day but the first indication of a change may not occur until the 45th or 46th day, which is 1/8 of the year or 365 days. 1/16 of the year is 23 days. Therefore, both the 46-day and 23-day periods are important to watch for change in trend.

Next in importance is 63 to 65 days because 7 x 9 is 63 and the square of 8 is 64. 81 days or the square of 9 is also of great importance. 90 to 91 days is 1/4 of the year or 7 x 13. This is of very great importance to watch for change in trend. Of course, of next importance is around 182 days or 1/2 of the year.

YEARS

Later we will refer to the four seasons or the divisions of the year, which are Spring, Summer, Fall and Winter and important to watch for change in trend. However, the divisions of Time are from the date of the actual important high and low prices.

The important yearly cycles are 1, 2, 3, 5, 7, 9, 10, 12, 14, 15, 18, 20, 21, 22½, 24, 25, 27, 28, 30, 40, 45, 49, 56, 60, 84, and 90 which is the Great Cycle. We divide the cycles into 1/2, which is the most important, and also into the periods of 1/8, 1/3 and 2/3, and watch these proportionate parts of the cycles for a change in trend. For example:

The Great Cycle of 90 years equals 1080 months;
                 1/2 is 45 years or 540 months
                 1/4 is 22½ years or 270 months
                 1/8 is 11¼ years or 135 months
                 1/16 is 5-5/8 years or 67½ months
The 30 year cycle or any other cycle is divided up in the same way.

MULTIPLES OF 7 YEARS: The multiples of 7 years or 84 months are all important to watch for change in trend. These are 7 years, 14, 21, 28, 35, 42, and 49, which is most important because it is the square of 7. Next 56 and 63 are very important, 63 because it is 7 x 9. 81, the square of 9, is very important.

Prices can also be used in sevens. Example: 98, 2 x 49. 126, 2 x 63. 162, 2 x 81, etc.

YEARLY TIME PERIODS - TRIANGLES AND SQUARES: When 1/3 of a year from any important low comes out at the same time that 1/4 or 1/2 of a year from another important top or bottom comes out, it is of great importance for change in trend. 1/2 of a yearly time period is always the most important, just the same as 1/2 of the highest selling price and 1/2 of the range of the price is important for resistance levels. By practice, study and comparison and by placing the Calculator over the Weekly high and low Chart, you will see how all these prices and Time Periods work out.

TIME, PRICE, VOLUME, VELOCITY, PITCH OR TREND

When a Time Cycle is completed, Volume increases and the market begins to move up faster or move down faster.

The pitch or trend is determined mostly by the 45° angle, which is the most important, but other angles can be used to determine the trend. The pitch or trend is the 4th dimension and shows whether the market is slow or fast by the angles, whether very acute or above the 45° angle or flat and slow, below the 45° angle, which causes a slower creeping market that may later regain important angles and increase the pitch of the angle and start moving up faster.

All of this is shown on the Master Calculator or Square of 52.

3 WAYS TO SQUARE OR BALANCE TIME AND PRICE

(1) Balance the lowest price with time measured in weeks and balance the highest price with time.
(2) Balance the range, which is the total between the extreme high and extreme low.
(3) Get the 4th dimension by balancing Price and Time in weekly time periods as shown on the Master Square of 52.

PRICE SCALE

The price scale runs up and down to 104, 208, 312, 416, and 520, which balances out with the Time Periods. For GRAINS, this scale is four cents per bushel. For STOCKS, it is $1.00 per share. The Price Periods are divided up into 1/8 and 1/3, the same as the Time Periods.

Scale for COTTON, COFFEE, COCOA and EGGS – each 1/8 cent equals 10 points. Therefore, 52 would indicate 520 in price and 104 would indicate 1040 for Cotton or any other commodity trading in 100 points to 1¢.

EGGS – Weekly high and low chart – Eggs trade at a minimum of 5 points. We use 10 points to 1/8 inch on the daily high and low chart. Experience has proven that a scale of 25 points to 1/8 inch, which represents one week in Time, works best. Therefore, 52 spaces on the Calculator would indicate 1300 or 13¢ for Eggs; 104 would represent 2600; 156 would represent 3900; 208 would represent 5200 or 52¢ per dozen for Eggs, etc. One year Time Period would give a range of 13¢, 1/2 of this would be 6½ cents, 1/4 would be 325 and 1/8 would be 162. Therefore, if you want to get resistance levels for prices above 26¢, you would add 6½, which would give 32½, etc.

All of these are shown on the Table enclosed for prices which run up to the equivalent of 40 years calculated. All you have to do is run across the period marked "1/2" and get the exact date during each year. When the Time is at 1/2 or 182 days from an important high or low, and in the same way from the Table, you get the price resistance levels based on the Square of 52.

HOW TO USE THE MASTER CALCULATOR

One column on the Calculator can be used for one month or one year, but the Calculator is designed to be used on the Weekly high and low Chart for determining the important changes in trend.

HOW TO USE CALCULATOR ON WEEKLY CHART

Place the bottom or "0" of the Calculator on "0" below any price or place it on the low price, then you will see where the angles cross and the resistance levels are indicated.

Place the Calculator marked "Top" at the high price on the exact date the important price is made, then you can see the important angles for resistance from the top down.

THE INNER SQUARE OR 1/2 POINT

Place the Calculator on 1/2 of the highest selling price or 1/2 of the range. Place the Calculator where it is marked 1/2 or 26 weeks over the chart on the same line that low or high is made. Placing the Calculator on 26 over the 1/2 point will show the resistance and whether the price is in a strong or weak position.

THE INNER SQUARE OF 45° ANGLES

The Inner Square of 45° Angles starts from 26, which is 1/2 of 52, and moved up or down. It crosses at 26, which is 1/2 of 52. The 45° angle moving up from "0" crosses at 52 and 104, and the 45° angle moving down from a top or high-level crosses at 52 and terminates at "0". All of these important 45° angles from any important high or low cross on 1/4, 1/2, 3/4, etc., as you can see, and balance out Time and Price.

MOST IMPORTANT TIME PERIODS

The most important Time Periods are the anniversary date of 1, 2, 3 years or more from the dates of the important highs and important lows. Second in importance is 1/2 of the Yearly Time Period; third in importance is the 3/4 or 39 weeks in each year; fourth, the 1/3 point or 17 weeks and the 2/3 point or 35 weeks are also very important Time Periods for change in trend.

When you are working out Weekly Time Periods, you must also consider the importance of the 3-year cycle, the 5-year cycle, 7-year cycle, 10-year cycle, 15 years, which is 1/2 of the 30-year cycle, and 20 years, which is 1/3 of the 60-year cycle, and 30 years, which is a complete cycle of 360 months. The longer the time period from an important top or bottom, the greater the variation, because each year of the time period gains at least one day, and in leap year's gains and additional day before the end of the complete cycle.

The Table for Time and Price Periods shows the exact time in 52 weeks to a year or 364 calendar days. By figuring the leap years and the time gained at the rate of one day per year, you know how much time to subtract and can make the adjustment for the full period.

SEASONAL TIME PERIODS

In figuring Seasonal Time Periods, we do not start to calculate Time from January 1st but calculate the Time Periods from the date when the Spring Season starts on March 21. These periods are marked on the table in 1/8, 1/3, etc. they are as follows:

May 5	ends	1/8	or	6½	weeks from March 21
Jun. 21	ends	1/4	or	13	"
Jul. 23	ends	1/3	or	17	"
Aug. 5	ends	3/8	or	19½	"
Sep. 22	ends	1/2	or	26	"
Nov. 8	ends	5/8	or	32½	"
Nov. 22	ends	2/3	or	35	"
Dec. 21	ends	3/4	or	39	"
Feb. 4	ends	7/8	or	45½	"
Mar. 20	ends	1 year	or	52	"

MIDSEASON TIME PERIODS

These are May 5, August 5, November 8, February 4. Important changes in trend occur around these midseason dates, but all of the above Time Periods should be watched for important changes in trend.

The Table for Time Periods and important high and low prices is shown with the figures at the top running from 1 to 38. The important Time Periods are shown with exact dates, and if you want to look up something in the 7th year, you move over to the column marked "7" and moved down to the 1/2 point. You will find that 7½ years is 390 weeks, etc. and any price on this same line would be an important resistance level.

By studying, practicing and experimenting with the Master Calculator, you will learn how valuable these Time and Price Periods in multiples of 7 are.

W. D. GANN

January 10, 1955

HOW TO USE THE MASTER CALCULATOR
MAY SOY BEANS

First it is important to know how to use the scale for prices. The scale is the same for grain, for all grains and stocks. The scale on the left side of the calculator runs from 0 to 144. If the price is above 144 you subtract 144 and then place the scale in the correct position.

EXAMPLE: When May Beans is selling above 288 this is 2 squares of 144 up from 0 and you place the Master Calculator with 0 on 288 at the time of any important high or low levels and you get the correct position and the indicated trend on the Daily, Weekly or Monthly Charts.

The scale on each side running from 0 up to 4320 is for cotton, eggs and other commodities. For Cotton on the Daily Chart using a 10-point scale. 1440 is the top of the chart of 144 spaces up. For the Weekly Chart using a scale of 15 points to 1/8 inch the price at the top of the chart is 2160 and the second square is 4320. Using a scale of 30 points for 1/8 inch on the Monthly Chart, the top of the Master Calculator at 144 equals the price of 4320.

Using a 20-point scale the top of the chart equals 2880 and at 72 on the second scale up 72 equals 4320.

First it is always important to find out the price position in a square.

EXAMPLE: May Soy Beans extreme high 436-3/4. This is 3 x 144 which equals 432 and 4-3/4 in the fourth square.

The extreme low on Cash Soy Beans is 44¢. Subtract this from 456-3/4
gives a range of 293-3/4 , which is 2 squares of 144 and 104-3/4 over.
The extreme low of May Beans is 67¢. Subtract this from 436-3/4 gives 369-3/4 and 81-3/4 in the third square. Note that 81 is 9 x 9 and an important resistance level.

January 15, 1948 May Beans high 436-3/4. February 14, 1949 low of 90½
a decline of 235¼. Subtract 144 gives 91¼ and 90 in the second square is a strong resistance level.

From the low of February 14, 1949 to February 6, 1951 a high of 344½ gives an advance of 143½, which was just inside this first square of 144 and was, therefore, a strong resistance and selling level. This price would come out at the top of the square at 144.

You should always keep up the important half-way points so that you can place the Master Calculator at 72 on the half-way point at the time period of any extreme high or low. 1/2 of 436 is 218-3/8 and 1/2 between 44 and 436-3/4 is 240-3/8. 1/2 between 436-3/4 and 201½ gives 319-1/8. Calculate all of the other half-way points in the same way.

WEEKLY TIME PERIODS

The time from one important top to a bottom and from bottom to bottom and top to top is very important in using the calculator.

These time periods will show when you place the calculator on the chart at any top or bottom.

1948, May high to February 14, 1949, 38 weeks
1948, January 15, to October 16, 1950 low 232½, time 143 weeks
The low came just at the end of the 1st square of 144.
1948, May to October 16, 1950, 125 weeks
1948, January to February 6, 1951, high 344½, 159 weeks
1948, May to February 6, 1951, 141 weeks
1948, January to July 9, 1951, low 269, 181 weeks
1948, May to July 9, 1951, 163 weeks
1948, January to December 10, 1951, 203 weeks
1948, May to December 10, 1951, 185 weeks
1948, January to August 13, 1951, 238 weeks
1951, February 6 to August 13, 1951, 79 weeks
1952, August 13, to February 13, 1953, 26 weeks
1949, February 14, to October 16, 1950, 88 weeks
1949, February 14, to February 6, 1950, 104 weeks
1949, February 14, to July 9, 1951, 126 weeks
1949, February 14, to December 10, 1951, 148 weeks
1949, February 14, to August 13, 1952, 183 weeks
1949, February 14 to February 13, 1953, 209 weeks

When the time period is more than 144 in time periods you subtract 144 and start the second square. 144 from 209 would give a balance of 65 in the 2nd square.
You would, of course, look up the price on the time period of 65 to see the position on the Master Calculator.

By laying the top of the Master Calculator on 436-3/4 you will see that the green angle, which is 2 x 1 moving down 1/2¢ per week crosses for the week ending March 7, 1953 at 267 weeks. 1/2 of this gives 303-1/4 and a price below this angle still shows down trend.
On February 6, 1951 high 344½ to March 7, 1953, time 108 weeks. One half of this is 54 and the angle crosses at 290½.

We can always add proportionate parts to the bottom or subtract from the top. To 201½ low we add 90, which gives us 291½. To 201½ we add 96, which is 2/3 of 144 and this gives 297½ as a resistance level. If we subtract 144 from 436-3/4, it gives us 292-3/4.

If we subtract 48, which is 1/3 of 144, from 344½ we get 296½ as a resistance level.

PRESENT POSITION OF MAY SOY BEANS

For the Weekly High and Low Chart place the bottom of the calculator at 0 on 201½ and you will see that November 17, 1951 is 144 weeks and ends the first square of 144. You then move your calculator over and place the bottom or 0 on 201½ at the end of the first square of 144 on November 17, 1951. You will then see that the week ending March 7, 1951 [1953] is 212 weeks from Feb. 14, 1949 and the time is 68 weeks in the second square of 144. The price at 298 is at 96 on the price scale. This is the green line and is 2/3 of 144, a resistance and selling level. The red 45-degree angle from the top from 18 crosses 296 and the 45-degree red angle from 18 moving up crosses 296. Note that 18 is 1/8 of 144. Therefore, when the price of May beans is below 296 is the weaker position. 4 weeks later the time will be 72 weeks, which is 1/2 of 144. This will be important for change in trend.

Next place the bottom or 0 on the Master Calculator at 232½, the low of October 16, 1950, and time is 124 weeks, which is the first square of 144 and a price of 300 is at 68 on the scale or 68 up in the square of 144. In two weeks it will be 126 or 7/8 of 144, which is important for a change in trend. When the price is below 295 it is below the green angle of 2 x 1 from 232½, and is a weaker position.

February 1, 1933 low 280, was on the 45-degree angle from 72. THIS IS THE INNER SQUARE AND IS VERY STRONG AND IMPORTANT. The price at 48 up is 1/3 of 144 and strong resistance and buying level. From 280 to 298 is 18 points up, 1/8 of 144, and normal rally.

Next place the calculator on 269, the low of July 9, 1951 and you will see that March 7, 1953 is on the 85th week and the price at 297 is at the 3 x 1 angle from 269 and 295 is on the red line 27 and also the 2 x 1 green line from 72 crossed at 297 making this a resistance level. And below 297 is a weaker position.

Next place the top of the calculator over 344½, the top on Feb. 6, 1951 and for the week ending March 7 is 108 weeks or 2/3 of 144. This indicates a time for change in trend. The price of 299 is on the red price line of 99, a resistance and selling level.

Next place the top of the calculator on 314½, the high of Aug. 13, 1952 and the time is 29 weeks. The green angle 2 x 1 from 144 or the top of 314½ crosses at 300 in the week ending March 7 making this a resistance and selling level. A price of 296½ is on line 126 down and 18¢ from the high, which is 1/8 of 144.

For August 13, 1952 place 72, the price scale, on 273½, which is 1/2 of 201½ to 344½. You will see that 298 is on line 96 which is 2/3 of 144 and the 45-degree angle from 126 crosses at 299 making this a selling level.

Place the Master Calculator, that is the top of the calculator, on 310, the high price of December 15, 1951. March 7, 1953 comes out on the 64th week; which is the square of 8. The price line is on 132, which is 11 x 12 and is important for a change in trend.

TO GET POSITION FROM 0

For the week ending November 15, 1951 which was 144 weeks from February 14, 1949 when the low was 201½. As this was the end of the square of 144 you place the bottom of the calculator on a price of 288, which is 2 squares up in price, and you will see the position from 0 for the week ending March 7, 1953. The price of 297 is on 9 in the third square of 144 and 9 is 1/16 of 144. The 2 x 1 green angle from 144 to 0 crossed at 297 and in 3 weeks will be at 72 which is 1/2 of 144 and important for a change in trend.

MONTHLY INDICATIONS

You use the Master Calculator in the same way on the Monthly Chart to get the position for time and price.

December 28, 1932 low of 44. For the period ending March 28, 1953 is 243 months. You subtract 144 and this gives 99 in the second square. Set the Master Calculator at 0 on a price of 288 and on the 99th month and the price of 299 is at 9 in the 3rd square of 144. The second red angle comes out on 99 and this is 9 up in price, which is 1/16 of 144. The 45-degree angle from 90 and the 45-degree angle from 108 on the Master Calculator crosses 299 making this a resistance or selling level.

Place the Master Calculator on 0 on 201½, and note that the 2 x 1 green angle crosses at 299 and the 45-degree angle from 344 crosses at 295. When the price is below 295 it is in a weaker position. A price of 296 is on line 96, which is 2/3 of 144.

1948, January 15, to March 15, 1953 is 62 months. Set the Master Calculator at 436-3/4. This will be on the time period 62 months and 297, which is 144 down at 436-3/4. Note the heavy line 63, which is 7 x 9, is below 297 and in the second square of 144 down from 436-3/4 and when the price declines to 295 it will be in a weaker position.

On July 27, 1939 low 67¢ place the Master Calculator, that is 0, on 67 and Feb. 27th is 163 months and March 27, 1953 is 164 months. If we add 144 to 67 this gives 211 as the top of the first square in price. Set the calculator on 211 and 164 is 20 months in the second square of 144. Note that the 45-degree angle from 108 crosses at 299 making this a selling level.

1920, February 15, high 405, time to Feb. 15, 1953, is 396 months or 2 squares of 144 and a 108 in the third square. Set the Master Calculator on 202½, which is 1/2 of 405 and place 108 for Feb. 1953 and this gives a price of 298, which is 96 on the scale and 2/3 of 144 the resistance level.

Set the calculator at 344½, for Feb. 6, 1951 and 299 is on 99 price scale and the 45-degree angle from 72 crosses at 297. THIS IS THE INNER SQUARE AND RESISTANCE LEVEL and when the price closes below 296 it is a weaker position and indicates further decline.

It is well to remember that at this time of the year a reversal in prices can take place or an advance can continue, therefore, a stop loss order of 3¢ above 299 should be used making the stop-loss order 302. Should the price of May Soy Beans decline and close below 287 which will be back into the second square from 0 they will be in a weaker position. After March 15, if the price of May Beans is below 286 they will be below the 45-degree angle from Dec. 23, 1932 when the price was 44¢.

If you will practice with the Master Calculator and place it on all important tops and bottoms and half-way points on the Daily, Weekly and Monthly Charts you will soon see how well it works and will learn to get trend indications very quickly.

March 6, 1955

MASTER PRICE AND TIME CHART

SQUARES 1 TO 33 INCLUSIVE
PRICE AND TIME 1 TO 1089

This chart starts with the square of 1 in the center, and moves clockwise around with the odd squares coming out on the 45 degree angle. These are 1, 9, 25, 49, 81, etc. The even squares run in the opposite direction on a 45 degree angle, beginning with the square of 2, which is 4 and continuing on this angle. This produces a variable in time and price of 2. That is 2 points in price, 2 days, 2 weeks, or two months in time. This chart proves why prices move so much faster at higher levels, and measures exact resistance levels in the squares.

Example: May soy beans extreme low 44¢. This is in the square of 7. From 43 to 49, is 90 degrees. When the price was at 436-3/4, from 421 to 441 covered 90 degrees. Therefore to swing between these angles required 20 points while at low levels it was only 5 points. It is the same with the time periods. At the present time May soy beans is in the 253rd month from December 28, 1932 and you will note that from 241 to 257 is 90 degrees, or 16 points, in price or 16 periods in months, weeks and days. You will note that the 253rd months is on the angle of 22½ degrees or 112½ degrees from the starting point and the opposite point of the angle is January 13, making January 13 to 15 important for a change in trend. The time periods starting at the left and in the East beginning March 21, are the seasonal time periods, and get the same position on time, you would start soy beans from December 28, which is just a little past the seasonal date of December 21, and January 15, is just 2 days from the 22½ degree angle, July 27, extreme low on May soy beans is just beyond July 14, where the 22½ degree angle comes out.

All of the important highs on May beans are marked with a green circle. The important lows are marked with a red circle. You will note that 44¢ was just one point from the 45 degree angle and 436-3/4 the extreme high was on this 45 degree angle. Also on a green angle of 22½ degrees. The extreme low on May beans, 67, on July 27, 1939, was on a green angle of 22½ degrees, and this angles runs to the date of Aug. 31, and Feb. 28. Also 202½ was on the same line with 67, and 405 was just 1¢ away from the angle of 221½ degrees. From the important highs and lows, I have drawn 45 degree angles and 90 degree angles in order that you can see the important resistance levels.

Example: The recent high of 311¼ on May soy beans made on December 2, 1953, was on the 90 degree angle or straight up from 436-3/4, and also on the angle of 22½ degrees which runs from 44 and 277, and you will note that 310 is on a 45 degree angle from 240 the low in August 1953, making this a strong resistance and selling level. The time period of 253 months is in red figures and the price of 305 is on the 90 degree angle from 233 low and 240 low. A price of 305 is below the 45 degree angle from 44¢, 344, and 240. It is on the angle of zero degrees from 240. When the prices sells at 303 it will be below the 45 degree angle from 240. A complete cycle or a round trip is most important to watch for a change in trend. From 240 to 305, was a complete square, cycle or round trip, but to reach on 90 degree angle, the price had to make 308. The natural resistance level from the 45 degree angle at 307, to the 90 degree angle at 316, or one half was 311, the natural resistance and selling level.

When May beans declined on December 17, to 296, they were on the 45 degree angle from 44, because the time period was 252 months and we 44 which gives 296, making this a temporary support and buying level. Also, it was 1¢ above the angle of no degrees or 180 degrees east of 44¢ extreme low.

You should always consider how many degrees the price has moved from an extreme high to an extreme low. From a high of 311, to 298 is 67½ degrees and is about 11¼ degrees, which would make 78-3/4 degrees or 7/8th of 90.

When the price had advanced from 240 to 305 it had moved 360 degrees or a complete circle. Therefore at 311, it had moved 33-3/4 degrees more than the circle of 360 degrees. For the price to decline to the next natural resistance level from 340 low would be 289 which would be on a 90 degree angle and on the square of 17 and on the 45 degree angle in the natural squares. To move to 90 degrees from 311 would be 285. The next important resistance level would be 277-276, which would be 180 degrees from 311 and on the same angle of 22½ degrees.

Bring up all time periods from monthly highs and lows and weekly highs and lows and see how they stand in the square in relation to the price.

Example: For the week ending January 9, 1954, May soy beans will be in the 20th week, from August 20th low. Note that the beginning with square 1 at 20 on the angle of 22½ degrees and should the price drop below 303 it will be below this time angle, and should it decline to 297 it will be on no degrees or 180 degrees from 20 in the time period.

February 15, 1920, high 405. November 15, 1953 was 405 months, therefore, December 15 was 406 months and January 15, will be 407 months and 303 is no degrees or 130 degrees from this time angle.

January 15, 1945 high to January 15, 1954 will 72 months. Look at 72 in the squares and you will find that 72 which is in the square of 8 is on the same line as 44, and running across the price is 295. Therefore, if the price is below this it is in a weak position.

January 15, 1954 to Feb. 15, is the 73rd month and this is on a 45 degree angle, naturally, making February important for a change in trend.

1939, July 27, May beans low, 67 to January 27, 1954, will be 174 months.

Note that 174 is opposite the price of 296, and that 176th month will be March 27, and this will be in the balance between the two red lines and that the seasonal time period is marked March 21, making this important to watch for a change in trend.

Suppose the price is at 288, this will be on a 90 degree angle of the time period of 176. And 176 of course, is opposite 69 low and 178 months which will be May 27 will be opposite 180 degrees from 67 the extreme low on May beans.

If you will put in the time to study and practice with this Master Chart, using all of the time periods and price levels, you will soon find that it is easy to determine a change in trend from this chart alone.

December 30, 1953   W. D. Gann

PRICE AND TIME CHART-CYCLE OF 0 DEGREES TO 360 TIME PERIODS 15 DAYS EQUALS DEGREES - 24 CYCLES 24 PRICE FOR DAILY TIME CYCLES

This chart is entirely different to the Master Square Chart and is to be used for grains and wool. It can also be used for stocks. The outer circle starts on the right marked "E" for East. March 20. This is the seasonal yearly time periods and because the earth revolves on its axis in 24 hours, we use 15 degrees of longitude, which is 1 hour of time or approximately 15 days. From March 20, when spring begins to May 6, is 45 degrees, or 3 hours of longitude and from March 20 to June 21, is ¼ of the year, 90 degrees or 6 hours of longitude. July 23 is 1/3 of a year or 120 degrees from March 20. This is 8 hours of longitude.

September 23rd is 180 degrees of longitude from March 20, or 12 hours of time. This is the annual revolution of the earth around the sun and the time periods are the same as the outer circle. One complete circle is 12 months of time or 365¼ days. For the monthly time periods, 360 months complete the circle, and for the weekly time periods, 360 weeks complete the circle, but 364 weeks is 7 times 52 or 7 years.

The price also moves around the 360 degree circle. The price of 44¢ for May soybeans is 1¢ below the 45 degree angle at the date of May 5, and the price of 405 is the same degree because it is 45 added to 360. A price of 67 extreme low on May beans is at 67½ degrees or ½ between 60 degrees and 75 degrees. The price 470-3/4 is at 76 degrees 45 minutes because it is one complete circle of 360 and 76-3/4 over.

You will note the inner circles and price and time periods begin with one at zero and end at 24 at 360, making a complete cycle or equal to one revolution of the earth upon its axis. These are to be used as prices for the daily fluctuation and these cycles as follows; 24, 48, 72, 98, 120, 144, 165, 192, 216, 240, 264, 288, 312, 330, 360, 384, 408, 432, 466, 480, 504, 528, 552, and 576 which is the square of 24. This means when these prices are reached that they are on the 24th hour in longitude and have completed the circle of 360 degrees.

Starting with 1 or 0, 3¢ a bushel equal 45 degrees. 6¢ per bushel equals 90 degrees or ¼ of the circle. 9¢ per bushel equals 135 degrees and 12¢ per bushel equals 180 degrees or ½ of the circle. 15¢ equals 225 degrees or 5/8 of a circle. 18 equals 270 degrees or 3/4 of a circle. 21¢ equals 315 degrees or 7/8 of a circle. 24 in price equals 360 degrees or the complete circle, and so on around. I have drawn a green circle around the extreme high prices for May beans and a red circle around the low prices, in order that you can see when price reaches 45 degrees, 90 degrees, 120 degrees, 135 degrees, 180 degrees, 225 degrees, 240, 270, 315, and 360 from any high or low.

A complete circle or round trip of 24¢ is important for a change in trend. 48¢ is next important and 3 times around or 72¢ is of still greater importance.

Example: May Soybeans low 239½. Note that 240 is the end of the 10th cycle and if we add 72 to this we get 311¼. Therefore when May Soybeans reach 311¼ they had made complete cycles and this was a strong resistance and selling level. When they declined from 311¼ to 296 a decline of 15¢ they had moved down 225 degrees or 5/8 of a circle making this a resistance level. Note that 296 in price is of 120 degrees and the time period is July 23, close to July 17, and 296 is 2 cycles down from 344, the last extreme high. Follow this angle across at 180 degrees and you will see that 296 is opposite 44, 65 and 144. You will also note that 295 is 180 degrees or opposite 67.

The extreme low price, and when the price declines 294, it is below this angle and also below the natural 90 degree angle. Next you would watch 287 which is a complete cycle of 24¢ down from 311, and if the price went below this level you would watch 284 which is the same cycle 44, 68, and 164 and 285 is the same cycle as 67. When the price advanced from the low of 201½ to 344½ it lacked just 1½¢ of being 6 complete cycles up from the low, but the price stopped at 344½ because it was against July 7th bottom and 180 degrees from 44 and 68 low.

Note that 436 was against the angle of 60 degrees on the date May 20th. This was 150 degrees from 67 low and approximately the same from 44 low as they were only 15 degrees apart. When price was at 436 it was up 369 cents. Note that 369 is against the 45 degree angle at 135 date August 8. A natural resistance angle and 180 from 44 low.

When the price declined from 436-3/4 to 301½ it was down 135¼ points and 135 is a 45 degree angle on the great circle and 202 is at 150 degrees or against August 23rd, and this was against the cycle at 154 and also opposite 311 the cent high price. 311 from 344½ gives 33 down. Look at 33 in price and you find it is against the 45 degree angle or 135 degrees, note Aug. 3. Another confirmation of the resistance.

From 201½ to 311½ is 110. Look at 110 and you find it is at 210 degrees and opposite a price of 314, an old top. The date for 210 is October 23. The price reached the high of 311¼ on 2, which was at the date March 8 angle 345. This was ahead of time and being up 72¢ a reaction was due. When the price dropped back to 305. It was below the time period which was December 7, angle 255 degrees.

Prices are governed by time and time causes prices to change and the time angles are the resistance to price. These are measured in hours of longitude, which are basic geometric angles and determine the changes in trend. By checking over past records you see how accurate this works out.

Example: Feb. 15, 1920 high 435. This price was against the 45 degree angle at 315 date Feb. 5 and you would watch for a change in trend because it was at the correct annual time period and the price was 45 degrees above 360 and 45 degrees below 360 in the 24 circle cycle which determines the daily fluctuations and the fast moves up and down. First you look to the weekly and monthly and see the position and next you look to the daily position and watch daily chart for resistance and on Dec. 2, the daily high and low chart gave the first indication of a change in trend and showed a time turn.

Because it was the completion of 3 twenty-four price cycles from the low of 239½. Why was 240 a support point? One reason was because 240 is 2/3 of a circle and from the high of 436-3/4 to the low of 44 gives the main half way point of 240-3/8. The next important halfway point is 218-3/8 or 1/2 of 436-3/4. Note that 219 is against the 45 degree angle date May 6, and 219 on the great circle is half way between 210 and 225 from 67 low to 436-3/4 high gives the half way point 251. Note the 252 on the 24 circle is at 180 degrees date Sept. 25 making this a resistance level of great importance and when the price advanced above this level it continued on up to 311 and never reached below 249 after it crossed 252. Suppose May beans should decline to 276. They will be at 180 degrees or 1 cycle up from the halfway point of 252.

Analyze price of the grains in the same way but use separate charts of this kind to make the high and low prices and the dates so the angles will come out.

1955   W. D. Gann

W.D. Gann's Hand-drawn
Charts and Tables

MASTER 360° CHART

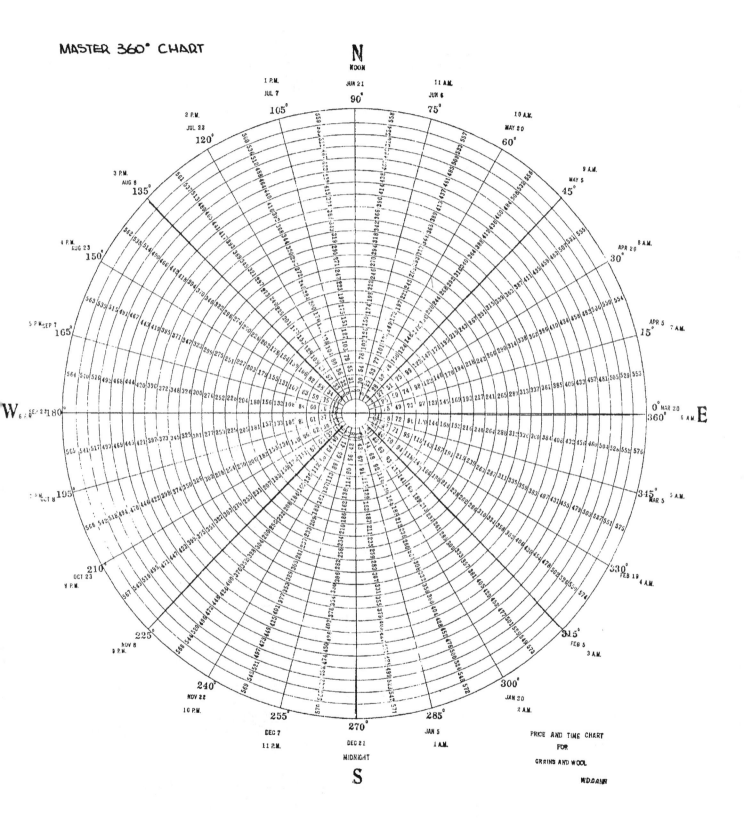

PRICE AND TIME CHART
FOR
GRAINS AND WOOL

W.D.GANN

1	44 = 22° ♓	28	314 3/4 = 15° ♓					
2	67	26 ♏	29	320 1/2 = 14° ♉		670 - 6		
3	68 1/2	8° ☊ ☉	30	323 1/2	8° ♊		8	6	13
4	69	13 " ☉	31	334	20 ♏		☐	5	
5	170	30 ♏	32	344 1/2	26° ♏	△	8	9
6	131 1/2	2° ♏	33	361	8° ♑	⚹	7	7
7	154 1/2	6° ♏	34	422	16° ♋	30°	4	
8	164	22° ♏	35	425	10° ♏	150	5	
9	182 1/2	4° ♈ ☉	36	486 3/4	14° ♐			
10	201 1/2	24° ♏	37	405 —	30° ♓			
11	202	18° "						
12	203	6° ☊ ☉		☿	☿	60	120	
13	210	30° ♏	26° ♏	☽	60 ♏	♑	8	
14	220 1/2	4° ♐	6	8	26	30 ♏	30°	
15	224	22° ♓	24	7	22	22°	24	
16	232 1/2	30° ♉	26	22	②	30	①	14
17	239 1/2	26° ♋	2	16	22		
18	239	22° ♋	10	28	26°	③	
19	276 3/4	24° ♉	⑥	30	⑤		
20	265 3/4	18° ♏		② 8			
21	268 1/4	16° ♓	♈ ☊	☐ ♐ ☐ ♋		
22	275 3/4	18° ♊	4° 16 8 —	4° 18 14°	8 28 6	
23	281	28° ♊	2	8	14	
24	255	22° ♏		3	② 3	
25	306 3/4 24° ♑ ✓		☐	⑤	(MOF.)	
26	309 17° ☉		Mean of 5	MOF - mean out	
27	309 3/4 18° ♈ ④		cal. of 8	- CE	

Mean of 5   MOF - mean out
cal. of 8 - CE
O of 8 - Cycle of Eight

h Scale a cycle

	♈	♉	II 60	♋ ♍
30	900 1800 2700 3600	4500	2570 5040 7560 100.80	157.20 1764
28	870 1740 2640 3540	4440		
	840	70 3570		
	810	4410		
	780			
4	720 1620 2520 3420	452	2100	4556
70	600 1500 2400 3300		1848 1680	
16	510 480 1380 2280 3180			
	1200 2176 3090		1260	15 1.89.00 Aug 23
				15 ♓ ♀ 184
12	360 1260 2160 3060			
			840	10 184°80
8	240 1148 2040 2940		756 672 588 504 420	
4	120 1080 1920 2820			
	1830	4530		
0	♋ 900 1800 2700 3600	4500	♈ 2574 5045 7560	10085 13712 17640
	♉ II 60 ♍		II 60	

4 Scale a cycle

	♈	♉	♊	♋	♍	♎	7 ♐	8 ♏	9 ♐	10 ♑	11 ♒	♓
0	360	720 1080 1440 1800			2160 2520 2880 3240 3600	2960 4320						
28	348	708 1068 1428										

(numerous handwritten numeric columns, largely illegible)

4 Jupiter Scale a cycle

☉ 15° in 15 Days −30 = 30 By
☿ 7½ 15° " 15 −30 "

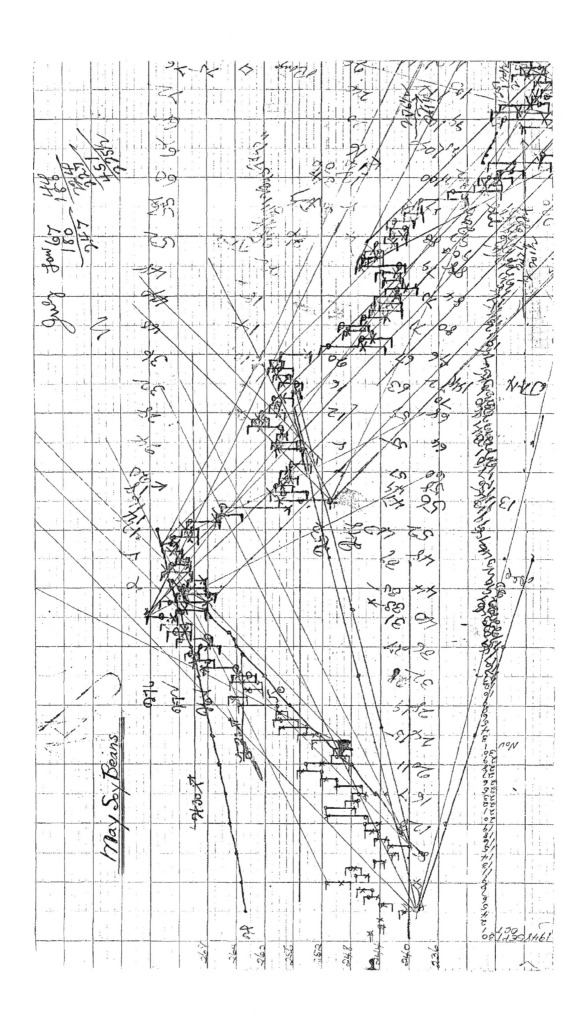

May Soy Beans

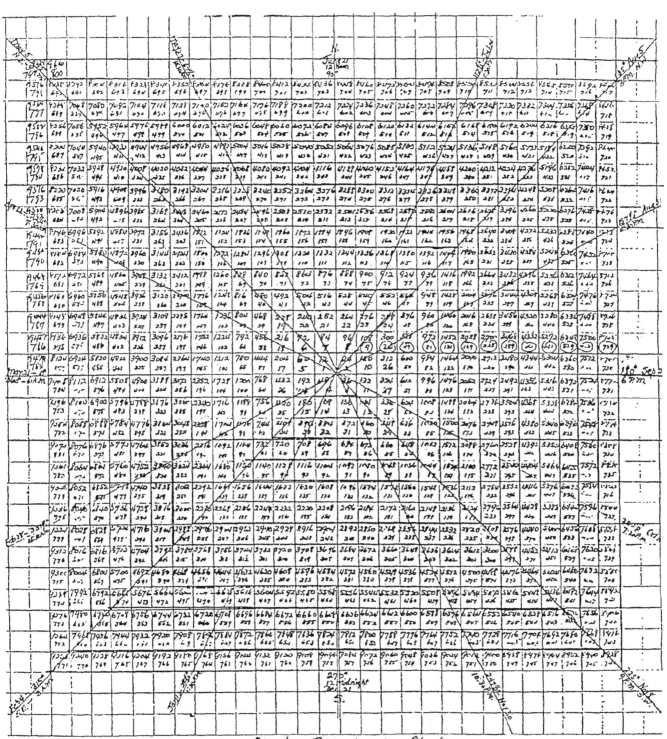

Master Price & Time Chart
for
Cotton, Coffee, Cocoa, Wool,
and Grain

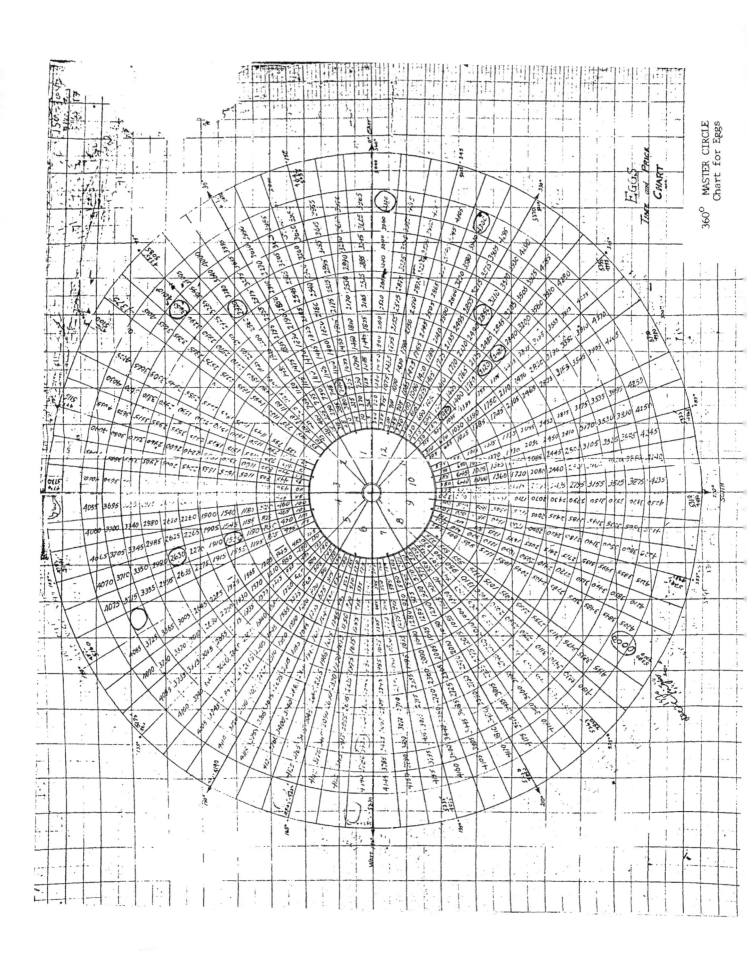

360° MASTER CIRCLE
Chart for Eggs

EGGS
TIME and PRICE CHART

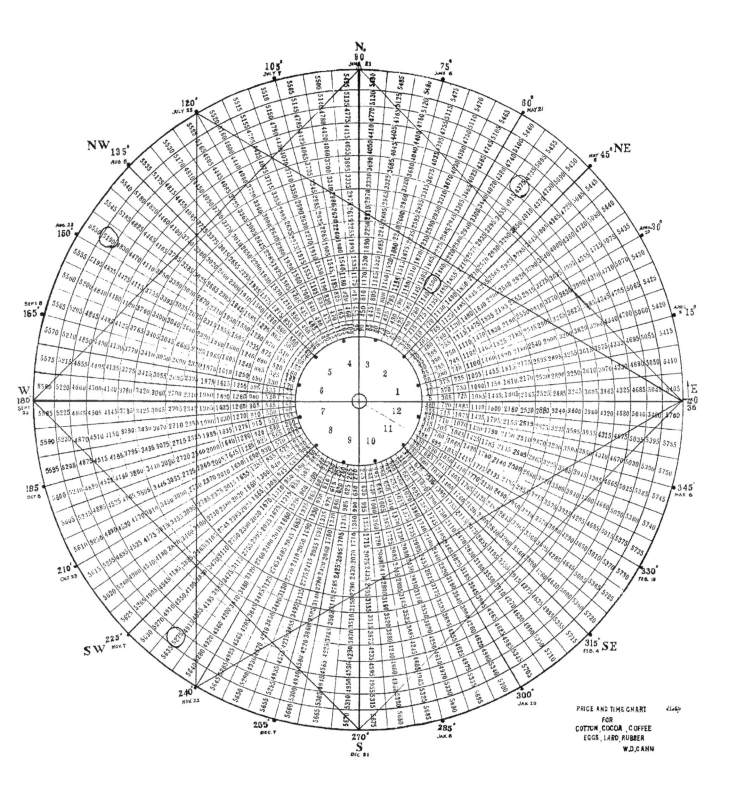

PRICE AND TIME CHART
FOR
COTTON, COCOA, COFFEE
EGGS, LARD, RUBBER

W.D.GANN

Eggs October Low May 28 1932

High 585 Sept 10 Aug 30

100 to 6460 → $1008.00 = 9.2160⁰ ⇒ Gain $8,208.00

1500 → $2,160.00 to 5855 = Gain $6,283.60

Egg V 70 Points to 1 Month

70 Points = $100.80/100

5855 = $8,445.60

6400 $9,216.00 → 70 → $1008.00

5460	5390	5320	5250	5180	5110	5040	4970	4900	4830
78	77	76	75	74	73	72	71	70	69
5530	3360	3230	3160	3080	3010	2940	2870	2800	4760
79	47	46	45	44	43	42	41	40	68
5660	3360	1680	1610	1540	1470	1400	1330	2730	4690
80	48	24	23	22	21	20	19	39	67
5670	3430	1750	630	560	490	420	1260	2660	4620
81	49	25	9	8	7	6	18	38	66
5740	3500	1820	700	140	70	350	1190	2590	4550
82	50	26	10	2	1	5	17	37	65
5810	3570	1890	770	210	280	1120	2520	4480	7000
83	51	27	11	3	4	16	36	64	100
5880	3640	1960	840	910	980	1050	2450	4410	6930
84	52	28	12	13	14	15	35	63	99
5950	3710	2030	2100	2170	2240	2310	2380	4340	6860
85	53	29	30	31	32	33	34	62	98
6020	3780	3850	3920	3990	4060	4130	4200	4270	6790
86	54	55	56	57	58	59	60	61	97
6090	6160	6230	6300	6370	6440	6510	6580	6650	6720
87	88	89	90	91	92	93	94	95	96

7 DAYS – 1 TO 10 YEARS

		1	2	3	4	5	6	7	8	9	10	11	12	13	14	15	16	17	18	19	20	21	22	23	24	25	26	27	28	29
MARCH 20																														
MAY 5	1/8	6½	58½	110½	162½	214½	266½	318½	370½	422½	474½	526½	578½	630½	682½	734½	786½	838½	890½	942½	994½	1046½	1098½	1150½	1202½	1254½	1306½	1358½	1410½	1462½
JUNE 21	1/4	13	65	117	169	221	273	325	377	429	481	533	585	637	689	741	793	845	897	949	1001	1053	1105	1157	1209	1261	1313	1365	1417	1469
JULY 23	1/3	17	69	121	173	225	277	329	381	433	485	537	589	641	693	745	797	849	901	953	1005	1057	1109	1161	1213	1265	1317	1369	1421	1473
AUGUST 5	3/8	19½	71½	123½	175½	227½	279½	331½	383½	435½	487½	539½	591½	643½	695½	747½	799½	851½	903½	955½	1007½	1059½	1111½	1163½	1215½	1267½	1319½	1371½	1423½	1475½
SEPTEMBER 22	1/2	26	78	130	182	234	286	338	390	442	494	546	598	650	702	754	806	858	910	962	1014	1066	1118	1170	1222	1274	1326	1378	1430	1482
NOVEMBER 8	5/8	32½	84½	136½	188½	240½	292½	344½	396½	448½	500½	552½	604½	656½	708½	760½	812½	864½	916½	968½	1020½	1072½	1124½	1176½	1228½	1280½	1332½	1384½	1436½	1488½
NOVEMBER 22	2/3	35	87	139	191	243	295	347	399	451	503	555	607	659	711	763	815	867	919	971	1023	1075	1127	1179	1231	1283	1335	1387	1439	1491
DECEMBER 21	3/4	39	91	143	195	247	299	351	403	455	507	559	611	663	715	767	819	871	923	975	1027	1079	1131	1183	1235	1287	1339	1391	1443	1495
FEBRUARY 4	7/8	45½	97½	149½	201½	253½	305½	357½	409½	461½	513½	565½	617½	669½	721½	773½	825½	877½	929½	981½	1033½	1085½	1137½	1189½	1241½	1293½	1345½	1397½	1449½	1501½
MARCH 20	1	52	104	156	208	260	312	364	416	468	520	572	624	676	728	780	832	884	936	988	1040	1092	1144	1196	1248	1300	1352	1404	1456	1508

WEEKLY TIME PERIODS 7 DAYS FROM HIGHS OR LOWS. THE YEAR IS DIVIDED INTO 1/6s AND 1/5s.

CASH AND MAY SOY BEANS

TIME AND PRICE PERIODS IN 7 DAYS, 1 to 40 years.

DAILY, WEEKLY, MONTHLY, TIME PERIODS

→ PRICE SCALE

MAY SOYBEANS
JULY 27 1939 LOW 674

SQUARE 12

	1	2	3	4	5	6	7	8	9	10	11	12
12	12	24	36	48	60	72	84	96	108	120	132	144
11	11	23	35	47	59	71	83	95	107	119	131	143
10	10	22	34	46	58	70	82	94	106	118	130	142
9	9	21	33	45	57	69	81	93	105	117	129	141
8	8	20	32	44	56	68	80	92	104	116	128	140
7	7	19	31	43	55	67	79	91	103	115	127	139
6	6	18	30	42	54	66	78	90	102	114	126	138
5	5	17	29	41	53	65	77	89	101	113	125	137
4	4	16	28	40	52	64	76	88	100	112	124	136
3	3	15	27	39	51	63	75	87	99	111	123	135
2	2	14	26	38	50	62	74	86	98	110	122	134
1	1	13	25	37	49	61	73	85	97	109	121	133

[Master 360° Square of 12 Chart for Eggs]

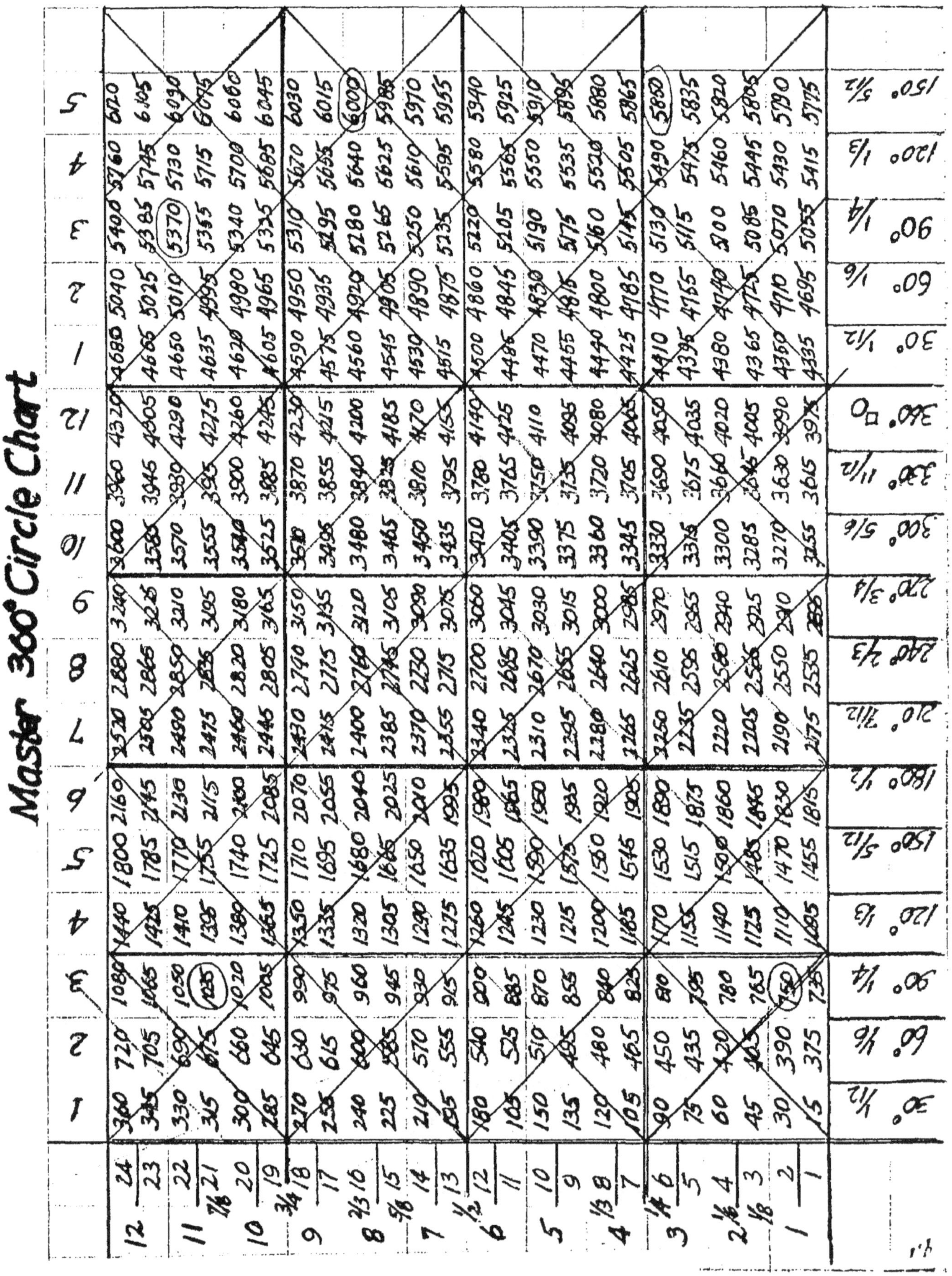

Master 360° Circle Chart

	5	4	3	2	1	12	11	10	9	8	7	6	5	4	3	2	1	
12	6120	5760	5400	5040	4680	4320	3960	3600	3240	2880	2520	2160	1800	1440	1080	720	360	
	6105	5745	5385	5025	4665	4305	3945	3585	3225	2865	2505	2145	1785	1425	1065	705	345	24 / 23
11	6090	5730	5370	5010	4650	4290	3930	3570	3210	2850	2490	2130	1770	1410	1050	690	330	22
	6075	5715	5355	4995	4635	4275	3915	3555	3195	2835	2475	2115	1755	1395	1035	675	315	7/8 21
10	6060	5700	5340	4980	4620	4260	3900	3540	3180	2820	2460	2100	1740	1380	1020	660	300	20
	6045	5685	5335	4965	4605	4245	3885	3525	3165	2805	2445	2085	1725	1365	1005	645	285	3/4 19
9	6030	5670	5310	4950	4590	4230	3870	3510	3150	2790	2430	2070	1710	1350	990	630	270	18
	6015	5655	5295	4935	4575	4215	3855	3495	3135	2775	2415	2055	1695	1335	975	615	255	17
8	6000	5640	5280	4920	4560	4200	3840	3480	3120	2760	2400	2040	1680	1320	960	600	240	2/3 16
	5985	5625	5265	4905	4545	4185	3825	3465	3105	2745	2385	2025	1665	1305	945	585	225	15
7	5970	5610	5250	4890	4530	4170	3810	3450	3090	2730	2370	2010	1650	1290	930	570	210	5/8 14
	5955	5595	5235	4875	4515	4155	3795	3435	3075	2715	2355	1995	1635	1275	915	555	195	13
6	5940	5580	5220	4860	4500	4140	3780	3420	3060	2700	2340	1980	1620	1260	900	540	180	1/2 12
	5925	5565	5205	4845	4485	4125	3765	3405	3045	2685	2325	1965	1605	1245	885	525	165	11
5	5910	5550	5190	4830	4470	4110	3750	3390	3030	2670	2310	1950	1590	1230	870	510	150	10
	5895	5535	5175	4815	4455	4095	3735	3375	3015	2655	2295	1935	1575	1215	855	495	135	9
4	5880	5520	5160	4800	4440	4080	3720	3360	3000	2640	2280	1920	1560	1200	840	480	120	1/3 8
	5865	5505	5145	4785	4425	4065	3705	3345	2985	2625	2265	1905	1545	1185	825	465	105	7
3	5850	5490	5130	4770	4410	4050	3690	3330	2970	2610	2250	1890	1530	1170	810	450	90	1/4 6
	5835	5475	5115	4765	4395	4035	3675	3315	2955	2595	2235	1875	1515	1155	795	435	75	5
2	5820	5460	5100	4740	4380	4020	3660	3300	2940	2580	2220	1860	1500	1140	780	420	60	1/6 4
	5805	5445	5085	4725	4365	4005	3645	3285	2925	2565	2205	1845	1485	1125	765	405	45	3
1	5790	5430	5070	4710	4350	3990	3630	3270	2910	2550	2190	1830	1470	1110	750	390	30	1/12 2
	5775	5415	5055	4695	4335	3975	3615	3255	2895	2535	2175	1815	1455	1095	735	375	15	1

Degree / fraction column (right side):
150° 5/12, 120° 1/3, 90° 1/4, 60° 1/6, 30° 1/12, 360° 0°, 330° 11/12, 300° 5/6, 270° 3/4, 240° 2/3, 210° 7/12, 180° 1/2, 150° 5/12, 120° 1/3, 90° 1/4, 60° 1/6, 30° 1/12

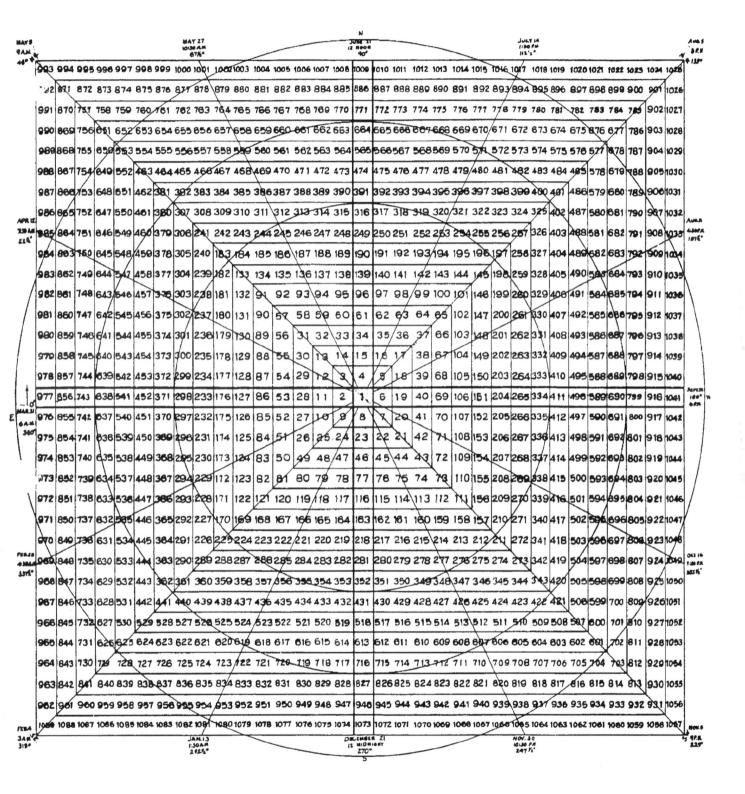

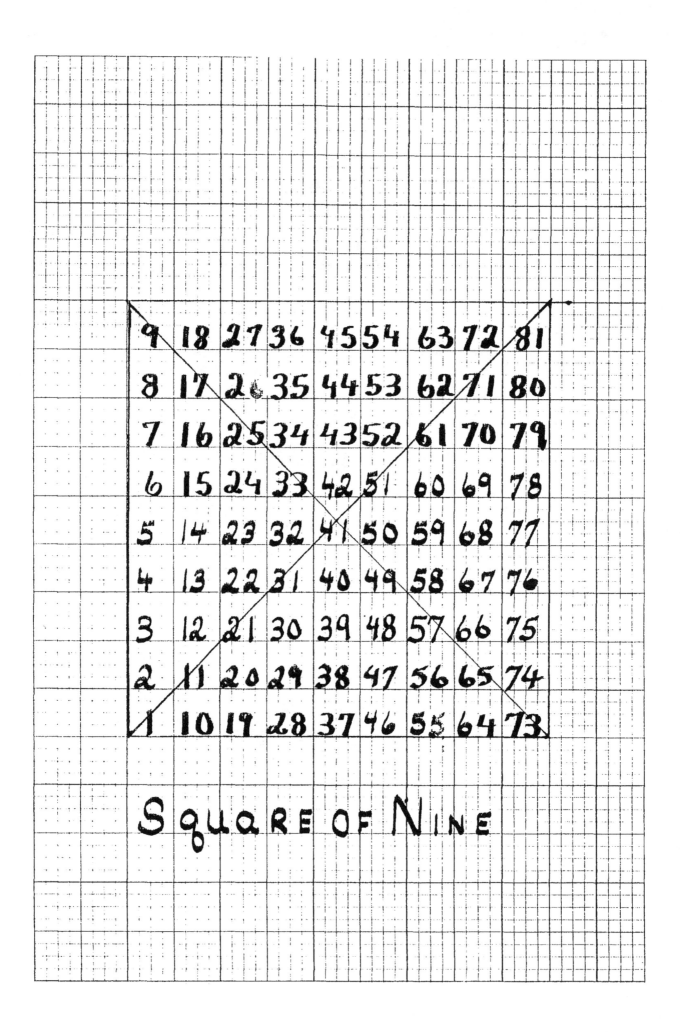

9	18	27	36	45	54	63	72	81
8	17	26	35	44	53	62	71	80
7	16	25	34	43	52	61	70	79
6	15	24	33	42	51	60	69	78
5	14	23	32	41	50	59	68	77
4	13	22	31	40	49	58	67	76
3	12	21	30	39	48	57	66	75
2	11	20	29	38	47	56	65	74
1	10	19	28	37	46	55	64	73

SQUARE OF NINE

Six Squares of Nine

9	18	27	36	45	54	63	72	81
8	17	26	35	44	53	62	71	80
7	16	25	34	43	52	61	70	79
6	15	24	33	42	51	60	69	78
5	14	23	32	41	50	59	68	77
4	13	22	31	40	49	58	67	76
3	12	21	30	39	48	57	66	75
2	11	20	29	38	47	56	65	74
1	10	19	28	37	46	55	64	73

90	99	108	117	126	135	144	153	162
89	98	107	116	125	134	143	152	161
88	97	106	115	124	133	142	151	160
87	96	105	114	123	132	141	150	159
86	95	104	113	122	131	140	149	158
85	94	103	112	121	130	139	148	157
84	93	102	111	120	129	138	147	156
83	92	101	110	119	128	137	146	155
82	91	100	109	118	127	136	145	154

171	180	189	198	207	216	225	234	243
170	179	188	197	206	215	224	233	242
169	178	187	196	205	214	223	232	241
168	177	186	195	204	213	222	231	240
167	176	185	194	203	212	221	230	239
166	175	184	193	202	211	220	229	238
165	174	183	192	201	210	219	228	237
164	173	182	191	200	209	218	227	236
163	172	181	190	199	208	217	226	235

252	261	270	279	288	297	306	315	324
251	260	269	278	287	296	305	314	323
250	259	268	277	286	295	304	313	322
249	258	267	276	285	294	303	312	321
248	257	266	275	284	293	302	311	320
247	256	265	274	283	292	301	310	319
246	255	264	273	282	291	300	309	318
245	254	263	272	281	290	299	308	317
244	253	262	271	280	289	298	307	316

333	342	351	360	369	378	387	396	405
332	341	350	359	368	377	386	395	404
331	340	349	358	367	376	385	394	403
330	339	348	357	366	375	384	393	402
329	338	347	356	365	374	383	392	401
328	337	346	355	364	373	382	391	400
327	336	345	354	363	372	381	390	399
326	335	344	353	362	371	380	389	398
325	334	343	352	361	370	379	388	397

414	423	432	441	450	459	468	477	486
413	422	431	440	449	458	467	476	485
412	421	430	439	448	457	466	475	484
411	420	429	438	447	456	465	474	483
410	419	428	437	446	455	464	473	482
409	418	427	436	445	454	463	472	481
408	417	426	435	444	453	462	471	480
407	416	425	434	443	452	461	470	479
406	415	424	433	442	451	460	469	478

SQUARE OF THE CIRCLE

	1	2	3	4	5	6	7	8	9	10	11	12	13	14	15	16	17	18	19
19	19	38	57	76	95	114	133	152	171	190	209	228	247	266	285	304	323	342	361
18	18	37	56	75	94	113	132	151	170	189	208	227	246	265	284	303	322	341	360
17	17	36	55	74	93	112	131	150	169	188	207	226	245	264	283	302	321	340	359
16	16	35	54	73	92	111	130	149	168	187	206	225	244	263	282	301	320	339	358
15	15	34	53	72	91	110	129	148	167	186	205	224	243	262	281	300	319	338	357
14	14	33	52	71	90	109	128	147	166	185	204	223	242	261	280	299	318	337	356
13	13	32	51	70	89	108	127	146	165	184	203	222	241	260	279	298	317	336	355
12	12	31	50	69	88	107	126	145	164	183	202	221	240	259	278	297	316	335	354
11	11	30	49	68	87	106	125	144	163	182	201	220	239	258	277	296	315	334	353
10	10	29	48	67	86	105	124	143	162	181	200	219	238	257	276	295	314	333	352
9	9	28	47	66	85	104	123	142	161	180	199	218	237	256	275	294	313	332	351
8	8	27	46	65	84	103	122	141	160	179	198	217	236	255	274	293	312	331	350
7	7	26	45	64	83	102	121	140	159	178	197	216	235	254	273	292	311	330	349
6	6	25	44	63	82	101	120	139	158	177	196	215	234	253	272	291	310	329	348
5	5	24	43	62	81	100	119	138	157	176	195	214	233	252	271	290	309	328	347
4	4	23	42	61	80	99	118	137	156	175	194	213	232	251	270	289	308	327	346
3	3	22	41	60	79	98	117	136	155	174	193	212	231	250	269	288	307	326	345
2	2	21	40	59	78	97	116	135	154	173	192	211	230	249	268	287	306	325	344
1	1	20	39	58	77	96	115	134	153	172	191	210	229	248	267	286	305	324	343

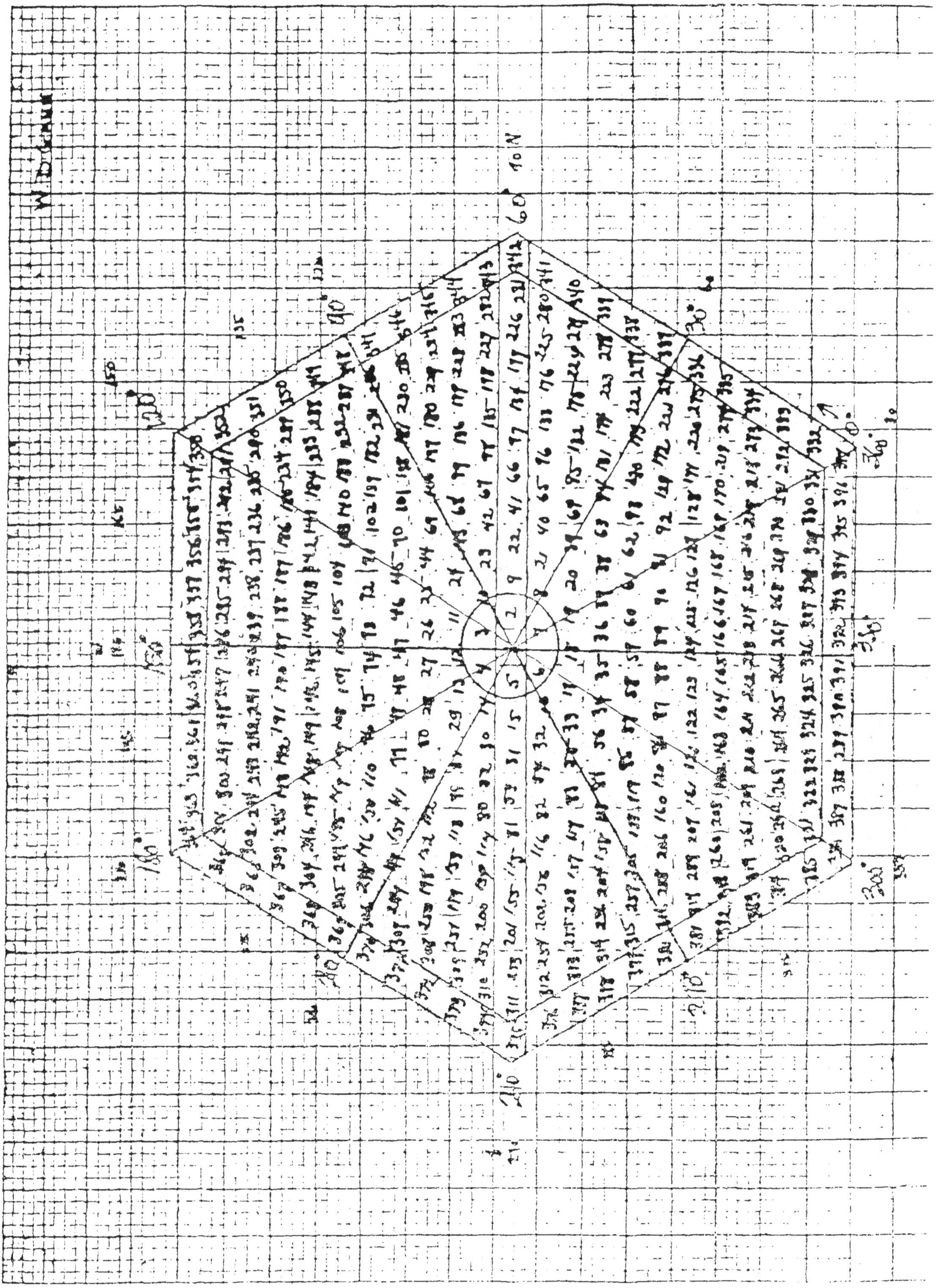

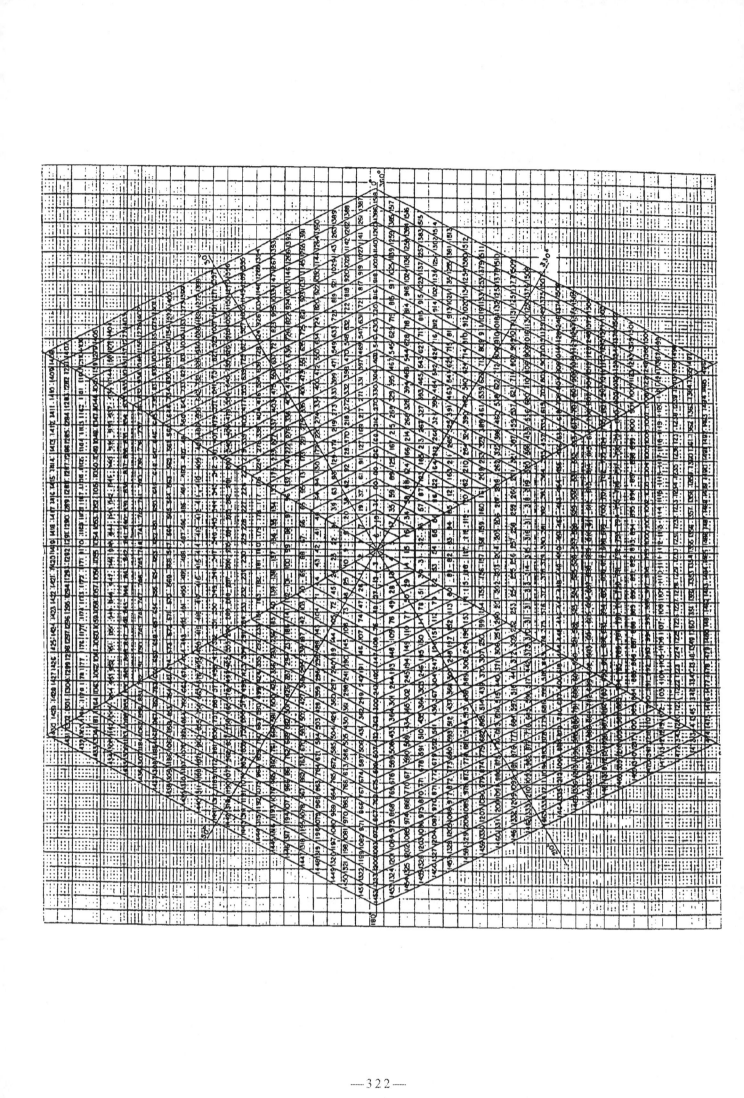

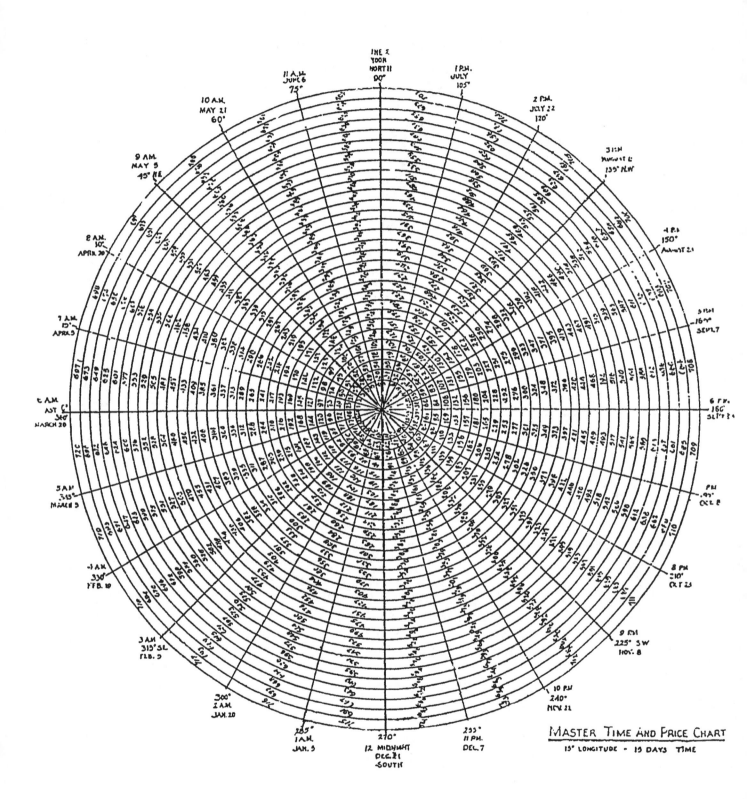

MASTER TIME AND PRICE CHART

15° LONGITUDE - 15 DAYS TIME

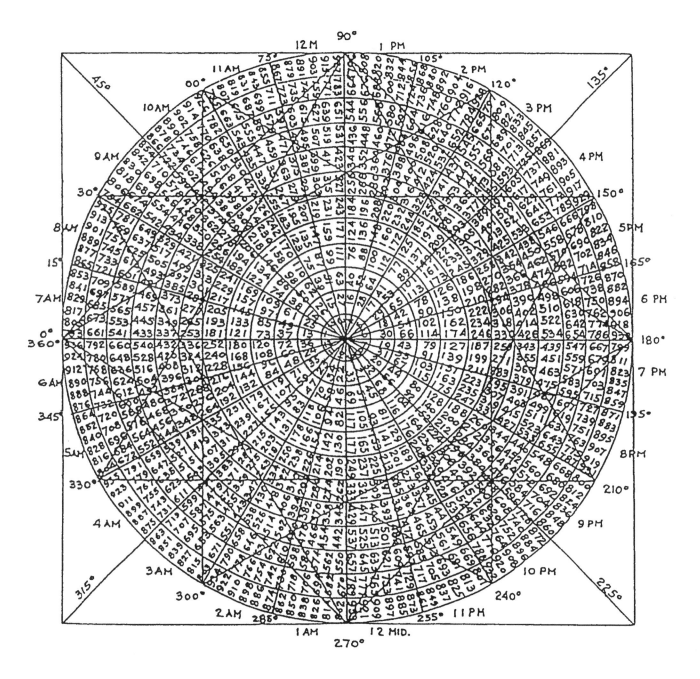

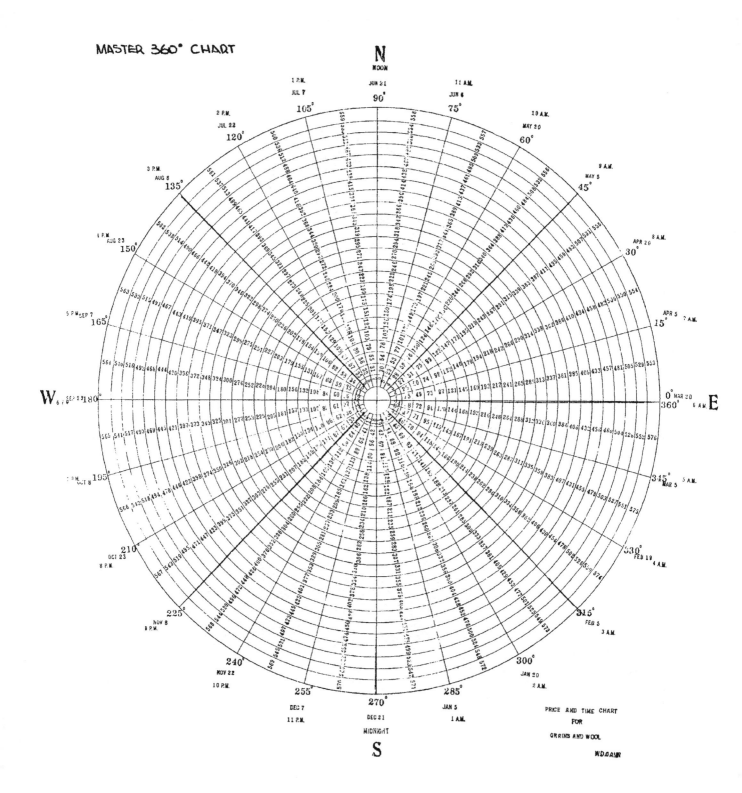

MASTER 360° CHART

PRICE AND TIME CHART
FOR
GRAINS AND WOOL

W.D.GANN

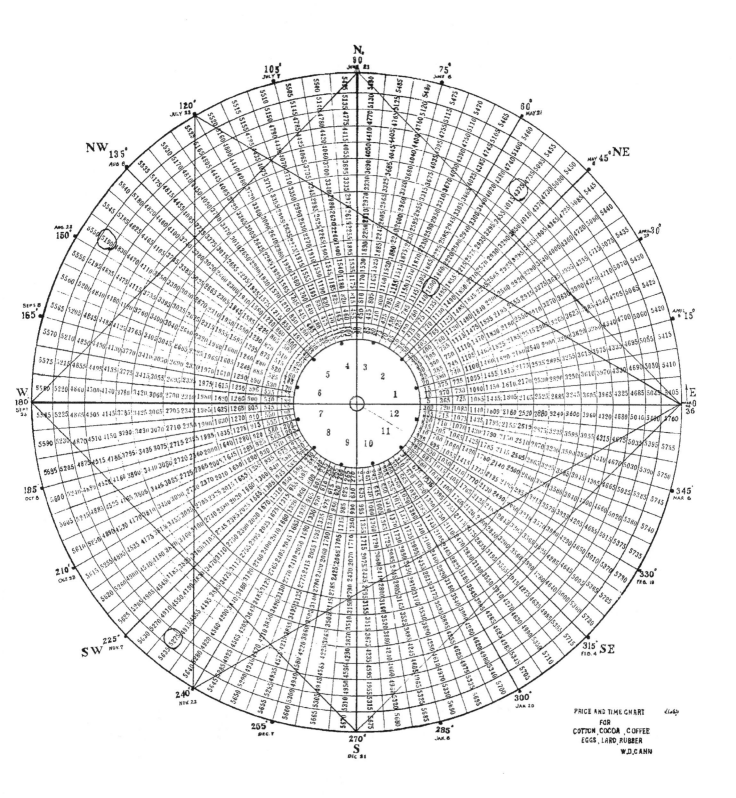

PRICE AND TIME CHART
FOR
COTTON, COCOA, COFFEE
EGGS, LARD, RUBBER
W.D.GANN

NYSE

PERMANENT CHART

1	2	3	4	5	6	7	8	9	10	11	12	13	14	15	16	17	18	19	20
20	40	60	80	100	120	140	160	180	200	220	240	260	280	300	320	340	360	380	400
19	39	59	79	99	119	139	159	179	199	219	239	259	279	299	319	339	359	379	399
18	38	58	78	98	118	138	158	178	198	218	238	258	278	298	318	338	358	378	398
17	37	57	77	97	117	137	157	177	197	217	237	257	277	297	317	337	357	377	397
16	36	56	76	96	116	136	156	176	196	216	236	256	276	296	316	336	356	376	396
15	35	55	75	95	115	135	155	175	195	215	235	255	275	295	315	335	355	375	395
14	34	54	74	94	114	134	154	174	194	214	234	254	274	294	314	334	354	374	394
13	33	53	73	93	113	133	153	173	193	213	233	253	273	293	313	333	353	373	393
12	32	52	72	92	112	132	152	172	192	212	232	252	272	292	312	332	352	372	392
11	31	51	71	91	111	131	151	171	191	211	231	251	271	291	311	331	351	371	391
10	30	50	70	90	110	130	150	170	190	210	230	250	270	290	310	330	350	370	390
9	29	49	69	89	109	129	149	169	189	209	229	249	269	289	309	329	349	369	389
8	28	48	68	88	108	128	148	168	188	208	228	248	268	288	308	328	348	368	388
7	27	47	67	87	107	127	147	167	187	207	227	247	267	287	307	327	347	367	387
6	26	46	66	86	106	126	146	166	186	206	226	246	266	286	306	326	346	366	386
5	25	45	65	85	105	125	145	165	185	205	225	245	265	285	305	325	345	365	385
4	24	44	64	84	104	124	144	164	184	204	224	244	264	284	304	324	344	364	384
3	23	43	63	83	103	123	143	163	183	203	223	243	263	283	303	323	343	363	383
2	22	42	62	82	102	122	142	162	182	202	222	242	262	282	302	322	342	362	382
1	21	41	61	81	101	121	141	161	181	201	221	241	261	281	301	321	341	361	381

MAY 17 1792

W.D. GANN

Coffee Riv. Jaw... Oct 2 1986

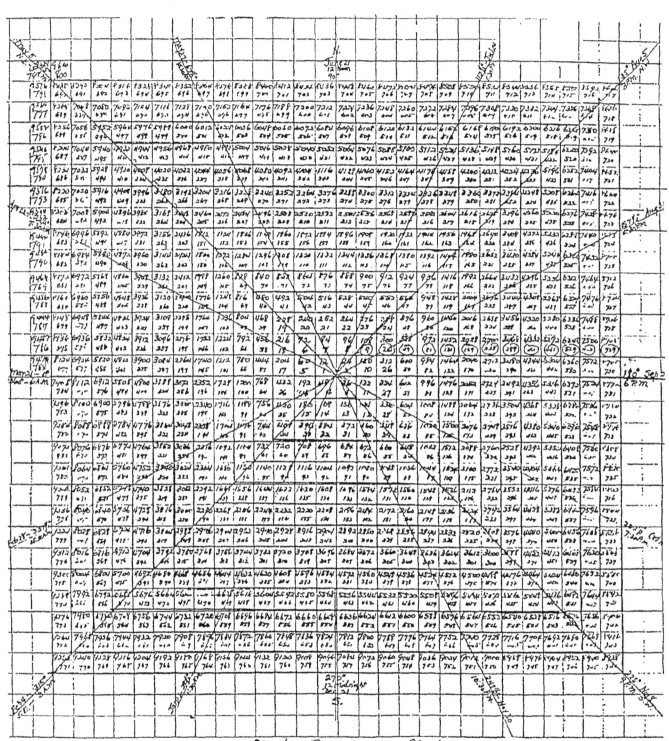

Master Price & Time Chart
for
Cotton, Coffee, Cocoa, Wool,
and Grains

Even Squares for Cotton & Eggs
— Time and Price —

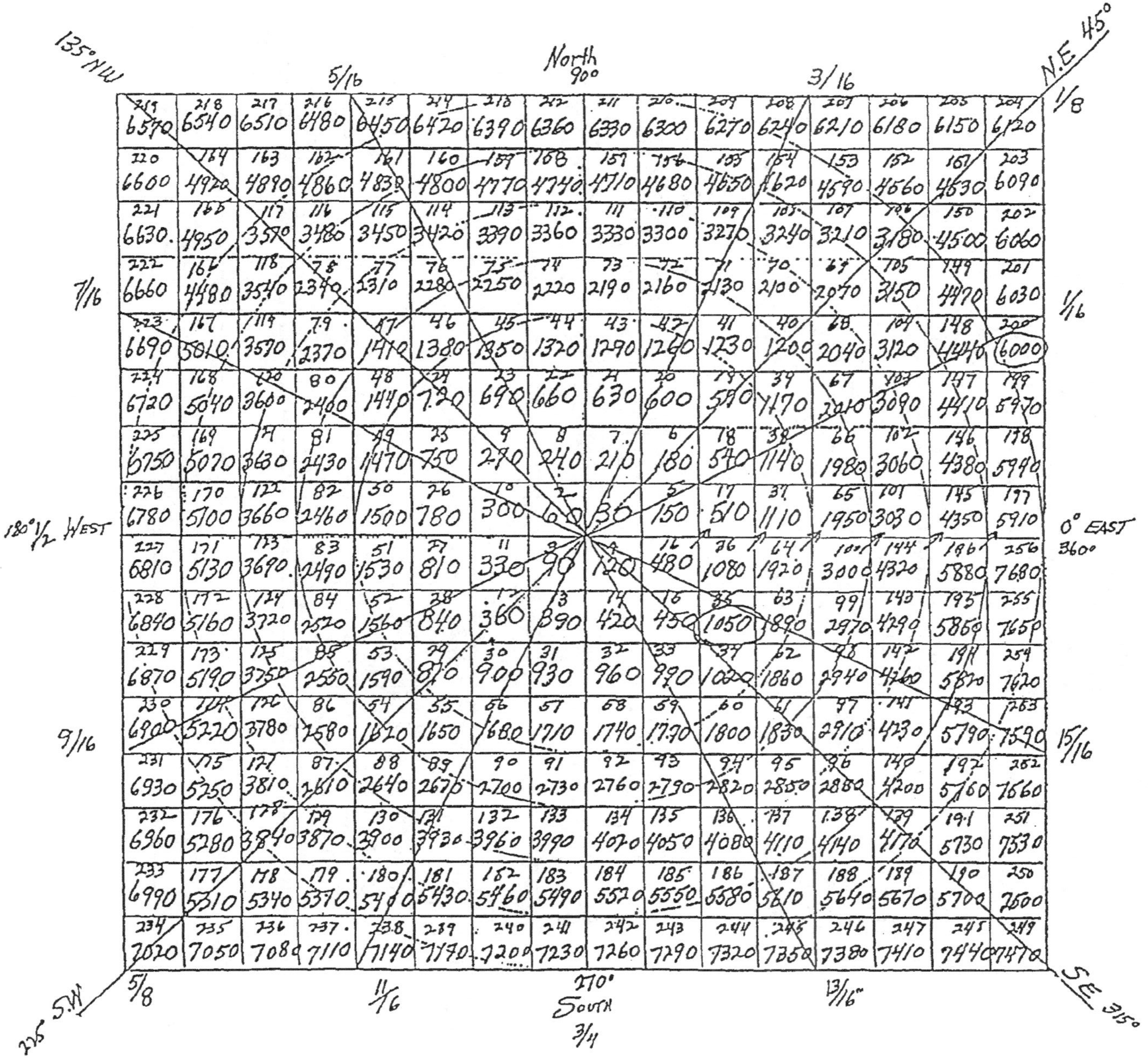

Dec-28-1870
Dec-28 844 = 336 Months
April-28-844 = 4 "
———————— = 340 "
July-28-844 = 343 "
" = 343 "
7×4×2 = 649

Dec 28-1920 – High 60 ¢
May 2-1944 = 1841 weeks
Square a circle

From □ 38 to 639
1/4 = 19 1/4 Weeks
1/2 = 38 1/2 —
1481+38 1/2 = 1482 1/2 —
May 13-849 = 1482 1/2

1440 = 4 × 360

May 30, 1949 = 45 weeks
In New 360 cycle.

N.E. 45°   1/8   1/4   3/16   0° EAST / 360   15/16   SE 315°
North 90°   South 270°
135 NW   180 1/2 WEST   9/16   S.W. 225°

---331---

Egg X October Low May 28 1932

Low high 585 Sept 10

90 Aug 30

Oct 15 / 135

4 5/14 July 14

N 57 1/4 / Nov 7

27 1/2 June

N 80 / Nov 29

Dec 24 / 202 1/2

337 1/7 May 8

Jan 2 / 325

July 4

Feb 26 / 270

March /

Dec 12 / 315

Fig.

—333—

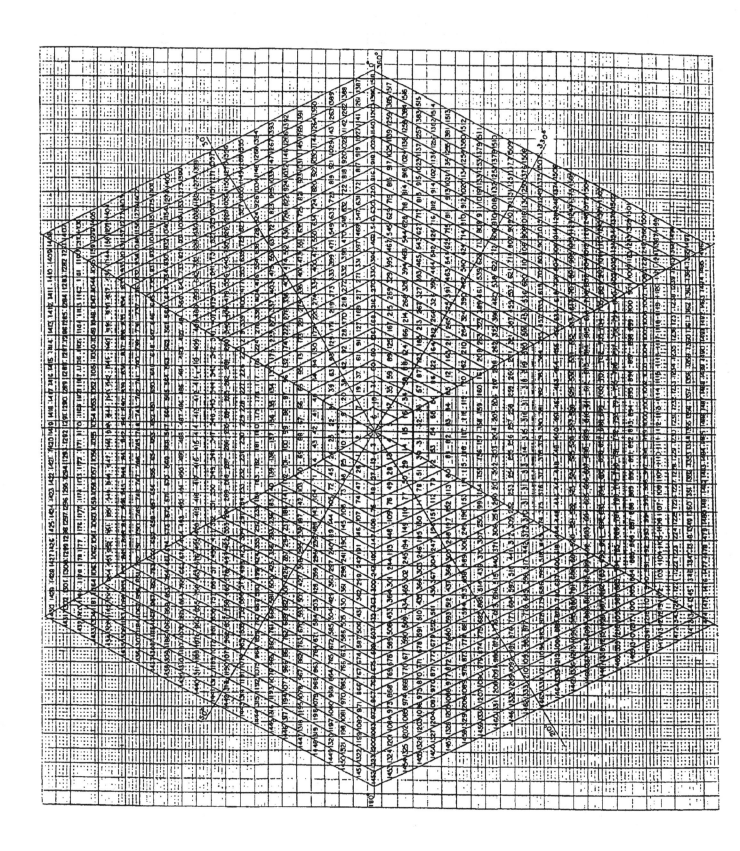

MASTER 360° CHART

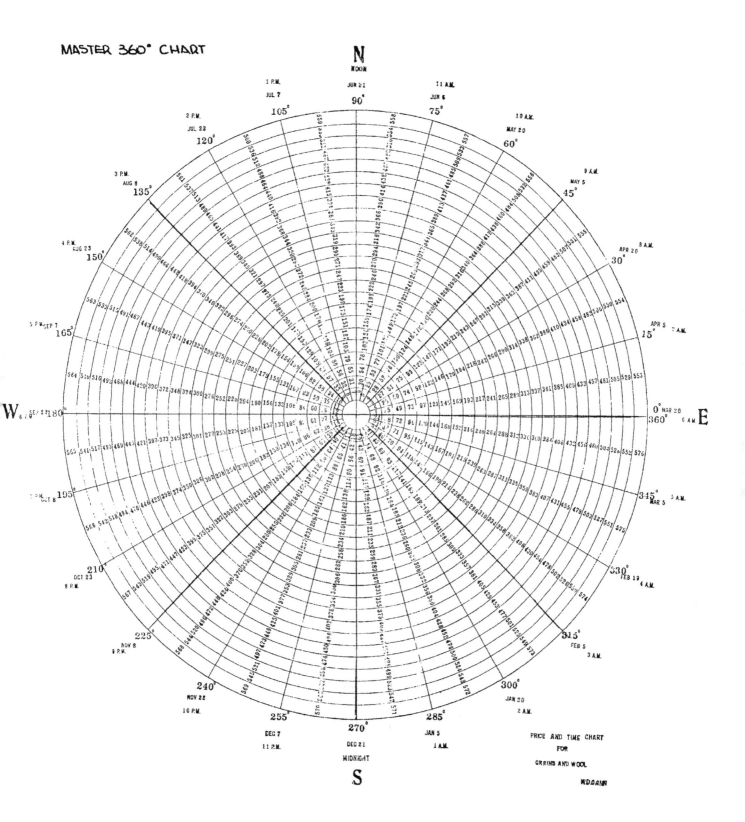

Coffee Riv. Survey Oct 2 1936

9300 9310 9360 9350 942 9450 9480 9510 9540 9570 9600 9630

8410 8480 9461 9760 9730 9770 8650 8680 8570 8500 9000 9030 9060 9120 9150 9180 9210 9240 9270

37520 7550 7580 8010 8040 8070 8100 8130 8510 8550 8587 8728 8280 8310 8340 8370 8440 8430 8460 6490 8520 8550 8580

7207 7230 7330 7380 7410 7440 7470 7500 7530 7620 7650 7680 7710 7770 7800 7840 7860 7890

6630 6660 6690 6720 6750 6780 6810 6840 6870 6900 6930 6960 6550 7420 7070 7080 7110 7140 7170 7200 7230

6060 6090 6120 6150 6180 6210 6240 6270 6300 6330 6360 6390 6420 6450 6480 6510 6540 6570 6600

5460 5490 5520 5550 5580 5610 5640 5670 5700 5730 5760 5790 5820 5850 5880 5910 5940 5970 6000

4410 4440 4470 4500 4530 4560 4590 4620 4650 4680 4710 4740 4770 4800 4830 4860 4890

3870 3960 3990 4020 4050 4080 4110 4140 4170 4200 4230 4260 4275 4350 4380 4350

3480 3510 3540 3570 3600 3630 3660 3690 3720 3750 3780 3810 3840 3870 3900

3060 3090 3120 3150 3180 3210 3240 3270 3300 3330 3360 3390 3420 3450

2700 2730 2760 2790 2820 2850 2880 2910 2940 2970 3000 3030

2310 2340 2370 2400 2430 2460 2490 2520 2550 2580 2610

1980 2010 2040 2070 2100 2130 2160 2190 2220 2250

1680 1710 1740 1770 1800 1830 1860 1890 1920 1950

1410 1440 1470 1500 1530 1560 1590 1620 1650

1170 1200 1230 1260 1290 1320 1350 1380

960 990 1020 1050 1080 1110 1140

780 810 840 870 900 930

560 660 690 770 750

510 540 570 600

340 450 480

360 390

390

Lev 300

MAY COFFEE SANTOS

MAY COFFEE SANTOS D
March 19, 1954
High 8729

Using a scale of one point to one degree, 8729 equals 29° Gemini.
Using a scale of 30 points to one degree, equals 21° Capricorn.
Using the Jupiter scale of 12 points to one degree, equals 7° 30' Aries.
Using one cent to one degree, equals 27° 16' Gemini.

The dollar value is $28,171.00 which equals 11° 45' Capricorn.
The average price of 5 options on March 19, 1954 was 8663 which equals 28° Aries, or 60° from the Heliocentric Jupiter. Heliocentric Jupiter is 20° 35' Gemini, which means that the price of 8729 was at this degree. Heliocentric Uranus is 21° 52' Cancer and the price at 21° Capricorn is opposite to this.

April 16, 1954 is 276 months from April 16, 1931, low 435. Using 50 points per month, the 45° angle crossed 8715 on March 19, 1954, and the Sun has moved 8253 degrees from April 16, 1931. Add this to 435 gives 8688 as the resistance angle.

MARCH COFFEE – October 1, 1936 low 300. Time to April 1, 1954 210 months at 30 points per month, the 45° angle crosses at 5600, and at 40 points per months, it crosses at 8700.

1931, April 16 to March 19, 1954 – Geocentric Saturn moved 285° 38'. This would give a price of 8572. 1936, October 1 to March 19, 1954 – Geocentric Saturn moved 231°, which would equal a price of 7230.

1940, May 15 to March 19, 1954 – Saturn moved 181° 35', which gives a price of 6990 and using 45 points to one degree would give 8715.

1940, August 19 – Saturn moved 173° 23'. At 45 points to one degree, this equals 8760 price.

HELIOCENTRIC SATURN – 1931, April 16 to March 19, 1954, Saturn moved 287° 15' which equals 17° 13' Capricorn, price 8632.

1936, October 1, Saturn moved 225°, which gives a price of 7150.

1940, May 15 Saturn gained 179° 44', price 5940.
1940, August 19, Saturn gained 176° 14', price 5842.

HELIOCENTRIC PLANETS, March 19,1954
    Jupiter 89° 35' equals 29° 35' Gemini.
    Saturn 214.44 equals 4° 44' Scorpio.
    Uranus 111.52 equals 21° 52' Cancer.

The average of these 6 planets is 164.17 or 14° 17' Virgo.

GEOCENTRIC PLANETS

Neptune 204.35 equals 24° 35' Libra.   --- Pluto 144 equals 24° Leo. -- Mars 221 equals 11° Scorpio.

The average of these 6 Geocentric planets is 173.26 or 25° 26' Virgo.

One-half of Jupiter to Saturn Helio is 152.09 or 2° 9' Virgo.
The average of Saturn, Jupiter, Uranus and Neptune is 155.10 equals 5° 10' Virgo. ½ of this average is 17° 35' Gemini. Jupiter, Uranus ½ is 100.43, equals 10° 43' Cancer Heliocentric.
½ of Geocentric Jupiter to Uranus is 93.48 or 3° 48 'Cancer.

IMPORTANT DATES EACH MONTH – 1st, 15th, 18th, and 19th. The present market is running close to these dates.
1953, June 19 - May Coffee low 5050 July 17, low 5555
August 17 - high 5765 Sept. 15 - low 5565
Sept. 21 - high 5710 Oct. 9 - Last low 5470
Oct. 19 - High 5660 Dec. 9 - High 6240
1954, Jan. 13 - High 7470 Jan. 19 - Low 6560 - This was 7 months from March 15 - High 5625 June 19.
March 18 - Low 5465 March 19 - High 8729 - This extreme high was 9 months from June 19, low , 2 months from Jan. 19 low, 6 months from Sept. 15, 1953 low and 5 months from Oct 19 high at 5860.

HELIOCENTRIC & GEOCENTRIC ASPECTS
1954, March 24 - Heliocentric Jupiter enters Cancer.
June 24 - Heliocentric Jupiter 120° of Saturn.
April 12 - Sun 60° of Jupiter Geocentric.
April 15 - Sun 180° of Neptune Geocentric.
April 13 - Jupiter 135° of Saturn Geocentric.
April 16 - Jupiter 60 of Pluto Geocentric.
April 26 - Jupiter 120 of Neptune Geocentric.
April 26 - Sun 180 of Saturn Geocentric.
The month of April is very important. There should be great activity and wide swings in prices due to these aspects.
GEOCENTRIC MAPS MOVEMENTS from low prices on Coffee --
1931, April 16 to August 7, 1953 - Mars has made 12 round trips.
1954, October 29 - Mars will be opposite or 180° from its place on April 16,1931.
1936, October 1 to September 19,1953 - Mars made 9 round trips of 360° each.
1954, Dec 9 - Mars will be 9½ round trips or opposite its place Oct. 1, 1936.
1940, May 15 to June 12, 1953 - Mars made 7 round trips or complete cycles.
1954, Apr 9 - Mars is 7½ cycles or opposite its place on May 15, 1940. Due to the retrograde position of Mars, it will again be 7½ on July 7 and on Aug. 17, 1954 or the third time in opposition to its own place, which is very important.
1940, August 19 to Sept. 15, 1953 - Mars had completed 7 round trips. Note low on coffee on that date.
1954, Dec 4 - Mars 7½ round trips or opposite its own place on Aug 19, 1940.

If Coffee starts to decline between March 22 and 24, 1954, it should continue down to around April 15, when the adverse aspects of Jupiter to Saturn and the Sun to Neptune are completed.

From these dates, you should watch for the possibility of a rally up to April 16, 1954 when

Jupiter is 120 of Neptune and the Sun 130 of Saturn. This might cause a quick rally followed by a sharp quick decline. By studying all of the data outlined above and applying it to Coffee, you will be able to learn more about what causes the changes in trend.

March 20, 1954   W.D. GANN

Coffee Rio January Oct 2 1936

LETTERS

Supply and Demand Letter

·RISING PRICES · · · · **FALLING·PRICES**

~~W. D. GANN & SON, INC.~~ · INVESTMENT ADVISERS · 82 WALL STREET, NEW YORK 5, N.Y.

W. D. GANN RESEARCH, INC.

COMMODITY LETTER

August 20, 1947

GRAINS Grain prices are being determined by speculation rather than economics. This is shown by the large open interest and daily volume, which is largely Commission House business. It is also shown by the history of price ratios. These will be discussed in the Special Circular on Corn which will be sent to our regular subscribers on Friday with our compliments. (Regular price - $3.00.) All the Grains are in a broad trading area, after a prolonged advance, presumably, they are making a top. But the market is feverish and highly dangerous. Wide and erratic swings are to be expected. Commitments either way are extraordinarily hazardous. But the probabilities favor the short side and the big shock, whether it comes from these or higher levels will be on the down side. You will always find that someone will sell at high prices if you are short. But, imagine yourself crowded to the only door when a fire breaks out. If you don't happen to be near the door, you wont have a chance. That is what can happen to you when a break in Grains, especially in Corn, comes.

A special Government Report on Corn will be issued after the close on Thursday. We expect it to be bullish. But it should be received with caution. Present prices have, probably, discounted most of it. Some rains have fallen in most of the Corn Belt since the data for the Report was compiled. And while we do not pretend to have any inside information, we do not believe that human nature is perfect. And we hear rumors up and down the street, that persons with good connections in Washington are heavily committed in Corn.

Special Advice on Grains - Because of present price relationships, we advise clients who are bullish to buy Wheat and clients who are bearish to sell Corn. A sale of Corn on strength and a purchase of Wheat on weakness should prove to be a profitable *arbitrage*. Use the May options.

December Wheat - The trend is now up. Breaking 237 will indicate lower.
May Wheat - Turned up. Breaking 233 indicates lower.

December Corn - Short sale with stop at 225. Breaking 217 indicates lower and breaking promises wide-open break.
May Corn - Short sale with stop at 220. Breaking 212 indicates lower.

Oats is following the pattern of Corn rather than Wheat.
Dec. Oats. - Closing above 107 indicates higher and breaking 102 indicates lower.
May Oats - Closing above 100 indicates higher and breaking 96 lower.

EGGS Made a new high for the present move but sold off and closed on the low of the day. October - Short sale with stop at 5280. Breaking 5160 indicates lower.

COTTON Heavy hedge-selling continues-which the market is unable to absorb and prices broke badly late today, closing near the lows. The main trend is down and we strongly advise short sales on any rally.
October Cotton - Short sale with stop at 3290. Breaking 3220 indicates lower and breaking 3180 very much lower.
December Cotton - Short sale with stop at 3250. Breaking 3180 indicates lower and breaking 3080 indicates 29¢.

W. D. GANN RESEARCH, Inc.

formerly

W. D. GANN & SON, Inc.

INVESTMENT ADVISERS

82 WALL STREET, NEW YORK 5, N. Y.

W. D. GANN
PRESIDENT

C. L. GILSON
VICE-PRESIDENT

LETTER

SCIENTIFIC ADVICE - STOCKS - COMMODITIES

WHAT PRICE CORN?

Recently September Corn sold higher than September Wheat. Corn has sold higher than Wheat about three times in history. In the past such a price relationship has always been "the beginning of the end" of a long run in Corn. We do not believe the present situation will prove to be an exception.

The present run in Corn started in January 1947 when the December option sold for 124. We believe it culminated in August 1947 when that contract sold at 229-3/4.

This position is supported by other statistics:

From their 1932 lows, Wheat is up less than 700%. Oats is up about 500%. Eggs approximately 350%. Corn, on the other hand, is up about 1050%. And hogs (Corn on the hoof) are up approximately 1400%.

Further, December Corn at its high, was up about 123 points from the January lows. That is nearly 100% in seven months. Corn has far out-distanced Wheat. The present price relationship between them is economically unsound and simply cannot be continued. Since Wheat is apparently in a broad trading range, at the top of a rally, and has been unable to respond adequately to the recent strength in Corn, we believe Corn is going to break sharply and advise short sales.

But speculators should remember that speculation in Corn has been overdone and that the market is volatile and highly dangerous. However we believe the potential profits justify the risk if trading is done on a moderate scale and capital is protected with stop loss orders as advised.

SPECIFIC ADVICE FOR CORN

September Corn – Do not trade in this option.
December Corn – If you are long, take profits and go short. It is a short sale with stop at 231. Breaking 225 will be a definite indication of lower prices and closing under 222 will initiate a down-trend.
May Corn – If you are long, take profits and go short. It is a short sale with stop at 227½. Breaking 220 definitely indicates lower prices and breaking 218 indicates much lower.
March Corn – Never trade in this option.
July Corn – Do not trade in this option until November.

SPECIAL CROP FORECAST

Corn crop prospects will be greatly improved if we get rain in the near future and the Fall frosts are delayed. Of course, they will get worse if the bad weather continues for any extended period of time or if we have early frost. Assuming average conditions, we predict that, for the country as a whole, the crop will be between 70% and 80% of last year's bumper crop which isn't so bad.

W. D. GANN RESEARCH, Inc.

SCIENTIFIC ADVICE
AND ANALYTICAL REPORTS
ON STOCKS AND COMMODITIES

CABLE ADDRESS "GANWADE"
PHONE BROAD 1035

April 1st, 1926.

Mr. John H. Spohn,
P. O. Box 95-96

Dear Mr. Spohn:

Your favor of March 28th received and I note that you have secured a list of names for which you expect to claim some business for my Service. I will be glad to furnish you any literature that you need, or if you want to send the list of names in I will circularize them and pay you commission just the same on anything you get.

There are thousands of people patronizing fakers and clairvoyants who know nothing about the market, and paying out their money for advice which causes them to lose their money in the market. Many of these people would subscribe for a good market advice if they knew about it.

I have read Professor Moore's book and the trouble with him was that he failed to get the right time factor and of course did not know the cause behind market movements.

You will find Schuster and Fourier theories helpful in analyzing the market.

Yours very truly,

W. D. Gann

WDG/PE

W. D. GANN
72 WALL STREET
NEW YORK

SCIENTIFIC ADVICE
AND ANALYTICAL REPORTS
ON STOCKS AND COMMODITIES
AUTHOR OF "TRUTH OF THE STOCK TAPE"

MEMBER
AMERICAN ECONOMIC ASS'N
ROYAL ECONOMIC SOCIETY
CABLE ADDRESS "GANWADE"

July 9, 1927

Mr. J. H. Spohn,
Post Office Box No. 95,

Dear Mr. Spohn:

You, as an intelligent man, know that
the way to succeed as a speculator or investor is to
have a successful plan and follow it.

Livermore has certain fixed rules which
he follows in his trading. He watches for certain signs,
then makes his trades. You will make the greatest success
WHEN you KNOW the scientific rules for forecasting stocks
and commodities, because you can trade with greater con-
fidence.

You are eligible to enter my Summer
Class of Stock and Commodity Scientific Forecasting which
opens August 2nd. My latest discovery - the Master Time
Factor - will be taught you. I will instruct you in the
seasonal trend of man which will enable you to KNOW the
times and seasons when you can succeed best. This is of
great value.

The price of the Forecasting Method will
be reduced because it is just as easy to teach 12 at the
same time as one. The Class will be limited to 12 Students. For those unable to come to New York for personal
lessons, I have prepared a Special Course of Instruction.

If you are interested, please fill out
and return the enclosed blank and you will receive full
details.

Yours very truly,

W. D. Gann

WDG-CM

Enclosures

SMALL SUPPLY.
LARGE DEMAND:
RISING PRICES.

SCIENTIFIC ADVICE
ON
STOCKS. COTTON. GRAIN.

LARGE SUPPLY.
SMALL DEMAND:
FALLING PRICES.

ANALYTICAL REPORTS
ON
MARKET CONDITIONS.

W. D. GANN
78 WALL STREET, NEW YORK

Sept 6th 1927.

Mr. John H. Spohn,
P. O. Box 95,

Dear Sir:

Your letter of September 2nd received with check for $10.00.

I am enclosing a copy of the horoscope of the Chicago Board of Trade for the second incorporation of February 18th, 1859.

I think that if you will use the opening time, 9:30 A.M., Chicago Time for the Ascendant, you will find it works out all right and also calculate the progress position according to this.

I am enclosing a copy of my Supplements on Cotton and Grain for the Month of September, however I don't see how this can be of much value to you as you do not have the Forecast and are not receiving the Tri-weekly Letters or Weekly Letters of any changes. I presume you simply want to watch it and that is why you have ordered it.

Yours very truly,

W. D. Gann

WDG-1
encl

W. D. GANN
520 S. W. 26TH ROAD
MIAMI 45, FLORIDA

December 30, 1952

Dr. John De Jonge
30 West 8th Street
Holland, Michigan

Dear Dr. De Jonge:

Your letter of December 23rd received together with Soy Bean
Charts which I am returning herewith. You are quite right in your
interpretation Soy Beans are getting ready for a big decline and I
believe they will decline eventually to $2 per bushel or lower.
The Time Period from December 28th 1932 to December 28th 1952 was
20 years and this is very important for a change. The next important
Time Period will be February 15th which is 33 years from the high of
405 Feb. 15, 1920. Therefore November 15, 1953 will be 405 months
the square of time with price from extreme high and as a rule in the
last stages of these great squares there is a sharp decline. Beans
have been in such a narrow range for such a long period of time that
they should now decline very fast. I am confident that General
Eisenhower will bring about peace in Korea and also reach an agreement
with Stalin which will prevent a third World War. This will be very
bearish on all commodities.

For forecasting 1953 you can use the past cycles on wheat using
the years 1853,63,73,83,93,1903,13,23,33,1943. Consider the 30 and 60
year cycles the most important. Also the 7 year cycles such as 14, 21,
28, etc.

You will note that the last extreme low was Feb. 27, 1933 and 1953
will be the 21st year and the trend should start down in February if
it has not already started down.

For many years I have been working on a Master Mechanical Time
and Trend Calculator which will not only save 90% of the work on Charts
but give accuracy in determining the trend, time periods, and resistance
level. I finished this Calculator in Sept. 1952 and have patented it
and have the charts made up. You do not have to put on any time periods
or put any angles on. You lay the Master Calculator on over your chart,
daily, weekly, or monthly and it gives you the trend at a glance
together with the next price or resistance level. One man who has used
this chart and made $78,000 in the past few months paid me $4000 in
addition to payments for all my courses. He says it is the greatest
invention since the "wheel". If you would like to have it I'll make
you a special price on it. Any human being can make a mistake but this
Master Calculator prevents mistakes of any kind.

Wishing you a Happy New Year and great success, I am,

Sincerely yours,

W. D. Gann

AUTHOR OF
TRUTH OF THE STOCK TAPE
WALL STREET STOCK SELECTOR
NEW STOCK TREND DETECTOR
45 YEARS IN WALL STREET
HOW TO MAKE PROFITS IN COMMODITIES

W. D. GANN
820 S. W. 26TH ROAD
MIAMI 45, FLORIDA

January 12, 1953

Dr. John De Jonge
30 W. 8th Street
Holland, Michigan

Dear Dr. De Jonge:

Your letter of January 7th received. Soy Beans are certainly acting right and the main trend id definitely down. I do not understand why you trade in September beans. They never work as good as the May, July and November options. To make a success in trading you must stick to the trend and change when it changes. Be neither a Bull or a Bear. Follow the rules strictly.

Unless there is a very sharp severe decline in Soy Beans in the month of February I do not expect them to make low for any important rally. They should run down until April or May.

My new calculator helps you to see the trend easily and quickly and if you will follow what it indicates you will make a greater success When a change is indicated you must get out of the market and take the other side. This new calculator is worth a fortune to any man who will follow it because it saves making mistakes and saves time. It is made on plastic and is much clearer than glass. You simply lay it over your charts and get the time periods, resistance levels and angles without doing any work. You know that I never try to sell you or any man something that they do not want but I do feel this will be of immense value to you. I am charging other people $1,000 in addition to the regualr prices of the courses. If you want it I will make the price to you of $500. You can pay me $250 cash in advance and pay the balance at the rate of $50 per month.

With kindest regards to you and the boys, I am,

Sincerely yours,

W. D. Gann

Recommended Readings

- 45 Years in Wall Street by W. D. Gann

- Truth of the Stock Tape by William D. Gann

- How to Make Profits In Commodities by W. D. Gann

- Options Made Easy: How to Make Profits Trading in Puts and Calls By W. D. Gann

- The Essence of Success by Earl Nightingale

CPSIA information can be obtained
at www.ICGtesting.com
Printed in the USA
LVHW061203080819
626692LV00025B/153/P